Our republic; a history of the United States for grammar grades

Franklin L. 1868-1929 Riley, Chandler, J. A. C. (Julian Alvin Carroll), 1872-1934, joint author

Nabu Public Domain Reprints:

You are holding a reproduction of an original work published before 1923 that is in the public domain in the United States of America, and possibly other countries. You may freely copy and distribute this work as no entity (individual or corporate) has a copyright on the body of the work. This book may contain prior copyright references, and library stamps (as most of these works were scanned from library copies). These have been scanned and retained as part of the historical artifact.

This book may have occasional imperfections such as missing or blurred pages, poor pictures, errant marks, etc. that were either part of the original artifact, or were introduced by the scanning process. We believe this work is culturally important, and despite the imperfections, have elected to bring it back into print as part of our continuing commitment to the preservation of printed works worldwide. We appreciate your understanding of the imperfections in the preservation process, and hope you enjoy this valuable book.

WESTWARD HO!

After the painting by Emmanuel Leutze in the National Capitol.

OUR REPUBLIC

A HISTORY OF THE UNITED STATES FOR GRAMMAR GRADES

BY

FRANKLIN L. RILEY
PROFESSOR OF HISTORY, UNIVERSITY OF MISSISSIPPI

J. A. C. CHANDLER
SUPERINTENDENT OF SCHOOLS, RICHMOND, VIRGINIA

J. G. DE ROULHAC HAMILTON
PROFESSOR OF HISTORY, UNIVERSITY OF NORTH CAROLINA

RICHMOND, VIRGINIA
RILEY AND CHANDLER
1910

E178
1
R58

Copyright, 1910, by
RILEY AND CHANDLER

©CLA271428

PREFACE

It may be asked at the outset, In what does this book differ from the many text-books of American history that have already been offered to the schools?

It is presumably the object of every author of such a book to show properly the trend of our country's development—how colonies grew into States, and they in turn into a united nation; to show, furthermore, how the people have lived, how the methods of making a livelihood have been changed by discoveries and inventions, producing new social conditions; and to set forth, in the course of such narrative, the acts of heroism and statesmanship that are conspicuous in our national biography. Presumably, too, school histories have been written to create an interest in the nation and the duties of citizenship—to foster patriotism and a sense of civic duty; to fix standards of morality by a comparison of human deeds; and, lastly, to stimulate love of the study itself.

These common ideals of the historian and the teacher are fundamental in the present book. But in offering to the schools of the United States a new book on American history, the authors have considered also certain other conditions to be met.

The children who enter the grammar grades have usually no knowledge of history outside of tales of heroism and adventure, and biographical sketches. They have little idea of the logical sequence of events. Therefore the study of history in these grades should lead them gradually from their former standpoint to a broader and more adult view of historical occurrences. In this book the subject is presented very simply at the outset, with abundance of illustration, and enough of what may be called the romantic element in history to sustain interest and stimulate the imagination; but as the child who studies the War of Secession, will be older by nearly two years than at the beginning of his study of the colonial period, the narrative is presented with due consideration of the pupil's mental growth in those two years. Yet nowhere is the pupil's ability overestimated. This book is, therefore, intended as a text for the sixth and seventh or seventh and eighth years of the elementary school.

Furthermore, children of these grades have but little idea of historical accuracy. A tale second-hand is quite as acceptable to them as a quotation from original sources. Any quickening of the historical perception in this direction has, obviously, a far-reaching moral bearing; and the authors have, both by quotations in the text, and by facsimile reproductions among the illustrations, tried to foster a desire for accurate information from original sources.

All the children of our country need to be trained to impartial observation and judgment. It is the broad basis of efficient citizenship. With this in mind, the authors have endeavored to give here a well balanced, accurate, and impartial account of the great period of sectional disputes. The children of the present must learn to view without prejudice this era of our history, reverencing and respecting whatever was nobly done and condemning the ignoble and the harsh.

The authors have endeavored to present difficult problems concisely and simply, omitting what is beyond the understanding of children. They have provided brief biographical sketches of many leading Americans; also some questions and exercises at the close of the text, to stimulate both memory and reasoning; and have listed a simple reference library for children, which can be had at little cost.

THE AUTHORS.

HISTORICAL LIBRARY LISTS FOR GRAMMAR GRADES

(Reference to these books will be found on page 472 and following.)

I.—A FIVE DOLLAR REFERENCE LIBRARY.

    Southworth: Builders of Our Country, Book I. D. Appleton & Co., New York. 60 cents.

    Southworth: Builders of Our Country, Book II. D. Appleton & Co., New York. 60 cents.

    McMurry: Pioneers of Land and Sea. The Macmillan Co., New York. 40 cents.

    Hart: Colonial Children. The Macmillan Co., New York. 40 cents.

    Guerber: Story of the Thirteen Colonies. American Book Co., New York. 65 cents.

    Fiske: The War of Independence. Houghton Mifflin Co., New York. 40 cents.

    McCarthy: Soldier Life in the Army of Northern Virginia. B. F. Johnson Publishing Co., Richmond, Va. 50 cents.

    Hall: Half Hours in Southern History. B. F. Johnson Publishing Co., Richmond, Va. 75 cents.

    Williamson: Life of General Robert E. Lee. B. F. Johnson Publishing Co., Richmond, Va. 25 cents.

    Williamson: Life of General Stonewall Jackson. B. F. Johnson Publishing Co., Richmond, Va. 30 cents.

II.—A TEN-DOLLAR REFERENCE LIBRARY.

Add to the list given above, the following books:

    Gordy: American Leaders and Heroes. Charles Scribner's Sons, New York. 60 cents.

    Blaisdell and Ball: Hero Stories from American History. Ginn & Co., New York. 50 cents.

    Chandler and Chitwood: Makers of American History. Silver, Burdett & Co., New York. 60 cents.

    Mowry: American Inventions and Inventors. Silver, Burdett & Co., New York. 65 cents.

Johonnot: Stories of Our Country. American Book Co., New York. 40 cents.

White: The Making of South Carolina. Silver, Burdett & Co., New York. 60 cents.

Connor: Story of the Old North State. J. B. Lippincott Co., Philadelphia, Pa. 35 cents.

Massey and Wood: The Story of Georgia. D. C. Heath & Co., New York. 35 cents.

Littlejohn: Texas History Stories. B. F. Johnson Publishing Co., Richmond, Va. 50 cents.

Karns: Tennessee History Stories. B. F. Johnson Publishing Co., Richmond, Va. 50 cents.

CONTENTS

I. PERIOD OF EXPLORATION

CHAPTER		PAGE
I.	European Countries in 1492	1
II.	Geographical Knowledge in 1492	7
III.	The Plan of Columbus	11
IV.	The Voyages of Columbus	16
V.	The Unknown Lands a New World	21
VI.	Other Spanish Explorations	25
VII.	French and Dutch Explorations	31
	1. French Explorations	31
	2. Dutch Explorations	34
VIII.	English Explorations	35
IX.	The American Indian	42

II. SETTLEMENT OF THE THIRTEEN ORIGINAL COLONIES

X.	The Settlement of Virginia	49
XI.	The Struggles of the Jamestown Colony	53
XII.	The Growth of Virginia	58
XIII.	Virginia under Charles I and Cromwell	62
XIV.	The Liberty-Loving Virginians	64
XV.	The Plymouth Colony	67
XVI.	The Massachusetts Bay Colony	71
XVII.	The Expansion of New England	75
	1. Rhode Island	75
	2. Connecticut	77
	3. The New Haven Colony	80
	4. New Hampshire and Maine	81
XVIII.	The United Colonies of New England	81
XIX.	New England under Charles II and James II	85
XX.	New England under William and Mary	88
XXI.	The Settlement of Maryland	91

CONTENTS

CHAPTER		PAGE
XXII.	Government and Progress of Maryland, 1649–1700	96
XXIII.	The Beginnings of the Carolinas	98
XXIV.	North Carolina and South Carolina	101
	1. North Carolina	101
	2. South Carolina	103
XXV.	Georgia	105
XXVI.	New York a Dutch Colony	109
XXVII.	New York an English Colony	113
XXVIII.	The Colony of New Jersey	117
XXIX.	Pennsylvania and Delaware	119
	1. Pennsylvania	119
	2. Delaware	122

III. INTERCOLONIAL WARS

XXX.	French Settlements in America	124
XXXI.	King William's, Queen Anne's, and King George's Wars	128
XXXII.	Struggle over Western Lands	131
XXXIII.	The French Driven out of North America	134
XXXIV.	The Colonists and Their Homes in 1763	137
XXXV.	Various Phases of Colonial Life	143

IV. PERIOD OF REVOLUTION

XXXVI.	Dissatisfaction with England's Policy	150
XXXVII.	The Stamp Act and the Townshend Acts	153
XXXVIII.	England Insists on the Right of Taxation	158
XXXIX.	Opening of Revolutionary War, 1776	163
XL.	The Organization of an Army, 1775	167
XLI.	War in the South, 1776	171
XLII.	Washington's Campaigns, 1776—The Declaration of Independence	172
XLIII.	Events of the Year 1777	179
XLIV.	The War North and South in 1778	184
XLV.	The Winning of the West	187
XLVI.	Events of the Year 1779	190
XLVII.	Events of the Year 1780	195
XLVIII.	The War in the Year 1781	198
XLIX.	Peace with England	203

V. CRITICAL PERIOD

CHAPTER		PAGE
L.	First Constitution of the United States	206
LI.	Dissatisfaction with the Articles of Confederation	209
LII.	Making a New Federal Government	211
LIII.	Social Conditions in 1789	215

VI. MAKING OF THE REPUBLIC

LIV.	Organization of the New Government Washington's First Administration, 1789–93.	221
LV.	Foreign and Domestic Relations Washington's Second Administration, 1793–97.	227
LVI.	End of Federalist Rule John Adams's Administration, 1797–1801.	231
LVII.	Triumph of Republican Principles Jefferson's First Administration, 1801–05.	237
LVIII.	Struggle for Commercial Rights Jefferson's Second Administration, 1805–09	241
LIX.	England Forces War Madison's Administration, 1809–12.	245
LX.	First and Second Years of the War of 1812 Madison's Administration, 1812–13	249
LXI.	Third Year of the War of 1812 Madison's Administration, 1814.	254
LXII.	The American Republic Respected Abroad End of Madison's Administration, 1814–17	256
LXIII.	New Problems at Home and Abroad Monroe's Administration, 1817–25.	258
LXIV.	The United States in 1820	263
LXV.	Formation of New Parties John Quincy Adams's Administration, 1825–29.	269
LXVI.	Triumph of the New Democracy Jackson's First Administration, 1829–33.	272
LXVII.	Nullification and the Bank Jackson's Second Administration, 1833–37. Van Buren's Administration, 1837–41.	277
LXVIII.	Development of the Country, 1820–40.	284
LXIX.	Failure of the Whig Program Harrison's and Tyler's Administration, 1841–45.	294

CONTENTS

CHAPTER		PAGE
LXX.	WAR WITH MEXICO AND ITS RESULTS	299
	First Years of Polk's Administration, 1845–48.	
LXXI.	WESTWARD EXPANSION AND ITS PROBLEMS	305
	End of Polk's Administration, 1848–49.	
LXXII.	THE CALIFORNIA COMPROMISE	307
	Taylor's Administration, 1849–50.	
LXXIII.	FAILURE OF THE COMPROMISE OF 1850	312
	Fillmore's Administration, 1850–53.	
LXXIV.	EFFORTS TO ACQUIRE NEW TERRITORY FOR SLAVERY	315
	Pierce's Administration, 1853–57.	
LXXV.	ACUTE STAGE OF THE SLAVERY CONTROVERSY	319
	Buchanan's Administration, 1857–61	
LXXVI.	PROGRESS OF THE COUNTRY, 1840–60	323

VII. WAR OF SECESSION

CHAPTER		PAGE
LXXVII.	THE ELECTION OF 1860	330
LXXVIII.	THE BEGINNINGS OF SECESSION	333
LXXIX.	GROUNDS FOR SECESSION	335
LXXX.	THE FORMATION OF THE CONFEDERACY	338
LXXXI.	THE SOUTH TRIES TO PREVENT WAR	342
LXXXII.	THE BEGINNING OF THE CONFLICT	345
LXXXIII.	THE STRENGTH OF THE TWO NATIONS	348
LXXXIV.	THE WAR IN 1861	350
LXXXV.	WAR ON THE SEA	353
LXXXVI.	THE WAR IN 1862—ADVANCE ON RICHMOND	359
LXXXVII.	THE WAR IN 1862—CAMPAIGNS IN MARYLAND AND NORTHERN VIRGINIA	363
LXXXVIII.	THE WAR IN 1862—CAMPAIGNS IN KENTUCKY AND TENNESSEE	366
LXXXIX.	THE WAR IN 1862—CAMPAIGNS IN MISSISSIPPI AND TENNESSEE	369
XC.	POLITICAL AND ECONOMIC CONDITIONS IN 1862	373
XCI.	THE WAR IN 1863—CAMPAIGNS IN THE WEST	378
XCII.	THE WAR IN 1863—CAMPAIGNS IN VIRGINIA AND PENNSYLVANIA	382
XCIII.	THE WAR IN 1864—CAMPAIGNS IN THE LOWER SOUTH	386
XCIV.	THE WAR IN 1864—CAMPAIGNS IN VIRGINIA	390
XCV.	LINCOLN REËLECTED—PRISONERS OF WAR	393
XCVI.	THE WAR IN 1865—THE CONFEDERACY OVERCOME	395
XCVII.	SOME FACTS ABOUT THE WAR	400
XCVIII.	SACRIFICES AND MAKESHIFTS OF THE WAR	403

VIII. PERIOD OF NATIONAL DEVELOPMENT

CHAPTER		PAGE
XCIX.	The Problem of Reconstruction	407
C.	Congressional Reconstruction	412
	Johnson's Administration, 1865–69.	
CI.	Foreign and Domestic Affairs	416
	Johnson's Administration, 1865–69.	
CII.	Congressional Reconstruction a Failure	418
	Grant's First Administration, 1869–73.	
CIII.	A Period of Distress and Corruption	423
	Grant's Second Administration, 1873–77.	
CIV.	Sectional Feeling Begins to Die	429
	Hayes's Administration, 1877–81; Garfield's and Arthur's Administration, 1881–85.	
CV.	Democratic Triumphs and Defeats	435
	Cleveland's First Administration, 1885–89; Harrison's Administration, 1889–93.	
CVI.	Democrats in Control of the Government	441
	Cleveland's Second Administration, 1893–97.	
CVII.	The War with Spain	445
	McKinley's First Administration, 1897–1901.	
CVIII.	Fighting in American Waters	450
	McKinley's First Administration, 1897–1901.	
CIX.	The Problems of Imperialism and the Panama Canal	454
	McKinley's First Administration, 1897–1901; McKinley's and Roosevelt's Administration, 1901–05.	
CX.	Recent Events	460
	Roosevelt's Administration, 1905–09; Taft's Administration, 1909.	
CXI.	Progress of the Country, 1865–1910	463

Questions and Exercises 473

Appendices:
   I. Declaration of Independence 513
   II. Constitution of the United States 517
   III. Table of Presidents and Vice Presidents of the United States . 530
   IV. Table of the growth of the United States 531

Pronouncing Index 533

LIST OF MAPS

	PAGE
Trade Routes to the East in the Fifteenth Century	8
The Part of the World Known to Europeans before 1492	10
Toscanelli's Map	12
Early Voyages Across the Atlantic	26
The Circumnavigation of the Globe by Magellan and Drake	36
Location of the Principal Indian Tribes of Central North America	44
The Division of Virginia Between the London and Plymouth Companies	50
The Region of Jamestown and Roanoke	52
The Colonies of New England	78
The Maryland Grant and Settlements	95
The Grants of the Carolinas	102
The Development of Georgia	107
The Middle Colonies	118
Forts and Settlements Established by the French Before the Close of the Eighteenth Century	127
Ohio Valley Region	133
European Possessions in North America in 1755 and in 1763, *colored*, *facing*	137
The Campaign around Boston	170
The Campaigns around New York and Philadelphia	175
Burgoyne's Campaign	180
The Pioneer Route to the West and the Frontier Settlements	189
Marches and Countermarches of the Forces in the South, 1780–81	201
The United States with Her Western Territory at the Close of the Revolutionary War, *colored* *facing*	207
The United States in 1800	235
The Louisiana Purchase, *colored* *facing*	239
The Routes of Lewis and Clark, and Pike	240
The Northern Frontier During the War of 1812	250
The Campaign around Washington	254
The Territory Affected by the Missouri Compromise	260
The Disputed Boundary of the Oregon Country	298
The Disputed Boundary of Texas	301

LIST OF MAPS

	PAGE
Marches of the American Army in the Mexican War	303
Territory Acquired from Mexico by the Treaty of 1848	304
Changes in Free and Slave Territory from 1820 to 1850, *colored*, facing	308
Territory Acquired by the United States from 1789 to 1853, *colored*, facing	315
The Division of the Country in Regard to Slavery after the Passage of the Kansas-Nebraska Bill	318
The Electoral Vote of 1860	331
The Union and the Confederate States in 1861, *colored* facing	341
The Harbor of Charleston in 1861	345
Campaign in Virginia in 1861	350
The Peninsula Campaign	359
Forts and Battlegrounds of the Western Campaigns	367
The Vicksburg Campaign	378
The Campaign near Chattanooga	381
From Chancellorsville to Gettysburg	384
Sherman's March to the Sea	388
Virginia Campaign of 1864–65	391
Limits of Confederate Occupation from 1861 to 1865, *colored*, facing	399
The Electoral Vote in 1876	428
The Hawaiian Islands	443
The Philippine Islands	448
The War in the West Indies—The Pursuit of Cervera's Fleet	451
The Panama Canal Zone and Route of the Canal	456
Alaska and the Klondike	457
How the Centers of Population and Manufacture Have Been Moving Westward	464
The United States and Its Territorial Possessions, *colored*, facing	464

OUR REPUBLIC

I. PERIOD OF EXPLORATION

CHAPTER I

EUROPEAN COUNTRIES IN 1492

Civilized countries in 1492.—At the close of the fifteenth century, the known world was very different from what it is to-day. Its population was probably not over two hundred millions; the world that we know to-day has probably more than two thousand millions. At that time the cities were small, and the mode of living was rude. All the modern conveniences of home and business and travel were unknown.

The centers of civilization were the countries of Europe west of Russia. With a few exceptions, the governments of these were poorly conducted. The people had nothing to do with the making of the laws or the selection of the rulers. To-day we believe that the masses of the people should have a voice in governing themselves, but four hundred years ago there was no such view of the rights of man.

Germany.—Among the chief civilized nations was Germany. It was called an empire, and the ruler of it was spoken of as emperor. It was not, however, one country, but many little countries and free cities. In the free cities the people had some voice in the management of affairs, but usually the city governments were controlled by the wealthy. In the small kingdoms of Germany, the kings were the sole rulers, making all laws and often putting men to death at will. The German emperor was

A GERMAN LANDSCAPE OF THE MIDDLE AGES
Castles of powerful lords control the peasant villages below.—After a drawing by Hirschvogel.

not himself a powerful ruler; for the small kingdoms and the free cities did not submit without resistance to his rule. When the emperor tried to control them, there were frequent civil wars, causing great loss of life and property. Because of its disorganized condition, Germany had nothing to do with the discoveries in the western world.

France.—To the west of Germany lay France, which not many years before 1492 had been just as disorganized as Germany. But the many dukes and lords had been conquered, and France was now fairly well united under one king, Charles VIII. He made the laws and, through his judges, decided all cases. With the exception of the middle class in some of the cities, the masses of the people had little opportunity for advancement in culture or wealth. The great bulk of the land was owned by the king, the nobles, and the Church. The common people were only tenants, and in many instances almost slaves.

Italy.—Once the entire peninsula of Italy had been under the control of Rome; but with the breaking up of the empire over which the city of Rome held sway, Italy became greatly divided. By 1492 it was in even greater

ENTRANCE TO THE PORT OF VENICE IN THE FIFTEENTH CENTURY
In the foreground, merchant vessels at the wharves; shipbuilders completing a man-of-war.—After a fragment of the *Civitas Veneciarum* of Breydenbach.

confusion than Germany; for there was no central government, and strife among the small states was an everyday occurrence. Several of the Italian states were regarded as part of the German Empire. As a rule, the larger Italian cities were free states. Noteworthy in history were such city-states as Venice, Genoa, Florence, and Pisa. They were the most cultured and refined cities of Europe. The masses of the people in some of the city-states of Italy had no small part in their own government—almost as much, in fact, as the residents of one of our large American cities. Much of the trade of Europe, at this time not very large, was in the hands of these Italian cities.

England.—Of all the European countries, England was probably the best governed. It had just emerged from a long and bloody war, by which a strong king, Henry VII, had acquired the throne. The lords had been subdued, and the king was encouraging the middle class to develop industries and trade in their towns and villages. Ireland was a possession of England, though many of the native Irish rulers refused to be governed by the King of England. Scotland was still an independent kingdom, but it had little influence in shaping the history of Europe.

HENRY VII OF ENGLAND
After the portrait at Kensington.

Spain.—Spain had just become a united kingdom. By the close of 1492 it was possibly the greatest power in Europe, though but a few years before the country had been composed of a number of independent states. By the marriage of Ferdinand and Isabella, the chief states, Aragon and Castile, had been united. In 1492, after a bloody war, the Moorish state of Granada in southern Spain had been conquered. Thus the whole country had been made into a strong state, which at once began to shape the course of history. There was much wealth in the land, due in great measure to the skill of the Jews and the Mohammedans.

Portugal. — Portugal was an independent kingdom under King John. This monarch was one of the most progressive in Europe. Being a wise man, he tried to build up his little kingdom by establishing trade with all parts of the world. Thus Portugal had the same idea as the Italian city-states and modern England.

ISABELLA OF SPAIN
After the portrait in the Royal Palace at Madrid.

Turkey. — During the whole of the fifteenth century an Asiatic people, the Turks, were making conquests in eastern Europe. These people were Mohammedans and were much disliked by the Christians. In 1453 they seized Constantinople, the most important city in southeastern Europe. From that city as a base, they penetrated into central Europe. For a time it looked as if they would overrun all the southern part of the German Empire; but the Germans by brave resistance finally checked them. However, Europeans were never able to rescue Constantinople from the "unspeakable Turks" and to restore its Christian rulers. So the Turks remained its proud possessors, adding to their territory in western Asia not only this city upon the Bosporus but northern Africa, which they likewise conquered.

Other countries.—Greece was a part of Turkey. Russia was semi-barbaric and almost unknown to civilized Europe. Holland and Belgium were not independent countries, but subject from time to time to Germany or to Spain. The countries of northern Europe—Norway, Sweden, and Denmark—were more or less at war with one another. Constant warfare at home and a desire for adventure drove many of these Northmen to wander over the seas.

The Norsemen.—In their wanderings the Northmen, or Norsemen, touched Iceland, Greenland, and other lands. Many of the Norsemen had settled in England. Some under Chief Rollo had gone to France, and others as far south as Sicily. It is said that one, Leif Ericson, a Norse prince, about the year 1000 had crossed the Atlantic Ocean and touched upon a coast well timbered and filled with many varieties of wild fruits.

A NORSEMAN'S VOYAGE
Sketched after the Norse ship reconstructed for the Columbian Exposition, and now in the Field Museum, Chicago.

Thereupon he had called the land Vinland. An account of this discovery is to be found in the old stories of Iceland, known to history as the Sagas. Judging from these stories, the country visited by these Norsemen was undoubtedly the region along the coast of New England.

Although the discovery of New England by the Norsemen had no influence on the course of American history, it is nevertheless interesting because it shows to what extent these people explored the seas. According to the old reports, Leif built some houses in Vinland. A few years later a bold Norseman, Karlsefni, having talked with Leif about the new land, determined to settle it. With his beautiful bride, Gudrid, and a number of settlers, he sailed to the New World. He found the rude houses that Leif had constructed, and in these he lived for a short time. There Gudrid bore a son, known to us as Snorri — the first European child reported to have been born in America. The natives were so fierce, however, that Karlsefni, with his wife and son and companions, soon returned to Greenland. They carried with them lumber and furs. According to an old story, Karlsefni bought from the natives for a few strips of red flannel furs worth hundreds of dollars.

STATUE OF LEIF ERICSON, BOSTON, MASSACHUSETTS

Miss A. Whitney, Sculptor.

But reasons other than mere adventure and conquest were responsible for a great voyage, which made America known to Europe.

CHAPTER II

GEOGRAPHICAL KNOWLEDGE IN 1492

Trade conditions in 1492.—At the time that the Turks established themselves along the eastern and southern shores of the Mediterranean Sea, the European peoples were enjoying a profitable trade with India, which was then, as now, one of the wealthiest countries of the world. Three important trade routes to Asiatic countries had been opened up. One route was by ship through the Mediterranean and Black Seas, and thence overland by caravan into China, or northern India. Another route was by

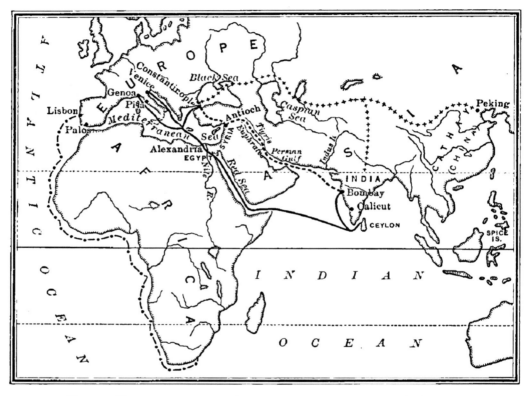

TRADE ROUTES TO THE EAST IN THE FIFTEENTH CENTURY

caravan from some port, usually Antioch, on the eastern shore of the Mediterranean Sea, to the Persian Gulf, and thence by ship to India. A third route was overland by way of the Isthmus of Suez, and thence by ship through the Red Sea and the Indian Ocean. By means of this trade—largely in silks, jewels, and spices—many merchants had grown rich; and Venice, Genoa, and Pisa had become the trade centers of Europe.

As soon as the Turks had secured themselves in eastern Europe and western Asia, they began to interfere seriously with all of the trade between Europe and Asia. It became evident that unless new trade routes could be established, the great cities of Italy would decline in wealth, and Europeans would have to do without many of the luxuries that India had furnished.

The adventures of Marco Polo.—In this day of progress and knowledge, it is hard to realize how difficult it was four hundred years ago to establish new routes of trade. In the latter part of the thirteenth century, a rich merchant of Venice, Marco Polo, in a spirit of adventure went across Asia to China. He was absent from home for twenty-four years. On returning to Venice he had much difficulty in securing his house, as no one would at first believe that the real Marco Polo could have returned in safety. Wonderful stories he told of China and its wealth, so strange, indeed, that few would credit him. He claimed that the emperor of China had made him an officer of the court, and had given him great riches. To prove this he displayed to his friends quantities of rubies, emeralds, and diamonds, which fairly dazzled their eyes. From the accounts of Marco Polo, all Europe gradually learned of the fabled wealth of China, or Cathay as it was then called. Many, therefore, longed to reach China and India without the interference of the Turks.

Geographical knowledge in 1492.—The degraded condition of most of the people, and the superstitions of the times blocked the way of rapid progress. The known world was Europe, western and southern Asia, and northern Africa. Explorers had been accustomed to travel east, but the great ocean to the west of Europe was unexplored. It was popularly thought to be filled with awful monsters, which would destroy any ship that ventured out upon it. The great body of the people believed that the world was flat, so that any suggestion of reaching Asia by way of the west was at once regarded as visionary. Moreover, the promoter of such an idea

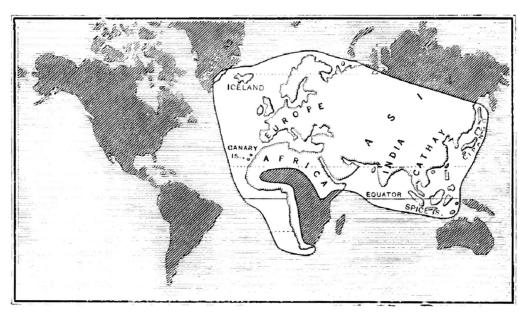

The Part of the World (White on the Map) Known to Europeans before 1492

might be considered by many as a heretic, since it was still taught that, according to the Scriptures, the world was flat and had four corners. As these ideas were general and people were slow to do anything contrary to accepted beliefs and customs, few men were bold enough to try to solve the problem of a new route to India.

There were at this time two geographies, each written many centuries before, that were still relied upon by scholars. One of these, written by Mela, said that

Africa was a small country and that its southern limit did not reach to the equator. The other, written by Ptolemy, claimed that Africa was a long continent, which made a great bend and united with southeastern Asia, thus inclosing the Indian Ocean as a large inland sea. The acceptance of Ptolemy's view meant that India could not be reached by sailing around Africa. No one had actually proved, by sailing around the coast of Africa, the truth of either view.

Earlier in the century there had lived in Portugal a prince known to history as Prince Henry the Navigator, who determined to test the matter by actual experiment. Accordingly he sent out many expeditions to sail southward along the African coast in the hope that his sailors might find a way to India. In 1471, after Prince Henry's death, some Portuguese sailors crossed the equator; but as they failed to reach the southern part of Africa, they concluded that Ptolemy was right and Mela was wrong. On their return they declared that India could not be reached by sailing around Africa; and their conclusion was readily accepted, for strange stories had been told about the southern seas. Some said that the water at the equator was boiling hot, and the sun so burning as to blacken permanently the skin of a white man.

CHAPTER III

THE PLAN OF COLUMBUS

Toscanelli.—Despite the folly or heresy of declaring that the earth is round, some rose above the superstitions of their times. Among the ancient Greeks and among the Christians of the Middle Ages could be found now and then a scholar who believed this and dared to make public his opinion. In the fifteenth century there lived in Italy an astronomer named Toscanelli, who claimed that the earth is not flat. In his speculations he drew a map, locating the different countries upon the earth as

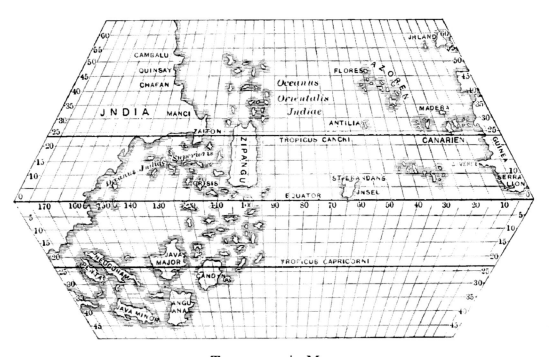

Toscanelli's Map

Restored and somewhat simplified.

a sphere. As the continents of the western hemisphere were then unknown, they do not appear on the map. According to Toscanelli's idea, Japan (Zipangu) was about the same distance from Spain as is modern Mexico; and the circumference of the earth was only about 17,000 or 18,000 miles instead of 25,000 miles, as we know it to be. In 1474 Toscanelli gave a copy of this map to a young friend who was deeply interested in the study of geography.

The early life of Columbus.—This friend of Toscanelli was no other than Christopher Columbus, one of the bravest characters of history. He was born about 1446 in the city of Genoa, Italy, and spent his youth following the occupation of his father, who was a humble wool comber. But during such hours of leisure as his father allowed him, he used to go down to the busy wharves of Genoa to listen to the stories of the sailors. Every bit of geography and adventure that he heard he treasured eagerly and pondered over as he combed the wool in his father's shop. At last he himself became a sailor. Once he was shipwrecked on the coast of Portugal; and there he learned of the exploring parties sent out by Prince Henry the Navigator, and of their failure to find an all-water route to the shores of India.

CHRISTOPHER COLUMBUS
After the portrait in the Royal Palace at Madrid.

The desire of Columbus.—During his residence in Portugal, Columbus thought of the accomplishment of a westward voyage to Asia, across the unknown seas. The vision grew from a mere wish to a determination. He studied carefully Toscanelli's map. Moreover, he was greatly influenced by a book on geography, published in 1409, which declared that the earth is round. He was convinced that Asia could be reached by sailing westward; and if this were accomplished, not only could western Europe trade with Asia unmolested by the Turks, but knowledge of the earth would be increased. There seems to have been in his mind no thought of a new world lying between Europe and Asia, but the desire to find a new route with new opportunities for trade between the old countries of Asia and the western countries of Europe.

His search for help.—Columbus sought aid for his enterprise first in Genoa and then in Venice, but the merchants only laughed at him. He was full of zeal, however, and offered his services as an explorer to the king of Portugal. Crafty old King John delayed giving Columbus a decisive answer. In the meantime he sent some sailors west to explore the ocean. They soon returned and reported that the plan of Columbus was visionary and that no European ship could brave the rough waves of the Atlantic and the terrible sea monsters that filled its waters. Thereupon the king declined to avail himself of the offer of Columbus, and thus to Portugal was lost the honor of sending out this great man on a wonderful undertaking.

Undismayed, Columbus applied to King Ferdinand and Queen Isabella of Spain. This country had just entered upon an era of great prosperity. Moreover, it was ruled by two ambitious monarchs, ready to undertake whatever might bring glory to their country. But the plan proposed by Columbus appeared to them so foolhardy that they were unwilling to further it without the approval of the learned men of Spain. These were consulted freely. For many reasons they ridiculed any notion of a western voyage; but particularly on the ground that the earth was not round. They said that if the earth were round, the people living on the other side would be walking with their feet upward.

Columbus thereupon departed to go into France; but on the way, wearied by his journey, he stopped at a Spanish monastery. To the abbot of this monastery he explained his whole plan and convinced him that a

COLUMBUS AT THE COURT OF FERDINAND AND ISABELLA
After the painting by Brozik in the Metropolitan Museum of Art, New York City.

western voyage was possible. The abbot presented the matter to Queen Isabella, and the good queen determined to equip ships for the undertaking. She was willing even to pledge her jewels, should government money be withheld. Thus it was that the wisdom of an abbot and the foresight of a clear-headed woman prepared the way for a voyage that was to change the course of history.

CHAPTER IV

THE VOYAGES OF COLUMBUS

The memorable voyage of Columbus in 1492.—As soon as he had secured the support of Queen Isabella, Columbus began to make preparations for his voyage. Three ships, the *Santa Maria*, the *Pinta*, and the *Niña*, were soon equipped. After much persuasion—for many refused to go for fear of sea monsters—a crew was secured. On the 3d of August, 1492, Columbus set sail from Palos. Hardly had the ships reached the high seas when the rudder of one vessel broke. The expedition was forced to go to the Canary Islands for repairs. When everything had been properly righted, Columbus started due west. For thirty-odd days he sailed on against the protests and murmurings of the sailors. Day by day their opposition grew more bitter, till they refused to continue the voyage. Then Columbus resorted to strategy, deceiving them into thinking that the distance sailed was not half so great as they had believed. The crew was at the point of mutiny; hope of land was about to be given up, when lo! some branches containing berries were seen floating on the waters. Soon carved pieces of wood appeared, and birds such as the sailors had never seen before soared about their ships.

Land discovered.—As darkness came on, everyone felt that the vessels were approaching land and eagerly awaited some visible sign. About two o'clock on the morning of October 12th, one Rodrigo de Triana called out, "Land! Land!" After waiting a few hours in inense anxiety, by the light of the early dawn they saw, t a short distance from the vessels, a beautiful green land. At early dawn Columbus landed and took ossession of the country in the name of Ferdinand and

Columbus's Departure from Palos
After the painting by Bacala.

sabella. The island was probably one of the Bahama roup. It was inhabited by a race of people whom olumbus named Indians, for he thought that he had ouched upon the coast of India. From this island Columbus sailed southward and discovered Cuba and Haiti.

Wherever he went, crowds of men, women, and children, bringing food and drink, came to see him and his sailors. They believed that the white men were gods.

Spain aroused.—In a short time Columbus turned his course homeward. It was an eventful day in the his-

Three Drawings from Columbus's Letter of 1493

An ocean vessel—the Admiral's caravel.   Columbus lands on Haiti and surprises the natives.   Columbus builds a fort and colony at Haiti.

The letter of Columbus first recounting his discovery was translated into Latin and sent to Rome to be published immediately after his return to Spain (March 15, 1493). These drawings, from an edition of the letter, are thought to have been copied from sketches made by Columbus himself.

tory of Europe when Columbus reëntered the harbor of Palos, from which he had sailed seven months before. Of the three little ships, only two reached the home port, one having been wrecked in a storm off the coast of Haiti. The arrival being reported throughout the town, the people rushed to the wharf to hear accounts of the voyage. They marveled at several Indians whom Columbus brought with him. Indeed, they listened intently to every story of adventure told by any member of the crew. There were no telegraph lines to spread the news of the wonderful voyage; but a swift messenger was dispatched to the city of Barcelona, where the Spanish sovereigns held court. Hither Columbus proceeded by slow journeyings. Wherever he went, he was greeted as a prince; and his journey was in all respects a march of triumph. On reaching Barcelona he was received as one of royal blood and had great honors conferred upon him.

The second voyage of Columbus.—Columbus's report on the lands he had seen created an intense desire to send out other expeditions. It was thought that a new route to India had been found, and for the time there was no thought of a new world. As the rulers of Spain were impressed by the accounts of the richness of the country, they at once sent Columbus upon a second voyage. There was no difficulty in securing sailors for this trip. This time hundreds were ready to go. In September, 1493, the expedition set sail. Again Cuba was reached, and shortly afterward Jamaica was discovered. Columbus visited also Haiti, where, on his first voyage, he had left a garrison of forty men. These had all perished or had been massacred by the natives. A second colony was then planted in Haiti. This colony did not flourish; for the men quarreled and had no thought of work, hoping merely to secure wealth quickly from the natives. Their oppression of the Indians made the success of the colony impossible. Finally Columbus was forced to return to Spain.

The third voyage of Columbus.—The king and queen, while disappointed with the results of the second voyage of Columbus, still remained friendly. Another expedition was equipped, and he was again sent out to find India and China. In the hope of reaching Asia, Columbus sailed farther south than he had done before; but, instead of reaching the coast of Asia, he touched (1498) upon the northern coast of South America. Though realizing that these lands were more than an island, he failed to grasp the fact that he had discovered a new world. His desire was to continue until he should find a passage to India, but he was taken ill and forced to sail to Haiti. There he found the Spanish colony in great turmoil. Some of the colonists were in rebellion against their governor, and a bitter war was being waged with the natives. Columbus was seized, put in chains, and sent back to Spain to answer the charge of creating sedition. The Spaniards, however, were his friends; and great was their indignation when the explorer was brought back to Spain a prisoner. The queen immediately ordered his release.

Vasco da Gama

A water route to India discovered.—Shortly after Columbus started on his third voyage, all Spain was aroused by the report that Vasco da Gama, who had left Portugal in 1497 at the head of an exploring party, had sailed around the south of Africa, crossed the Indian Ocean, and reached India. Two years later he returned to Portugal, his ships laden with the products of the far-famed India. Thus while Columbus was exploring the West, Portuguese sailors had reached the goal toward which the merchants of Europe had for centuries longingly turned their eyes. After all, Portugal had outstripped Spain in finding the long desired route to the East. These facts were known in Spain when Columbus was brought back in chains from his third voyage. Hence, though he held the sympathies of the people, it was, nevertheless, generally felt that his voyages had as yet brought no profit to the Spanish kingdom.

The fourth voyage of Columbus.—In 1502 the Spanish government determined to send Columbus upon a fourth expedition. This time he searched carefully along the coast of Central America, hoping to find a passage to India. After an absence of two years, he gave up his search and returned to Spain practically a broken-hearted man. Two years later he died. It is probable that Columbus never knew that he had actually discovered a new world. He thought that Cuba was an island off the coast of Asia, but possibly regarded South America as a new continent. Though Columbus himself accomplished little to enrich Spain, his voyages were incentives to others; and in a few years, as the result of his brave effort, Spain had possession of a large part of North and South America. Moreover, men's ideas of geography were completely changed, and a new era of opportunity was opened.

CHAPTER V

THE UNKNOWN LANDS A NEW WORLD

The Cabots.—No European country was willing that Spain should reap all the benefits that might result from western discoveries. Hence England, Portugal, and France entered the contest of exploration. England was among the first. Her king, Henry VII, was ready to undertake anything that would build up English trade. He commissioned John Cabot, an Italian seaman living in England, to sail westward. In 1497, Cabot began his voyage, but he found only a barren coast, probably Labrador; and his ship was almost destroyed by icebergs. Then, heading southward, he reached a fertile island, probably Cape Breton. When he returned to England, he was given by the "stingy" king ten pounds for the discovery of the new island, was allowed to dress in silken clothing, and was called Admiral. The next year with his son, Sebastian Cabot, he sailed westward and northwest, but finding the seas perilous with ice turned south and, according to report, explored the coast of North America from the shores of Nova Scotia to the Carolinas. On his return he gave a glowing description of the region; for he had seen many varieties of fruit and forest. Because of these discoveries, the English many years later laid claim to the greater part of North America.

Sebastian Cabot
After a portrait credited to Holbein.

As yet no one seemed to realize that a new world had actually been discovered.

Americus Vespucius.—About the time that the Cabots were sailing the northern part of the Atlantic Ocean, another Italian, whose home was the city of Florence, was exploring the Atlantic far to the south. His name was Amerigo Vespucci, or, in Latin, Americus Vespucius.

By occupation he was a merchant, but by inclination he was a student of geography and an explorer. While on a business trip to Spain in 1493, he had met Columbus, just returned from his first voyage, and had at once determined to be an explorer himself. Soon afterward he made two voyages under the flag of Spain. Later he entered the service of the King of Portugal and made several voyages along the coast of Brazil, sailing far south of the equator, and discovering a great expanse of territory.

The New World called America. — Americus Vespucius wrote an account of his explorations, which was published in many languages of Europe. The learned men recalled that the ancient geographer Mela had said that there was a fourth unknown continent. At once some of them began to say that Americus had in reality discovered a new world. In 1507 a German geographer named Waldseemüller published a little geography describing the new continent, which he called America. This America was

CABOT'S SHIP ON THE COAST OF LABRADOR

only South America; but in after years, when it was found that the northern lands were not a part of Asia, the name America was given to all the New World. Thus it happened that the hemisphere in which we live took its name from Americus Vespucius, not from Christopher Columbus.

AMERICUS VESPUCIUS
After a contemporary portrait by Bronzino.

Balboa's discovery of the Pacific Ocean. — In 1513 a Spanish explorer named Balboa was wrecked on the Isthmus of Darien. He and his men found some Indians, whom they robbed of all their gold. When they demanded more, the Indians told them to go to the west. After climbing the tops of mountains in their quest, they saw a broad expanse of water, which Balboa called the South Sea. In the name of Spain, he claimed the ocean and all its islands. This discovery was reported in Spain, and soon the news had spread that evidently a great sea lay between the New World and Asia.

Magellan's expedition proves that the earth is round. — Strange to say, no exploration had yet proved anything as to the shape of the earth, and no one had yet found out whether Asia could be reached by sailing westward. With a determination to explore South America and to reach Asia if possible, in 1519 Ferdinand Magellan fitted out an expedition of five ships. Sailing along the coast of South America, he reached the narrow passage since called the Strait of Magellan. He passed through this strait and out upon the broad ocean which he called the Pacific. Turning northward he skirted the western shore of South America for some distance, then heading abruptly westward sailed across the Pacific. In time he reached the Philippine Islands. Here, in a quarrel with some of the natives, Magellan was killed. But his followers continued the voyage, and sailed around Africa. Finally (1522), one vessel, manned by thirty-six survivors and laden with spices, returned to Spain.

FERDINAND MAGELLAN

At last the world had been circled! It was no longer a theory but a fact that the earth is round. The ideas of Toscanelli and Columbus about the shape of the earth were now known to be true.

CHAPTER VI

OTHER SPANISH EXPLORATIONS

The line of demarcation.—In 1493 Pope Alexander VI, by a famous document, divided all the newly discovered lands between Spain and Portugal. By a treaty, soon afterward, a north and south line three hundred and

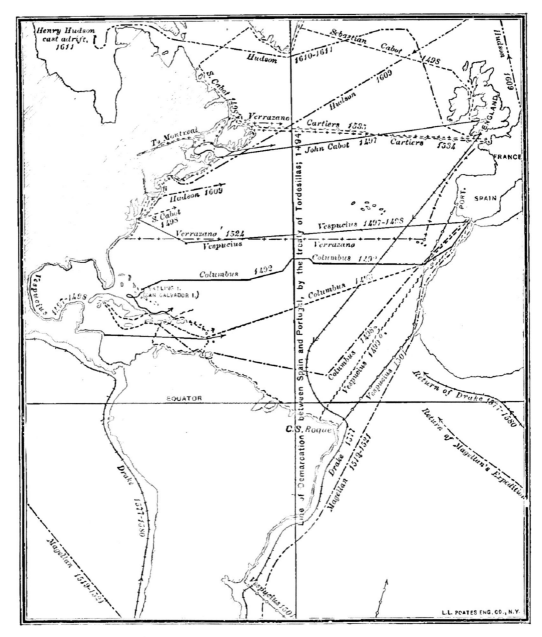

EARLY VOYAGES ACROSS THE ATLANTIC

seventy leagues west of the Azores became the so-called "line of demarcation." All lands discovered east of this line should go to Portugal, all west to Spain. Since this line passed through Brazil, Portugal secured that country

OTHER SPANISH EXPLORATIONS

and made no further efforts to acquire territory in America. Thus the New World was left practically to Spain.

Ponce de Leon.—Spanish explorers followed up the work of Columbus and discovered most of the islands in the West Indies. Early in the sixteenth century Porto Rico was settled; and in 1513 Ponce de Leon, the governor of that island, sailed to Florida. He was then an old man.

DE SOTO AND HIS MEN AT TAMPA BAY
After a drawing by Captain Eastman.

He had heard that somewhere in the new land there was a fountain of youth; and he was in quest of it when, on an Easter morning, he touched the shores of Florida. In 1521 he sailed again to Florida to make a settlement there; but on landing, he was mortally wounded by some Indians. So, for a time, Spaniards made no further attempt to settle Florida.

Hernando de Soto.—In 1539 the governor of Cuba was Hernando de Soto. Like others of his race, he was seeking gold. With a band of six hundred men he crossed to

Florida, disembarked at Tampa Bay, and proceeded northward. The fevers of the Florida swamps overcame many of his men. He left them behind him, dead or dying, pushed on, and entered what is now Georgia. Here he bent his course westward. With his followers growing daily fewer and fewer, he pressed on till he reached the great river that the Indians called Mississippi.

HERNANDO DE SOTO

Up to this point he had traversed four of the present Southern States, Florida, Georgia, Alabama, and Mississippi. He crossed the great river, made his way into what is now Missouri, turned southward, and, traversing Arkansas, again reached the Mississippi near the present site of Natchez. At this point he was taken ill with a fever from which he died. He and his followers, as the Spaniards had done many times before, had pretended to the natives that they were gods and could not die. Now it was necessary that De Soto's men should, for their own safety, keep the Indians ignorant of this deception. So by night they lowered his body into the Mississippi, thus burying him in the great waters he had discovered. Then the few survivors of the expedition passed down the river and along the coast, and after much wandering reached some Spanish settlements in Mexico. Here they made known the facts of De Soto's explorations. Knowledge of North America was gradually widening.

Other Spanish explorers.—A Spaniard named Cortez conquered Mexico in 1519; and in 1531 another, Pizarro, seized Peru.

In 1528 Narvaez reached the west coast of Florida and explored the shores of the Gulf of Mexico as far as Texas. Here he was shipwrecked, and he and all his men except four perished. These four, after six years of wandering, reached Mexico. An account of their adventures was given by one of their number, Cabeza de Vaca.

Some years later a certain Francisco de Coronado heard from Indians that there were rich villages north of Mexico called the cities of Cibola, and in 1540

An Indian Pueblo (Town) Built of Sun-Dried Clay

he went in search of them. He crossed southern Nevada, New Mexico, and Arizona, and probably reached Kansas and Nebraska. But when he turned back, it was without having found the reported cities of wealth. He had seen only the crude villages of the Pueblo Indians. This exploration, with De Soto's, proved that North America was no narrow strip of land, but a vast continent. Many geographers thought, however, that farther north the continent became very narrow. Some believed that there was a passage to the north by which Asia could be reached.

Earlier in the century a Spaniard, D'Ayllon, had sailed

north along the Atlantic coast and entered Chesapeake Bay. He meant to establish a colony within the present borders of Virginia, but his death there ended the plan.

The settlement of Florida. — By the explorations of Ponce de Leon, Narvaez, and De Soto, the Spaniards learned of Florida. In 1559, by authority of King Philip II, Velasco, with fifteen hundred soldiers and many missionaries, settled at Pensacola Bay. Two years later, on account of the climate, the settlement was abandoned. However, in 1565 Pedro Menendez arrived in Florida with five hundred troops and began the building of the town of St. Augustine. This is the oldest city in the United States. The Spanish colony of Florida grew slowly. Here and there smaller settlements were made; and Catholic missionaries established schools and missions, and undertook to convert the Indians to Christianity.

A CORNER OF FORT SAN MARCO (FORT MARION) ST. AUGUSTINE

Showing the lookout tower on the wall and the moat below.

Spain's colonial policy.—The result of the Spanish explorations in America was the occupation of all South America except Brazil, nearly all the islands of the West Indies, the present State of Florida, Central America, and Mexico, the latter then including Texas and California. Spain's policy was to secure all the wealth possible from these colonies. In the West Indies the natives were worked to death by their Spanish masters, and soon negro slaves were imported to take their place. In the South American colonies and Mexico the Spaniards made friends with the natives and in many cases intermarried with them. Spanish missionaries went into these countries and established mission schools. None of the Spanish colonies had any great amount of freedom; all were forced to contribute largely to the mother country. By this policy Spain lived upon the resources of the colonies and kept them in subjection. It was not until the early part of the nineteenth century that they began to free themselves from Spanish rule.

CHAPTER VII

FRENCH AND DUTCH EXPLORATIONS

1. *French Explorations*

Jacques Cartier.—Hardly had lands been discovered in the West before French vessels were exploring the Atlantic. In the early part of the sixteenth century French fishermen were found on the banks of Newfoundland. About 1523 the King of France sent an Italian named Verrazano to explore the North American coast. About twenty years later Francis I turned his eyes longingly to the New World. Being at war with Spain, he wished to cripple the Spanish power across the seas. He sent out Jacques Cartier, who explored Newfoundland and Labrador, and entering the Gulf of St. Lawrence, ascended the St. Lawrence River to the point

JACQUES CARTIER
After the portrait at St. Malo.

where Montreal now stands. Cartier claimed the whole country in the name of France. In 1541 he attempted a settlement on the St. Lawrence River, but the severe climate forced him to give up the undertaking.

The Huguenots in South Carolina and Florida.—In France there was a large Protestant body, known as Huguenots, who were severely persecuted by Charles IX, a son of Francis I. They wished to secure religious freedom, so they applied to King Charles for permission to establish a colony in America. The leader in this movement was a Protestant, Admiral Coligny, a man of noble birth. He sent out a colony under Jean Ribault. In 1562 Ribault planted a settlement in South Carolina on Port Royal Harbor. Then he continued his explorations as far south as the St. John's River in Florida and claimed the whole region in the name of France. After Ribault had returned home, his colonists, who were on the verge of starvation, built a small vessel and set out to sea. Fortunately an English ship picked them up and carried them safely home. Two years later the French planted another colony under Laudonnière on the St. John's River in Florida. They called their settlement Fort Caroline. This colony, too, suffered greatly from hunger and would have perished but for the timely arrival of Ribault with supplies and more settlers—men, women, and children.

French driven out of South Carolina and Florida.—The French settlements in the New World were watched jealously by Spain; for the growth of France on the continent so near to the West Indies meant interference with Spanish commerce. It was not long, therefore, before a Spanish fleet was dispatched against the settlement on the St. John's River. There were five hundred soldiers aboard, and the whole was commanded by Pedro Menendez. Ribault sailed out to meet the Spaniards, but his ships were scattered by a storm. Menendez then attacked the French colony and totally destroyed it. It was at this time that the town of St. Augustine (page 30) was founded.

France lost possession of South Carolina and Florida because the French king was not friendly to the Huguenots. However, Dominique le Gourges sold his estates, fitted out an expedition, and sailed to Florida to get revenge. Every Spaniard in the garrison on the St. John's River was killed.

SAMUEL DE CHAMPLAIN
After a portrait by Moncornet.

The French then sailed away, and Spain was allowed to hold Florida as far north as Port Royal.

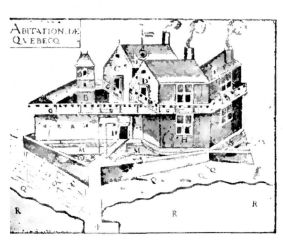

CHAMPLAIN'S SETTLEMENT AT QUEBEC
Reduced facsimile of a drawing by Champlain.

Canada occupied by the French.—For thirty-five years France ignored the new land. In 1604 King Henry IV, having heard of the excellent opportunity for trade in furs along the St. Lawrence River, granted entire control of this trade to De Monts on condition that he should settle the country.

One of the colonists sent over by De Monts was Samuel de Champlain. He explored the coast of New England

and the St. Lawrence River, and discovered the lake that bears his name. He urged the French to settle the region. Under his direction, in 1608 Quebec was founded. The beginnings of Quebec were three houses and a courtyard. This settlement became permanent, and soon other French

HUDSON RECEIVING HIS COMMISSION FROM THE DUTCH EAST INDIA COMPANY
After a painting by Chappel.

colonies were planted. For twenty-five years Champlain remained the leader of the French in Canada.

2. Dutch Explorations

Henry Hudson.—The three chief competitors in American exploration were Spain, France, and England. However, the growing republic of the Dutch had in the early part of the seventeenth century developed a great trade with the East Indies, and was therefore interested in the search for a westward passage to Asia. With this in view, in 1608 the Dutch East India Company sent out an exploring party under an English seaman, Henry Hudson. The next year, in his ship, the *Half Moon*, Hudson searched the coast a short way southward, then, turning north, sailed into New York Bay and up the Hudson River as far as the site of the present city of Albany. He reported to the Dutch the possibility of a large fur trade with the Indians, and this stimulated the Dutch in later years to make a settlement in this region. Because of the explorations of Hudson, the Dutch claimed all the territory between the Connecticut and Delaware rivers.

CHAPTER VIII

ENGLISH EXPLORATIONS

Rivalry between Spain and England.—For more than a half century after the explorations of the Cabots, the English gave no thought to the New World. With the exception of a few fishing vessels which sailed to and from Newfoundland, no English ships entered American waters. With the reign of Queen Elizabeth, however, a spirit for trade and commerce sprang up in all England; and stories from foreign ports roused interest in America. Moreover, England became the leading Protestant nation. Spain was the leading Catholic nation, and a religious antagonism existed between the two. This antagonism did not at first take the form of open warfare; but seldom did a Spanish and an English ship meet without a challenge. It was partly this rivalry on the seas that led England to compete with Spain in America.

An English sea rover.—Most prominent among those who constantly engaged in fights with Spanish vessels was Sir Francis Drake. He pillaged Spanish ships wherever he found them and carried home to England quantities of gold and silver captured from the Spaniards. In 1577 with five ships he set out to plunder some of the Spanish towns in South America. Four of his ships were destroyed; but with the one remaining, the *Golden Hind*, he sailed around South America, reached the ports of Chili and Peru, and seized booty valued at many millions. He continued northward

SIR FRANCIS DRAKE
After an old English engraving.

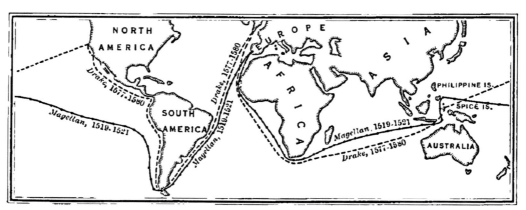

THE CIRCUMNAVIGATION OF THE GLOBE BY MAGELLAN AND DRAKE

in the hope of finding the "Northwest Passage," touched the shores of Oregon, and claimed the country for England.

ENGLISH EXPLORATIONS

Failing to find the "Northwest Passage,"[1] he crossed the Pacific Ocean and returned to England by way of the Cape of Good Hope. Drake was the first Englishman to sail around the world.

Gilbert's scheme.—Sir Humphrey Gilbert favored an English settlement in America for two reasons: first, it would make it easier for the English to oppose the growth of Spain; second, it would increase the commerce of England. Under a charter secured from Queen Elizabeth he tried to establish a colony in Newfoundland (1583), but was compelled to abandon it. On his voyage to England he was lost in a storm. It was reported that as the ship went down he said to his comrades, "Be of good cheer. It is as near to heaven by sea as by land." Sir Humphrey Gilbert and Sir Francis Drake were typical Englishmen of the time of Queen Elizabeth. They were strong believers in the Bible and in prayer, but they were rough and uncouth and cruel to their enemies.

Sir Walter Raleigh.—Sir Humphrey Gilbert had a half brother, Sir Walter Raleigh. At the time of the death of Sir Humphrey Gilbert, Raleigh was in great favor with the queen. It was reported that he had first won her confidence by spreading his cloak over a muddy place before her in one of the walks around her palace. At his request Queen Elizabeth granted him a charter to a greater portion of the English claims in America.

The explorations of Amadas and Barlow.—In 1584 Raleigh sent Captains Amadas and Barlow to explore the coun-

---

[1] It is to be remembered that the Cabots when they discovered North America were looking for a route to India. Such a route was supposed to exist and later was spoken of as the "Northwest Passage." In 1576 Frobisher sailed in search of this route and in 1585, Davis.

try. After a tedious voyage these men landed on the coast of what is now North Carolina. Great was their delight at the magnificent woods, the game, and the many varieties of vegetables they saw. They took with them to England several of the natives and specimens of potato, tobacco plant, and Indian corn. Their reports created such interest in the new country that, in honor of the "Virgin Queen," as Elizabeth was called, it was named Virginia.

SIR WALTER RALEIGH
After a portrait dated 1602.

The first colony on Roanoke Island.—The encouraging reports of Raleigh's exploring party made it easy for him to organize a band of settlers. They sailed from England in 1585, guarded by a fleet under the command of Sir Richard Grenville. Ralph Lane was in charge of the colony. He was an enterprising man; and as soon as the colonists landed on Roanoke Island, everyone was made to go to work. A fort was built, and a number of rude houses were quickly constructed. Grenville with his fleet sailed back to England. Unfortunately, on reaching Roanoke the settlers had some trouble with the Indians; so when their provisions were exhausted, none could be had from the natives. The colony was forlorn when, a year later, Sir Francis Drake came up from the West Indies where he had been plundering Spanish commerce. He took the half-starved colonists on board his ships and carried them back to England. A few days later, a supply ship arrived, and finding the colonists gone, returned to England leaving fifteen men at Roanoke.

The second colony on Roanoke Island.—Raleigh's determination to colonize the new country was not crushed out by the failure of his first attempt. He organized a company to aid in a second effort and sent out one hundred and fifty persons. John White was appointed governor. The new colony reached Roanoke in 1587. The garrison were all dead, but the old houses were found standing and were soon repaired, and the settlement was re-established under what seemed to be favorable conditions. Soon after, 1587, a child was born here—Virginia Dare, the first child born of English parents in the New World. Her mother was Eleanor, the daughter of Governor White and the wife of Ananias Dare. With the colony well under way, Governor White returned to England for supplies. On reaching home, he found that England and Spain were about to engage in a great conflict. Philip II of Spain had openly declared war against the

Raleigh's Colonists Planting the English Standard at Roanoke

English nation and was sending a mighty fleet, known in history as the Spanish Armada, to conquer the British Isles. All England was aroused, and every ship was pressed into service to fight the Spaniards. But Raleigh did not forget his colony at Roanoke. He dispatched

"The Arrival of the Englishemen in Virginia"

Reduced facsimile of one of several drawings made in Virginia in 1585 by John White; first reproduced to illustrate an account of the voyage written by John Hariot, one of the settlers, as a report to Raleigh. The original drawings are in the British Museum.

a ship with supplies. The ship, however, was destroyed by storm. It was three years later before Governor White could return to the aid of the colony on Roanoke Island. When at last he reached the settlement, all the houses were in ruins. The only sign to guide his search was the word "Croatoan" carved on one of the posts of a rough stockade.

The lost colony.—White had made an agreement with the colonists that if they should leave the settlement they would carve on a tree, or on the doorposts of their houses, the name of the place to which they would go. If they should leave in distress, a cross should be carved above the word. No cross appeared above the word "Croatoan," so White concluded that the settlers were not in dire circumstances when they abandoned Roanoke. But where was Croatoan? Five expeditions were sent out to find the place, but no sign of the settlers was ever seen. As a matter of fact, however, no search was made far from the coast. There are to-day in North Carolina some people known as the "Croatan Indians." Many of them have blue eyes and light hair, indicating that in their veins runs the blood of the white man. So, by some historians it is thought that the lost colony of Roanoke went to the lands occupied by the Croatan Indians and intermarried with them.

ELIZABETH, QUEEN OF ENGLAND 1558-1603
After a portrait at Kensington.

With the Roanoke colony perished Raleigh's efforts to colonize America. It was twenty years before the English attempted another settlement. Still Raleigh had done more to point the way to the new land than had any other Englishman of his day. North Carolina has done well in naming her capital city for this soldier, scholar, and far-seeing man. The fate of Raleigh is sad. After the death of Queen Elizabeth, her successor, James I, imprisoned him. Many years later, in 1618, to pacify the Spaniards Raleigh was beheaded by order of the king. Raleigh had lived long enough, however, to know that his plans for American colonization had met with success.

CHAPTER IX

THE AMERICAN INDIAN

The natives of the New World.—Wherever in America the Europeans went, they found vast tracts of land uninhabited except where, here or there at some spot favored by nature, small settlements had been made. These settlements were chiefly along the streams where fish were abundant, or in some region plentiful with game or fruit and vegetables. Everywhere the natives had practically the same characteristics and undoubtedly belonged to the same race. The name by which they have long been known was given to them by mistake. When Columbus first landed on the Bahama Islands and saw some of these natives there, thinking that he had touched the shores of India in Asia he called them Indians (page 17).

Mound builders.—In many parts of the country along the Mississippi and Ohio rivers and in the Appalachian Mountain range are found numerous mounds. Examination of these mounds has revealed human skeletons, many kinds of implements from a bone needle to a stone hand mill, and ornaments ranging from the crudest copper bracelet to a beautiful string of pearls. By some it is thought that the mound builders were the mother race of the Indian tribes of America. Judging from these mounds, the New World had been inhabited for many centuries before Europeans came to it.

Population.—The Indians were not numerous in that part of America which makes up the United States. By some it is estimated that there were not over two hundred thousand in all. Others think that there may have been a million. The Indian settlements, therefore, were very far apart. The people were divided into many small tribes. In some of these there were not more than fifty fighting men. In Mexico and Peru, where the Indians had advanced to some state of civilization, the population was probably greater.

The Indians of the United States are usually classified according to their mode of living into two classes, savage and barbarous.

The savage Indians.—The savage Indians occupied the country north of Mexico between the Pacific Ocean and the Rocky Mountains. They lived in a very rude way, had rough stone implements and subsisted chiefly on wild fruits and such game as they could trap.

The barbarous Indians.—It is with the barbarous Indians that we are chiefly concerned; for they were the ones with whom our English forefathers came in contact. They lived east of the Mississippi River and were divided into three races—the Muskhogees, the Iroquois, and the Algonquins. The territory now embraced in the States of Mississippi, Alabama, Georgia, Florida, North and South Carolina, and Tennessee was the home of the Muskhogees. There were many small tribes, among them being the Chickasaws and Choctaws of Mississippi and Alabama, the Seminoles of Florida, the Creeks of Georgia, the Yemassees of South Carolina, and the Catawbas o North Carolina.

The Iroquois, made up of five tribes, lived chiefly ir New York; but one branch of them, called the Tuscaroras had their home in the Carolinas and Tennessee. Nea them lived the Cherokees, by some regarded as of th Iroquois branch, by others as of the Muskhogees.

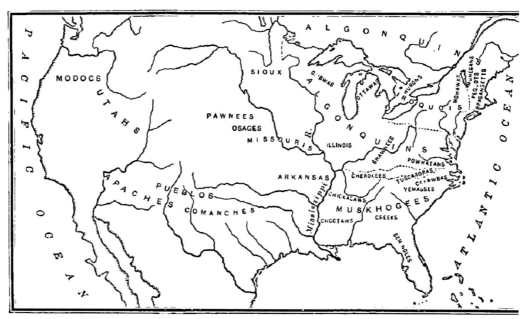

LOCATION OF THE PRINCIPAL INDIAN TRIBES OF CENTRAL NORTH AMERIC

All the country not occupied by the Iroquois north o the present southern boundary of Virginia and Kentuck and east of the Mississippi River was controlled by th Algonquins. Among the tribes were the Powhatans c Virginia, the Narragansetts and Pequots of New Eng land, and the Shawnees of the Ohio Valley.

Mode of living among the barbarous Indians.—The In dians were before all else hunters and warriors. This be ing the case, what little domestic work was done amon them was in the hands of the women. The women reared the children; cultivated little patches of Indian corn and tobacco; crushed the corn in a stone mortar with a pestle; did the cooking, and often constructed the wigwam in which the family lived. The Indian woman was called a squaw. Her life was, for the most part, that of a household drudge.

While the squaw stayed at home and worked, the warrior, or brave, went out to hunt or fight. He roamed the forest and with his bow and arrow shot down deer or wolf or bear. Often he prepared a trap or net in which he caught birds or larger game. In his canoe he frequented the small streams in search of fish. The Indian of the tidewater region was fond of oysters, and an oyster roast was as great a feast to him as it is to the modern American.

AN ALGONQUIN FAMILY

After a painting by C. Y. Turner, on the wall of the Baltimore Court House. By courtesy of the artist.

The Indians east of the Mississippi River had no domestic animals except the dog; and wherever they went, they traveled either on foot or in canoes. The various tribes were not friendly one with another, and war was common among them. The warrior delighted in taking the scalp of his enemy, and the most honored man in a tribe was he who had secured in war the greatest number of scalps.

The Indian child's life was a hard one. As a baby he was carried around tied to his mother's back. In some tribes the heads of the babies were put between boards to make them long. Little children were not allowed to go freely into the forest for fear of wild animals.

WARFARE BETWEEN THE TRIBES ON LAKE SUPERIOR

They were kept around the wigwam and helped the squaws in the work. At an early age, however, the boys were taught the use of the bow and arrow; and as they approached the age of manhood, they were allowed to fish and hunt preparatory to becoming warriors. The girls learned to cultivate vegetables, to build rude houses, and to weave grasses or other fibers into baskets, mats, or clothes.

Tribal organization.—As previously stated, the Indians were organized into small tribes. Each tribe had its ruler called king, chief, or sachem. Usually he was elected by the warriors. In time of war, these warriors constituted his council. The hunting grounds and the small open pieces of ground for the cultivation of Indian corn, tobacco, and melons were the property of the tribe. No individual owned any land. All that a warrior could call his own were his bow and arrow, his tomahawk, and the crude clothes he wore. It was because of this tribal organization that the Indians were

An Indian Chief and His Warriors in Council

seldom able to unite against the white men; and this was one cause of their failure to check the progress of the colonists.

Personal characteristics.—The Indian is often called the red man because his skin is copper-colored. He has high cheek bones, small, keen eyes, and straight black hair. He is slender and tall. From youth he is trained to undergo many hardships and to practice many feats of outdoor skill. He can go without sleep for days together and will endure without murmur intense cold or heat. He is swift of foot, and sure of aim. His senses are keen. He knows all the birds and beasts of the forest by their cry or bark. His sense of smell is almost as well developed as is that of a dog. He has observed so carefully all marks and signs in forest or prairie that he can readily track beast or man.

By nature the Indian is cruel. In approaching an enemy he is sly and stealthy, preferring to fight in ambush rather than in the open. He trusts few people. Those whom he loves he loves devotedly and will do anything in his power to help. With his friends he smokes the pipe of peace. The smoking of the peace pipe was a ceremony always observed when tribes that had been at war made peace with one another.

The characteristics of the western Indian to-day are not nearly so distinct as they were in his ancestors of a hundred years ago. His contact with the white man has been changing him.

"THE TOWNE OF SECOTA"
One of John White's Virginia drawings of 1585, showing an Indian village owned in common. Instead of wigwams there are lodges, or one-roomed houses. The plantation contains fields of corn and tobacco, and a grove filled with deer. In the foreground Indians are performing a festival dance. In the last field on the right an Indian sits under cover, doing duty as a "scarecrow."

II. THE SETTLEMENT OF THE THIRTEEN ORIGINAL COLONIES

CHAPTER X

THE SETTLEMENT OF VIRGINIA

Reasons for English colonization of America.—In England Raleigh's scheme (page 38) was not forgotten. In 1602 Bartholomew Gosnold visited the American coast and was convinced that England should occupy the country. About this time several reasons were advanced why this should be done:

1. Other European countries were making settlements in America.

2. Many people in England had nothing to do. England was filled with beggars. Moreover, the younger sons of English noblemen did not inherit any part of the land or estate of their fathers. They were poor; yet they were classed as gentlemen, and as such they felt that it was degrading to work. They wished to go to some new land where they might secure wealth. They noted that many Spaniards had grown rich in the New World. They thought that Virginia might be to them what the West Indies and South America had been to the Spaniards. Many reports had reached England that the natives of Virginia made all their utensils of gold.

3. Great Britain should extend her trade. Far-seeing men knew that with so little land in England, the

English would have to give up living by agricultural pursuits. Nature had decreed that England should be a manufacturing and trading country.

The three reasons given above and many others,

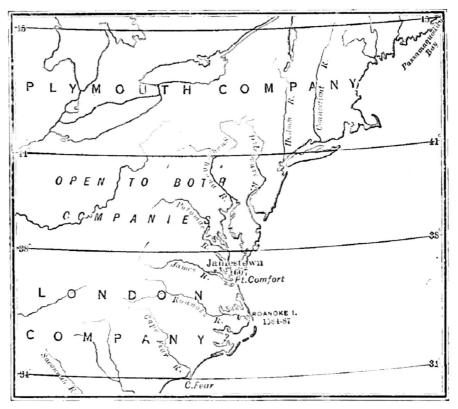

The Division of Virginia between the London and Plymouth Companies

among them the christianizing of the Indians, were urged by Richard Hakluyt, an English clergyman. As a result of the efforts of Hakluyt, Gosnold, and others, the Virginia Company was chartered to settle the New World.

The London and Plymouth companies of Virginia.— In 1600 Queen Elizabeth granted a charter to the East India Company. In a short time the English merchants who were stockholders in this company were growing

THE SETTLEMENT OF VIRGINIA

rich. Therefore, when the proposition was made to King James I to charter a company for the settlement of Virginia, he naturally accepted the charter of the East India Company as a model. In 1606 the king chartered the Virginia Company in two divisions, one as the London Company and the other as the Plymouth Company. Each company was to have a council residing in England to be presided over by a president and treasurer. The money paid into these companies for stock, as we say to-day, was to be used in sending out settlers and in establishing a line of ships, as it were, from England to America.

To the London Company was given the right to settle anywhere from the 34th to the 41st degrees of north latitude, which, roughly speaking, means anywhere along the Atlantic coast from the mouth of the Cape Fear River to the mouth of the Hudson. The Plymouth Company could send settlers into the country anywhere between the 38th and the 45th degrees of north latitude, which, roughly speaking, means from the mouth of the Potomac River to Nova Scotia. It was provided that if either of the companies established a colony in the overlapping territory between the mouth of the Potomac and the mouth of the Hudson, the other company could not settle within one hundred miles of that colony. The whole territory from the 34th to the 45th degrees of north latitude was designated Virginia.

JAMES I, KING OF ENGLAND
1603–1625

Jamestown, the first permanent settlement.—The first company to send out a band of colonists was the Plymouth Company. In the fall of 1606 Sir Ferdinando Gorges planted a colony in Maine; but on account of the severity of the climate, the settlers abandoned the country the following spring.

THE REGION OF JAMESTOWN AND ROANOKE

Likewise, in the fall of 1606 the London Company equipped three ships, the *Sarah Constant*, the *Goodspeed*, and the *Discovery*. These vessels sailed from London on December 20, 1606, and after a difficult voyage passed the capes off the coast of Virginia, April 26, 1607. One of these capes the colonists named Charles and the other Henry in honor of the two sons of King James I. Landing at Cape Henry, they took possession of all the country in the name of the English king. Then they passed slowly up the river, stopping at several points, and on the 13th of May came to a peninsula, now an island, where a settlement was made. In honor of their king, they called the river the James and the town James City. This town, afterwards known as Jamestown, was the first permanent English settlement in America.

The first English settlers.—The number of English who

settled at Jamestown was one hundred and five. Many were classed as gentlemen but only twelve as laborers. The gentlemen were unused to hard work, and consequently did not know how to use the hoe or the ax. They had not come to till the soil. It was due to this fact as much as to anything else that the early days of the colony were hard ones. Moreover, the government was poorly managed. It was in the hands of a council resident in the colony. The members had been appointed by the king; but, with the exception of Captain John Smith, they were not trained to endure hardships. Added to these disadvantages, a terrible fever in the summer of 1607 swept away all but forty-six of the colonists.

CHAPTER XI

THE STRUGGLES OF THE JAMESTOWN COLONY

Captain John Smith.—One of the most interesting characters in American history is Captain John Smith. All his life he had been an adventurer. As a boy, he had run away from home. When a young man, he joined the Germans to fight against the Turks. In the wars between these peoples he was made a prisoner and sold as a slave to a Turkish lady. After suffering the chains of slavery he managed to escape and returned to England.

On reaching home he heard of the proposed Virginia company. He volunteered to go to the new land, and so interested himself in the matter that King James appointed him—adventurer though he was—a member of the council. Smith seems, however, to have been a very boastful man and given to arguing with people. These characteristics provoked trouble on the voyage; and on the charge of stirring up strife, he was put under arrest. No sooner, however, had the colonists landed at Jamestown than he was tried and acquitted of the charge.

Smith captured by the Indians.—Edward Maria Wingfield, president of the Virginia council, paid little attention to Smith; so during the early days of the colony Smith spent his time in exploring. While exploring the Chickahominy River, he was taken prisoner by the Pamunkey Indians, whose chief was Opecancanough.[1] He was taken before the chief of the Powhatans, usually spoken of as Powhatan. According to Smith's statement, he had been condemned to death and his head was about to be crushed by a great stone when Pocahontas, a young daughter of Powhatan and his favorite child, fell upon Smith and by her entreaties caused her father to relent. A few days later Smith returned to Jamestown. This was early in 1608.

CAPTAIN JOHN SMITH
Reduced facsimile from Smith's map in the 1624 edition of his "Generall Historie."

---

[1] Smith in his history says that the Indians were about to put him to death when he drew from his pocket a small compass. They were so amazed at the action of the needle that he was able to save his life by making signs—for he could not speak the Indian language—explaining the use of it. The Indians probably thought he was more than a mere man.

The Jamestown Colony in the winter of 1607-8.—When Smith returned to Jamestown, he found the colony in a terrible condition. Wingfield had proved incapable of managing the colonists. They had spent their time during the summer in searching for gold instead of planting crops; hence when winter came there was but little food in the storehouse. Moreover, during the late summer and early fall many of the men had died from fever. About the time that Smith rejoined his companions, Newport came from England with settlers and supplies. There were now about two hundred people in the colony. For a few months everyone was hopeful.

Smith president of the council.—Discord soon came again. One man after another was made president of the council, but failed to accomplish anything. Finally Smith was elected. Thereupon he appealed to the London Company for a change of policy and begged it to send over mechanics and laborers. In the meantime, however, he put the gentlemen to work. He made them build houses and stop searching for gold. Being unused to hard labor, they had great blisters on their hands from working in the forest and the field. It is said that they swore loud oaths, for which offense Smith punished them by pouring a can of water down the culprit's sleeve for every oath. The result of Smith's measures was that by the middle of 1609 the colony was in a prosperous condition. Some good houses had been built, and much land was in cultivation. All told, there were about five hundred people in Jamestown in the fall of 1609. Unfortunately for the colony, Smith at this time was injured by the explosion of a bag of gunpowder and was forced to return to England for medical treatment.

The new charter of 1609.—The letters that Smith had written to the company in England influenced it to make

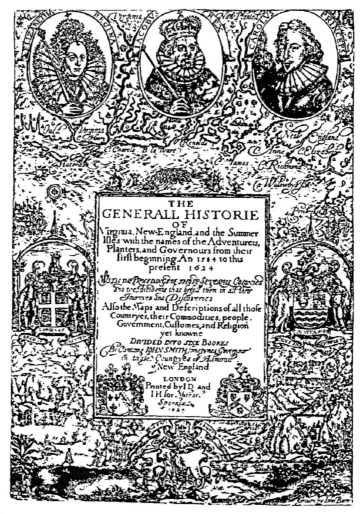

Reduced Facsimile of the Title Page of John Smith's "Generall Historie of Virginia, New-England, and the Summer Isles [Bermudas]," published in London, 1624

The portraits are of Queen Elizabeth, James I, and his son Prince Charles (afterward Charles I).

some changes in the government of Virginia. A new charter was obtained, by which the London Company was allowed to appoint a governor with entire control of

THE STRUGGLES OF JAMESTOWN

the colony. Lord Delaware was made first governor. About five hundred settlers under Gates and Somers were sent from England in ten ships. The two ships containing Gates and Somers were separated from the others by a storm and wrecked on the Bermuda Islands. The other immigrants arrived at Jamestown with no one in charge. They were left there, and the ships returned to England. On board one of these ships was the wounded Smith.

The terrible winter of 1609-10.—The arrival of the new colonists without the governor or his assistants was unfortunate. They came at a season when little work could be done and supplies were short. The result was that before the winter was over there was nothing for the colonists to live upon. By the first of June not more than sixty were left alive. Many crimes were committed during that winter. After Smith left the colony, Pocahontas, who had befriended him and had on several occasions sent provisions to the colonists, came no more to Jamestown with aid. In May, 1610, Sir Thomas Gates and Sir George Somers, having constructed two small ships out of the wreckage on the Bermudas, reached Virginia. Seeing the wretched condition of the settlement, they at once took the survivors on board and set out for England. Thus Jamestown was abandoned.

The colony saved.—In the spring of 1610 Lord Delaware, the governor, sailed for Jamestown. As Gates and Somers, steering seaward, neared the mouth of the James River, they met a small boat which announced that Delaware had appeared between the Capes and would the next day reach Jamestown. Thereupon, they turned back; and Jamestown, which had been abandoned on June the seventh, was reoccupied the next day.

CHAPTER XII

THE GROWTH OF VIRGINIA

Lord Delaware and Thomas Dale.—Under Lord Delaware, a new era was inaugurated in Virginia. The governor ruled well. He made everyone work regular hours every day, gentlemen as well as laborers. When he returned to England in 1611 and was succeeded by Sir Thomas Dale, the colony was on the road to prosperity. There were then six hundred settlers in Virginia.

Dale inaugurated martial law and introduced a new system of working the lands. Up to his time all the cultivated lands were held by the colony as a whole, and everything was worked in common. All that was produced went into a common storehouse and became the property of the company. The company, on the other hand, had to supply each settler with his daily provisions. Dale, however, decreed that every man should have a certain piece of ground to work by himself, and that whatever he made on that should be his own. Still every man had to give a certain part of his time to the cultivation of the lands that were held by the company.

The Princess Pocahontas.— In Dale's administration Pocahontas was captured and brought to Jamestown. While a prisoner, she was converted to Christianity and was baptized, assuming the Christian name, Rebecca. John Rolfe, one of the men who had been shipwrecked on the Bermuda Islands with Somers and Gates, persuaded the princess to accept his hand in marriage. In the little wooden church which had been built at Jamestown there was celebrated, in 1614, the marriage of John Rolfe and Pocahontas.

Soon after this Dale returned to England, and Rolfe and his wife went with him. The princess was received at court, and the story goes that King James reproved Rolfe for having married a princess without royal sanction. It is said, too, that Pocahontas met John Smith and was greatly surprised to know that he was alive. She claimed that the settlers at Jamestown had said that Smith was dead. In 1617 Pocahontas died in England, when she was about to return with her husband to America. She left one son, Thomas Rolfe, from whom many of the distinguished families of Virginia claim descent.

THE PRINCESS POCAHONTAS
After the famous portrait painted in England in 1616, now in Booton Hall, Norfolk, England.

The tobacco industry.— From the coming of Dale to Virginia until 1619 the colony prospered more and more. Rolfe was one of the first to introduce the cultivation of tobacco, the smoking of which had become very common in England since the time of Raleigh. Tobacco was soon the great commercial product of the colony. It was even used as money.

Governor George Yeardley.—One of the most prominent governors of Virginia in colonial days was George Yeardley. He encouraged the cultivation of tobacco and the bringing over of cattle of all kinds. He saw that if Virginia was to grow, she must raise at home what the people would need. He saw, too, that no colony could be really important which did not have settlers who intended to live there permanently. When he became governor, the great majority of the settlers were men who had come to Virginia only to make money and then return to England. There were few women and children in the colony. Therefore, in order that permanent homes might be built in the new land, in 1619 the London Company sent over a shipload of young women who had volunteered to come to Virginia and become wives of the settlers. Each colonist had to pay one hundred and twenty pounds of tobacco to cover the transportation of the young woman whom he selected for his wife.

African slavery.—Yeardley's administration saw African slave labor introduced into Virginia. In 1619 a Dutch man-of-war brought twenty negroes to Jamestown and sold them to the planters. Eight of these negroes were bought by Governor Yeardley and sent to his plantation on the James River. At this time the planters had also a number of white servants called "indented servants," who had been brought to the colony and "indented," or bound to service, for a term of years. This indented servant system grew in the colony side by side with African slavery. After 1675 the indented servants gradually grew fewer, while the slaves increased rapidly in number.

The first legislative assembly in America.—Another important event of Yeardley's administration was the calling together of the first legislative assembly that ever met in the New World. In 1619 there were nearly two thousand settlers in Virginia; so, under direction of the London Company, it was decreed that a legislative assembly should be established. The Assembly met at Jamestown on July 31st. It consisted of twenty-two representatives chosen by the people. With these sat the governor and his council. This first House of Burgesses passed laws against drunkenness, gambling, and idleness. It also requested the London Company to send over carpenters to construct a college in the colony.

The London Company overthrown.—In 1612 the London Company received a new charter, which somewhat enlarged the rights of the company. James I unintentionally made the company free to manage Virginia as it pleased. When the company gave the colony a liberal government with a legislative assembly, the king was displeased. But when it refused to elect as its president and treasurer one of his friends, he became more displeased. He only awaited an opportunity to destroy the company. He made this opportunity when, in 1622, there was a terrible Indian massacre in the colony. Commissioners were appointed to investigate the affairs of Virginia, and they reported against the management of the London Company. Thereupon, in 1624, King James caused the charter to be repealed, and Virginia became a province to be governed directly by the king. At this time the colony was prosperous despite the Indian uprising in 1622, when three hundred and fifty settlers had been killed. In 1624 the population was nearly four thousand, distributed among about fourteen important settlements.

CHAPTER XIII

VIRGINIA UNDER CHARLES I AND CROMWELL

Twenty-five years as a royal province.—James I died before he had a chance to change the government of Virginia to suit himself. Charles I, his successor, finally allowed the same kind of government in the colony that had existed under the London Company, except that the governor and the council were to be appointed by him. The king, of course, owned all the land; and no one could have any land unless it was granted to him by the king. During the period from 1624 to 1642 there were several governors. One, Sir John Harvey, is remembered because the Virginians did not like him. They suddenly rose up and put him out of office. This greatly angered Charles I, and he made the Virginians restore Harvey to the governorship. Harvey, however, found his life in the colony so unpleasant that before long he went back to England. In 1642 Sir William Berkeley came over and remained as governor ten years, until Virginia passed into the hands of a new government in England.

Charles I ruled so badly in England that his subjects rebelled against him, and many of his followers were forced to leave the country. Charles himself was seized, tried for his actions, and beheaded (1649). A new government, known as the Commonwealth, was immediately established in England, under the direction of Oliver Cromwell.

The followers of King Charles had been dubbed Cavaliers in England. Many of those who fled came to

Virginia; and this coming of the Cavaliers not only increased very greatly the population of the colony, but somewhat changed its character. Eight counties had been established in 1634; and by 1652, on account of the increase of population, there were twenty counties. The general mode of living improved much during this period, and some brick houses and better wooden ones were built.

A Cavalier

Virginia under the Commonwealth.—The establishment of the Commonwealth in England caused a similar disturbance in the English colonies in America. The Virginians at one time thought of refusing to yield to the new government and talked of proclaiming Prince Charles their king. But when the English commissioners, headed by William Claiborne and Richard Bennett, arrived in Virginia, demanding allegiance to the English Commonwealth, Governor Berkeley and the House of Burgesses yielded. It was not, however, as a conquered province, but rather as one country making a treaty with another; for the terms of Virginia's agreement with the Commonwealth were that the Virginia House of Burgesses should elect its own governors and that the colony should have free trade with England and the other countries of Europe. During the Commonwealth period, which lasted in Virginia for eight years, three governors were elected by the House of Burgesses.

The Virginians belonged chiefly to the king's party, though at this time there came a number of the followers of Oliver Cromwell. One of these was the Richard Bennett mentioned above, who was elected governor of the colony.

The Restoration in Virginia.—When royal government was restored in England with Charles II, the Virginians, who had always been more or less loyal to him, quickly proclaimed him their king; and at once Sir William Berkeley became governor again. In recognition of Virginia's loyalty to him, Charles II, it is said, dubbed the colony "the Old Dominion."

CHAPTER XIV

THE LIBERTY-LOVING VIRGINIANS

Virginia again under royal control.—With the restoration of Charles II as king, Berkeley seemed to think that he might ignore all the notions of freedom that the Virginians might have. He forgot that in 1619 the first House of Burgesses had talked of disregarding such acts of the London Company as they did not approve; and that in 1624 the Burgesses had said that no tax, except such as was approved by them, ought to be levied in Virginia. He forgot, too, that Governor Harvey had been driven out of office and forced to return to England, and that the Virginians had enjoyed a great deal of liberty during the Commonwealth. Disregarding all these facts, Berkeley kept the House of Burgesses elected in 1660 in power for sixteen years.

The colony was being endangered by Indian attacks on the frontier plantations. Berkeley, however, was engaged in trade with the Indians and therefore discouraged every effort to put down the attacks, lest he should lose the profits of his trade. Berkeley, moreover, was an aristocrat; that is to say, he wished only the land owners to vote or to hold office. In dealing with men, he was haughty and overbearing. He had no regard for the feelings of others. This made him generally hated by the masses of the people.

Furthermore, the Virginians had a grievance against the king himself. They resented his policy of granting large tracts of land in the colony to his friends.

Bacon's Rebellion.—In 1676 the Indians began to give additional trouble along the frontier, which at that time was a line drawn at the head of the tidewater region. At this time, Nathaniel Bacon, a daring young Englishman of education, raised troops to go against them. He was at first commissioned by Berkeley, but immediately afterward has ordered to disband his troops. Disregarding the governor, however, Bacon moved against the Indians and defeated them in a terrible battle.

BACON, WITH HIS FORCES, DEMANDS A COMMISSION TO FIGHT THE INDIANS

The affairs of the colony were in such a state that Berkeley was forced to ask for the election of a new House of Burgesses. This House was on the whole friendly to

Bacon, who was himself elected a delegate from Henrico. On reaching Jamestown, Bacon was arrested; but later he was pardoned by the governor and again given a commission to fight the Indians. No sooner, however, had he and his army left Jamestown than he was a second time ordered to disband his troops. Again Bacon, not heeding the governor, fought the Indians. Then he turned back and besieged Jamestown. Berkeley fled to the Eastern Shore, and Bacon and his men captured and burned the capital of Virginia, so that it might not be reoccupied by his enemies.

The colony of Virginia, which numbered forty or fifty thousand people, was now sorely rent. Next-door neighbors became enemies and were ready to burn each others' homes and plantation houses. The followers of Berkeley were especially strong in Gloucester County. Bacon went there to put them down, but was taken ill with fever and died. With their leader dead, Bacon's army was easily conquered. Berkeley ordered twenty-two of Bacon's "rebels" to be hanged. This so enraged Charles II that he recalled the old governor to England, where soon after Berkeley died a broken-hearted man. The king is said to have remarked, "That old fool put to death more men in that barren colony than I did for the death of my father."

Virginia in 1700.—At the time of Bacon's Rebellion, settlements had gone no farther west than tidewater. By 1700 there were probably seventy-five thousand people in Virginia, fifteen thousand of whom were slaves and twenty thousand indented servants. There were few schools, and these were conducted chiefly by ministers of the Church of England, the established church in the colony.

THE PLYMOUTH COLONY

The rich planters, however, were generally well educated for that day, many of them having been taught by tutors at home, and some having attended the colleges in England.

In 1693 the College of William and Mary was established, and soon it came to be an important institution.

ALEXANDER SPOTSWOOD

In 1710 Alexander Spotswood was appointed governor of the colony. He encouraged the iron industry and established several foundries. Under his direction the Blue Ridge Mountains were crossed and the Shenandoah Valley explored. In a few years settlers went into the western valleys and the mountain regions, and by 1750 Virginia was well settled to the foot of the Alleghany Mountains.

CHAPTER XV

THE PLYMOUTH COLONY

The Pilgrims.—It happened that Virginia was colonized as a great commercial enterprise. Quite other causes were responsible for the settlement of New England. In the reign of Elizabeth, the Church of England was divided. Some of its members had begun to disapprove both its government and the way in which its services were conducted. Of this number some separated from the church, or would not attend worship held according to its ritual. These were called Independents or Separatists, and were persecuted for their religious beliefs.

There was a small congregation of Independents in the town of Scrooby in western England. After they had endured not a little persecution, they moved to Holland. In Holland this little body of Christians could worship God as they liked; but they were English at heart and did not want to see their children brought up to speak Dutch and to lose their identity as English people. Therefore they appealed to the London Company and received a grant of land in America. Those who were to go in the first shiploads crossed to England and set out for the New World in two vessels, the *Mayflower* and the *Speedwell*. The latter became disabled and had to return; but the *Mayflower* continued its course and, after a rough voyage, reached the North American shore.

Plymouth established.—It was December 21, 1620, when finally the Pilgrims, as these wanderers were called, reached the harbor which they called "New Plymouth." On Captain John Smith's famous map the region had already been named "New England." The rough winds had driven them farther north than they had expected to go, so they had failed to find the settlements of the London Company in Virginia. Before going ashore, they drew up a contract, known as the "Mayflower Compact," agreeing to abide by the rule of a majority of their number. John Carver was elected first governor. It was a terrible undertaking to plant a colony in a bleak northern climate in the dead of winter. But, with brave hearts, they built rude huts and shaped a little town. The

THE PLYMOUTH COLONY

weather throughout that winter was so cold that many died from exposure. One of these was Governor Carver. William Bradford was elected his successor.

Miles Standish.—The Indians proved unfriendly; but fortunately for the colony it had for its leader a good soldier, Captain Miles Standish. He is said to have been a little man with sandy hair and a high temper, but of undoubted bravery. His wife died the first winter, but his faith in his cause only made him more determined.

WATCHING THE "MAYFLOWER" SAIL BACK TO ENGLAND, SPRING OF 1621
After the painting by Bayes.

At one time, when the Indians were harassing the colony, Standish with nine men conquered the largest village of the unfriendly tribe and forced them to make peace with the colonists. The Indians feared Captain Standish and tried repeatedly to capture him; but he was so shrewd that all the neighboring Indian tribes finally made peace with the settlers at Plymouth.

The first American Thanksgiving feast.—With the coming of spring, 1621, the settlers took new courage.

They learned from the Indians how to grow corn, and the weather proved favorable to all their plantings. In the fall when they had gathered their crops, they kept, according to their custom, a day of thanksgiving for God's blessing on their efforts. And this time, at the suggestion of Governor Bradford, they held a feast to mark with special neighborliness the gratitude they felt. To this feast they invited Massasoit, the chief of the friendly Indians, and a number of his braves.[1]

GOVERNOR BRADFORD'S HOUSE AT PLYMOUTH
The house and gardens are fenced in by a high stockade as protection against the Indians.

The growth of Plymouth. — Bradford remained governor of Plymouth thirty-one years. The settlers secured from the old Plymouth Company a grant of a small tract of land in what is now eastern Massachusetts. Other settlers soon joined them, and in four or five years the Pilgrim fathers of Plymouth were prospering. In this colony they worshiped God according to their beliefs. Strange to say, just as the Church of England had persecuted them, so they in turn sent from their midst any who differed from them in their religious opinions.

---

[1] For this first American Thanksgiving feast, a party of hunters had killed many wild turkeys and a number of deer. The feast lasted three days, and ninety Indians were present. Many outdoor sports were held with friendly contests between the settlers and the Indians.

The Pilgrims were a frugal people, and very industrious. When they came to America, they had borrowed money from the London merchants; but in seven years, by perseverance, they had shipped to England enough lumber, fur, and fish to pay their debt. By 1643 the colony had about three thousand people and seven or eight towns. Following the example of Virginia, they established a General Assembly, in which every town had two representatives. In 1691 Plymouth was made a part of the neighboring colony of Massachusetts Bay.

CHAPTER XVI

THE MASSACHUSETTS BAY COLONY

The Puritans.—Among the disapproving members of the English Church were some who wished to "purify" it by abolishing all its forms and ceremonies. These people were called Puritans. They had not left the church, but were not satisfied with it. Some of them, therefore, sought new homes where they might have opportunity to worship according to their own ideas. As early as 1628 some of the Puritans had settled in what is now Massachusetts, at Salem. Their leaders had secured from the old Plymouth Company the grant of a strip of land lying between the Charles and Merrimac rivers. To develop this territory they organized a company, which was chartered by the king. It was known as the Company of the Massachusetts Bay in New England.

Later settlements in Massachusetts.—Soon settlers in numbers came over and established Boston, Cambridge, and other towns. In two or three years a thousand or fifteen hundred men, women, and children had arrived.

JOHN ENDICOTT
After the original portrait.

The Massachusetts Bay Company, unexpectedly to the king and the people of England, moved over as a company, bringing all their officers with them. Thus they slipped out from under the control of the English king. Before long the towns formed by the Puritans were known as Massachusetts Bay, later as Massachusetts.

The prime movers in the settlement of Massachusetts were John Endicott and John Winthrop. For a number of years Winthrop was governor of the colony. Under his influence the Puritans gave up their connection with the Church of England and established a new church. This grew into what is now known as the Congregational Church. The church controlled the government of the colony, as only church members could vote or hold office.

JOHN WINTHROP
After the portrait in the Massachusetts Senate Chamber.

Government of Massachusetts.— With the establishment of a number of small towns, it was necessary to have some form of town government. The one adopted was the township system. Under this system, all the church members in a town met together to pass such laws as might be needed for their government. At this meeting they also elected the town officers. This township system, somewhat changed, is now found in many parts of the United States. For the general management of the colony, a system was introduced not unlike the one in Virginia—a General Assembly or general court, to which delegates were elected from each town. In this Assembly sat also the governor and his "assistants," or councilors.

PURITANS RETURNING FROM CHURCH

Religious troubles.— Since Massachusetts was a colony controlled by a religious denomination, the laws were very strict. No man was allowed to be absent from church on Sunday. If a man used a blasphemous word, he was branded on the forehead. In church a woman, if she went to sleep, was waked by being tickled around her ears with a squirrel's tail; but men and boys were aroused by a sharp stick or a deer's hoof fastened to the end of a long pole. A liar was punished by being put in the stocks. Scolding women were tied in a ducking stool and let down into the water.

Naturally there were some men who did not believe as the Puritans wished. One of these was Roger Williams, the minister who had charge of the church at Salem. He did not believe in harsh laws. Moreover, he thought that every man should be allowed to follow his own religious convictions, and that men, whether church members or not, should be allowed to vote. For holding such views, Williams was tried. It was ordered that he should be sent out of the colony, but he escaped into the wilderness.

THE FIRST CHURCH AT SALEM

About the time that Williams fled from the colony, there came to Boston a clever, strong-minded woman, Mrs. Anne Hutchinson. She freely criticised the preachers of the town, and soon large crowds flocked to hear her. Her doctrines were in conflict with those of the Puritans; and two years after Williams fled from Massachusetts, she also was banished.

Massachusetts a permanent home.—The first settlers of Virginia had come to gather wealth and expected to return to England. This was not the case with the Puritans. Consequently, when they settled in Massachusetts, they went to work to establish permanent homes and to build up such industries as would help them gain a livelihood.

Ships began to carry dried fish from the New England coast to Spain and Portugal. Frequently these ships went to the South African coast and would bring back cargoes of slaves. These slaves were disposed of in the West Indies or in the English colonies of the South, or were brought north. When the slaves were sold in the West Indies, the ships returned to New England with cargoes of molasses to be converted into rum. The rum would be sold to the other colonies. Before the seventeenth century had closed, the New Englanders had ships engaged in trade in many directions.

As soon as they had well established their towns, the people of New England founded a college. There could have been no stronger proof of their intention to remain in America. The college was named Harvard College in honor of John Harvard, who had left his library and a sum of money to the institution. The colony passed a law requiring every town that had fifty families to support a primary school, and every town of one hundred families, a grammar school. The ministers as a rule were well educated, many of them being graduates of the English universities; but as Harvard College grew, the young men of the colony were educated there.

The progress of Massachusetts was, therefore, very rapid. In twelve years from its first settlement, it numbered nearly twenty-five thousand people.

CHAPTER XVII

THE EXPANSION OF NEW ENGLAND

1. Rhode Island

Roger Williams plants a colony.—Roger Williams, as you have read, fled from Massachusetts because of religious persecution. It was then the dead of winter. The snow was knee deep; but with grit and determination he pressed through the wilderness southward from Boston. When he came to the Seekonk—now the Providence—River, he went to the wigwam of Massasoit, the old chief who had been friendly to the settlers at Plymouth.

It was not long before Williams was joined by some of his friends who believed as he did, and together they journeyed down the stream, beyond the boundaries of the Plymouth colony. When they reached the territory of the Narragansett Indians, they purchased a tract of

ROGER WILLIAMS RECEIVED INTO THE LAND OF THE NARRAGANSETTS

land and began a settlement (1636), which they called Providence.

Settlements by Mrs. Anne Hutchinson and others.—When Mrs. Anne Hutchinson (page 74) was driven from Massachusetts, she too went south to Portsmouth which had been founded by some of her followers (1637). Two years later, a settlement was made at Newport. These two settlements and Providence were finally united (1644) by a charter, which Roger Williams obtained from the English government. This charter established the colony that later became the State of Rhode Island.

The government of Rhode Island.—The charter that Williams received was a liberal one. The people were to govern themselves. Williams, however, was the real ruler. Everyone agreed to abide by the rule of the majority. It was also determined that there should be no established church and that the people should not be taxed to support any church. In other words, there was to be religious freedom. All men over twenty-one years of age were to have the right to vote, no matter what their religious beliefs. This scheme was quite different from that of Massachusetts. Yet this very idea of not basing on church membership the right to participate in government is what everyone in the United States now believes in. Rhode Island was the first colony to have entire religious freedom.

Under the government established by Williams, Rhode Island grew, and the people lived in peace with their neighbors, developing industries and acquiring wealth.

2. *Connecticut*

Conflict between the English and the Dutch.—Since the discovery by Henry Hudson, the Dutch had been settling the Hudson valley. Gradually they had been extending their settlements eastward, claiming likewise the lands along the Connecticut River. In 1633 they built a fort on the Connecticut River and began trading with the Indians. But the people of Massachusetts and Plymouth also claimed the Connecticut valley, and at once sent settlers into the region. The Dutch, however, drove them out. In 1635, under the direction of two English nobles, Lord Saye and Sele and Lord Brook, young Winthrop, a son of Governor Winthrop of Massachusetts, established a colony near the mouth of the Connecticut River. He called it Fort Saybrook.

The Dutch were driven away from the Connecticut region; and, though they tried again and again to reoccupy the country, the English succeeded in keeping them out.

THE COLONIES OF NEW ENGLAND

Thomas Hooker.—The people of Massachusetts gradually moved westward. Settlers from Massachusetts established the town of Windsor on the Connecticut River (1635), and a little later others came and farther down the stream built Wethersfield.

Following these, many inhabitants of Cambridge then sold their homes (1636) and, under the direction of their pastor, Thomas Hooker, moved to the Connecticut valley. Hooker's view was not unlike Williams's, in that he held that all men should have a voice in their own government. On the other hand, he believed that the Congregational Church should be the established church supported by taxation. About one hundred people followed Hooker through the wilderness, taking with them their cattle, horses, and such personal property as they could carry. They settled at Hartford. Around this settlement the colony of Connecticut was built.

Connecticut's constitution.—These three towns—Hartford, Wethersfield, and Windsor—drew up a written constitution (1639), providing for a government entirely by the people. Every free man in the colony was given the right to vote. An interesting thing about this constitution of Connecticut is that it contained no reference to the king. It was made by the people who were to be governed by it. No other colony had as yet made for itself, independently of king, proprietor, or church, such a code of laws. For this reason it is sometimes called the first written constitution of America.

Trouble with the Indians.—Hardly had the English planted themselves in Connecticut before they were at war with the Indians. A powerful tribe, the Pequots, lived in the eastern part of Connecticut. When they saw the English occupying their lands, they started out to burn and pillage. The Connecticut colony raised an army of one hundred men and placed it under the direction of Captain John Mason (1637). Surprising a palisaded village in which there were seven hundred Indians, he set fire to it. Nearly all the Indians perished in the flames or were shot down. From this time Connecticut grew rapidly, and many small towns were established.

3. The New Haven Colony

John Davenport.—At the close of the Pequot War there came from England a Puritan minister with his entire congregation. He believed that in every government the laws should be based entirely upon the Bible. Therefore, none of the New England colonies were satisfactory to him. So he settled (1638) south of the Connecticut colony on Long Island Sound and built the town of New Haven. By agreement, the colony was to be governed entirely by laws based on the Old Testament. Since trial by jury was not to be found in the Bible, it was not allowed in New Haven. Everything was centered around the church, and government and church were more closely united in the New Haven colony than anywhere else in New England. By 1643 there were a number of towns in Davenport's colony.

A SUGGESTION FROM ENGLAND

Showing how "a godly dissenting brother" may greet pleasantly a "godly brother" of different belief.—From a pamphlet of 1646, making a plea for harmony.

When, shortly after Cromwell's death, Charles II was restored to the throne of England (1660), he found that two members of the court that had put Charles I to death had fled to New Haven and were being harbored there. This so angered the king that he made New Haven a part of Connecticut (1662). Thus the colony lost its independence, and was thereafter governed under Connecticut's liberal constitution.

4. *New Hampshire and Maine*

John Mason and Ferdinando Gorges.—After the Plymouth Company failed to make a settlement in New England, James I granted (1623) all the country from the Merrimac River northward to the Kennebec and westward as far as Lake George to two friends, John Mason and Ferdinando Gorges. Settlements were soon established at what are now Portsmouth and Dover in New Hampshire. The colonists were much like the early settlers of Virginia—not religious dissenters, but members of the English Church trying to establish a commercial enterprise.

A few years later (1629), Mason and Gorges divided their grants, Mason taking what is now New Hampshire, and Gorges taking what is now Maine. On the death of Mason, New Hampshire passed, after some turmoil, into the hands of Massachusetts (1641). Eleven years after that, Massachusetts bought the claim of Gorges to Maine. The territory of Massachusetts was now many times its original extent. When the transfers were made, there were not many inhabitants in either Maine or New Hampshire—in Maine, only a few fishing stations and trading posts, and in New Hampshire but four or five towns.

CHAPTER XVIII

THE UNITED COLONIES OF NEW ENGLAND

New England as a whole.—Except for the few settlers in New Hampshire and Maine, the character of the people throughout New England was much the same. They differed somewhat among themselves in religious belief; but they were all opposed to the Church of England. They were all agreed in wishing to be free as far as possible from the English Government. It is true, however, that the religious freedom established in Rhode Island was not pleasing to the other colonies, and that at times Rhode Island was ignored by the rest of New England.

CHARLES I, KING OF ENGLAND
1625-1649
After a portrait by Van Dyke.

New England Confederation.— In 1643 the colonies of Massachusetts, Plymouth, Connecticut, and New Haven formed a union under the title of the United Colonies of New England. New Hampshire and Maine were included in this union because they were at this time a part of Massachusetts. Rhode Island was left out because it did not support the Congregational Church as the established church of the colony. The object of this union was protection against the Indians, against the Dutch, and against the French. The Dutch were troubling the settlers in the Connecticut valley. The French had settled along the St. Lawrence River and were pushing into northern New England. The government of this union was placed in the hands of commissioners, two from each colony, who were to decide what important matters the united colonies should undertake together.

Attitude toward the Indians.—All the later New England colonies followed in the steps of Massachusetts in providing means for educating their children; and not only their children, but the Indians around them. There came to Massachusetts the Reverend John Eliot, a devout man, who went among the Indians preaching Christianity. It is said that at one time in New England there were four thousand Indians who had given up their superstitions and accepted the Christian beliefs. Eliot wished to have these Indians taught, and planned to establish schools for them. He accomplished the stupendous work of translating the Bible into their language. John Eliot has been fitly called the Apostle to the Indians.

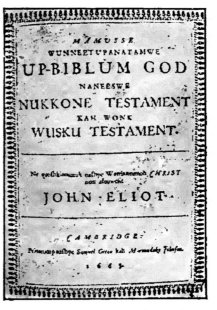

TITLE PAGE OF ELIOT'S INDIAN BIBLE

Translation: "The whole Holy Bible of God, both Old Testament and also New Testament. This translated by the Servant of Christ who is called John Eliot. Cambridge: Printed by Samuel Green and Marmaduke Johnson, 1663."

Twenty years of independent growth.—For about twenty years after the establishment of the New England Confederation, the colonies of New England governed themselves without any interference from England. For the first six years of this period, Charles I was at war with his subjects in England and could pay no attention to the American colonies. For eleven years following the execution of the king (1649–1660), Oliver Cromwell and the Puritans ruled England as a representative government, or commonwealth. They were in sympathy with the settlers of New England and interfered but little in their affairs. Thus the people of New England came to feel that they were almost independent. They had united themselves without consulting the Government in England, and they felt that the Confederacy would be fully able to manage its own affairs. They could enforce their own laws without first sending them over to England to be approved, as the Virginia Assembly was obliged to do. They could coin their own money without permission from the English Government. The shilling that Massachusetts coined bore the picture of a pine tree. A "pine-tree shilling," as it was called, is to-day a rare coin and worth a great deal of money.

OLIVER CROMWELL
LEADER OF THE ENGLISH
COMMONWEALTH
1649–1658

After a painting by Samuel Cooper, in the University of Cambridge, England.

Attitude toward Quakers.—The laws of Massachusetts were severe against Quakers. These people were at first sent out of the colony, but many returned. It was then enacted that their ears should be cut off; later, that every Quaker who would not stay out of the colony should be put to death. In Boston one woman and three men of this sect were hanged. The Quakers thought it their duty to preach freedom of worship; and this, to the authorities of Massachusetts, seemed like preaching anarchy.

A PINE-TREE SHILLING

CHAPTER XIX

NEW ENGLAND UNDER CHARLES II AND JAMES II

Charles II's interference.—When Charles II became King of England, his feeling was hostile to the New England colonists. Though England herself persecuted the Quakers, Charles felt that Massachusetts had gone too far and ordered that in New England no more Quakers should be put to death. The king had good reason to dislike Puritans; and he thought that the rebels in England who had overthrown his father's government had been encouraged by the Puritans across the sea. Furthermore, New England was now a harbor for rebel refugees. It was Charles's intention to punish all who had served in the court that had condemned his father to death. Two of these men, Edward Whaley and William Goffe, had escaped to New England, avoided arrest in Boston, and been concealed in New Haven (page 80). The spirit of independence, thought the king, was growing too strong.

How the king treated Massachusetts.—Charles did not interfere with the charter of Massachusetts, but he demanded that certain laws should be changed: first, that the right to vote should not be restricted to church members, and that worship according to the rites of the Church of England should be allowed; second, that all the people of Massachusetts should take the oath of allegiance to him as their king. The people of Massachusetts complied in only a half-hearted way with the instructions of their king. Fortunately for Massachusetts, Charles was engaged in a war with Holland and, for the time at least, thought it better not to force the colony into open rebellion.

The charters of Connecticut and Rhode Island.—The Connecticut colony, realizing that it might be politic to try to please the king, made application for a royal charter. This pleased the king so much that the charter he gave Connecticut (1662) was a most liberal one. The colonists were allowed all the liberties that they had previously enjoyed. They could elect their own governor and their own officials, and they did not have to send their laws to England for approval. Moreover, the boundaries of the colony were extended by the addition of the New Haven colony, which had so displeased the king (pages 80, 85.) Thus the Connecticut of to-day was created. This charter of 1662 was so satisfactory to the people that no change was made in it until 1818.

KING PHILIP, CHIEF OF THE WAMPANOAGS

On the petition of Roger Williams a charter was granted to Rhode Island similar to the one given Connecticut. And this charter, too, created such good government that it was 1842 before Rhode Island found need to change it.

King Philip's War.—In 1675 occurred a general uprising of the Indians of New England. It was headed by King Philip. He was a son of Massasoit, the chief who as long as he lived had been a friend of the English. King Philip invaded the Plymouth colony and burned several small villages. At once the commissioners of the New England Confederation met, raised an army, and prepared to attack the Indians in their stronghold in Rhode Island. This stronghold was an inclosure surrounded by a stockade of logs, within which the Indians had placed their wigwams and moved their families for the winter. The white men surprised the fort by a sudden attack, and set it on fire. One thousand of the Indians were killed. King Philip was able to escape and to carry on the war a short time longer; but after a year he was killed, and the Indians scattered in all directions. His sons were taken prisoners and sold into slavery. It had been a severe struggle; for during the course of one year, more than twelve of the New England towns had been destroyed, and nearly fifty had suffered from Indian attack.

Andros sent to New England.— The time had come when the people of Massachusetts were to pay the price of disobedience to their king. You remember how they had hesitated to alter their laws (page 85). For a time Charles II took no steps to force them. But in 1679 he showed that he had not forgotten the incident; for he took New Hampshire from Massachusetts and made it a royal province. His second step was to revoke the charter of Massachusetts and make that, too, a royal province (1684).

Sir Edmund Andros
After the portrait in the State Library at Hartford.

Hardly had this been done when Charles died.

His brother, James II, pursued the same policy of trying

to humble and restrain the colonies. He determined to unite them all under one governor. To carry out this plan, he sent Sir Edmund Andros to New England (1686). Rhode Island was forced to surrender its charter. But Connecticut refused to do so, and Andros went to Hartford to demand the charter. It is said that as the General Assembly, or General Court as it was called, of Connecticut was debating the matter, a member blew out the lights, seized the charter, and rushed out and hid it in an oak. This tree was for many years preserved in Hartford and pointed out as the "charter oak." Andros was made governor of New Jersey and New York; and Boston was made the capital, as it were, of all the territory that he governed.

About this time, 1688, there was another rebellion in England, and James II was driven from the throne. Thereupon the people of Boston put Andros into prison, and the different New England colonies began to rule themselves as they had done before his coming.

CHAPTER XX

NEW ENGLAND UNDER WILLIAM AND MARY

King William readjusts matters in New England.— As soon as political affairs had been straightened out in England, and King William and Queen Mary were reigning, New England received the attention of the king. William appreciated the friendship that the New Englanders had shown him; but on the other hand he knew the unruly spirit of the New Englanders, especially of those in Massachusetts. Therefore, he did not restore to Massachusetts the same charter that it had had before the coming of Andros, but gave it a new one. The new charter granted to all freemen the right to vote; but it reserved to the crown of England the right to veto any law passed by the General Court of Massachusetts, and it specified that the governor of Massachusetts must be appointed by the crown.

Needless to say, the charter was very distasteful to the people. Somewhat to make amends for it, William

WILLIAM I AND QUEEN MARY, SOVEREIGNS OF ENGLAND 1689–1702
After portraits by Sir Godfrey Kneller, at Kensington Palace.

annexed to Massachusetts the Plymouth colony. He allowed Massachusetts to keep Maine, but he did not return the territory of New Hampshire. That he kept as a royal province.

To Connecticut and Rhode Island he restored the charters granted by Charles II.

The political divisions of New England as King William adjusted them remained fixed as long as the colonies continued to be provinces of England.

Salem witchcraft.—By 1700 New England as a whole was no longer troubled by friction between religious sects. It had been forced by the English Government to give up religious persecution. The harsh spirit of the first Puritans had gradually been softened in their descendants. Shortly before 1700, however, some of the people had worked themselves into a strange state of mind that was at that time common in some parts of Europe. That is, they believed in witchcraft. In Salem almost the whole town was excited by this religious frenzy. A witch, they thought, was a special agent of the devil. All the troubles that had come upon them, they said, were caused by wicked witches who lived among them. Many a poor old woman was accused of being a witch. All told, no less than nineteen persons were put to death. Finally, those who were responsible for the persecution realized the terrible crime they had committed. Some made open confession of their mistake, whereupon the witchcraft delusion was over.

TITLE PAGE OF AN EIGHTEENTH CENTURY EDITION OF THE "NEW ENGLAND PRIMER"

The chief reading and spelling book in the colonies from about 1690 to 1800. Facsimile but slightly reduced from original size.

New England in 1700.—At the close of the seventeenth century New England was in great prosperity. More and more merchantmen were pushing across the sea. They were trading with Spain and Portugal in fish, with Africa in slaves, with the West Indies in molasses, and with the southern English colonies in rum and cereals. Each year more ships were built, and gradually the foundation was being laid for manufacturing enterprises. The forests of Massachusetts did not furnish so much lumber and fuel as were needed, but ships soon brought wood in plenty from Maine. In the early days Boston had suffered severely for want of wood to burn. The people lived simply. Their laws even forbade them to wear fine clothes.

Nearly all the boys were sent to school. The girls, however, were not, as a rule, taught much from books. It was thought that learning would keep a girl from becoming a good housekeeper. School lasted from seven o'clock to eleven in the morning, when the children were given a two hours' recess. They came back at one and stayed till four. The subjects taught were reading, writing, spelling, and ciphering. The Bible was the chief reading book.

In 1700 the population of New England was probably about one hundred and five thousand. Of this number about five thousand were African slaves.

CHAPTER XXI

THE SETTLEMENT OF MARYLAND

English settlements in 1633.—Before 1633 only three English colonies had been established in America. The first was Virginia (1607); the second was Plymouth (1620); the third was Massachusetts (1628). The relation of all the New England colonies with one another was so close that we naturally think of the growth of New England as a whole, even though some of her colonies were settled later than colonies farther south. The fourth settlement of the English in America was Maryland.

Lord Baltimore.—In the time of King James I there lived in England a good Catholic named George Calvert. Because of his statesmanship he was much admired by the king, who made him Lord Baltimore. At that time the English Government did not allow Catholics freedom in religious worship; so Lord Baltimore thought it would be well to form a colony in the New World, where Catholics could live and worship as they pleased.

GEORGE CALVERT, FIRST LORD BALTIMORE

With this in view he visited Virginia, exploring the country along Chesapeake Bay. When he returned to England, he secured from Charles I, then reigning, a grant of land north of the Potomac River. This country he called Maryland in honor of the queen, Henrietta Maria. His charter was a liberal one. It made him ruler and owner of the province with the understanding that he should grant to the king one-fifth of the gold found in the province and should pay yearly to him a tribute of two Indian arrows at Easter time.

Maryland a proprietary colony.—Maryland was the first permanent colony in America to receive a charter in which its founder was declared the owner, or "pro-

THE SETTLEMENT OF MARYLAND

prietor." Hence Maryland was known as a "proprietary colony." In a royal province such as Virginia the governor and the members of the council were appointed by the king, to whom all the laws were submitted for approval. In a proprietary the proprietor was himself king, as it were. He appointed the governor and members of the council, and to him the colony had to submit its laws for approval.

CECIL CALVERT, SECOND LORD BALTIMORE
After a portrait dated 1657.

Maryland settled, 1634.—The first Lord Baltimore died before he could carry out his plans. His son, Cecil Calvert, the second Lord Baltimore, proceeded to fulfill his father's wishes by sending over about one hundred settlers. Most of them were Catholics, but there were a few Protestants. They disembarked on the western shore of Chesapeake Bay, in what is now St. Mary's County, and began a settlement there. They bought the land from the Indians, who in this region were tillers of the soil. The land proved fertile, and during the first summer the colonists raised a goodly crop of corn. Game was plentiful, too; so the early Marylanders did not undergo the same hardships as the first settlers of Virginia and New England.

Religious toleration.—The second Lord Baltimore was a liberal man; and he instructed Leonard Calvert, his brother, whom he sent over as governor, to establish religious toleration. In fifteen years, as many Protestants as Catholics had come into the colony. In 1649, the General Assembly of Maryland passed a law known as the Toleration Act, which decreed that no Christian should be disturbed because of his religious belief. This Act has often been quoted; for it showed

GOVERNOR CALVERT BUYING LAND FROM THE INDIANS
From the frieze in the Baltimore Court House. By courtesy of the artist, Mr. C. Y. Turner.

the broad spirit of Lord Baltimore and the early settlers of Maryland. The mother country had at that time no such liberal law.

Troubles between Maryland and Virginia. — William Claiborne and a number of Virginians had established a colony on Kent Island in Chesapeake Bay, under a charter secured before Maryland was settled. The boundaries of Maryland, as given in Lord Baltimore's charter, included Kent Island. Claiborne, however, claimed that Lord Baltimore had no rights in the island because Lord Baltimore's charter, in designating the boundaries, had said that he should have authority only over uninhabited lands. According to Claiborne's view, Kent Island was already inhabited and was not, therefore, a part of Maryland. A year after the Maryland colony was planted, the settlers, by Governor Leonard

THE MARYLAND GRANT AND SETTLEMENTS

Calvert's instructions, seized the island. Claiborne appealed to the English Government, but the decision was in favor of Maryland's claim.

When England was torn by the civil war between Charles I and his subjects, Claiborne made one more effort to secure his possession. He found that the Puritans of Maryland were about to rise in rebellion against the proprietor, so he interested them in his cause and by their aid seized Kent Island. The rebels were so strong that they even captured St. Mary's and drove Governor

Calvert from the colony. But a year later, 1646, Calvert returned and regained control of Maryland. Claiborne was forced to give up Kent Island; and when Cromwell became Lord Protector, he decided for once and all that Claiborne had no right to Kent Island.

CHAPTER XXII

GOVERNMENT AND PROGRESS OF MARYLAND, 1649–1700

Maryland under the English Commonwealth.—When the Toleration Act was passed, there were already many Puritans in Maryland. Soon others came; and several settlements were made, among them one at Annapolis, which afterwards became the capital of Maryland. With the establishment of the Commonwealth in England under the rule of Oliver Cromwell, the Puritans of Maryland determined to overthrow Lord Baltimore and to deprive the Catholics of freedom of worship. However, Lord Baltimore did not give up without a struggle. William Stone, whom Lord Baltimore had appointed governor, raised a force and tried to overthrow the Puritan government; but he was defeated at the Severn River (1655). Then Lord Baltimore took the whole matter before Oliver Cromwell, who restored the proprietary government (1658).

Thirty years of growth.—Charles II recognized the proprietary rights of the second Lord Baltimore, and until 1675 this good man continued to direct the affairs of Maryland. He was kind and liberal, and approved of all laws that the colony passed to further its growth. Settlers came each year; and the people devoted themselves to the raising of tobacco, wheat, and some cattle. Slavery was early introduced into the colony, so the Maryland plantations were not unlike those of Virginia.

In 1675 the second Lord Baltimore died; and George Calvert, the third Lord Baltimore, became proprietor. Because the right of voting was restricted to land owners and because the government did not quickly put down Indian uprisings, there was a rebellion in Maryland not unlike Bacon's Rebellion in Virginia. This was soon quelled, however; and order was restored.

PURITANS OF MARYLAND
From the frieze in the Baltimore Court House. By courtesy of the artist, Mr. C. Y. Turner.

Maryland a royal province. — When William and Mary, who were strongly Protestant, came to reign in England, the Protestants of Maryland, who outnumbered the Catholics three to one, expelled the governor; for the governor was a Roman Catholic and represented Lord Baltimore. They appealed to William and Mary to make Maryland a royal province. Their request was granted, and for the next twenty-five years the Maryland government was in all features like that of Virginia.

Maryland again a proprietary colony.— In 1715 the then Lord Baltimore was a Protestant, having given up the religion of his fathers. After some difficulty, he had his right as proprietor of Maryland restored; and for more than fifty years Maryland remained a proprietary colony. The people were never entirely satisfied, however, with the rule of the proprietor. They could not understand why they should be taxed for his benefit.

The conditions of life in Maryland in colonial days were practically the same as in Virginia.

CHAPTER XXIII

THE BEGINNINGS OF THE CAROLINAS

Early settlements south of Virginia.—The first attempt at an English settlement in America was made, you remember, at Roanoke Island, in what is the present State of North Carolina (page 39). In what is now South Carolina, at Port Royal, the French made their first attempt (1562). The country was named Carolina by the French, in honor of their king, Charles IX, *Carolus* being the Latin for Charles; and in 1629 the name was retained in honor of King Charles I of England.

The Virginia colony was growing westward toward the mountains, rather than southward. However, before 1660 some Virginians had settled in the region to the south. There were various reasons why these settlers separated from the other Virginians: most of them wished to occupy the rich lands which lay at their disposal and to find good grazing country; many were adventurers who disliked to live in settled communities; and some had gotten into trouble in Virginia. Later many Quakers and other dissenters came to escape religious oppression. The first permanent settlement in North Carolina was made (1653) by Roger Green and a party led by him, in the region between the Roanoke and Chowan rivers. More settlers followed, and this was the beginning of the Albemarle colony. A few years later others came, some from New England and some from the Barbadoes, settling on the Cape Fear River; but they soon abandoned the settlement, and the Cape Fear section was not permanently settled until 1725.

The Carolina proprietorship.—When Charles II became king in 1660, a new era was begun for English colonization in America. Up to this time there were only three portions of America settled by the English—Virginia, Maryland, and New England. Between Maryland and New England the Dutch had settled. South of Virginia was a large strip of territory, uninhabited, extending to Florida. The English people saw the importance of grasping the whole Atlantic coast. Therefore, at the same time that they planted settlements south of Virginia they began a war against the Dutch colonies between Maryland and New England.

A charter to the territory south of Virginia had been granted by Charles I, in 1629, to Sir Robert Heath; but no colony was planted. It is doubtful whether Charles II knew how many settlers had already gone into this southern region. In any event, he determined to establish a proprietary for this southern country. In 1663 he granted Carolina to eight lords-proprietors, among them being the Earl of Clarendon, the Duke of Albemarle, and Sir William Berkeley, then governor of

Virginia. About the only restriction placed upon the proprietors was that they should recognize the land claims of any settlers who might already have gone into the territory, and that the laws should conform to those of England.

Albemarle and Clarendon settlements.—Colonists came over and in a short time began settlements around two centers: one to the north in what was known as the Albemarle colony, where the Virginians had first gone; and the other to the south on the Ashley River, to which the immigrants from the Barbadoes went. In a few years these two settlements were well-to-do. The soil was more fertile than in the colonies to the north, and the crops were good. The Bahama Islands were then (1670) added to the Carolina grant, which now included all land south of Virginia and north of Florida, running from the Atlantic to the Pacific. The proprietors established something like local self-government, allowing an assembly of the people like the assemblies of Virginia and Maryland.

THE EARL OF CLARENDON
From a portrait dated 1667.

Locke's scheme of government, 1669.—Unfortunately for Carolina, there lived in England a philosopher, John Locke, who devised a new plan of government for Carolina. He was a friend of one of the Carolina proprietors, and so it happened that he was asked to draw up a constitution for the province. This constitution is known as the "Grand Model," because Locke and the proprietors thought that it would be a model form of government for all the colonies. Locke had in mind the interests of the lords-proprietors. His scheme divided the people into several classes, graded from nobility down to land laborers with no privileges at all. They could not even leave the land on which they lived. But when the proprietors undertook to enforce this scheme in America, the result was an absolute failure. The people of Carolina already knew what it was to have freedom. The outcome was that after several years of discord, the new government had to be abandoned.

CHAPTER XXIV

NORTH CAROLINA AND SOUTH CAROLINA

Two colonies in Carolina.—For many years (1663–1729) there were two distinct colonies in Carolina, but the proprietors tried to govern them as one. Most of the governors lived in the southern or Clarendon colony with a deputy in the Albemarle settlement, but there was often a governor for each colony. Constantly during this period there was a struggle between the people and the governor representing the proprietors. But in spite of these difficulties the colonies grew. For convenience we will speak of the northern colony as North Carolina and the southern colony as South Carolina.

1. *North Carolina*

The growth of the Albemarle colony.—The Albemarle colonists prospered from the beginning, many raising cattle and planting corn and tobacco. They built up a flourishing trade with New England in defiance of the navigation acts, and the king's officers there had much trouble in collecting the customs duties. At one time (1678) the people put into prison Deputy Governor Miller, who was also the collector. It was several years before the proprietary governor could make the people yield to the laws of England, and they did not yield until the proprietors gave them more responsibility in their own government. When this had been done, people flocked to North Carolina because they believed they could have liberty in that colony. The liberty-loving spirit of the North Carolinians showed itself when Seth Sothel was governor. Though he was one of the proprietors, they would not submit to his tyranny, but drove him from the colony (1688). Again, in 1704, there began a long struggle over the right of the Quakers to hold office. This was known as the Cary Rebellion, and during it the people of the colony forced two governors out of office.

THE GRANTS OF THE CAROLINAS

Indian troubles. — For a while, North Carolina was disturbed by the Tuscarora Indians, but the tribe was at last defeated (1711-13) by the joint forces of the two Carolinas. Most of the surviving Indians, who belonged to the great Iroquois family, then migrated north to the home of their ancestors, east of the Great Lakes.

North Carolina a royal province. — The proprietors, having failed in their management of the Carolinas,

NORTH CAROLINA AND SOUTH CAROLINA

finally, with one exception, sold their claims to the crown (1729). Thereupon the two Carolinas were formally separated, and each was made into a royal province. They thus came to have a form of government in which the governor was appointed by the king.

2. South Carolina

Charleston.—The first body of settlers to come directly from England to South Carolina landed along the Ashley River. In 1670 William Sayle planted a colony at the junction of the Ashley and Cooper rivers on the site of the present city of Charleston. Sayle received the support of the proprietors, and his settlement grew rapidly. On his death, he was succeeded as governor by Yeamans, who was very unpopular with the colonists. Into this region came a number of French Protestants called Huguenots, who had been persecuted in France. They were industrious, thrifty people and added much to the growth of the colony.

Many governors a curse.—South Carolina would have grown more rapidly if it had not had so many governors. Unfortunately, each good governor was followed by a succession of bad ones. These governors tried to enforce the laws of trade on the high seas and the collection of customs, included under the navigation acts, and to raise taxes for the benefit of the proprietors. But the people resisted bitterly and drove out governor after governor. In 1695 John Archdale came to the colony as governor. He quieted matters, raised a moderate tax for the proprietors, and established peace with the Indians.

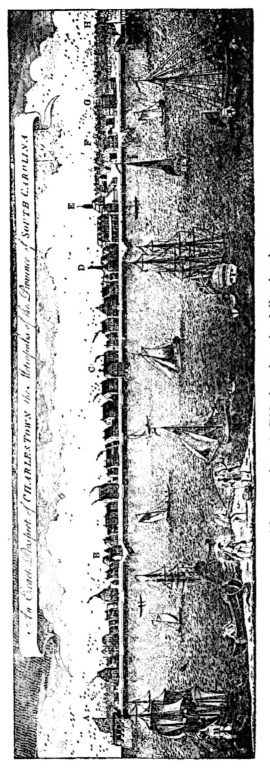

After a print of 1762, bearing the following key:
A. Granville Bastion. B. Court House. C. Council Chamber. D. Meeting House. E. St. Philip's Church. F. Custom House. G. Secretary's Office. H. Craven's Bastion.

The growth of South Carolina. — By 1700, with the coming of many Huguenots and English, there were some five or six thousand people in the colony. About one half, however, were slaves—a larger proportion than was found in any of the other colonies at this time. The plantation system grew rapidly, many of the large planters living on their plantations in the summer and in Charleston in the winter. Thus Charleston became the center of social life in the South. It was also an important seaport.

The people in South Carolina hated the Spaniards in Florida and were anxious to engage in war with them. This was discouraged by the governors and proprietors. However, Charleston harbor was a point from which many sea-rovers went out and preyed on Spanish commerce. These expeditions, together with the disregard of the navigation acts, added much to the wealth of the colony.

South Carolina a royal province.—During the years following 1700, the government of the proprietors was very bad and finally, in 1719, the people deposed the governor and asked the king to appoint one. The petition was granted, and in 1729, George II purchased from the proprietors their claims to the colony.

CHAPTER XXV

GEORGIA

Conditions in England in 1730.—About the time that the Carolinas became two royal provinces, the conditions of life in England were in many ways deplorable. A few noblemen owned most of the land. The wealthy merchants owned all the ships and controlled trade. There was little opportunity for the great middle class of people to better themselves. They had almost no voice in the government. Because of the conditions of trade, many men were in a dire state of poverty. Those who were unable to pay their debts were thrown into prison. The country was overrun with paupers and beggars.

General Oglethorpe.—To relieve this condition of affairs, General James Oglethorpe planned to establish a new colony in America. He was a kind-hearted and wealthy man of noble family. He had been educated at Oxford University, had entered the English army, and had fought bravely in wars on the continent of Europe. In 1729 he was a member of Parliament and as such was trying to pass laws to improve conditions in England. He wished to take the poor debtors out of prison and give them a chance to start anew in life. With this in view, he suggested that a colony be planted between South Carolina and Florida. It would not only help the debtors and poorer people but would also serve as a barrier to the increase of Spanish power in America.

JAMES EDWARD OGLETHORPE
After the painting by Ravenet.

The Georgia charter.—A number of generous men became interested in General Oglethorpe's plan. A sum of money was subscribed to send out a colony, and a charter was secured from King George II. The territory granted was called Georgia in honor of the king. General Oglethorpe and others named in the charter were designated as trustees. This title indicated that the colony was not planted for the benefit of those to whom the grant was made, but for the benefit of the settlers. Oglethorpe and his associates were to serve without pay and were to derive no profits from the undertaking. So anxious was General Oglethorpe for the success of the enterprise that he consented to come over with the first colonists. Such interest was taken in the matter that Parliament even voted a sum of money to promote the undertaking.

The founding of Savannah.—In 1732 Oglethorpe arrived in America with one hundred and fifty settlers. They were debtors released from prison, but persons of good character. After some little delay a high bluff on the Savannah River was selected as the site for settlement, and here was begun (1733) the city which to-day bears the name Savannah.

Oglethorpe's relation with the Indians.—One of the first things that General Oglethorpe did was to have a conference with the chief of the Yamacraw Indians, who lived near by. Their chief was an old man, Tomo-chi-chi. A treaty of alliance was made with him, and this precaution saved Georgia from Indian onslaught and plunder.

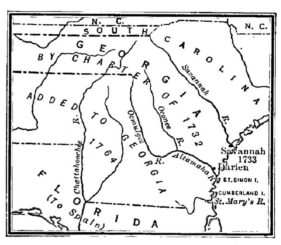

THE DEVELOPMENT OF GEORGIA

The growth of the colony.—It was fortunate for Georgia that Oglethorpe established friendly relations with the Indians, for the first settlers could not have contended with them. In fact, they were not fitted to establish a colony in the wilderness. They were not industrious; and had Georgia been compelled to rely for its growth upon the debtor class, the colony would have gone to ruin. Slavery and the sale of whisky were prohibited; for Oglethorpe intended that the colonists should themselves learn to labor, and he hoped to keep them out of bad habits. Other settlers soon came, among them some Protestants from Germany known as Salzburgers.

These were followed by Moravians, and later by Scotch Highlanders. They all built good towns and were a thrifty people. From South Carolina came traders, who gave Oglethorpe much trouble; for they insisted on bringing whisky for the Indians and the settlers. Finally, the laws prohibiting whisky and slavery were repealed.

Troubles with Florida.—One of the purposes for which Georgia had been colonized was to prevent the Spaniards from moving northward. In carrying out this plan, an English settlement had been made on St. Simon's Island. This brought on a war between Georgia and Florida. A few years later, when England and Spain were at war, Oglethorpe invaded Florida; but after a fruitless siege of St. Augustine, he was compelled to return home. The Spaniards retaliated by invading Georgia. By dint of military skill, Oglethorpe kept the Spaniards back until an English fleet arrived and the Spanish troops were forced to withdraw (1742).

Two great preachers.—There came to Georgia to preach to the settlers and to the Indians John Wesley, who was to be the founder of the Methodist Church. After working among the Indians and making many converts, he returned to England. His work in Georgia was taken up by George Whitefield. The first orphans' home established in Georgia was founded by Whitefield. These two great preachers had a very wholesome influence, which spread into the other American colonies.

Georgia a royal province.—In 1743 General Oglethorpe returned to England. He had been the guiding hand in the development of Georgia, and after his departure the colonists slipped back into bad habits of quarreling and idleness. The leaders left in charge disagreed, and the trustees in England were dissatisfied with the management of affairs. On the other hand, the Georgians were dissatisfied with the trustees. In 1752 the trustees surrendered their charter; and Georgia, like all the other southern colonies, became a royal province. From this time the growth of the colony was rapid.

JOHN WESLEY PREACHING TO THE INDIANS

CHAPTER XXVI

NEW YORK A DUTCH COLONY

The Middle Atlantic coast.—Between the English colonies of the South and of New England there was a broad strip of land which has become in many ways the wealthiest portion of the United States. In this district lie the States of New York and Pennsylvania, New Jersey and Delaware. At one time it looked as if the English claims on the Atlantic coast would remain separated; for all this middle tract was claimed by Holland, which, in the seventeenth century, was one of the great commercial countries of Europe.

How the Dutch got a foothold in America.—You remember that it was the Dutch East India Company that sent Henry Hudson to find a passage to India (page 35). As the result of his discoveries, Dutch traders came frequently to the Hudson region and began to trade with the Indians in furs. The country around was called New Netherland. Two small trading posts were established—one in 1613, on Manhattan Island; and the other a few years later, near the present site of Albany. This latter was a stronghouse, which was called Fort Nassau. In 1621 the Dutch West India Company was organized. This company immediately began to send settlers to New Netherland. Some made a settlement on the Delaware River, not far from the present site of Philadelphia. A number went up the Hudson River, and built Fort Orange where Albany now stands. Some went to Long Island, and others located on Manhattan Island.

The growth of New Netherland.—In 1626 the Dutch West India Company sent over Peter Minuit to govern New Netherland. He purchased Manhattan Island from the Indians for about twenty-four dollars' worth of blankets, knives, and trinkets. Then, out of the little settlement already on the island he began at once to develop a town, which he called New Amsterdam. This was the beginning of the City of New York.

The other settlements did not grow rapidly at first, but about 1630 the Dutch West India Company established what is known as the "patroon system." "Patroon" means a patron or proprietor. To each patroon who would bring over a colony of fifty persons, the company granted a tract of sixteen miles along the Hudson River, running as far into the interior as each patroon might wish to go. A patroon was to have the right to treat his tenants in the same way that a great lord in Europe did those who lived on his estates. The tenants would have to work a certain number of days in the year for the patroon; to grind all their meal in the patroon's mill, paying him for the use of it; and to do other things that

NEW AMSTERDAM IN 1656
From a contemporary Dutch print.

would be equivalent to paying rental for their land. This established a system almost like that of the nobility in Europe. Many of the prominent men of New York to-day are descended from the patroons who took grants of land along the Hudson River.

The company's trade with the Indians grew, and soon New Amsterdam was a thriving town. There were also more settlements along the Delaware. The patroon system of securing settlers, however, was abandoned after a few years, because it did not increase the number of settlements as rapidly as the company had hoped.

Governor Stuyvesant.—Governor Minuit was succeeded by Governor Kieft, under whom the colony did not grow because of war with the Indians. In 1647 he was in turn succeeded by Peter Stuyvesant, a cross and peevish old man. Stuyvesant tried to rule the colony with a rod of iron. He was unpopular; but he was a strong governor, and the colony grew rapidly under his administration. Like the rest of the colonists who had come to America, the Dutch wanted some voice in their own government; they would not, for example, be taxed against their will. So Stuyvesant was forced to have a council from among the people.

During Stuyvesant's governorship, there came to New Netherland many races of people. It is said that at this time eighteen different languages were spoken in New Amsterdam.

Stuyvesant conquers the Swedish settlement.—While Kieft was governor, the Southern Company of Sweden had sent out a colony. It was under the charge of Peter Minuit, who had previously been governor of New York. He built Fort Christiana (1638) about where Wilmington, Delaware, now stands. The country around was called New Sweden. The Dutch asked the Swedes to leave the country, but they would not; and when the Dutch built a fort near by, the Swedes seized it. Then Stuyvesant went with an armed force into the Delaware region and droves the Swedes out, and all this country was made a part of New Netherland (1655).

CHAPTER XXVII

NEW YORK AN ENGLISH COLONY

New Netherland conquered by the English. — The Dutch of New Netherland had frequent quarrels with their English neighbors east and south. Dutch farmers tried to occupy Connecticut along the shore and as far as the Connecticut valley, but were driven out by the English settlers (page 77). On the other hand, the English desired the territory along the Hudson and Delaware rivers. Some Englishmen settled on the Delaware, and others went to New Amsterdam because there the opportunities for trade were good.

PETER STUYVESANT, GOVERNOR-GENERAL OF NEW AMSTERDAM IN THE PROVINCE OF NEW NETHERLAND

When Charles II became King of England, he saw the advantage of having his people occupy the whole of the Atlantic coast. They already owned the territory from Maryland to Florida and the coast of New England. He determined to secure all the land claimed by the Dutch. So in 1664 he sent a fleet of four ships with four hundred and fifty soldiers to New Amsterdam and demanded its surrender. Stuyvesant did not wish to yield. "I had rather be carried to my grave," he declared. But the Dutch burghers were unwilling that the town of New Amsterdam should be ruined by a bombardment; so the old governor was forced to yield to their entreaties and surrender. Before the year was out, the English had taken possession of all the country occupied by the Dutch. At once the name New Netherland was changed to New York in honor of the Duke of York, who was brother of the king and afterwards became King James II. The city of New Amsterdam, too, was called New York. Charles did not make New York a royal province but gave it to his brother, the Duke of York, as a proprietary.

The action of the English in conquering New York was an important one. It saved the English colonies from being cut in two. It gave the English a solid front of territory along the Atlantic coast between Florida and Nova Scotia.

New York as a proprietary.—For twenty-one years the Duke of York, as proprietor, ruled over the colony. He appointed the governor, but otherwise the affairs of New York went on much as they had in the days of the Dutch. When the English rule began, the city of New York had a population of about sixteen hundred, and the population of the whole colony was about ten thousand. The city was a fairly well built town. Many of the houses were of brick. Boston and New York were the largest cities on the coast. But they were quite unlike; for the Dutch style of architecture and Dutch fashions of living were very different from the English. However, many English came to New York, and the town was much changed in manners and customs.

New York a royal province, 1685.—When the Duke of York became King of England under the name James II, New York was made into a royal province. The system of government that had been established while

New York was a proprietary was allowed to remain, except that the governor was to be appointed by the king. The colony had been divided into counties, and in each county were a number of towns where the town-meeting system of New England prevailed. Thus very early in the colony there was a mixed system of local government, made up of the county system of Virginia and the

A Street in New Amsterdam
From Valentine's "History of New York."

township system of New England. Governor Thomas Dongan, who began his administration in 1683, under instructions from the proprietor, the Duke of York, established a legislative assembly, which had power to levy all taxes. When the Duke of York became King James II, he declined to approve of the course of the governor, and abolished representative government in New York. Further, he ordered the governor to establish the Church of England in the province.

Leisler's Rebellion.—In 1688 New York was joined to New England under Governor Andros (page 88). Shortly after this, news was received that James II had been driven from the throne of England. Thereupon, Jacob Leisler, a German shopkeeper, stirred up a rebellion in New York and drove the deputy governor, Francis Nicholson, out of the colony. Leisler then undertook the government himself.

The first thing he did was to call a meeting of all the American colonies. This was the first Colonial Congress in America. It met at Albany in February, 1690. The object of this Congress was to organize the colonies to resist the French and their Indian allies.

In 1691 Leisler was forced to resign his control to Henry Sloughter, the governor appointed by William and Mary. Soon after this, Colonel Sloughter had Leisler put to death as a rebel and traitor.

The growth of the colony.—New York grew rapidly. The legislative assembly practically managed affairs. Under the Earl of Bellomont, governor in 1698, the pirates who frequented New York harbor were driven out. This colony seemed to be the point to which most of the immigrants from Europe came; yet, in 1700, the Dutch still constituted the majority of the white population. The total population at the time was about twenty-five thousand, and perhaps two thousand five hundred of these were negro slaves. The settlers dwelt chiefly along the shores of New York Bay and on the banks of the Hudson.

CHAPTER XXVIII

THE COLONY OF NEW JERSEY

Berkeley and Carteret.—At the time that the English conquered New Netherland, a few settlements had been made within the present State of New Jersey. They were regarded as a part of New Netherland. The Duke of York granted (1664) all the land between the Hudson and the Delaware to Sir George Carteret and Lord Berkeley. Carteret had once been governor of the Island of Jersey, off the coast of England—a fact which explains the name New Jersey given to all this territory. Immediately after this grant had been made, Englishmen located at Elizabeth and other points. From the time of these settlements until 1674, there were many disputes between the settlers and the proprietors as to taxes. As a rule, the settlers would pay no taxes. In disgust Lord Berkeley sold out his interest, and it was finally acquired (1676) by William Penn and several others. The king then divided the colony into East Jersey and West Jersey, East Jersey going to Carteret and West Jersey to Penn and his associates.

Penn's government of the Jerseys.—Penn's idea was to establish a Quaker colony in New Jersey. He set up a liberal government with a representative assembly, and about four hundred Quakers came over in one year (1677). When Carteret died, Penn purchased East Jersey from his heirs, and a government was established not unlike that in West Jersey. Both of these colonies prospered under Penn's administration.

New Jersey a royal province.—When James II came to the throne, his idea, you remember (page 87), was

THE MIDDLE COLONIES

to get all New England, New York, and New Jersey under one government. The right to govern was surrendered to the king, but Penn was allowed to retain his rights in the lands. Penn found it impossible, however, to collect the rents on the lands; so, in 1702, he and all other claimants turned over all their rights to the crown. The two colonies of New Jersey, now united, became a royal province; but for thirty-six years the province was governed by a deputy governor under the governor of New York. Practically the same form of government existed in New Jersey as in New York.

The people were not so wealthy as those of New York. There were but few owners of large plantations. Nearly all the small farmers, however, were prosperous. The colony of New Jersey never had trouble with the Indians; and its growth was, therefore, less interrupted than that of any other colony. In 1700 the population was probably fifteen thousand. The majority of the people were Quakers. Of the others, some were Puritans from New England and some Scotch-Irish.

CHAPTER XXIX

PENNSYLVANIA AND DELAWARE

1. Pennsylvania

The Quakers.—In reading about New England (page 84) and New Jersey (page 117), you have learned that a number of Quakers came to America. The true name for these people is the Society of Friends; but in ridicule they were called Quakers. This religious body originated in England about the middle of the seventeenth century. They were what we term a democratic people; that is, they believed that all men are equal in the eyes of God and should therefore be of equal rank in this world. They were opposed to titles of nobility. They thought that a king should be respected no more than any other man, nor would they take off their hats in the presence of a king. They were opposed to war, and in England refused to pay taxes for carrying on wars. They were opposed to church rituals and ceremonies and refused also to pay their share of the taxes that supported the English Church. For these and other reasons the Quakers were persecuted.

OBEISANCE TO THE KING
From "The Courtier's Calling," a pamphlet on etiquette, published during the reign of Charles II.

William Penn. — Prominent among the English Quakers was William Penn, a son of Admiral William Penn, who had distinguished himself in the English navy. The Admiral was a member of the Church of England, and it grieved him very much to see his son become a Quaker. Young Penn was expelled from Oxford University because of his belief and soon became a Quaker preacher. Several times he was imprisoned. But in spite of warnings from his father and the king, he would not change his course.

Pennsylvania founded.—On his father's death William Penn inherited a large fortune. He wished to use it to establish a colony where the Quakers could worship without being persecuted. With this in mind, he bought a part of New Jersey (page 117). To New Jersey there came, as you remember, many Quakers. But there was such quarreling over Penn's rights here that he planned a new colony for the Quakers.

Charles II had owed Admiral Penn £16,000 which, now that the Admiral was dead, he owed to the son. William Penn agreed to cancel the debt if the king would grant him a tract of land in America west of the Delaware River. The king did so, and in honor of Penn's father, he called the grant Pennsylvania, which means "Penn's woods." In 1681 Penn sent out a band of colonists. The next year he came himself and laid out a city that he called Philadelphia, which means "brotherly love." Penn was a progressive man. He advertised the lands in the new territory at a very low price and soon persuaded a number of settlers to come to the colony. In three years there were two thousand people in Philadelphia, and many small settlements had been made near by. Soon Germans came in large numbers, and Penn's colony was spreading toward the present boundaries of the State of Pennsylvania.

PENN'S HOUSE IN PHILADELPHIA
Built of English brick and roofed with slate.

Being opposed to war, Penn determined to live peaceably with the Indians. One of the first things that he did was to make a binding treaty with the Indians and to pay them something for their land.

The government of Pennsylvania.—Pennsylvania was a proprietary like Maryland, and so remained as long as it was a colony. Despite Penn's wisdom and kindness, the people of Pennsylvania did not like a proprietary government any more than did the people of Maryland; and frequently they refused to pay the tax to the proprietor. After Penn's death (1718) his heirs still ruled as proprietors, appointing the governor but allowing the people to have a representative assembly. There was religious freedom in the colony from the start.

PENN PAYING THE INDIANS FOR THEIR LAND
From a print of the eighteenth century.

2. *Delaware*

The first settlements.—The first people to settle in what is now the State of Delaware were some Dutch who built a fort (1631) near the site of the present town of Lewes. The Indians destroyed the colony. A few years later (1638) the Swedes settled near the site of Wilmington. This settlement of the Swedes was soon seized by the Dutch (page 112). In 1664 Delaware, as a part of New Netherland, fell into the hands of the English. It was claimed by both Maryland and New Jersey.

Delaware secured by Penn.—As soon as William Penn came to Pennsylvania (1682), he saw that his colony must have open passage to the sea. So at once he negotiated with the Duke of York for Delaware, and secured it in spite of the protest of Lord Baltimore. To this territory Penn gave a separate government, so that Delaware grew independently of Pennsylvania. The governor of Pennsylvania, however, always acted as governor of Delaware.

Mason and Dixon's Line.—For many years there was a dispute between the proprietor of Pennsylvania and Delaware and the proprietor of Maryland as to the northern boundary of Maryland. Finally, in 1767, an agreement was reached and a line marked by two surveyors, Charles Mason and Jeremiah Dixon. Thus was established the boundary called "Mason and Dixon's Line," so frequently spoken of as the dividing line between the North and the South.

The growth of Pennsylvania and Delaware.—Large bands of Germans, Swedes, Welsh, and Scotch-Irish continued to settle this middle region between New York and Maryland. By 1700 Pennsylvania and Delaware together had twenty thousand colonists. A generation later, Pennsylvania was the third colony in population, Virginia being first and Massachusetts second.

III. INTERCOLONIAL WARS

CHAPTER XXX

FRENCH SETTLEMENTS IN AMERICA

The French occupy Canada.—You have already learned of Jean Ribault's unfortunate settlement (page 32) and of the explorations of Cartier and Champlain (pages 31–33). Champlain's explorations led to the settlement of Quebec (1608). From this city as a center, the French spread gradually throughout Canada. They moved westward and southward, reaching the Great Lakes and finally passing into the northern part of what is now the United States. The fur trade with the Indians proved profitable, and everywhere along the Great Lakes could be found French traders. These traders made friends with the Indians and, intermarrying with them, became their firm allies. There came to Canada also a number of priests of the order of the Jesuits. They were zealous to make converts to the Roman Catholic faith, and went here and there preaching to the Indians. This missionary spirit made explorers of the priests.

The Mississippi River explored.—Jesuit missions were established on the shores of Lake Superior and in Illinois. Stationed at one of these missions in Illinois was Father Marquette. Here he heard from the Indians of a great river to the west, and determined to go in search of it.

In 1673, accompanied by his friend Joliet, he went down the Wisconsin River and into the Mississippi. Onward he went until he came to the mouth of the Arkansas

THE DEATH OF FATHER MARQUETTE
The figures are typical of the Jesuit and the French trader.

River. Then he turned back; but before he reached the Jesuit missions, he died in the forest on the shores of Lake Michigan.

La Salle.—About this time there came to Canada Robert de La Salle. In 1682, he went down the Mississippi River to its mouth. There he set up a cross, claiming all the lands drained by the Mississippi in the name of King Louis XIV of France, and naming them in his honor, Louisiana.

La Salle had dreams of a great French empire in the New World. Like most of his race, he scorned the English. He believed that if the French could occupy the entire valleys of the Mississippi and St. Lawrence rivers, the English colonies would be shut in to the east of the Appalachian Mountains. Thus France could build a great empire in America, though England might control the Atlantic coast. This scheme greatly pleased King Louis XIV, who authorized La Salle to make a settlement at the mouth of the Mississippi River.

LA SALLE CLAIMING THE VALLEY OF THE MISSISSIPPI IN THE NAME OF LOUIS XIV OF FRANCE

La Salle set out from France with four ships and about three hundred settlers (1684). The ships were steered in the wrong direction and, instead of reaching the mouth of the Mississippi, went into Matagorda Bay off the coast of Texas. Here La Salle and his companions landed and attempted to plant a colony. Finally, when they were nearly starved, La Salle started on foot for Canada. He had gone but a short distance when he was murdered by one of his companions.

French settlement of Mississippi, Louisiana, and Alabama.—For a time La Salle's plans for French colonization were abandoned; but at length (1698) Louis XIV sent over another band of settlers, two hundred in all, under Iberville as governor (1699). After a search for a satisfactory site, a settlement was made at Biloxi in the present State of Mississippi. Three years later another party arrived and located on Mobile Bay in Alabama.

Each year new settlers came. Some stopped east of the Mississippi, and some went west. In 1718 the town of New Orleans was founded, and farther up the river St. Louis was begun. Soon new settlements were made on the Great Lakes, and the French had laid the foundation

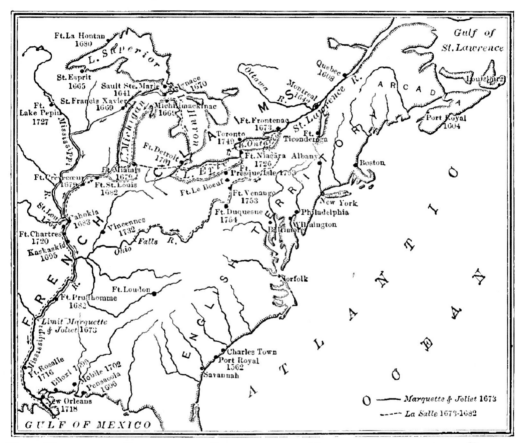

THE PRINCIPAL FORTS AND SETTLEMENTS ESTABLISHED BY THE FRENCH BEFORE THE CLOSE OF THE EIGHTEENTH CENTURY

of Detroit and several towns in what is now Indiana. The next step was to bring the settlements of the north in touch with those of the south. This was done by building a chain of forts through the Mississippi valley. By 1750 it looked as if La Salle's hope of a French empire in North America might be realized.

CHAPTER XXXI

KING WILLIAM'S, QUEEN ANNE'S, AND KING GEORGE'S WARS

Wars between England and France.—After James II had been deposed (1688) and William and Mary had become rulers of England, France showed herself a bitter enemy. Louis XIV of France had long wished to bring the Dutch under French rule, but William, who had formerly been ruler of Holland, prevented this. Furthermore, William was a Protestant; James II was a Catholic; and Louis XIV thought it his duty as the most powerful Catholic monarch in Europe to help James back to the throne. At least, if this were impossible, he would do all he could to weaken England; for England was the most powerful of the Protestant countries. Moreover, Louis had another cause for resentment. When he had driven the Huguenots—the Protestants of France—out of his kingdom, the English had allowed them to settle in the American colonies.

King William's War.—This attitude of Louis XIV brought on a war in Europe, which lasted for eight years (1689-97). The French and the English in America took up the quarrel; and the war here is known as King William's War. The American colonies were not drawn very deeply into it. New York and New England, however, were brought into conflict with the French of Canada, who had the support of the Indians. Schenectady in New York; Salmon Falls in New Hampshire, Portland in Maine, and other places in New England were burned;

and the colonists lived in great terror. Sir William Phipps raised a force and destroyed Port Royal in Acadia. An invasion of Quebec was attempted, but failed. When the war came to an end in Europe, hostilities ceased in America without any of the differences having been settled.

Queen Anne's War.—In the reign of Queen Anne, who followed William and Mary, another war broke out in Europe, lasting eleven years (1702–13). England allied herself with the enemies of France, fearing that Louis XIV would gain too much power. In America the colonies that took part in the war were chiefly New York and those of New England. Many small towns were destroyed by the French and Indians. The New Englanders succeeded in again capturing Port Royal in Acadia, which had been rebuilt; and when the war closed, England kept Acadia, now known as Nova Scotia.

In this war Spain was an ally of France. So the southern colonies were opposed by the Spaniards of Florida. A force from South Carolina captured St. Augustine. On learning that Spanish soldiers were approaching to retake the town, the English colonists burned St. Augustine and returned to Charleston. A small combined French and Spanish fleet then attacked Charleston, but was driven away.

The war ended in Europe with the treaty of Utrecht. Besides acquiring Nova Scotia, England got control of the entire African slave trade to America. This was unfortunate. Many years afterward, when the English colonies wished to break up the slave trade to America, the English Government refused its approval because a number of English merchants would be deprived of a profitable business.

King George's War.—From 1714 to 1744, during the reigns of George I and George II, England and France were outwardly at peace; but each was suspicious of the other. English settlers were pushing across the Alleghany Mountains and making homes for themselves

THE BURNING OF THE FRENCH SHIPS OFF LOUISBURG

in the valley of the Mississippi; and meanwhile the French were spreading over the Gulf territory and moving up the valley. There were fewer missions at that time and more forts; fewer Jesuits and more traders and soldiers.

Another war broke out (1744) among the countries of Europe, in which France and England had a part; and England took the side opposing France. Again the American colonies were drawn into the war. The New Englanders under a New England leader, Sir William Pepperell, who had gradually won high rank, captured Louisburg on Cape Breton Island, after a most daring siege. But many of the border towns in New York and New England were burned by the French and their Indian allies.

The southern colonies were again pitted against Florida, because the Spaniards, as allies of the French, had tried to capture St. Simon's Island and defeat the new colony of Georgia (page 108). Fortunately General Oglethorpe was able to drive the Spaniards back. When a treaty of peace was signed (1748), Louisburg on Cape Breton Island was given back to the French. This angered the New Englanders who had fought so bravely for it. After fifty years or more of war, the French and English holdings in America were practically unchanged, except that Nova Scotia had passed under English rule.

CHAPTER XXXII

STRUGGLE OVER WESTERN LANDS

Preparation for a greater conflict.—As far as America was concerned, the struggle between England and France had scarcely begun. The English determined to occupy the Mississippi valley; and the Ohio Company, formed chiefly of Virginians, was preparing to go into the valley of the Ohio. The French also had come into that valley and built Fort Duquesne about where Pittsburg, Pennsylvania, now stands. Moreover, the French had gone through the Ohio valley and put down lead tablets, each engraved with an inscription claiming the land for France.

Virginia prepares for resistance.—In coming into the Ohio valley, the French were encroaching upon Virginia's territory. Governor Dinwiddie of Virginia sent George Washington as a messenger to the French to request them to withdraw. Washington at that time was a young man about twenty years old.

George Washington was born in Westmoreland County, Virginia, in 1732. When he was a mere boy, his father died; so he was reared by his mother, Mary Washington, who is known in history as the "Mother of Washington." It is said that through all his life George Washington was noted for his truthfulness. We are told that as a boy he loved to play soldier, and at school would organize his companions into bands and have sham battles. Because his mother wished it, he gave up his desire to be a sailor boy. Instead of going to sea, he learned surveying.

At sixteen years of age he was surveying all the country in the Shenandoah valley. His life was a hard one, sleeping on the ground at night and constantly in danger of being killed by Indians. As a member of the Ohio Company, he was put in charge of a body of militia. It was at this time that Governor Dinwiddie called upon him to be the messenger to the French.

After a hard journey Washington reached Fort Duquesne, where the French received him pleasantly, but declined to remove from the valley.

Virginia sends troops into the Ohio valley. — After Washington made his report, Dinwiddie sent him in command of a body of troops to drive out the French. The enterprise was unsuccessful. Fort Necessity, which Washington built, was attacked by the French; and, after a stubborn resistance, the Virginians were forced to surrender. Washington had conducted the campaign so well, however, that he was able to make terms with the French, by which his men were allowed to march away, retaining their arms (1754).

Franklin's plan of union.—Other colonies became interested. Dinwiddie called a conference of the governors of several colonies, including Maryland and Pennsylvania, to be held at Annapolis. Later a conference was called at Albany (1754). At this conference Benjamin Franklin proposed a plan for the union of all the colonies under a president-general to be appointed by the crown and a council to be elected by the colonies. The plan was not accepted, however. The English Government thought that the colonies would have too much power, while the

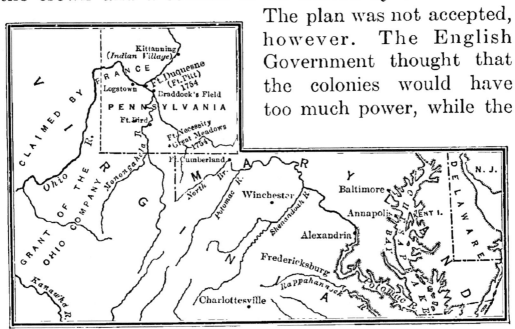

OHIO VALLEY REGION, 1755

colonies feared union under a ruler appointed by the king. Nevertheless, this conference produced one result—a more friendly spirit among the colonies and a determination on their part to drive the French out of America.

Braddock's defeat.—Again war broke out in Europe. Prussia, Austria, France, and England were the chief combatants. The English sent General Braddock to help the colonies take Fort Duquesne. Braddock joined the Virginia troops at Alexandria (1755). He was a trained soldier and a brave man, but he knew nothing about fighting in the American wilderness. He marched toward Fort Duquesne with drums beating and flags flying. As he approached the fort, he was suddenly attacked on all sides by the French and Indians in ambush. Braddock was shot down and soon afterward died from his wound. The whole army would probably have been destroyed but for the bravery of Colonel George Washington. He rallied the fleeing troops so that they made a stand behind the trees and, under cover of bushes, fought in regular American style.

CHAPTER XXXIII

THE FRENCH DRIVEN OUT OF NORTH AMERICA

Other campaigns.—A campaign against the French was begun all along the frontier line, but the English commanders were incompetent. The entire frontiers of Virginia, Pennsylvania, and New York, and northern New England were left exposed to the attacks of the French and their Indian allies. The leader of the French was Montcalm. Had the French population of America been larger, he undoubtedly could have made great inroads into the English colonies. But there were only about eighty thousand French in America; the white population of the English colonies was about a million.

Acadian Exiles.—The English had reasons to fear that the French living in Acadia, or Nova Scotia, might rebel and aid their mother country in this war. An order was therefore issued for the forcible removal of them from their homes. It was a sad day for these unfortunate people; for some families and many relatives and friends were permanently separated. They were scattered among the different colonies. Many of the exiles found their way to the French colony of Louisiana where their descendants are living to-day.

William Pitt's plans.—The French had been victorious everywhere. The English Government needed a good counselor. He was found in the person of William Pitt. As Prime Minister of England (1757), he determined to push the war vigorously and to put new and efficient men in service. The old generals were recalled; and a young man, James Wolfe, was given charge of the British army in America. A general move was to be made against the French from Virginia to the mouth of the St. Lawrence.

English successes.—Louisburg, on Cape Breton Island, was taken from the French in 1758. The same year, Fort Duquesne and Niagara were captured. Thus the French were practically driven out of the territory claimed by the English.

The fall of Quebec.—Pitt wanted to do more than merely drive back the French. He wanted to conquer their territory. So he sent General Wolfe against Quebec. Montcalm had five thousand regulars, ten thousand Canadian militia, and several thousand Indian allies, while Wolfe had about nine thousand regular troops to lead against the city. When he had failed to take the city by storm, he laid siege to it. After many weeks he discovered that the cliffs upon which a portion of the city was built were not well guarded; and, in the dead of night he moved a part of his army in boats quietly by the city and began an ascent of the steep cliffs. With great difficulty his men climbed up a narrow path, in single file. To the amazement of the French, on the morning of Sep-

THE DEATH OF GENERAL WOLFE ON THE PLAINS OF ABRAHAM
After the painting by Benjamin West.

tember 13, 1759, they saw about four thousand English troops drawn up on the Plains of Abraham. Montcalm rallied his troops and went out to battle. He was in the thickest of the fight and was mortally wounded. Wolfe, too, exposed himself to the enemy and was likewise wounded. He was being carried to his tent when he heard the cry, "They fly! They fly!"

"Who?" asked Wolfe.

"The French," was the reply.

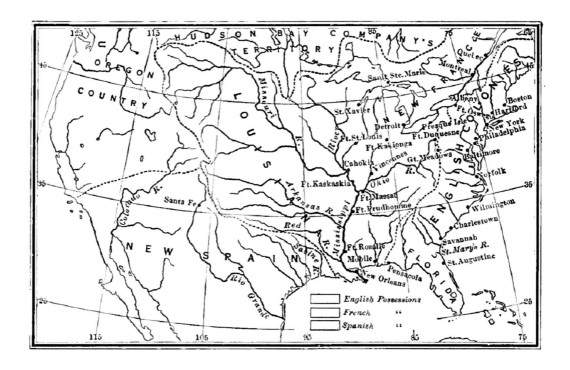

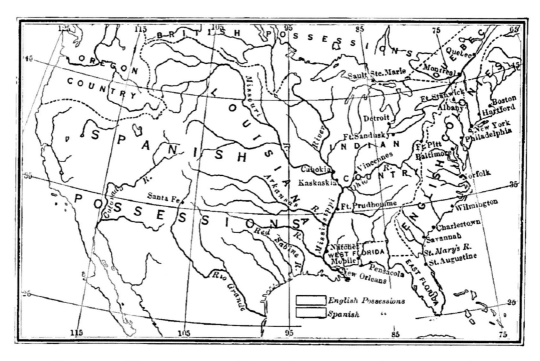

EUROPEAN POSSESSIONS IN NORTH AMERICA IN 1755 AND IN 1763

"Then I die happy," he said. These were his last words; and so England lost the brave soldier to whom she owes her possession of Canada.

The end of the war.—In 1763, the terrible struggle that had gone on in Europe was brought to an end by the Treaty of Paris. Since Spain had been an ally of France, England demanded from Spain all of Florida. From France she secured Canada and all the French possessions east of the Mississippi River except the "island of Orleans." France compensated Spain for the loss of Florida by ceding to her all the territory west of the Mississippi River. Thus France surrendered her entire possessions in North America, and the dream of La Salle (page 125) for a North American empire vanished. It then seemed that England might have a colonial empire in America. At the same time that she had driven the French out of North America, she had driven them out of India. With such large possessions, it looked as if England could easily outstrip all the other European countries.

CHAPTER XXXIV

THE COLONISTS AND THEIR HOMES IN 1763

Population.—When the war between England and France closed with the Treaty of Paris in 1763, there were thirteen colonies stretching from Maine to Florida, in addition to the possessions aquired from France. In no colony was there a very large population, the total population of all being about one million four hundred thousand, of whom probably two hundred and fifty thousand were African slaves. Virginia was the most populous,

Massachusetts was second, and Pennsylvania third. The population was about equally divided between the North and the South. Some settlers had passed beyond the Alleghany Mountains, but the English colonies were really along the Atlantic seaboard.

MARTHA WASHINGTON WHEN A YOUNG WOMAN

A type of Southern aristocracy.

Of the white population at least ninety per cent were English. The Dutch, Germans, Swedes, and French, with a sprinkling of other nationalities, made up the rest. There were more French in South Carolina and more Germans in Pennsylvania than in the other colonies. The Dutch, of course, were numerous in New York. The English people differed greatly in their point of view, the people of New England being sturdy, stern, and serious-minded; those of the South more given to amusements, and great admirers of English social life.

Social classes.—Everywhere in the colonies there were class distinctions. The aristocrats of New England were for the most part officials, ministers, and the descendants of the first settlers. In the first catalogues of Harvard College the students' names were arranged in the order of their social standing. The aristocrats of New York

COLONISTS AND THEIR HOMES IN 1763 139

were chiefly the descendants of the old Dutch patroons and wealthy English merchants of Manhattan Island. In Pennsylvania the influential class were the Quaker planters; in the South, the owners of large plantations. Below the aristocrats there was in all the colonies a second class composed of small farmers, traders, and shopkeepers. In a sense, most of the colonies contained a third class com-

"THE TOBACCO MANUFACTORY IN DIFFERENT BRANCHES"
Showing slaves and "indented servants" at work on a Southern plantation.—After a print engraved for the *Universal Magazine*, London, 1750.

posed of artisans and laborers not bound to a term of service. A fourth class was made up of the "indented servants"—white persons bound to service for a term of years. This class was found in all the colonies. During their period of indenture, as it was termed, they could be bought and sold like slaves. The African slaves made up the fifth class. This class existed in all the colonies; but in South Carolina the slaves outnumbered the white population, and in Virginia they were nearly equal in number to the whites. In Massachusetts they were not more than one fortieth of the whole population.

Social life.—The New England people were stern in manner and in their family life. Children were given few amusements and were taught that too many pleasures were sinful. Their amusements were generally of a useful kind—quilting parties, spinning bees, and the like; so what little pleasure they got out of life was in social gatherings where useful things were made. The Quakers of Pennsylvania and New Jersey were only slightly more lenient, but they did not look unkindly upon all follies and amusements.

In the South and New York, conditions were somewhat different. There was much gaming, horse-racing, and dancing, and amusement of one kind or another for all classes of the people. The life of the aristocratic Dutch patroon of New York and the lordly planter of the South was one of ease and pleasure, filled with many noble ideals. There were frequent gatherings that lasted for many days. The days were spent in hunting or in the discussion of important matters relating to politics and the development of the country, and the evenings were spent in music and dancing.

The people in their homes.—The home life of the people differed greatly. Among the lower classes in all the colonies there was a real struggle for existence. The wife and mother did all the housework and made all the clothes, and frequently the boys and girls were bound to service to some wealthy man of the neighborhood. The head of this frugal home worked as a common laborer or as a tenant, if he did not own a small piece of land. His wage was small, and his hours long. From sun to sun was the working day in colonial times.

The house of a humble family such as we have described was usually a crude log or clapboard structure without plastering and frequently with a dirt floor. Tables were sometimes made from stumps of trees; and stairways, of notched logs. One room sufficed for bed-chamber, parlor, kitchen, and dining room. Frequently there was no bedstead, and pallets of straw or grass or leaves were made upon the floor.

The cooking was done in the fireplace, as there were no stoves. In the summer time it was done out of doors, and often the meals were served under the trees. There was very little variety of food. Dried meat or salt pork or dried and salt fish made up the meat diet, with peas, onions, weeds, and flowers for vegetables. Coffee was seldom used, and many a poor family did not have a pound of sugar during the whole year. For sugar, they depended upon molasses brought from the West Indies. The tableware of the poorer classes was rough or carved wooden blocks; the well-to-do middle classes had plates and dishes of pewter or very common china.

PLAIN COUNTRY FOLK

From a print dated 1772.

The wealthy throughout all the colonies had brick houses or well-constructed frame buildings. There were not, however, a great number of large mansions. These homes were well furnished. Among the Southern planters most of the furnishings were imported from England, but in New England much of the furniture in common use was made at home. In the South, the best mansions were in the tidewater region. The pioneer's home, though his acres might be large, more nearly approached in appearance and furnishings the homes of the humbler people of tidewater.

THE HOUSE OF A PENNSYLVANIA PLANTER

The clothing of the wealthy was also imported from England; and the ships that carried cargoes of tobacco and other exports across the ocean came back with silks and satins for the ladies and velvets for the men. In 1763 gentlemen wore knee trousers and silk stockings with swallow-tail coats and fancy waistcoats. The trousers were often green, the waistcoat red or yellow, and the coat blue. The hair was worn long, and was either fastened in a bag, or made into a queue, at the back of the neck. It was common for both men and women to powder their hair.

There were many servants in the homes of the wealthy. Most of the slaves owned in New England were house servants. In New England the farm work

JOHN WESLEY WALKING BETWEEN TWO FRIENDS, A PHYSICIAN AND A CLERGYMAN

Showing the sober dress of professional men of the day. —After a sketch from life, made in 1790.

was done chiefly by white laborers; also all the work at the shipyards and the carpenter work of every kind. On the large Southern plantations, however, by 1763 practically all the work was done by negro slaves. Some slaves could spin and weave. Some were trained to farm, some to be carpenters and brick masons, and others blacksmiths. Thus, with the exception of those articles that were imported from England, everything needed was produced on the plantation.

The food of the wealthy was far better than that of the poor. Many fresh meats were served, and the garden on a great plantation was filled with all kinds of vegetables.

CHAPTER XXXV

SOME PHASES OF COLONIAL LIFE

Industries.—The New Englanders were the chief seafaring people of America. In every town on the New England coast there was a small shipyard, and the New England vessels went all over the world. Fishing was profitable; and Spain, Portugal, and other European countries afforded good markets. Among the New Englanders, however, were a number of prosperous farmers, particularly in the Connecticut valley.

In the middle colonies agriculture was the chief occupation, though cattle were raised in New York and Pennsylvania, and there were many manufacturing enterprises. The cities of New York and Philadelphia were important shipping centers, from which large quantities of grain were exported.

Maryland, Virginia, the Carolinas, and Georgia were almost wholly agricultural. Tobacco and wheat were

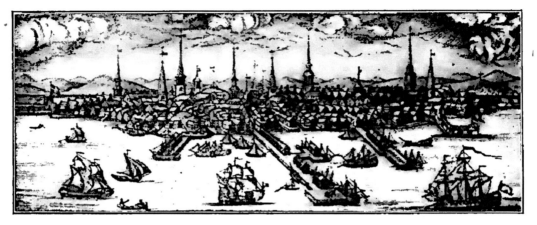

THE CITY OF BOSTON IN 1744
After a drawing by Turner, of Boston, made in that year.

the products of Maryland and Virginia; cattle, tar, and turpentine of North Carolina; indigo and rice of South Carolina; while all these colonies raised an abundance

RICE FIELDS OF SOUTH CAROLINA
After a sketch by Basil Hall.

of grain. In Virginia a few iron furnaces had been established.

Travel.—In all the colonies travel was difficult. Where the streams were large enough, the best way was to go by sailboat. Even in traveling from New York to Philadelphia it was better to go by boat. In the early part of the eighteenth century, lines of stagecoaches began to run between New York and Philadelphia and between New York and Boston. The stagecoaches were heavy, and the roads always bad. The result was that travel was very slow. It took three days and many relays of horses to go by coach from New York to Philadelphia, a distance of ninety miles.

From one settlement to another within any colony, the roads were practically nothing more than bridle paths; and travel was chiefly on horseback. The migration westward from the tidewater into the Piedmont or upland sections of all the colonies was made under great difficulties, because of lack of well-defined roads. The emigrants usually rode, while some slave or "indented servant" brought such household goods as they dared to carry in rude ox carts.

WILLIAM AND MARY COLLEGE

Education.—As a rule, as soon as each colony was founded, some steps were taken to establish schools. Virginia had at Hampton the first free school in America. It was endowed by one Benjamin Syms. The first free school system for an entire colony was established in Massachusetts; and the first college,

Harvard, was in the same colony. The first college in the South was the college of William and Mary. By 1763 foundations had been laid for Yale, Princeton, and three or four other colleges. They were established for the benefit chiefly of ministers and Indians. Elementary and secondary education in the middle colonies and in the entire South was practically in the hands of privately employed tutors, though here and there was a free school.

The culture of the people was not broad compared with modern times. Books were few. Most houses could show only a volume or two besides Shakespeare and the Bible. There were, however, some fine private libraries in the South and in New England. William Byrd, of Virginia, who died in 1732, had a library of about four thousand volumes. Among the white people were many who could neither read nor write. This was true of New England as well as of the South. A vast majority of the property holders in every colony, however, had at least an elementary education.

Communication.—News spread slowly from colony to colony, there being no telegraph or other means of rapid communication. Mail routes were established between the chief towns. The deliveries, however, were not regular, as the mail was never sent out until postage enough had accumulated to pay the carrier. There were no daily newspapers; and such newspapers as were published were small sheets, sometimes no larger than a pamphlet, and containing at most four pages. The first newspaper printed in America was started in Boston, in 1711. It was called the *Boston News Letter*. The first newspaper in the South was the *Virginia Gazette*, begun in 1736. The papers were under government censorship.

Government.—In 1763 the colonies were of three classes —the corporate charter colonies, the proprietary colonies, and the royal provinces. Rhode Island and Connecticut belonged to the first class. Under a charter from the king they elected their own governors and made their own laws without any interference from England. To the second class belonged Pennsylvania, Delaware, and Maryland. Pennsylvania and Delaware were owned by the heirs of William Penn. Maryland was under the control of the Lords Baltimore. The governors in these provinces were appointed by the proprietors, and all laws before they became binding had to be approved by the proprietors. To the class of royal provinces belonged New Hampshire, New York, New Jersey, Virginia, the two Carolinas, and Georgia. In this class may also be placed Massachusetts, which differed from the others in that it was a royal province with a charter. In the royal provinces the governors were appointed by the king; and the laws passed by their Assemblies had to be approved by the king, or by a committee of the Privy Council of England representing the king.

THE OLD COURT HOUSE AT WILLIAMSBURG, VIRGINIA

Local government.—In local affairs there was great diversity. In New England the town or township was the unit; and the people met together in a mass meeting, made their own rules for the government of the locality, and elected the local officers. In the South the unit was the county; and as a rule, the officers were only a sheriff and his deputies and a number of justices of the peace, who, meeting together, formed a county court. These owed their appointment directly or indirectly to the governor. In the middle colonies local government was a combination of town and county government, there being a county system, though in the counties there were frequently many towns governed as towns were in New England.

Religion.—By 1763 all the Southern and middle colonies, except Delaware and Pennsylvania, recognized the Church of England as their established church. It was supported by levies made upon the people of the parish, whether they accepted the doctrines of the established church or not. In all of New England, except Rhode Island, the established church was the Congregational, which also was supported by taxation. In Rhode Island, Pennsylvania, and Delaware, there was no established church; and no one was taxed to support any church. There was a sprinkling of various religious denominations in all the colonies. In 1763 no one religious organization contained a majority of the people in English America.

IV. PERIOD OF REVOLUTION

CHAPTER XXXVI

DISSATISFACTION WITH ENGLAND'S POLICY

Some results of French and Indian wars.—The continued wars from 1697 to 1763 had created in the colonies a spirit of self-reliance. The people had found that they knew more about conducting their own wars than did the best trained English soldiers. Moreover, these wars had brought the colonies more closely together, and they were ready to aid one another. During this same period of war there had been more or less struggle with the royal governors; and, as a rule, the people did not like the king's representatives in America. The colonists were ready to oppose any proposition that looked like an imposition.

Troubles over the established church. — In those colonies where the Church of England was established, many persons, not being members of that church, felt that it was an imposition to be taxed to support it. Were it not for the English Government, they thought, they would not have to pay taxes for religious purposes. At one time the King of England had refused to approve a Virginia law that reduced the salaries of ministers. Nevertheless, the salaries were reduced; and the ministers brought suit, in the famous "Parsons' Case," to recover the amounts that had been withheld. But Patrick Henry so earnestly advocated the rights of the people to determine what they should pay to the ministers, without interference from England, that the jury gave the parsons only one penny damages.

Opposition to governors.—Another cause of dissatisfaction was oppression by the royal governors. In North Carolina the governor, in order to build a palace, tried to raise the necessary money by taxing the people. In New England the governors did not give sufficient support against the French and Indians. In Virginia and North and South Carolina, the governors repeatedly dismissed the Assemblies whenever the representatives of the people expressed any criticism of English policy. The people's representatives were able to a certain extent to overcome these governors by refusing to appropriate money or to levy taxes. The latter was the usual course, especially in North Carolina. An effort to establish in America a government by aristocrats did not appeal to the people. There was a growing democratic spirit in all the colonies.

The Hanover Court House, in which Patrick Henry Argued the Parsons' Case

Delays in approving laws.—In all the royal provinces every law that was passed had to be sent to England for approval. This delayed putting laws into operation, and frequently good laws were disapproved by the king. Sometimes, when the king did not act on the law, the people would put it into operation despite him. Later the king would disapprove it. Much confusion and discord would necessarily follow. To the people in general there seemed to be a constant changing of their laws. Under such circumstances it was not strange that they came to regard the crown as arbitrary.

The Navigation Acts.—In the days of Oliver Cromwell regulations were passed to control colonial commerce. From that time to 1763 no less than thirty-three acts were passed relating to colonial trade. The sum and substance of these acts was that goods must be shipped out of the colonies only in English vessels or vessels bound for English ports, and that goods should be shipped into the colonies only in English vessels or vessels sailing from English ports. This was a great restriction on colonial trade; for it meant that no goods could be imported or exported except through English merchants.

The colonies were practically forbidden to manufacture certain articles (for instance woolen goods), in order that the trade might go to English manufacturers and dealers in these articles. These laws were not obeyed by the Americans, particularly the New Englanders. Furthermore, the British Government placed heavy duties on certain articles shipped to colonial ports. These duties were frequently evaded by the merchants. New England vessels were engaged in trade with many points, and often brought goods to the colonies without paying duties.

Writs of Assistance.—In order to enforce the Navigation Laws, special courts were established to try smugglers. With a view to giving these courts more power to prevent smuggling, Writs of Assistance were issued as in England. These writs gave authority to the officers to search for smuggled goods in any places where they deemed wise to look. When the officers attempted to search some homes in Boston, the townsfolk made a vigorous protest on the ground that it was wrong to go into the house of any citizen on a general search warrant.

In 1761 James Otis, a lawyer of Boston, was employed by some prominent merchants to fight in the Superior Court of Massachusetts all Writs of Assistance. The argument that he made before the court was that any act of Parliament which established these writs was null and void, because such a writ was contrary to the charter of Massachusetts and against all the principles of the English constitution. He lost the case; but he won the sympathy of the people, whose indignation towards England was greatly aroused.

CHAPTER XXXVII

THE STAMP ACT AND THE TOWNSHEND ACTS

England's American problem in 1763.—The Treaty of Paris at the end of the French War gave England all the territory east of the Mississippi and north of the Great Lakes (page 137). How she was to control this vast territory was the question that Parliament had to settle.

A standing army was necessary, because of the large number of Indians in the Mississippi valley and along the Ohio River and the Great Lakes. The Indians of the Northwest had already bestirred themselves; and the Ottawas, under a leader named Pontiac, finally broke into rebellion. Pontiac knew that the English settlers in America would not intermarry with the Indians, but would eventually drive them westward. All the Indians from the mouth of the Mississippi to the Great Lakes joined in Pontiac's conspiracy. At one time all the forts in the Northwest, with a few exceptions, were held by Indians. An English army sent into this territory finally subdued the Indians, and peace was restored.

England felt that settlers would soon be pushing across the Alleghany Mountains, and that new conflicts with the red man would follow. Moreover, the English possessions in the New World might be attacked by some European power.

All of these considerations caused Parliament to wish to keep a standing army in America. But, as the English Government was unwilling to bear the entire expense of this army, it was proposed to tax the American colonies.

GEORGE III, KING OF ENGLAND
1760–1820

The frontispiece in "Watt's Compleate Spelling Book," from which many colonial children were taught.

King George III especially was anxious to tax the colonies and he influenced Parliament to pass a law providing for such a tax.

The Stamp Act.—The public debt of England had been doubled by the wars with France, and the support of a standing army in America would increase England's colonial expenses fivefold. To raise money from the American people, a stamp act was passed in 1765. By this measure all bills of merchandise, all legal writings, all licenses, newspapers, almanacs, etc., must have upon them a stamp, the cost of which varied from one cent to fifty dollars, according to the character of the document. This was a system of indirect taxation which the English Government thought that the Americans would accept. It was estimated that this tax would pay one-third of the expenses of a colonial standing army.

Opposition to the Stamp Act.—The colonies declared that they had already borne their full share of the burdens of the French war, and that they did not need a standing army. They also called attention to the well-known saying of Englishmen: "Taxation without representation is tyranny." They did not mean by this that they wished to be represented in the English Parliament, but that they wished to pay only taxes raised by their own Assemblies.

In many parts of the country secret societies were organized, called the Sons of Liberty. Their object was to force all officers who had been appointed to sell the stamps, to resign their positions, or else to drive them from the country. Riots occurred in a number of places. Many of the merchants agreed not to have any dealings with English merchants until the Stamp Act had been repealed. Documents were drawn up on paper that contained no stamp, and in a silent way the colonists accepted these as legal.

An English Revenue Stamp for the Colonies

The governors in all the colonies tried to enforce the Stamp Act. In New York the people burned the governor in effigy. In North Carolina hundreds of armed men, led by Waddell, Ashe, and Harnett, defied Governor Tryon and by force even against English vessels, prevented the sale of stamps in the colony. The officers elected by the people were, as a rule, opposed to the Stamp Act. The Assembly of Virginia was the first to speak openly against it. In May, 1765, Patrick Henry carried through the Virginia Assembly a series of resolutions denouncing the Stamp Act and declaring that the right to tax the people of Virginia lay entirely with that Assembly. In discussing these resolutions, Patrick Henry in the midst of cries of "Treason, Treason!" said: "Caesar had his Brutus; Charles I, his Cromwell, and George III may profit by their example. If this be treason, make the most of it." Eight days later Massachusetts took the first move toward union, by calling for a Congress of the colonies to consider what action seemed best. This call was not heeded until the Assembly of South Carolina accepted the invitation and urged the other colonies to do likewise. But for this action of South Carolina no "Congress would then have happened."

The Stamp Act Congress.—In October, 1765, the Congress called by Massachusetts met in New York, the South Carolina delegates being the first to arrive. The meeting was composed of twenty-eight representatives from nine of the colonies. They passed a Declaration of Rights, which was sent to the king and Parliament with a petition for a redress of grievances. The substance of this Declaration was that the Americans were English subjects and entitled to the same rights and privileges as the residents of England; and that there should be no taxation without representation.

The repeal of the Stamp Act.—When the time came to put the Stamp Act into operation, all the collectors had resigned. A number of English statesmen became convinced that the Stamp Act was an unwise, if not an unjust, measure. Edmund Burke questioned the wisdom of the tax, while the great William Pitt questioned the right of Parliament to levy it. As a result, Parliament repealed the Stamp Act because it was unwise; but it clung to the view that Parliament had a right to tax the colonies as it pleased. This idea was expressed in what is known as the Declaratory Act.

The Townshend Acts.—The colonists accepted with great joy the repeal of the Stamp Act. But in 1767 a series of acts, offered by Charles Townshend, passed Parliament. One of them levied a tax on all tea, lead, paper, glass, sugar, and wine imported into the colonies. The opposition to these acts was as great as to the Stamp Act. Again the people made agreements not to import English goods, and again representatives of the English Government were burned in effigy.

Action by the colonies.—The General Court of Massachusetts issued a circular letter to all the colonies asking them to help in procuring the repeal of the Townshend Acts. The Assemblies of Virginia, North Carolina, South Carolina, and Georgia responded by the adoption of resolutions pledging their hearty support in this effort. All of these Assemblies were dissolved by their governors according to instructions from England. When the Virginia Assembly was reconvened in 1769, it passed the celebrated "Resolves", again declaring that the sole right of taxation belonged to the colonial legislatures. These resolutions were promptly endorsed by all the colonies.

Riots in the colonies.—One night in March, 1770, an alarm of fire was given in Boston; and many citizens and soldiers rushed into the streets. Some citizens unfortunately began to pelt the soldiers with snowballs. The soldiers became enraged and fired into the crowd, killing five men. This is known in history as the Boston Massacre. A few weeks before this some British soldiers had cut down a liberty pole in New York City. A riot had followed, which resulted in the death of one citizen.

War with the royal governor in North Carolina.—In the midst of the revolutionary movement, some citizens of North Carolina, who believed themselves oppressed, had organized in various parts of the colony into bands called "Regulators." Appeal was then made to the governor for relief from excessive taxes, dishonest officials, and other abuses. But relief was not granted, and the "Regulators" resorted to violence and rose in revolt. The Assembly then declared them outlaws and Governor Tryon marched against them at the head of an army. At Alamance, in 1771, a battle was fought between the governor and the "Regulators." The victory lay with the governor, as many of the "Regulators" were practically unarmed. About thirty of them were killed in battle, and seven of the prisoners taken by the governor were hanged.

Royal government hated in the South.—The Georgia Assembly was made indignant because the governor would not permit it to choose its speaker. In South Carolina the people were aroused by the appointment of Englishmen to office and by instructions limiting the right of the Assembly in passing money bills. The governor of Maryland practically asserted the right to levy taxes. George III instructed the governor of Virginia to veto her law stopping the slave trade. Her petition to the king on this subject was "the last prayer Virginia ever made to mortal man" (1772).

CHAPTER XXXVIII

ENGLAND INSISTS ON THE RIGHT OF TAXATION

Repeal of the Townshend Acts.—When the Virginia Assembly was dissolved by the governor in 1769, the members agreed not to import any goods from England until the Townshend Acts had been repealed. Societies were formed in all the colonies to prevent the importation of English goods. British merchants lost so much money by this, that Parliament finally repealed the Townshend Acts (1770).

Tax on tea.—In repealing the Townshend Acts, Parliament still insisted on the right to tax the colonies and did not take the duty off of tea. To deceive the American people, it was arranged that no tax should be collected in England on tea sent to the colonies. As the colonial tax on tea was made less than that levied in England, American merchants could buy tea at a lower price (including the tax) than was paid by merchants in England. However, the Americans were not deceived and still refused to receive English goods. Ships loaded with tea were sent to all the principal American ports. In Boston some citizens disguised themselves as Indians and threw all the tea overboard into the harbor (1773). At Annapolis, Maryland, the owner of a ship, the *Peggy Stewart*, was forced to set fire to it because he had paid the tax on seventeen packages of tea in its cargo. The

North Carolinians declared that they could not "suffer East India tea to be used in their families and would consider all persons who did so to be enemies of their country." At Edenton, certain patriotic ladies, in 1774, resolved that they would use no more tea while the tea tax lasted. The South Carolinians seized two hundred and fifty-seven chests of tea, which were sold for the benefit of the Revolutionary cause. Seven chests of tea were emptied into the Cooper River "amid the acclamations of the people."

A spirit of violence and resistance was everywhere found. A

RESIDENTS OF ANNAPOLIS WATCHING THE BURNING OF THE TEA SHIP "PEGGY STEWART"
After the wall painting by C. Y. Turner in the Baltimore Court House. By courtesy of the artist.

year before the destruction of the tea in Boston Harbor, the people of Rhode Island burned an English vessel, the *Gaspee*, which had been trying to catch New England smugglers. In every colony the citizens held meetings and organized to maintain their right not to be taxed except by their own representatives.

Five acts of Parliament.—The action of the citizens of Boston in destroying the tea, and of other colonies in resisting the law, so enraged Parliament that five important measures were passed (1774), in substance as follows:

1. The Boston port was closed, and it was ordered that no vessel should trade with Boston until the tea had been paid for.

2. The local government of Massachusetts was changed. Town meetings were abolished, and all officials were to be appointed by the governor.

3. A colonial official or a soldier who killed any person in Massachusetts might be sent out of the colony for trial.

THE BOSTON TEA PARTY

By this measure all royal officers and soldiers felt that they had nothing to fear from the people of Massachusetts.

4. Citizens of Boston were compelled to take soldiers into their homes and feed them.

5. All the country between the Ohio River and the Great Lakes was added to the province of Quebec. (This

measure was a blow at the western territory of several of the colonies, Virginia especially.)

Everywhere the people were aroused. Virginia observed the day on which the Boston Port was to be closed (June 1, 1774) as a time of "fasting and prayer." Many made contributions for the poor people of Boston. It is said "the donations from South Carolina exceeded, both in money and supplies, any other colony, not excepting Massachusetts itself."

Steps to union.—A system of correspondence between the towns of Massachusetts was begun in 1772. In 1773 the House of Burgesses of Virginia appointed a committee to correspond with all the colonies. Thus there was established a general correspondence by which each colony was kept in touch with the others. As a result of the five oppressive acts of Parliament, Virginia made a proposition to hold a general meeting of representatives from all the colonies to consider what should be done. This meeting was held (1774) in Carpenter's Hall, Philadelphia, and is known as the first Continental Congress. All the colonies were represented except Georgia, which was prevented by the royal governor from sending delegates. Among the leaders were Samuel Adams of Massachusetts, Richard Henry Lee and Patrick Henry of Virginia, Roger Sherman of Connecticut, and the Rutledges of South Carolina. The total membership was fifty-five men, who represented the best American citizens. Peyton Randolph of Virginia was elected president of the meeting. About ten documents and resolutions were passed, declaring in one way or another that the English Government was mistreating its American colonies. Additional steps were taken to keep all the colonies well posted about conditions throughout the country. In this meeting Patrick Henry said: "The distinctions between Virginians, Pennsylvanians, New Yorkers, and New Englanders are no more. I am not a

CARPENTER'S MANSION, AFTERWARD CARPENTER'S HALL, PHILADELPHIA
From a contemporary lithograph.

Virginian, but an American." This Congress adjourned, to meet again in 1775.

The resolutions and petitions passed by the Continental Congress were presented to the English Government. But George III would not concede that the Americans were in any way mistreated or had any just grievances. In the meantime, conditions in America were moving rapidly toward war.

CHAPTER XXXIX

OPENING OF THE REVOLUTIONARY WAR, 1775

General Gage in Boston.—General Gage, who had been sent to Boston with several regiments of soldiers, became military governor of Massachusetts. The Bostonians detested the troops and scorned the authority of the governor; and the whole province resented being placed under military control. The colonists were rapidly becoming divided into two distinct factions—the Tories, as they were called, who sided with the king; and the Patriots, who protested against his tyranny. The Patriots organized a provincial government; and gradually and quietly citizens were enlisted and armed, ready to fight, if need be, at a minute's notice. They were called "Minutemen." Meanwhile, arms and supplies were being assembled at Lexington and Concord.

A MINUTE-MAN

After the statue by Daniel French, in Concord. On the pedestal are engraved Emerson's lines:

" By the rude bridge that arched the flood,
Its folds to April's breeze unfurled,
Here the embattled farmer stood,
And fired the shot heard 'round the world."

The battle of Lexington and Concord.—The British planned to march secretly from Boston to Concord, to capture Samuel Adams and John Hancock at Lexington and to seize the military stores at Concord. But for the timely warning given by Paul Revere, a silversmith of Boston, they might have succeeded. Revere had arranged with friends in Boston that in the event of any movement of the British troops, a signal light should be shown in the tower of Old North

THE STONE MARKING THE LINE OF THE MINUTE-MEN AT CONCORD
Engraved with Captain Parker's command.

Church. As soon as he saw the gleam, he rode swiftly toward Lexington and Concord, shouting to every household to prepare for the coming of the British.

When the British appeared at Lexington, more than fifty minute-men were already on the village green, and Adams and Hancock had disappeared. The British commander, Major Pitcairn, rode forward and shouted to them, "Disperse, ye rebels!" They refused to obey, and he ordered his men to fire. Sixteen fell dead. The others returned the fire and then escaped from the green. Thereupon, the British pushed on to Concord, hoping to seize the ammunition and stores. They found, however, that everything had been removed. On their way back to Boston, they were fired upon by the minute-

OPENING OF REVOLUTIONARY WAR, 1775

men from behind fences and out of ambush. In the fight that day (April 19, 1775) the British lost about three hundred soldiers, and the Americans about ninety-three.

Anti-British movements in the spring of 1775.—While Massachusetts was in open conflict with the British, the feeling against British rule was growing stronger in all the colonies. In Virginia steps had been taken to resist Lord Dunmore, the British governor. Patrick Henry had introduced resolutions in the Virginia convention, to raise troops with which to fight the governor.

THE BRITISH RETREAT FROM CONCORD

"The next gale that sweeps from the North will bring to our ears the clash of resounding arms," said Henry—prophetic words, for they were spoken about a month before the battle of Lexington and Concord.

Acting upon Henry's resolutions, Virginia raised two

companies of troops. Governor Dunmore had seized some gunpowder that belonged to the colony; but Henry led an armed force in the direction of Williamsburg, and the governor paid for the powder.

St. John's Church, Richmond
Here Patrick Henry spoke before the Virginia Convention.

On May 10th a body of New England troops under Ethan Allen marched into northern New York and took Forts Ticonderoga and Crown Point.

The Georgia Patriots seized a quantity of powder (May 11, 1775) and prevented a celebration of the king's birthday. They also commissioned a schooner which helped to capture a British vessel with about 16,000 pounds of powder. The South Carolinians captured a British ship with nearly 12,000 pounds of powder. Georgia was the first Southern colony to commission a ship for use in the war (1775). South Carolina equipped her own navy of eleven ships, and North Carolina and Virginia also had a small number of ships. Maryland equipped privateers, "by some estimated at two hundred and fifty or more." In 1775 all the colonies were making preparations for armed resistance.

CHAPTER XL

THE ORGANIZATION OF AN ARMY, 1775

The Second Continental Congress.—May 10, 1775, the second Continental Congress met in Philadelphia, in the state house now known as Independence Hall. John Hancock of Massachusetts was elected president of the convention. Congress at once proceeded to order military supplies and to organize an army, of which Colonel George Washington of Virginia was made commander-in-chief. The New England militia were regarded as a part of the army, and Washington set off at once to Boston to take charge of the force assembled there. This Congress had no authority to do anything; but it assumed the authority, believing that the colonies would approve its action.

Battle of Bunker Hill.—Before Washington could reach Boston, the New England militia had shut the British up in that city. Learning that the British intended to fortify Bunker Hill, the Patriots fortified Breed's Hill, which lay between Bunker Hill and Boston. When General Gage, the British commander, observed this, he sent a detachment of three thousand men, under General Howe, to dislodge them. Here on June 17th, occurred a bloody struggle. The brave British troops charged up the hill until they were within fifty yards of the American line. The Americans, who with equal bravery had stood without firing a gun, then poured a terrific volley into the British ranks. The British retired and charged again. But they were again driven back with great slaughter. A third charge followed; and this time the

Americans, for want of ammunition, were forced to leave the hill. It was a desperate struggle and cost the Americans four hundred and forty-nine of their bravest men. Among the slain was General Warren, a Boston physician who had been president of the Provincial Congress of Massachusetts before he was put in command of her forces.

"THE BATTLE OF BUNKER HILL"

Soldiers from the British ships march up Bunker Hill,[1] and the British burn Charlestown.—From an English print made soon after the battle.

Washington in command of the troops.—Early in July Washington reached Cambridge, Massachusetts; and there, under an old elm tree near Harvard College, the young Virginia colonel assumed command of a body of brave but untrained men. He was soon joined by troops from the South. A portion of these were led by Daniel Morgan, whose banner contained the memorable words of Patrick Henry, "Give me liberty or give me death!"

---

[1] The battle was fought on Breed's Hill, but by an error has always been called the battle of Bunker Hill.

THE ORGANIZATION OF AN ARMY, 1775

Washington was a calm, cool calculator. His policy was not to rush madly into battle, but to train his troops and be ready to take advantage of any mistake the British might make. The first difficulty that confronted him was to control an army made up of farmers and others who were away from their work and their families. They were all anxious to fight and go home. A second great difficulty was that the colonies had not really formed a nation, so that Congress had no positive authority to raise troops, to coin money, or to enforce any acts of government. It had to depend upon the goodwill of each of the colonies. A third great difficulty was the securing of arms. The best cannon that Washington had were those that were seized at Ticonderoga by Ethan Allen.[1] (Page 166.)

Throughout all the summer and fall of 1775, Washing-

DANIEL MORGAN

In the buckskin garb (adapted from Indian dress) of a frontiersman. Many of Washington's soldiers wore similar dress for lack of cloth uniforms. At Morgan's right hangs his powder horn.

---

[1] Powder was hard to get, as the British Government had not allowed the colonists to make powder. The colonists had only what they seized

ton planned to keep the British shut up in Boston and at the same time to train his men.

The American invasion of Canada.—Washington feared an invasion from Canada; and to prevent this, he thought

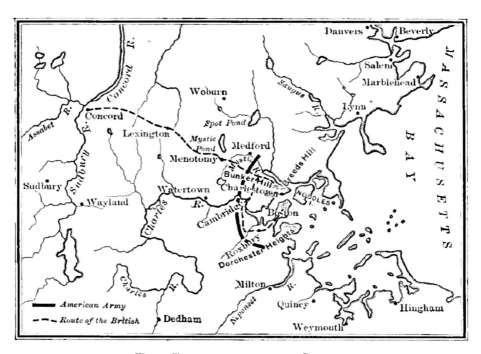

THE CAMPAIGN AROUND BOSTON

Showing: (1) the British march to Concord; (2) the encampment of Washington's army during the following months.

it would be a good plan to attack Quebec. In the fall of 1775 he sent General Montgomery with a small army

---

from the British. In a small fort in New Hampshire the British had stored some powder. One night this fort was surprised by twenty-eight Patriots, who captured ninety-seven barrels of powder. This was six months before the battle of Lexington. Some of this powder was used at Bunker Hill. In August, 1775, the powder supply was so low that the soldiers in Washington's army had only nine charges each. An appeal was made to the New Hampshire Patriots, who then sent to Washington's army all the powder they had left. Much powder was also sent from Georgia and South Carolina (page 166).

into Canada. Other troops under Benedict Arnold and Daniel Morgan were to aid in this invasion. The attack on Quebec failed. Montgomery was killed, and the Americans were forced to give up this undertaking.

CHAPTER XLI

WAR IN THE SOUTH, 1776

War in Virginia. — In Virginia at the close of 1775, Governor Dunmore was still at war with the Virginia militia. He was defeated at the battle of Great Bridge, near Norfolk, by the Virginians under General Woodford and the North Carolinians under Colonel Robert Howe. Dunmore then burned Norfolk and, with a British fleet, plundered the counties along Chesapeake Bay. Finally, July, 1776, he was driven out of the colony.

War in North Carolina.—In February, 1776, an important battle was won in North Carolina by the Patriots. Governor Martin planned for a rising of the Scotch Highlanders, who believed that the British Government should be supported; they were to join him at Wilmington, and assist a large British fleet and army in subduing North Carolina and the rest of the South. About fifteen hundred of these Highlanders assembled at what is now Fayetteville and marched toward Wilmington; but a small body of Patriots, led by Colonels Caswell and Lillington, met them at Moore's Creek and totally defeated them, thus thwarting an important British plan and saving the Patriot cause in the South.

War in South Carolina.—About the middle of the year, a British fleet attempted to capture Charleston. But the Patriots had built on Sullivan's Island, in Charleston harbor, a fort of palmetto logs, which they fortified with thirty guns. They called it Fort Moultrie, after its commander. The fort was attacked by the British (June 28th). Though the king's troops had ten times as many guns as the Patriots, they could make no impression upon the fort; for the balls buried themselves in the soft palmetto logs.

WILLIAM MOULTRIE

In this fight a British ball cut down the flag of South Carolina; and Sergeant Jasper, leaping down over the side of the fort, seized the flag, fastened it to a pole, and replaced it on the ramparts. For this brave deed he was offered a lieutenant's commission; but he refused it, feeling that he was better fitted to serve his country as a sergeant. He said that he could not read or write, and felt unworthy to associate with officers.

After a day of hard fighting, the British sailed away. The battle of Moore's Creek and the struggle off Charleston left the Carolinas free from British interference for two years.

CHAPTER XLII

WASHINGTON'S CAMPAIGNS, 1776—THE DECLARATION OF INDEPENDENCE

The British leave Boston. — Throughout the winter (1775-76) Washington was drawing the lines tighter and tighter around Boston. In March (1776) his forces seized and fortified Dorchester Heights overlooking the city. Thereupon General Howe, then in command of the royal troops, withdrew his army from Boston, sailing first to Halifax in Nova Scotia. Washington, believing that the British would attempt to occupy New York City, moved his army there.

Efforts at reconciliation.—The Continental Congress was still in session. It still desired to make terms with the mother country. It sent to England, by Richard Penn, a Tory, a careful and moderate statement of the grievances of the colonies. But George III was angry. He said that the Americans were only rebels, and he would not listen to anything they had to say. He sent twenty thousand more troops to America, chiefly Hessians hired in Germany. He could have done nothing more tactless; for this forced the Americans into more radical measures.

Steps to independence.—Events were moving rapidly towards independence. In May, 1775, the citizens of Mecklenburg County, North Carolina, had met at Charlotte, and, after passing resolutions of independence, resolved to set up a county government "independent of Great Britain". Practically all the colonies in 1776 had their own governments by conventions in opposition to their old royal governments. South Carolina in March, 1776, had established an independent government with John Rutledge as president. On April 12, 1776, the North Carolina convention instructed its delegates in Congress to concur with those of the other colonies in declaring independence. A little later the Virginia Convention of 1776 passed a resolution instructing its delegates to propose that the colonies should declare themselves free and independent.

The Declaration of Independence. — In obedience to instructions from the convention of his State, Richard Henry Lee of Virginia, on the 7th of June, 1776, moved in Congress "that these United Colonies are, and of right ought to be, free and independent States, and that all political connection between them and the State of

THE STATE HOUSE, OR INDEPENDENCE HALL, PHILADELPHIA
As it looked when the Declaration of Independence was signed there.

Great Britain is, and ought to be, dissolved." These resolutions were adopted, and a committee was appointed to draft a declaration of independence.

The honor of writing this declaration fell to Thomas Jefferson of Virginia, the youngest member of the committee. It was adopted on the 4th of July, 1776, and was later signed by all the members of Congress except

John Dickinson of Pennsylvania. Thus by formal act Congress assumed the right to sever connection between England and the colonies. Henceforth they were known, not as colonies, but as the United States of America.

The British attack New York.—Hardly had the Declaration of Independence been proclaimed before Lord Howe, at the head of a large British force of about thirty

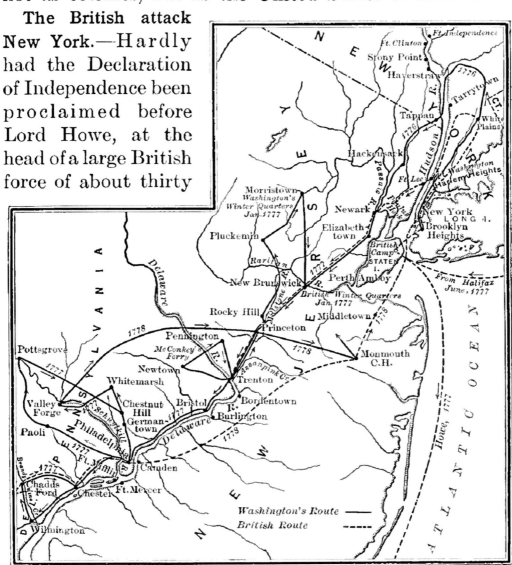

THE CAMPAIGNS AROUND NEW YORK AND PHILADELPHIA

thousand troops, entered New York harbor and occupied Staten Island. Washington had but eighteen thousand men. In August he met Howe in battle on Long Island

and came near losing his army; but by skillful generalship, on a foggy night he succeeded in crossing the East River into New York. He retreated to White Plains,[1] crossed the Hudson River, and took up his position in

THE BRITISH FORCE TAKING HARLEM HEIGHTS ON MANHATTAN ISLAND

New Jersey. The British occupied New York, and seized Fort Washington on Manhattan Island and Fort Lee on the opposite side of the Hudson.

---

[1] Before Washington left New York, he desired to know the strength of the British. This meant that he wished some one to go as a spy into Long Island. The undertaking was so perilous that no one at first offered to go. Finally, a brave young officer, Nathan Hale, a graduate of Yale College and a school-teacher, decided that it was his duty to his country to go into the British lines. Disguised as a teacher, he went to Long Island. For two weeks he gathered information; but just as he was about to escape, he was recognized by a Tory and arrested. He was treated with all kinds of indignities; he was not allowed a Bible, and his letters to his mother and sweetheart were torn to pieces before his eyes. He was hanged as a spy. As he was led out to his fate, he said, "I only regret that I have but one life to lose for my country."

After Washington had retreated into New Jersey, there were still left on the east side of the Hudson seven thousand of his troops under the command of General Charles Lee, a native Englishman. Washington ordered Lee also to cross the Hudson and come into New Jersey. Lee had hoped to be commander-in-chief of the army himself; and now, not approving of Washington's retreat into New Jersey, he refused to obey. Meantime, Washington was pursued out of New Jersey and was forced to cross the Delaware River into Pennsylvania. Lee then crossed the Hudson into northern New Jersey, and was captured; but, fortunately for the Americans, his troops crossed the Delaware and joined Washington.

Washington then had an army of only five thousand men. Many of his soldiers had gone home; some of them because their terms of enlistment had ended, others because they had nothing to live on, and still others because they felt compelled to return to their families.

The battle of Trenton.—It looked as if all were lost. But Washington determined to make a bold stroke. He knew that there was a large body of Hessian troops in Trenton, New Jersey; and he determined to cross the Delaware River and attack them on Christmas night, while they were absorbed in their Christmas jollity. In small boats, through falling snow and floating ice, he crossed with two thousand men. At daylight he reached Trenton and surprised the Hessians, putting them completely to rout and seizing a large quantity of arms. A thousand prisoners were captured, and many Hessians were killed. Washington at once returned to the Pennsylvania side of the river, and this move ended the campaigns of 1776.

The close of 1776.—The outlook for American success was not encouraging. In the first place, the States themselves were not united. In every one there were many Tories. Although the Tories were in the minority, they kept the majority from sending troops to fight the British. Among the Patriots many were Quakers who, not believing in war, would not join the army. There was no money but the paper currency issued by Congress, which was practically worthless. Merchants would not take it in exchange for supplies, and the soldiers would not take it as pay. There was little ammunition, and the army lacked even teams to haul supplies. But for the help of Robert Morris, one of the wealthiest men of Philadelphia, the army would probably have been compelled to disband. Morris raised fifty thousand dollars in gold and silver on his personal credit to pay the soldiers and to furnish the army. But at the close of '76, everything pointed to the failure of the Patriot cause. The only encouraging incidents had been the battle of Trenton and the failures of the British in the Carolinas.

Paper Currency Issued by the Continental Congress

Robert Morris

CHAPTER XLIII

EVENTS OF THE YEAR 1777

The battle of Princeton.—After the battle of Trenton, Washington remained in Pennsylvania only a few days. He again crossed into New Jersey and fell upon the British under Cornwallis at Princeton. So wisely did he plan, that when he made his attack at sunrise, on January 3, 1777, the British were completely surprised. The people of New Jersey were so delighted at this success that the militia went actively into service. Washington went into winter quarters at Morristown Heights. The British gradually left New Jersey, returning to New York City. This city they held till the end of the war, making it their base of supplies.

BARON STEUBEN
Who taught military tactics to the Continental army.

The short and decisive campaign that Washington waged in New Jersey in the dead of winter showed that he could be an aggressive leader as well as a master of defense. The campaign had a wholesome influence, and Washington found it possible to secure many recruits for his disorganized army. There was great need of money for both the war and the government, and the success in New Jersey stimulated a number of Patriots to make contributions for the support of the army. Washington led in this patriotic movement by pledging his entire estate for the support of the Revolutionary cause. This success also brought to America a number of brave European officers to help the colonists in their struggle for freedom. Among them were the Marquis de Lafayette of France; Baron de Kalb, a Bavarian who had served in the French army; and Baron Steuben, a distinguished Prussian officer whom we remember as the great drill master of the American soldiers.

BURGOYNE'S CAMPAIGN

The British plan of campaign. — The British then planned a double campaign. First, they hoped to conquer all of New York State and thus separate New England from the rest of the country. Second, they desired to capture Philadelphia, the capital of the new government, and, if possible, to capture the members of the Congress.

Burgoyne's campaign and defeat.—General Burgoyne marched from Canada with the idea of seizing the Hudson valley. He first took Fort Ticonderoga. As he

EVENTS OF THE YEAR 1777

marched south from Ticonderoga, he was opposed by General Schuyler, who ordered that trees and other obstructions be put in the roads. This forced Burgoyne to march so slowly that his provisions became scarce. Thereupon he sent Colonel Baum at the head of a Hessian force to look for provisions in Vermont, and to secure some Tory recruits. This force was defeated at Bennington, Vermont, by a small body of Americans headed by General John Stark.[1] When, therefore, Burgoyne reached Saratoga, his resources were much reduced; and the failure of other English forces to come up placed him in an awkward position.

Opposing him was an army of Americans under the command of General Schuyler, assisted by Benedict Arnold and Daniel Morgan. Just at this point, jealousy in Congress between the New York and New England factions caused the removal of Schuyler and the appointment of General Horatio Gates in his stead.[2] Gates

---

[1] A saying of General Stark, made as he was about to engage in battle, has been quoted for many generations: "There are the redcoats! We must beat them to-day or Molly Stark is a widow."

[2] At this time it was very difficult to get soldiers for the American cause. The fact that Burgoyne had some Indian allies who burned and pillaged everywhere and who put to death and scalped a beautiful girl, Jane McCrea, made some, out of fear of the Indians, join the army. The story is told that a little boy, Richard Lord Jones of Connecticut, only ten years old, hearing of the great need of troops, volunteered. He was accepted and put under the charge of the bandmaster and was soon the best fifer in his corps. Shortly after, he was taken prisoner. The British officer inquired, "Who are you?" "One of King Hancock's men," the boy replied. "Can you fight one of King George's men?" he was asked. "Yes, sir," Richard replied, slowly adding, "if he is not much bigger than I." Thereupon, the officer called the son of one of the ship's crew, a boy twelve years old, and commanded the two to strip and fight. It was a hard fight, first one and then the other on top. At last the

was very inefficient; and it is doubtful whether he would have succeeded but for the assistance rendered him by Arnold and Morgan, who pushed to the rear of the British army. Burgoyne saw that he was surrounded, and surrendered (October 17, 1777) about six thousand prisoners and a large quantity of war supplies.

CROWN AND EFFIGY OF GEORGE II

Torn from the wall of Christ Church, Philadelphia, after the Declaration of Independence was signed.

This victory was of supreme importance to the Americans, as it gave them hope of success. The British had failed to get possession of New York and thus separate the middle States from New England.

War in Pennsylvania.—The second part of the campaign of the British was to capture Philadelphia so that they might control the Delaware River. In August, 1777, Howe advanced upon Philadelphia with an army of eighteen thousand men. The Americans first made a stand at Brandywine. Here they were defeated with a loss of about one thousand men. At this battle Lafayette was wounded. Washington was forced to retreat to Philadelphia, then a few days later to evacuate the city. Howe took possession of the capital (September, 1777), but Congress had fled. In October, Washington

---

English boy cried, "Enough!" The British officer was so pleased with Richard that he released the young prisoner. Richard lived to be an old man. It was always a delight for him to tell his grandson how he fought the English boy.

attacked the main division of the British army at Germantown, and was severely defeated.

For the next two months Washington remained north of Philadelphia, watching the British army and finally going into winter quarters at Valley Forge in Pennsylvania.

Attempt to remove Washington.—Some of the New Englanders, among them Samuel Adams and John Hancock, began to talk against Washington. They believed that Horatio Gates was a greater general. General Conway formed a conspiracy, known as the "Conway Cabal," to have Gates appointed commander-in-chief of the Continental army. Among those who wished to see Washington removed from command was that General Charles Lee who had the year before disobeyed Washington in not retreating across the Hudson. However, throughout the whole winter at Valley Forge, Washington's bravery and forbearance won him the entire confidence of Congress, and caused the utter failure of the plans of the "Conway Cabal."

BENJAMIN FRANKLIN
A portrait modeled while Franklin was in France

French alliance.—France hated England, and her own republican party was eager for a chance to help the Americans. Shortly after the Declaration of Independence, Benjamin Franklin was sent to Paris. Wherever he went he was received with great favor. He had an old brown coat that he said he would wear till independence was won; and whenever he went on the streets dressed in this coat, crowds gathered to see the great American.

When Burgoyne's defeat was known in France, Franklin persuaded King Louis XVI to aid the Americans; and soon (1778) a treaty of alliance was signed. Franklin was able to borrow money in France to help the Continental army.

CHAPTER XLIV

THE WAR NORTH AND SOUTH IN 1778

The winter at Valley Forge. — The American army suffered terrible hardships while in winter quarters at Valley Forge. After the British occupation of Philadelphia, the powers of Congress grew less and less. It was unable to borrow money, and to furnish supplies to Washington's army. His men had little to eat and very scanty clothing. It is said that a quantity of supplies were collected within thirty miles of Valley Forge, but that there were no teams to haul them to the encampment. Frequently the bare feet of the men left blood stains on the snow. There were not log huts enough to accommodate the soldiers, and numbers had to sleep in the snow by the camp fires. Many of them died that winter, and some deserted.

WASHINGTON'S HEADQUARTERS AT VALLEY FORGE
Now preserved by the Valley Forge Park Commission.

No one had any faith in Congress; but, remarkable to relate, Washington never despaired of final success. Baron Steuben trained the soldiers during the entire winter; and when spring came, in spite of deaths and hardships, those who had lived through the terrible crisis were better soldiers than ever before. With spring there came also renewed hope; for French ships were on the way to help the Americans gain their independence.

Change of British plans.—When the British learned of the coming of the French, General Clinton, who had superseded General Howe, withdrew from Philadelphia and marched to the British stronghold, New York. On the way he was attacked by Washington at Mon-

IN CAMP AT VALLEY FORGE

mouth, New Jersey. The British would have been totally destroyed but for the treachery of General Charles Lee, who for no cause whatever ordered his division of six thousand men to retreat. Washington came up and in great fury rebuked Lee, re-formed the troops, and saved the day. During the night the British withdrew and succeeded in reaching New York.[1]

---

[1] General Charles Lee was then court-martialed and dismissed from service. It was fortunate for the Americans; for many years after the Revolu-

War in the South.—When the British, returning to New York, agreed upon a new plan of campaign beginning with Georgia, they hoped to conquer the colonies— England had never acknowledged that they were other than colonies still—one by one, and force them into submission. According to this plan, a British fleet appeared before Savannah in the latter part of 1778. As there was only a small American force to resist the attack, the town fell into the hands of Colonel Campbell, the British commander (December 29th).

The close of the year.—After the battle of Monmouth little fighting was done in the North.[1] The French fleet, under Count d'Estaing, made an effort to capture New York. Failing in this, it made an unsuccessful attempt to capture Newport, Rhode Island. Then the fleet retired to Boston, having suffered from a severe storm and needing repairs. Washington waited in New Jersey between Philadelphia and New York, watching the British and preventing them from leaving New York City to attack other parts of the country. He went into winter quarters in New Jersey. The year 1778 had not been disastrous to the Americans. Though Savannah

---

tion, papers were discovered which proved that, when Lee was captured in 1777 (page 177), he had turned traitor to the extent of furnishing Howe plans to enable him to take Philadelphia.

[1] While Washington was watching the British, Tories in western New York were burning and pillaging. With some Iroquois Indian allies, they massacred the Patriots of Cherry valley, New York. While the men of Wyoming valley in Pennsylvania were away with Washington, Tories fell upon the defenseless women and children, burning some alive and torturing others for hours. General Sullivan was sent by Washington to break up these bands of murderers. The Indians were routed near Elmira, New York, and the power of the Iroquois was finally destroyed.

THE WINNING OF THE WEST

was lost, Philadelphia was regained and the British were driven out of the great Northwest. Lack of supplies and money was the most discouraging condition.

CHAPTER XLV

THE WINNING OF THE WEST

Western migration. — While the war was going on along the Atlantic coast, north and south, some people were thinking of the country west of the Appalachian Mountains. There were not many settlers in this great territory. About the time of the passage of the Stamp Act, in 1765, some pioneers had crossed these mountains and explored the country along the Tennessee and the Ohio River. Among those who went into this wild region were John Sevier and James Robertson. A settlement was formed at Watauga (1769), which is not far from the present city of Knoxville. The settlers came chiefly from North Carolina and Virginia.

DANIEL BOONE, THE PIONEER TO KENTUCKY

When Governor Tryon of North Carolina began to oppress the people with burdensome taxes, many of them moved westward to get out of his reach. One of these emigrants was Daniel Boone, who had gone to North Carolina from Pennsylvania. After a number of years of exploration, he went into Kentucky and settled with his family and a few friends at Boonesboro (1775). Many were Boone's experiences in fighting with the Indians. Several times he was captured, but managed to escape.[1] Frequently his little settlement was on the point of destruction.

THE SETTLEMENT AT BOONESBORO
Typical of pioneer times. The houses themselves form part of the palisade; and a blockhouse, or fort, stands at each corner.—From Boone's sketch.

Many Georgia patriots, being disgusted with the English governor of that colony, moved westward into the districts that are now Alabama and Mississippi.

Just before the Revolutionary War (1774), General An-

---

[1] On one occasion Boone was taken prisoner and carried to the home of the Indians near the Great Lakes. He was adopted into the tribe by having his hair slowly pulled out by the roots, after which he was washed in a stream to rid him of his white blood. He was such a fine shot that the Indians allowed him to keep his rifle, that he might kill game for them, but gave him very little ammunition. One day, hearing that the Indians were planning to go to Boonesboro and destroy the place, Boone determined to escape. Going into the forest on the pretence of hunting, he rushed wildly southward and after four days reached Boonesboro. He had traveled one hundred and sixty miles, and on the way had eaten only one meal, a wild turkey that he had shot.

drew Lewis, commanding a force of Virginians, crushed the Indians at Point Pleasant on the Ohio River and made the Ohio region available for English settlements. Within two years there was such a large number of settlements in Kentucky that it was organized as a county of Vir-

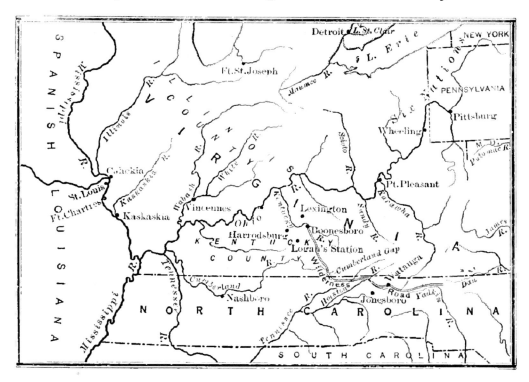

THE PIONEER ROUTE TO THE WEST AND THE FRONTIER SETTLEMENTS

ginia. Among the first representatives sent to the Virginia legislature was George Rogers Clark.

Under the Quebec Act (page 160), the British Government had annexed all the territory north of the Ohio River to the province of Quebec and established garrisons at Vincennes in what is now Indiana, and at Kaskaskia and Cahokia in Illinois. All this territory was claimed by Virginia, though it was occupied by the British. The white people living in this region, however, were chiefly French, who had occupied the country before 1760.

War in the West.—George Rogers Clark pointed out the necessity of driving the British out of the territory between the Ohio River and the Great Lakes. With a commission from Governor Patrick Henry of Virginia, he raised four companies of troops in that State, chiefly in the counties west of the Blue Ridge Mountains and in the county of Kentucky. With these troops he pushed into Illinois, and took Kaskaskia and Cahokia (1778). After a hard march through the drowned lands of the Wabash, he took Vincennes (1779) and sent Colonel Hamilton, the British commander, a prisoner to Williamsburg. Thus by the bravery of George Rogers Clark and his Virginia troops all this western territory was saved to the United States. Illinois became a county in Virginia (1778) and remained so until it was given to the general government.

CHAPTER XLVI

EVENTS OF THE YEAR 1779

The British plans.—Washington had been far more successful in his conduct of the war than the colonists realized. By the beginning of 1779 the British were practically driven out of the States of New York and New Jersey and out of Philadelphia. It is true that they held New York City, but they could make no headway against Washington. You remember that the British had, at the close of 1778, succeeded in taking Savannah (page 186). In the spring of 1779 they determined to renew their effort to subdue all of the Southern colonies. In doing this, they hoped to draw Washington from the vicinity of New York, and then to get control of New York State, New Jersey, and Pennsylvania.

War in the South.—During the year the fighting in the South was chiefly in Georgia. Colonel Campbell of the British army had taken Savannah, with the aid of some Tories. In the meantime the British had sent General Prevost to take charge of the "Province of Georgia." The American troops in the South were placed under General Benjamin Lincoln; but the British gained control of all the important points in Georgia. In September a French force joined General Lincoln in laying siege to Savannah. In a desperate assault on the city, the Americans were repulsed and lost Count Pulaski, a Polish patriot, and Sergeant Jasper, who had distinguished himself at Fort Moultrie. The French commander, D'Estaing, thought it best to give up the siege of Savannah; so he took his men aboard his ships and sailed away. General Lincoln was forced to withdraw to Charleston, South Carolina, leaving Georgia in the hands of the British.

GENERAL BENJAMIN LINCOLN

Washington's work in 1779.—When the British moved southward in the spring, Washington still remained in New Jersey, watching New York City and hoping to recapture it. About all the fighting done in the North was the capture by the Americans of two forts on the

Hudson. At Stony Point there was a strong British fortification (see map, page 175). In the dead of night (July 15th) the daring General Anthony Wayne with one thousand men seized the fort. All the stores and cannon were captured, and the fort was destroyed. At Paulus Hook also, now Jersey City, the British had built a fort. This was captured by Major Henry Lee on August 19th, and a number of the garrison were made prisoners.

The beginnings of the American navy.—As soon as the Declaration of Independence had been adopted, Congress

MEDAL PRESENTED TO JOHN PAUL JONES BY THE CONGRESS OF THE UNITED STATES

The portrait in relief was modeled from life by the French sculptor Houdon.

attempted to get together a navy by buying some vessels. Ships owned by private citizens (called privateers) were also given authority by Congress to plunder the merchant vessels of the enemy. Among those who commanded ships fitted out by Congress was John Paul Jones.[1] As early as 1777 he was working havoc on

---

[1] John Paul was born in Scotland. When a lad he became a sailor, and crossed and recrossed the Atlantic. Sometimes his vessel went to Virginia for tobacco; sometimes to Africa for slaves. He had a brother in Virginia, and on his death John Paul came to Virginia to take charge of the plantation. There he changed his name to Jones. With the

EVENTS OF THE YEAR 1779

English merchant vessels in the English and Irish channels and off the coast of Scotland. In September, 1779, with his vessel, the *Bon Homme Richard,* he met in battle the English man-of-war, the *Serapis.* After a desperate fight the *Serapis* was captured; but the fight cost the loss of the *Bon Homme Richard,* which was sunk. Nevertheless, it was a victory, and an important one. It gave the Americans a reputation as good fighters on the sea. It also brought on war between England and Holland; for Jones took the *Serapis* into a Dutch port, whereupon England demanded that the Dutch surrender the ship. This, Holland refused to do; and at once England began to plunder Dutch commerce, and war followed. Thus on the sea England was fighting the allied countries of France and Spain, and also Holland and all the privateers chartered by Congress. English commerce was in great danger. These conditions prevented England from sending many troops to America. Although England then had a standing army of about three hundred thousand, she did not have on American soil at any one time more than thirty-five thousand troops; and a large percentage of these were Hessian mercenaries.

---

opening of the Revolution he offered his services to Congress, and was given command of the ship *Alfred.* He hoisted the American flag on this vessel, the first American flag ever to fly over a ship. It was not the American flag of to-day, but the stars and bars with "the pine tree and rattlesnake emblem" on it with the words: "Don't tread on me." The next vessel under Paul Jones was the *Ranger.* Once the English vessel *Drake* hailed her and asked what vessel. The reply came back, "The American Continental *Ranger.* Come on, we are waiting for you." After an hour's fight, the *Drake* surrendered. After the Revolution Paul Jones lived most of the time in Russia and France. He died in Paris in 1792. His body was brought to this country in 1905 by Ambassador Horace Porter, to be interred at Annapolis, Maryland.

The close of 1779.—As far as the war was concerned, the year 1779 closed with much hope for the Americans. In the South the English had secured Georgia, but in the North they had lost ground. On the high seas England was engaged in war with three countries besides the United States. Unfortunately for the Americans, however, the war had dragged on so long that it was difficult to keep men in service. Moreover, Congress had no authority. Its most aggressive leaders had gone to the field of battle. Continental money was worthless, and it was difficult to secure loans from individuals. A few small loans were secured in Holland and France. Had there been a well-organized government with good resources, the situation would not have been bad for the States.

Paul Jones Directing the Fight with the "Serapis"

CHAPTER XLVII

EVENTS OF THE YEAR 1780

British plans. — The British now planned an active campaign, by which they hoped that Sir Henry Clinton would conquer the rest of the Southern colonies. The plan was the same as that of 1779, but it was to be executed in a more vigorous way.

Charleston captured. — With eight thousand men, Sir Henry Clinton sailed from New York. He laid siege to the city of Charleston, which was defended by General Lincoln. Lincoln had a very weak force, his army having gone to pieces in the winter. Although the five thousand men under his control bravely defended the town, he was forced to surrender (May, 1780) after the city had been almost destroyed by bombardment.

War in many parts of South Carolina. — South Carolina was now practically in a hopeless condition. As Congress could give it no aid, nearly every part of the State was overrun and pillaged. But in the swampy country along the banks of rivers brave Patriots had assembled and were joined by others from North Carolina and Georgia. Marion, Sumter, and Pickens, with small bands of men, were constantly seizing British supplies and routing small forces of troops.[1] At last Congress made an effort to organize an army. Washington asked that General Greene be put in charge, but Congress ignored his request

---

[1] McCreary says that of the one hundred and thirty-seven engagements in South Carolina in this war, one hundred and three were fought by South Carolinians alone. Congress could give but little aid.

and sent General Gates. At Camden, South Carolina, Gates rushed headlong into battle (August 16th) before his army had been well organized. The struggle had hardly begun before his militia fled from the field. Gates

THE BATTLE OF KING'S MOUNTAIN

was completely routed [1] by Lord Cornwallis, who had been made commander of the British, and compelled to retire to Hillsboro, North Carolina. In this battle the Americans lost Baron de Kalb, who had rendered faithful service to their cause.

---

[1] Many prisoners were taken by the English, among them Humphrey Hunter, a Charlotte (North Carolina) school boy. He was shut up in a prison pen in an old field. He had no hat or coat, these having been stolen from him. One day, as it was cold, he set out to get a coat from a near-by house; but he went beyond the bounds of his prison pen. Being arrested by a British soldier, who abused him, young Hunter determined to escape. Coming to a place where there were some lightwood knots,

EVENTS OF THE YEAR 1780

King's Mountain. — After the battle of Camden, Cornwallis determined to conquer North Carolina and Virginia. With this in view, he moved on Charlotte, North Carolina. Here he met with such sharp opposition that the British called that community (Mecklenburg County) "the hornet's nest." All, however, seemed lost to the Americans, when some Patriots from southwest Virginia and the Watauga settlements (page 187) got together under Colonel William Campbell and marched southward to aid their countrymen in South Carolina. They were joined on the way by many North Carolinians. At King's Mountain, on the border between North and South Carolina, they encountered Colonel Ferguson (October 7th), who had been sent to recruit troops from the South Carolina Tories. Ferguson's force of eleven hundred men was completely defeated, and Ferguson was killed. This victory prevented the southern Tories from enlisting in the British army. Cornwallis was left to fight out his campaigns with British troops only, and he retired to South Carolina.

Arnold's treason. — While the war was going on in the South, Washington still watched the British in the North. The winter of 1779-80 had nearly destroyed his army. When spring opened, he had only four thousand men under his command, and these were almost ready to mutiny. Provisions were scarce, and the money paid the men was worthless.

The British were planning to get control of the Hudson

---

he suddenly seized them; and before the soldier could shoot him with a pistol, he threw a lightwood knot so well aimed that it landed on the temple of the soldier, who fell stunned to the ground. Young Hunter then forced the soldier to surrender to him.

River. For this purpose they began secret negotiations with Benedict Arnold. He was a brave man in battle, but his heart was not in the American cause. He had been hostile to Washington, and for a number of indiscretions had been court-martialed at Washington's suggestion. Though acquitted, he always felt aggrieved. He persuaded Washington to give him command of West Point (map page 180), the most important post on the Hudson, where the chief supplies of the American army had been gathered. Arnold secretly arranged with the British to surrender this post to them. Fortunately for the American cause, the go-between, Major André, was captured. Arnold made his escape to the British ships, but the Americans held West Point. The British refused to exchange Arnold for André, so the latter was tried as a spy and hanged. Arnold was made an officer in the British army, though he was never respected by the English.

The close of the year 1780.—The situation at the close of 1780 was not so hopeful as at the beginning; for Washington's army had lost in numbers, supplies were more difficult to get, and there was less confidence than ever in Congress. The American army in the South under Gates had been annihilated. Georgia and South Carolina were in the hands of the British.

CHAPTER XLVIII

THE WAR IN THE YEAR 1781

The situation in the spring of 1781.—The troops in Washington's army mutinied because they did not have sufficient clothing and food. This condition was somewhat relieved by a loan which John Laurens of South Carolina, the American representative in France, was able to secure from the French. Congress then attempted to raise another army for the South. It removed Gates from command and followed Washington's advice in the appointment of Nathanael Greene.

War in South Carolina.—Greene began at once a vigorous campaign. He sent Daniel Morgan into western South Carolina to secure forces and get supplies, with the idea of ridding the State of the British. To prevent this, Cornwallis sent Colonel Tarleton. A terrible battle occurred between Tarleton and Morgan at the Cowpens in January, and the British were completely routed and many made prisoners.

GENERAL NATHANAEL GREENE

War in North Carolina.—Cornwallis with a large army advanced against Morgan, who quickly retreated into North Carolina. Greene hurried to Morgan's aid, and on account of the strength of Cornwallis retired into Virginia. The Americans had crossed the rivers of North Carolina none too soon. When Cornwallis came to them a few days later, he found them so swollen by rains that he was much delayed. Greene had time to collect his forces, and recruit and train them. Then he met Cornwallis at Guilford Courthouse near Greensboro (N. C.). It was a bitter struggle. The Americans were defeated, but Cornwallis's army was so weakened that he was compelled to withdraw to Wilmington,

North Carolina. He now determined to hasten to Virginia in order to be nearer aid from New York. The battle of Guilford Courthouse, though a British victory, had served the purpose of driving the British out of North Carolina.

South Carolina and Georgia freed of the British.—While Greene was fighting with Cornwallis in North Carolina, the Patriot leaders in South Carolina were driving the British troops out of the State and scattering the Tories. Soon General Greene himself started southward. He met the British under Colonel Rawdon at Hobkirk Hill and was defeated. But an attack in the rear by Sumter, Marion, and Light-Horse Harry Lee caused Rawdon to retire toward Charleston. After a campaign of six months, Greene met Rawdon in battle at Eutaw Springs. At first the Americans were successful; but the British rallied, and forced the Patriots from the field. Rawdon's forces were, however, compelled to retire to Charleston. By the last of September the British held only the two chief cities of the South, Charleston and Savannah.

War in Virginia.—Clinton sent from New York a band of troops under Benedict Arnold to raid Virginia. That State was unprepared for a struggle, as most of its troops had been sent either north to Washington's army or south to aid Greene. Arnold had no difficulty, therefore, in plundering the plantations along the James and in taking and burning Richmond. In the meantime Cornwallis moved from Wilmington, North Carolina, into Virginia. After taking Petersburg he began to pillage the country north of the James River; but he withdrew on the approach of Lafayette and Anthony Wayne, whom Washington had sent to check him. He

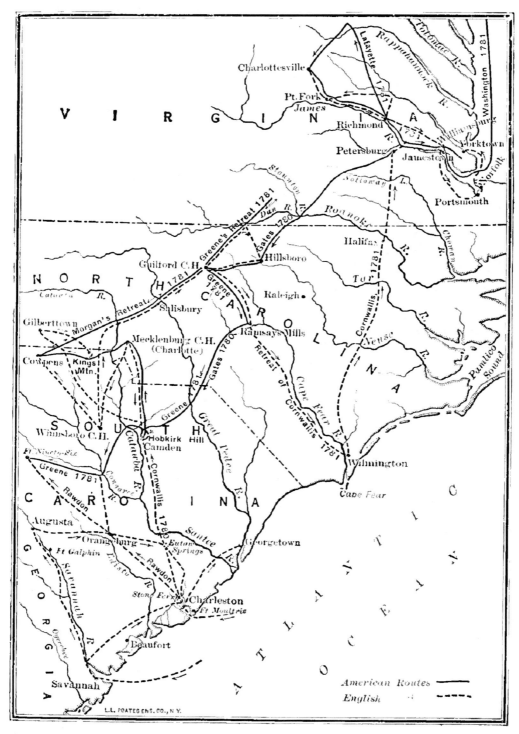

MARCHES AND COUNTERMARCHES OF THE FORCES IN THE SOUTH, 1780-81

then marched to Yorktown, where he hoped to establish connection with New York by sea.

The surrender at Yorktown. — Washington saw that the time had come for prompt action. After consultation with the French commander, Rochambeau, it was decided to march rapidly to Yorktown. In the meantime the French fleet under Count de Grasse sailed into Chesapeake Bay and blocked the mouth of the York River. Washington came up and, joining forces with Lafayette and Count Rochambeau, besieged Cornwallis in Yorktown.

The House at Yorktown Where the Terms of Cornwallis's Surrender Were Agreed upon

A British fleet under Admiral Graves was defeated in Chesapeake Bay, by Count de Grasse. After a stubborn resistance Cornwallis finally surrendered to Washington on the 19th of October, 1781. To receive the surrender of the British troops, Washington drew up his army in two divisions. On one side were the French, and on the other the Americans. Between these two lines the British marched and threw down their arms, while the band played "The World is Upside Down." Cornwallis did not come in person to deliver his sword, but sent it by General O'Hara. Washington required the British officer to deliver the sword to General Lincoln, who, in May, 1780, had been forced to surrender Charleston.

CHAPTER XLIX

PEACE WITH ENGLAND

Peace agreed upon.—Great was the joy of the country over the capture of Cornwallis at Yorktown! Everywhere the Americans regarded the war as over,[1] and at once commissioners were appointed to negotiate with England a treaty of peace. Finally, September 3, 1783, the English Government agreed to a treaty, which was duly signed and proclaimed. By the terms of this treaty the independence of each of the thirteen States was acknowledged. Florida was returned to Spain, but all the rest of the territory east of the Mississippi River and south of the Great Lakes and Canada was given to the thirteen States. The American States had been successful, but not entirely by the strength of their arms. They had been aided by England's enemies in Europe, against whom she had been obliged to use a large part of her resources. The hostility of the French, Dutch, and Spaniards toward England had been invaluable to the Americans.

The army disbanded.—More than two months elapsed after the signing of the treaty of peace before the British evacuated New York. A month later, December 23d,

---

[1] After a short time the British evacuated Charleston and Savannah, but they held New York City until after the Treaty of Peace was agreed upon. All the States had contributed many soldiers to carry on the war against the mother country. The North sent to the army one hundred men of every two hundred and twenty-seven of military age and the South one hundred for every two hundred and nine. The reports give the best record to South Carolina—thirty-seven out of every forty-two citizens capable of bearing arms. See Curry's "The Southern States."

Washington formally disbanded his army. The army was greatly dissatisfied with Congress because supplies had been scanty and the troops had not received their pay. It is probable that the soldiers would have rebelled and made Washington king, had he consented to such a movement. Instead, he discouraged every suggestion to overthrow the representative government that had been established.

The money of Congress was worthless. Over $200,000,000 in paper notes had been issued with no security whatever. It took $40 in paper to equal $1 in gold or silver. A barrel of flour cost $1,000 in Continental currency. The soldiers were unwilling to take this money as pay. Robert Morris again raised the money to pay the soldiers, borrowing on his own personal notes. After the army had been paid off and actually disbanded, Washington resigned his command to Congress and returned to his home at Mount Vernon in northern Virginia.

Monument at Yorktown, Commemorating the Surrender

Washington's services as commander.—It is not to be forgotten that the colonies could never have succeeded had there not been in the field an organized force to check the British. To the wisdom of Washington, therefore, we owe more than perhaps we realize. The fact that he did not risk the destruction of his army in battle was the salvation of the American cause. Washington never won any brilliant victories save that of Trenton, but the generalship that prevented his army from being

WASHINGTON AT MOUNT VERNON
After a painting by Chappel.

trapped or from suffering a disastrous defeat was the best evidence of his ability. His perseverance, his great faith in his cause, his unselfishness, his untiring personal effort —these were the qualities by which he held the army together. To the Patriots who stood by Washington we owe much; for never did men remain in service with such poor support from the government as did the Continental troops. It was only their love of country that made them endure so many hardships.

V. CRITICAL PERIOD

CHAPTER L

FIRST CONSTITUTION OF THE UNITED STATES

Congressional government.—You will recall that the Congress of the United Colonies had been started in a peculiar way. In 1765 only nine colonies had sent delegates to a meeting to discuss the Stamp Act (page 155). In 1774, after England had tried to enforce many oppressive measures (page 160), another Congress had been called, in which twelve colonies were represented. This was called the First Continental Congress. It adjourned to meet again in May, 1775. Many of the members at this second session were the same who had sat in the Congress of 1774. A number of vacancies had occurred, and had been filled by new members.

THE FLAG OF THE UNITED COLONIES

A variation of the British flag.

The Second Continental Congress, as it was called, had no authority other than to discuss and advise what was best to be done. With war at hand, it would have been impossible to submit all the questions to the various colonies. The result was that Congress began to act as if it were a legislative body. The States passed no resolutions

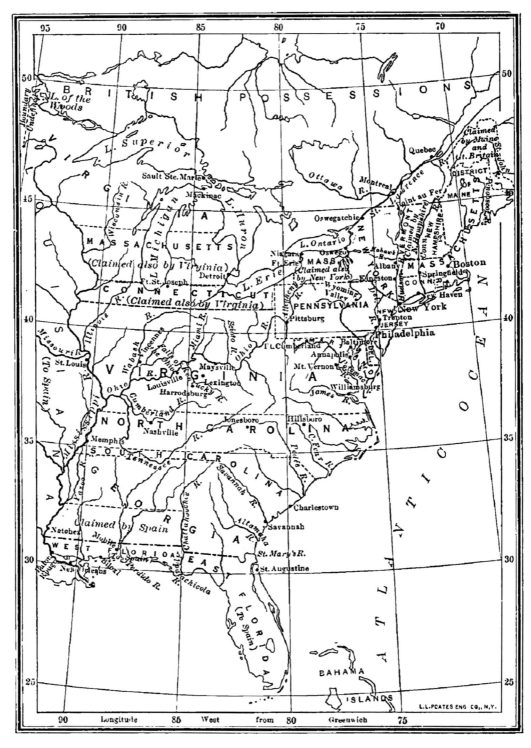

THE UNITED STATES WITH WESTERN TERRITORY AT THE CLOSE OF THE REVOLUTIONARY WAR

as to the powers of Congress, but simply accepted or rejected its acts at will.

When Congress, on the advice of some of the States, in 1776 declared the colonies free and independent (page 174), it at once proposed that there should be a union of all the colonies and that a constitution should be adopted. A committee was immediately appointed to draw up a constitution; and in 1777 Congress adopted a constitution called the Articles of Confederation, which had to be submitted to each State for approval before it became operative. In the meantime war was in progress, and the States were slow to approve the constitution.

Western land claims.—The reasons why the Articles of Confederation were not immediately approved by the States in 1777 were two:

1. Many of the States were too much engrossed in war to act.

2. Some of the smaller States were opposed to having large States, like Virginia, retain western lands.

Finally the Articles of Confederation were ratified by all the States except Maryland, which refused, declaring that she would not ratify until the States claiming western lands should surrender them to the general government for the common good. Connecticut and Massachusetts claimed a part of the Northwest Territory, which George Rogers Clark had conquered; but the greater portion of that territory had already been organized as a Virginia county (page 190). New York claimed a small strip of land along the Great Lakes. Since the claims of New York, Massachusetts, and Connecticut were comparatively small and, to say the least, doubtful, the surrender of their claims was not a great sacrifice. But in order that the union might be made, Virginia gave up all her territory in the Northwest, thus making the greatest sacrifice recorded in our history. Then Maryland ratified the Articles of Confederation (1781), under which a new Congress was elected. You observe, however, that the war was for the most part carried on by the old Continental Congress.

The Articles of Confederation.—The first constitution was not an instrument which bound together the States in a firm union. States' rights were fully recognized. It mattered not how many members any State might have in Congress; it was given only one vote. Thus the large States, such as Virginia and Massachusetts, counted for no more in the halls of Congress than small States like Delaware or Rhode Island. Moreover, there was in the new Government no real executive body. There was no president save the presiding officer of Congress, and no court like our modern Supreme Court of the United States to decide whether the action of a State was just or unjust. Therefore, Congress was, after all, only an advisory body. If troops were to be raised, Congress could ask the States to furnish them, but could not force the States to do so. If money was needed for the Government, the States could be called on to contribute according to their population; but there was no power to force them to comply with the request. Moreover, Congress could not make treaties of commerce with foreign countries and could not keep one State from levying a tax on importations from another. Though Congress issued a large amount of paper money, representing gold and silver, it had no power to guarantee that its face value would be paid; consequently, its paper currency was worthless. On the other hand, every State had the right to coin money or to issue paper currency.

No amendment could be made to the Articles of Confederation except by vote of all the States. Congress being helpless, the States did not respect it; and frequently not a majority of the States would have representatives in the body.

CHAPTER LI

DISSATISFACTION WITH THE ARTICLES OF CONFEDERATION

Efforts to revise the Articles of Confederation.—Before the actual disbanding of the army, Congress tried to get money to pay the soldiers. For this purpose it proposed an amendment to the Articles of Confederation, providing for a small import duty upon all goods brought to America. However, one State, Rhode Island, vetoed this, so that the measure was lost. A similar amendment to cover a period of twenty-five years was vetoed by New York. Another amendment offered by Congress regarding treaties of trade with other countries received even less consideration from the States than the other two. Thus every effort to amend the Articles of Confederation failed.

Internal disturbances.—In the meantime the State of New York was raising money by taxing the produce shipped into New York City by the farmers of Connecticut and New Jersey. The result was that the farmers refused to send their produce there, and trade was hampered.

In Massachusetts, in 1786, one Daniel Shays led an insurrection of the people, who refused to pay the taxes. The State troops called out under General Lincoln were able, however, to stop the disturbance. A revolt occurred also in New Hampshire. Vermont, which had been governed first by New Hampshire and then by New York, refused to live under the government of either. In 1782 the western counties of Virginia and Pennsylvania threatened to break away and organize a new State. What is now Tennessee, then a part of North Carolina, rebelled against the government of North Carolina and drew up a constitution, electing a governor and a legislature for itself as a new State to be called "Franklin." Kentucky talked of separation from Virginia; and Maine, from Massachusetts. Nowhere was there any confidence in the Government of the United States. Washington spoke of the Union as "the half-starved, limping government that appears always to be moving upon crutches and tottering at every step."

THE FIRST FLAG OF THE UNITED STATES

Proposal of a new constitution.—At this critical period, men like Washington, Hamilton, and Madison began to propose that some change be made. When Washington retired to private life, he sent a letter to the governors of all the States urging that something should be done to give more power to the Congress. From 1783 to 1787 he wrote to many prominent citizens of the United States urging this change. Madison and Hamilton likewise were writing letters to the most influential men in all parts of

The proposal of a Constitutional Convention.—Maryland and Virginia disputed the rights of each to navigate the Potomac River and Chesapeake Bay. A meeting was held at Alexandria to discuss the matter. As a result the legislature of Virginia called all the States to meet at Annapolis to consider what might be done to make better laws concerning commerce. Responding to this call, five States sent representatives to Annapolis in the fall of 1786. This conference recommended that there should be called a general convention to amend the Articles of Confederation. The resolution of the Annapolis Convention was presented to a meeting of Congress that did not fully represent the States. After some hesitation Congress passed a resolution approving of a general convention to meet in Philadelphia in May, 1787, to amend the Articles of Confederation.

CHAPTER LII

MAKING A NEW FEDERAL GOVERNMENT

The Convention of 1787.—Responding to the call of the Annapolis meeting and Congress, all the States except Rhode Island elected delegates to the Philadelphia Convention. There were some who declined places in the Convention because they felt sure that they could not approve a new constitution. Among these was Patrick Henry.

In May, 1787, the Convention assembled in Independence Hall, Philadelphia. Fifty-five members attended. Several of them had signed the Declaration of Independence, and twenty-nine out of the fifty-five were college-bred men. Among the representatives were George Washington and James Madison of Virginia; Alexander Hamilton of New York; Benjamin Franklin of Pennsylvania; Elbridge Gerry of Massachusetts; Roger Sherman of Connecticut; John Dickinson of Delaware; and the Pinckneys and John Rutledge of South Carolina. The Convention was organized by electing Washington president. It remained in session for two months, during which time the document known as the Constitution of the United States was framed. This Constitution was submitted to the States for their ratification. When nine States should have ratified it, the constitution was to go into effect. The document as adopted had been prepared chiefly by James Madison, who is therefore often spoken of as the "Father of the Constitution." It also contains thirty or more features from a plan submitted by Charles Pinckney of South Carolina, the youngest member of the Convention.

CHARLES PINCKNEY

Provisions of the Constitution.—The Convention declared that the central government should consist of three departments:

1. *An Executive, the President.*—There should be a President elected for four years, not by direct vote, but by a number of electors selected by the people in the various States.

2. *A Congress.*—There should be a Congress composed

of two houses, a Senate and a House of Representatives. There was considerable trouble in reaching an agreement in the Convention as to how the members of Congress should be elected. The smaller States wanted all the States represented on an equal basis. The larger States wanted representation according to the population of each. After much debate, it was decided that the States should be represented in the Senate by two members from each, whether large or small, and that these members should be elected by the State legislatures. Members of the House of Representatives, however, were to be elected by vote of the people; and the number of representatives from each State was to be determined according to the population of the State. This brought on a discussion between the free and slave States. The question long debated was whether slaves should be counted in the population. As a compromise it was finally decided that five negroes should be counted in the apportionment of representation as equal to three white persons. Out of this discussion grew another: whether slavery should be abolished. It was decided to put into the Constitution a provision by which the foreign slave trade might be abolished after twenty years; but no provision was made for the abolition of slaves within the States.

3. *A Supreme Court.*—One of the weak points in the old Articles of Confederation—the lack of a court to decide important matters—was met by the establishment of a Supreme Court to judge of cases arising under the laws of Congress, or of matters touching the relation of one State to another and of the several States to the Federal Government. This court was the greatest invention of the new Constitution.

The Constitution adopted.—As soon as the Constitution had been submitted to the States for ratification, the State legislatures called special conventions to pass on the document. In all the States the question discussed was to what extent the powers of the States would be interfered with. Several States hesitated about ratification because there was a feeling that the power of the States would be greatly restricted by so strong a central government. Among the States that hesitated were Massachusetts, Virginia, and New York. The general conclusion reached, however, was that States' rights would be limited, but not destroyed. By the end of July, 1788, the Constitution had been adopted by every State except Rhode Island and North Carolina. These two States did not ratify the Constitution until after the new Government had gone into effect, North Carolina coming in seven months after Washington had been inaugurated and Rhode Island six months later.

By a vote of Congress it was decided that the new Government should go into effect on the first Wednesday in March, 1789. As this day in 1789 was the 4th of March, it is the date every four years for the inauguration of the President, and every two years for the change from the old to the new Congress.

The Northwest Territory.—At the time that the people of the country were discussing a change in the Constitution, the old Congress of the Confederation, though frequently idle and poorly attended, passed a number of measures of importance. Probably the most important question it settled was that of the government of the Northwest Territory. You remember that this land had been ceded to the United States by Virginia, Massachusetts, and Connecticut (page 207). It was understood that the land should be sold for the common benefit of the States, Virginia included, and, according to Jefferson's plan proposed in 1784, the territory was to be divided into States as rapidly as the population would justify. Finally, in 1787, Congress passed the famous Ordinance for the Government of the Northwest Territory. This provided for a territorial government under the direction of Congress until the country should have sufficient population to warrant its division into States, and for the admission of these States into the Union on an equality with the original States. The form of government as outlined in this ordinance has been copied in the government of other territories which have been acquired by the United States since that time. One provision, which applied only to the Northwest Territory, forever excluded slavery from that region.

CHAPTER LIII

SOCIAL CONDITIONS IN 1789

Communication.—Twenty-six years had passed since, as colonies, the several States had begun to realize that they had interests in common (page 149). During that time, however, there had been but few changes in the way of living. The most important change was the result of the Revolutionary War. The continuous marching of troops through the States and the need of a more direct and rapid post had resulted in more and better roads and better means of communication. More stage-coaches were in use, and the mails were carried more frequently. By these means and by association in the army, the men of the South had come to know the men of the North.

Character of the people.—In spite of the fact, however, that the colonists had been frequently brought in contact during the Revolutionary War and had learned more about one another, there was still a great difference in the character of the people in the different localities. The New England people were engaged in commerce

HIGH STREET, PHILADELPHIA, AT THE CLOSE OF THE EIGHTEENTH CENTURY

An "American stage waggon" is collecting passengers for the trip to New York. From a contemporary print.

and had begun to do some manufacturing. They lived in small towns and depended chiefly upon their home industries for their living. They still retained the Puritanical spirit of their ancestors, though somewhat less severe. On the other hand, the Southern people lived on large plantations, every planter being almost a ruler at home. He was not accustomed to interference from any source. His views of life permitted of more amusement and pleasure than fell to the lot of a New Englander. There was a mixture of the two elements in the Middle States, where frequently one would find New England conditions side by side with conditions characteristic of the South.

Commerce.—At the beginning of the Revolutionary War the colonies were in a position to produce everything that they needed, but not many of the luxuries of life. With war, the imports from England rapidly declined, and the exports also fell off to a great extent. For a time, too, many of the young industries of the country were stopped. In order to provide properly for these matters, the new Constitution gave Congress absolute power to regulate commerce.

Development of the country.—At the close of the Revolutionary War the population was practically all east of the Alleghany Mountains, but the West was beginning to develop. By the time the new Government went into effect, many emigrant wagons might be seen going west through Pennsylvania to Pittsburg.

An Emigrant Wagon on the Westward Route
From an early print.

At Pittsburg the emigrants would transfer their possessions to flat-bottomed boats on the Ohio. They would pole their way down the river to make new settlements in the Northwest Country or Kentucky. In 1784,

Kentucky, then a Virginia county, received twelve thousand new settlers. In 1786, a number of immigrants began to go north of the Ohio River. In Georgia the mountain regions and what is now northern Alabama were being explored and soon crude towns were being built in western Georgia.

The largest city in the country was Philadelphia. It had about forty-two thousand inhabitants.

THE BEGINNINGS OF COLUMBUS, GEORGIA
A good illustration of a frontier village. After a sketch by Basil Hall.

The labor question. — One of the greatest changes produced in the period from 1776 to 1789 was the attitude of the country toward labor. The indented white-servant system went out to a great extent, so that white people were no longer bound for any long term of service or sold from one owner to another. A change also took place with reference to slavery. Many of the leaders in both the North and the South thought slavery a bad system, and the Ordinance of 1787 for the Government of the Northwest Territory forbade the introduction of slavery into that region. All the northern States, except New York, New Jersey, and Delaware, during this period provided for the abolition of slavery. Thus before 1789 slavery was excluded by law from practically half the area of the United States east of the Mississippi River. These changes were partly the results of the ideas of equality that grew with the Revolution, but chiefly due to economic conditions making slave labor unprofitable in the North. The country had set forth in the Declaration of Independence its belief that "all men are created equal." By the close of the century New York and New Jersey also had provided for the abolition of slavery; and the South would probably have done likewise but for the increase in the cultivation of cotton, which made slave labor very profitable.

Educational development.—The Revolution did much to aid in the culture of the people. More newspapers were printed, pamphlets were published, and books were circulated. Education was greatly hampered as long as the war lasted; but as soon as it was over, schools began to open, and the young Americans flocked to college. In the Ordinance of 1787 there was a provision that education should forever be encouraged in the Northwest Territory. As a result, all the new States formed from this territory received a portion of land in each township to be set aside for school purposes.

Dress, manners, customs, occupations.—The people still held to the dress, manners, and customs of 1763. The men who went West, it is true, gave up the more fashionable dress of the East—stopped powdering their hair and began to wear long trousers. It was not until about 1805 that men stopped wearing queues, and it was as late as 1830 before knee breeches were given up all over the country.

Occupations remained the same as in 1763, except that New England was doing more manufacturing. The South was still engaged principally in agriculture, and cotton was being developed as a staple product. So by the time of Washington's inauguration we note a number of important industrial movements, such as the development of manufacturing in New England, the cultivation of cotton in the South, the abolition of slave labor in the North, and the increased demand for slave labor in the South.

What the people did not have.—In 1789 the conveniences of life were few. There were no railroads, steamboats, telegraph or telephone lines. Communication was, therefore, very slow. The markets seldom showed bananas or oranges; for the slow sailboats could not bring these fruits any distance in good condition.

There were no matches with which to make a fire. Flint and tinder box were used instead, and people tried to keep some live coals through the night as a basis for the next day's fire. There were no gas or electric lights, and no kerosene oil lamps. The fuel was chiefly wood—people were just learning about coal; and the lights were for the most part candles. A student had a hard time to read at night a century ago.

There were few implements on the farm that were made of iron. Wheat had to be cut with a scythe. It was gathered with a wooden rake and, when dry, beaten out with sticks or trodden out by oxen. Most of the cloth was woven by hand, and all clothes were handmade. There were no patent looms or sewing machines.

VI. MAKING OF THE REPUBLIC

CHAPTER LIV

ORGANIZATION OF THE NEW GOVERNMENT

Washington's First Administration, 1789—93

First steps toward organization. — The Constitution only outlined a general plan of government. The details had to be settled by Congress, which was called to meet on the 4th of March, 1789. The members came in so slowly, however, because of the difficulty of traveling, that Congress was not organized before April.

In the meantime Washington[1] had been unanimously elected President; and when Congress met, the result was formally announced. After a triumphal journey from his home at Mount Vernon, he reached New

GEORGE WASHINGTON
After a painting by Gilbert Stuart.

---

[1] George Washington was born in Westmoreland County, Virginia, February 22, 1732. He became a surveyor, and while little more than a boy was sent on a mission to the French forces on the Ohio. He was an aide to Braddock and saved the remnant of his army from destruction.

York, then the National Capital, and was inaugurated at Federal Hall, April 30th, 1789.[1] John Adams of

WASHINGTON'S TRIUMPHAL ENTRY INTO NEW YORK, ON HIS WAY TO INAUGURATION

Massachusetts, who was elected Vice President, had already taken the oath of office.

In the French and Indian War he rose to the rank of colonel. He was frequently a member of the Virginia legislature and was a delegate to the Continental Congress in 1775. He was Commander-in-Chief of the American forces during the Revolution, but retired to private life in 1783. In 1787 he was President of the Constitutional Convention at Philadelphia. He was elected President of the United States and served two terms with distinction and ability. He died at Mount Vernon, December 14, 1799. He was a man of purest patriotism, of unusual ability and statesmanship, who well deserved the characterization, "First in war, first in peace, and first in the hearts of his countrymen."

[1] We are told by an eye-witness of the inauguration that Washington "was dressed in deep brown, with metal buttons with an eagle on them, white stockings, a bag [for the hair behind], and sword." His tall, erect

Congress now turned its attention to the great work of setting the machinery of government in motion. Four executive departments were established: State, Treasury, War, and Justice. The judicial system of the country was completed by the establishment of courts below the Supreme Court. Congress did its work well, and little of it has been undone since.

The Cabinet.—Washington appointed Thomas Jefferson, Secretary of State; Alexander Hamilton,[1] Secretary of the Treasury; Henry Knox, Secretary of War; and Edmund Randolph, Attorney-General. He began at once to ask their advice about the affairs of government, and this was the beginning of the Cabinet. Washington did not believe in political parties; and by selecting two men as

---

figure would attract attention in any gathering. He weighed about two hundred pounds and wore a number thirteen boot. He was strong and active—a skillful rider and an expert fencer. It is said that in a running jump he could cover a distance of twenty-two feet. He was one of the wealthiest Americans of his day, his estate being valued at as much as half a million dollars. Besides the family estate at Mount Vernon, which consisted of several thousand acres, he owned extensive tracts of fertile land near the Ohio River.

[1] Alexander Hamilton was born in St. Croix, an island of the West Indies, January 11, 1757. He was educated at King's College (now Columbia University), New York. He was in the army throughout the Revolution, rising to the rank of lieutenant colonel and serving on Washington's staff. He was several times a member of the New York Legislature and of the Continental Congress and was prominent in the movement which led to the meeting of the Federal Convention of 1787, which framed the Constitution. He was a prominent member of that body also. He was the first Secretary of the Treasury, and the credit of establishing our financial system belongs to him. He was a man of great personal charm and of unusual ability. He died from a wound received in a duel with Aaron Burr, July 12, 1804. He was the chief author of the series of papers called *The Federalist*, which were written to secure the ratification of the Constitution.

widely separated in political opinions as Jefferson and Hamilton, he hoped to prevent party government.

Rise of political parties.—Almost immediately, however, parties began to appear in the country. Party division was shown even in the Cabinet, by the great difference of opinion between Hamilton and Jefferson as to the nature of the new Government. Hamilton believed that the general Government should be given powers beyond those directly stated in the Constitution, while Jefferson held that the Constitution should be interpreted strictly. As those who agreed with Hamilton in a "loose" construction of the Constitution had favored the ratification of the Constitution, they took the name of "Federalists." All those opposed to Hamilton's method of construing the Constitution, with Jefferson as their leader, formed the opposition party. They were at first called Anti-Federalists; later, Republicans, and finally, Democrats.

HENRY KNOX, FIRST SECRETARY OF WAR

EDMUND RANDOLPH FIRST ATTORNEY GENERAL

Hamilton's financial policy.—As the first need of the country was an effective financial system, Hamilton made five suggestions, all of which were accepted by Congress. They were:

1. A tax on goods brought in from foreign countries.

This was intended to raise money to pay the expenses of the Government and the interest on the National debt. This was the origin of our tariff system.

2. A tax on distilled liquors. This was intended, not only to raise money, but to make the people respect the power and authority of the Federal Government.

3. The funding, or renewing, of the National debt in new bonds. This debt amounted to about fifty-four millions of dollars.

4. The assumption, or taking over, by the Federal Government of the debts of the States. This suggestion aroused so much opposition, especially from the Southern States, which had already paid part of their debts, that it was not accepted by Congress for some time. Finally a bargain was made by which the North agreed to locate the new Capital on the Potomac, and the South consented to the Federal assumption of the State debts. The State debts thus taken over by the general Government amounted to about twenty-one millions of dollars.

ALEXANDER HAMILTON, FIRST SECRETARY OF THE TREASURY

5. The establishment of a National Bank, which would take care of the money of the Government and assist it in regulating the currency. The United States was to own a part of the bank and thus benefit by its profits.

New states and amendments to the Constitution.— North Carolina at length (1789) ratified the Constitution, and Rhode Island entered the new Union the next year. In 1791 Vermont was admitted without slavery; and the year following, Kentucky also became a State, but with slavery. Vermont was formed from territory claimed partly by New York and partly by New Hampshire. As early as 1777 Vermont adopted a constitution. It contained a clause forbidding slavery—the first constitution in America with such a provision. Kentucky had been a county in Virginia (page 189), but its population grew so rapidly, and it was so far removed from Virginia's seat of government (Richmond), that the State of Virginia gave permission for the creation of this new State.

With a view to limiting the power of the Federal Government, the first ten amendments to the Constitution were ratified in 1791.

Indian troubles. — As the Indians in the Northwest Territory had given trouble for a number of years, General St. Clair was sent against them with a large force (1791). He was ambushed by Little Turtle at the head of two thousand Indians and was terribly defeated. Washington then sent "Mad Anthony" Wayne to command an expedition against them. The Indians were defeated near Maumee River (1794) and forced to make a treaty, the United States paying them for their lands.

Second Presidential election and inauguration.—In 1792 Washington was unanimously reëlected President, and John Adams again became Vice President of the United States. On March 4, 1793, Washington was inaugurated President for the second time.

CHAPTER LV

FOREIGN AND DOMESTIC RELATIONS

Washington's Second Administration, 1793-97

Relations with France. — The people of the United States were greatly interested in the establishment of the French Republic. After the execution of Louis XVI, France was at war with most of the European nations, including Great Britain. The Republicans in the United States wanted the Government to side with France, claiming that our country was still bound by the treaty made at the time of the American Revolution (page 184). But Washington, with the Federalists, held that the treaty had been made with Louis XVI and that it ceased to bind the United States when the French king was dethroned. A proclamation was accordingly issued, declaring that the United States would remain neutral; that is, that they would take no part on either side. This was a great disappointment to the people who sympathized with France. The French, too, were angry, because they claimed that the treaty was still binding.

About this time "Citizen" Genet came to America as minister from the French Republic and was at first received with great enthusiasm by the Republicans. But he attempted to rouse the people against the President and in favor of the French Republic. In violation of the neutrality proclamation, he sent out privateers from the United States to attack British commerce. Then he made the mistake of abusing Washington and the Government, and this caused him to lose most of his friends. Finally Washington demanded that he be recalled by the French Government. For a time it looked as if we should have war with France.

Relations with England.—France was not the only country with which the United States had strained relations. Great Britain still held the forts in the western part of the country, on the ground that the debts that Americans owed to British merchants had not been paid. In addition to this she not only restricted trade with the West Indies, but, after she had declared war with France, seized a large number of American vessels that traded with the French. The Americans claimed that "free ships make free goods," but England refused to acknowledge this.

JOHN JAY
FIRST CHIEF JUSTICE OF
THE SUPREME COURT

Nor were these the most serious grounds of complaint against England. The war with France caused need of more sailors in the English navy. As a consequence, American vessels were often searched by British officers, who seized and "impressed" into their service all sailors who appeared to be of English birth. They explained their action by saying that an Englishman could never become a citizen of another country. Many Americans were thus seized, taken from American ships, and forced to serve a foreign country.

Jay's treaty.—Feeling against England was so intense that Washington, in the hope of avoiding war, sent John Jay, the Chief Justice of the Supreme Court, to

FOREIGN AND DOMESTIC RELATIONS

England in the effort to reach an agreement. A treaty was signed (1794) by which England agreed to give up the forts in the West, and the United States agreed to secure the payment of the debts due British merchants. But England refused to pay for slaves that had been carried off by her troops. Neither would she agree to stop the impressment of seamen and the seizing of neutral ships. The treaty was a very poor one; and though it probably prevented war, it was deservedly unpopular in America, particularly with the Republicans.

ELI WHITNEY, INVENTOR OF THE COTTON GIN

Jay was accused of being a traitor to his country. Hamilton was stoned in New York for speaking in favor of the treaty, and excitement ran high. Washington had to use all his influence to secure its ratification by the Senate.

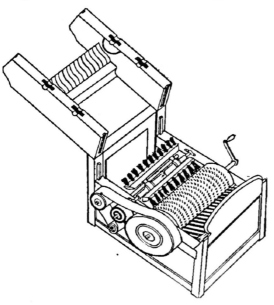

WHITNEY'S COTTON GIN
From a drawing after the original sketch.

Invention of the cotton gin.—In 1793 the widow of General Nathanael Greene (page 199) was living in Georgia on a cotton plantation. She gave a home to Eli Whitney, of Massachusetts, a young man who was then reading law. He was a graduate of Yale University. Noticing the slowness with which the seeds were separated from the cotton fiber by hand, he invented a machine which would separate as many seeds in a day as one man could do in fifty days. This was the "cotton gin."[1] Its invention was followed by a great increase in the production of cotton in the South.

The Whisky Rebellion.—In the summer of 1794 the farmers in western Pennsylvania, who were in the habit of disposing of their surplus grain by using it in making whisky, refused to pay the tax on whisky and at last rose in revolt. Washington then called out fifteen thousand militia from Pennsylvania, Virginia, Maryland, and New Jersey, which under Governor Lee of Virginia marched against the "rebels." But the uprising was over by the time the army reached Pittsburg. Two of the rebels were tried for treason and sentenced to death, but Washington pardoned them. The new Government thus proved its ability to enforce its laws, and so increased the respect of its citizens.

Admission of Tennessee.—In 1796 Tennessee, which had been ceded by North Carolina to the United States (1789), was admitted to the Union as a slave State.

Retirement of Washington.—Washington was growing old and was becoming very weary of the cares of his office and the abuse that was heaped upon him by the Republicans on account of his supposed sympathy with England. He therefore declined reëlection in 1796 and retired to private life at the end of his second term as President. Before returning to Mount Vernon, he published in a Philadelphia newspaper a "Farewell Address" to his beloved fellow countrymen. We still appreciate

---

[1] "Gin" is a shortened form of "engine"; that is, machine.

this address because of its patriotic foresight and for the soundness of its political advice. Washington spent his declining days on his magnificent estate, Mount Vernon, busily engaged with his domestic affairs. He died in December, 1799, at the age of sixty-eight.

Election of 1796. — The Federalists supported John Adams for President, in 1796; and the Republicans favored Thomas Jefferson. Jefferson had retired from the Cabinet in 1793, because he could not agree with Hamilton and objected to the policies of the administration. Washington was above partisan politics, but he inclined very much to the Federalists. Adams received a majority of the electoral vote and became President, while Jefferson, his opponent, receiving the next highest number, became Vice President.

CHAPTER LVI

END OF FEDERALIST RULE

John Adams's Administration, 1797–1801

The X. Y. Z. affair.—Adams[1] was inaugurated in 1797 and retained Washington's Cabinet. He attempted to follow Washington's policy of neutrality, but the relations

---

[1] John Adams was born at Braintree, Massachusetts, October 19, 1735. He was graduated from Harvard College and became a lawyer. He served in the Continental Congress and was one of its ablest members. He signed the Declaration of Independence and the treaty of peace with Great Britain in 1783. He was twice Vice President and in 1797 became President. He was defeated in 1800 and retired to private life. He died July 4, 1826. He was a faithful and patriotic statesman, but lacked tact and the ability to make friends. It is said that his last words were, "Jefferson still lives." Jefferson by a strange coincidence died the same day.

with France were a source of great trouble to him. French vessels still plundered American traders. France was much angered by the adoption of Jay's treaty with England (page 229), as she regarded it as an unfriendly act. In 1796 she dismissed Pinckney, the American minister, because he was a Federalist.

Later Pinckney and two other envoys were sent to France to make a treaty, but they were finally notified by three French agents known in history as "X. Y. Z." that a satisfactory treaty could be secured only by the payment of a large sum of money. Pinckney is said to have replied, "Millions for defense, but not one cent for tribute!" The envoys notified President Adams of the insult to them as representatives of the nation, and he at once sent a report of the whole matter to Congress. A wave of indignation against France swept over the whole country when the news was made public. Preparations for war were begun, and Washington was again asked to serve as Commander-in-Chief of the American army. A navy department was established, and American vessels were directed to attack French vessels. After several prizes had been taken by the Americans, France was glad to come to an understanding. The United States sent over a new embassy, and a treaty was made (1800).

JOHN ADAMS

The Alien and Sedition Laws.—Just at this time the Federalist party, which was now very popular with the people because it had always opposed the interference of the French, made a fatal mistake by passing the Alien and Sedition Laws. A new naturalization law was passed which required a residence of fourteen years before a foreigner could become a citizen of the United States. Two Alien Laws gave the President power to send out of the country all foreigners whom he might consider dangerous. The Sedition Law was intended to check the constant abuse of the Administration by Republican editors, many of whom were foreigners. It provided punishment for anyone who, by speaking or writing, tried to bring the Government, Congress, or the President into contempt. A Republican member of Congress from Vermont was fined one thousand dollars and sent to jail for four months for accusing the Government of "ridiculous pomp, foolish adulation, and selfish avarice."

The Virginia and Kentucky Resolutions. — The Alien and Sedition Laws brought out much opposition from both Republicans and Federalists. Many people believed that these laws allowed the National Government a dangerous exercise of power, a fact that hastened the downfall of the Federalists. Immediately two important statements of political doctrine were made. The legislatures of Virginia and Kentucky, at the suggestion of Madison and Jefferson respectively, passed resolutions which declared that these acts (by limiting free speech) were in violation of the Constitution; that the Constitution was a mere compact or agreement between sovereign States, and that the States therefore had the power to declare when a law violated the Constitution. The Virginia Resolutions called on the States to interfere; and the Kentucky legislature in 1799 passed a second series, which declared that a state could "nullify" an unconstitutional law—that is, refuse to allow it to be enforced.

Removal of the Capital.—In 1800 the Capital was moved to Washington, a new city whose site had been chosen by Washington. Although the city was then little more than a wilderness and grew very slowly for many years, it is to-day one of the most beautiful cities in the world. The District of Columbia, in which it is situated, was presented to the Federal Government by the State of Maryland.

Election of 1800.—The Federalists again supported Adams for President and nominated Charles C. Pinckney of South Carolina for Vice President. The Republicans supported Jefferson for President and Aaron Burr of New York for Vice President. There was much bitterness between the two parties, the Federalists claiming that Jefferson's election would result in anarchy, or the destruction of all government, and the Republicans asserting that the success of the Federalists would mean the establishment of a monarchy and the destruction of all the rights of the people. The Republicans also, with more reason, accused the Federalists of extravagance in the conduct of the Government.

The result was a Republican victory; but Jefferson and Burr received the same number of electoral votes, seventy-three each. No one had thought of Burr for President; but according to the Constitution, when there was a tie vote, the election went to the House of Representatives. After a long contest that body elected Jefferson, though the schemes of the Federalists to defeat him almost resulted in the choice of Burr. To avoid such a situation in the future, the Constitution was soon changed (1804) by

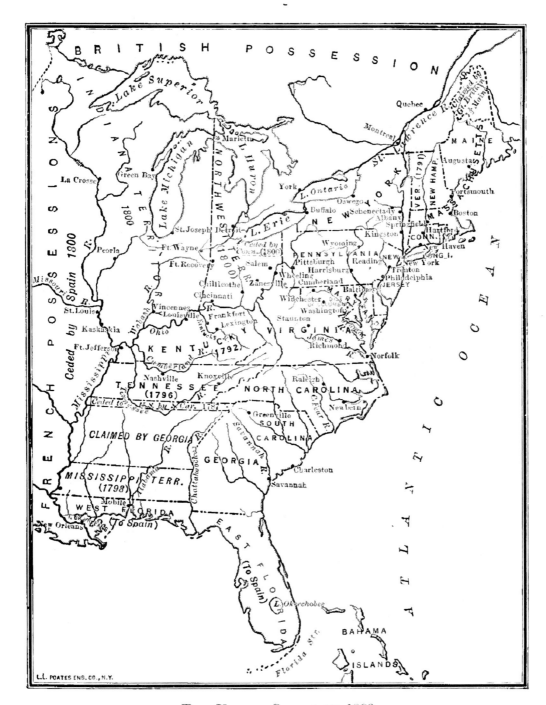

THE UNITED STATES IN 1800

Showing: (1) The thirteen original States.
(2) The States admitted since the Union, with dates of admission.
(3) The Territories, with dates of organization.

an amendment providing that each elector should cast separate votes for the offices of President and Vice President (Constitution, Amendment XII).

Services of the Federal Party.—The Federalists never came into power again; for this party had lost the confidence of the people. Through its lack of sympathy with them, it had ceased to be safe and progressive. But it had successfully organized the Government and deserves great credit for that important service. By the appointment of John Marshall[1] of Virginia to the place of Chief Justice of the Supreme Court, President Adams gave to the country its greatest judge. Chief Justice Marshall strengthened the National Government by his interpretation of the Constitution.

JOHN MARSHALL

---

[1] John Marshall was born in Fauquier County, Virginia, September 24, 1755. For a time during the Revolution he served in the army, but resigned to practice law. He was a member of the Virginia Convention that met to ratify the Constitution of the United States, and he was several times elected to the Legislature. He was also a member of the Virginia Constitutional Convention of 1829. He was at different times special envoy to France, member of Congress, Secretary of State, and Chief Justice of the Supreme Court. He died July 6, 1835. He was the greatest judge in our history and through his decisions he has influenced greatly the development of the nation.

CHAPTER LVII

TRIUMPH OF REPUBLICAN PRINCIPLES

Jefferson's First Administration, 1801—05

Meaning of Jefferson's election.—It was with great joy that the Republicans saw the election of Jefferson[1]. More than any other man in the country he represented the views of the mass of the people. This fact, coupled with his great ability, had made it possible for him to organize his followers into the compact Republican Party. He believed in the people and sought always to secure their rights. He joined with them in opposing every tendency toward a strong central government and in doing away with all ceremony and show. His election, therefore, meant that the rights of the people would be considered more by the Government than formerly. To the theory of a government *for*

THOMAS JEFFERSON

---

[1] Thomas Jefferson was born in Albemarle County, Virginia, April 13, 1743. He was educated at William and Mary College and began the practice of law. He was often a member of the Virginia Legislature and was a member of the Continental Congress. He wrote the Declaration of Independence and signed it. He was later governor of Virginia, minister to France, Secretary of State, Vice President, and President for two terms. He was the greatest political writer and thinker in America and was the founder of the Democratic-Republican Party.

the people had now been added that of a government by the people.

Jefferson's policy.—Jefferson came into office with a definite policy. He urged economy in the administration of government, the lowering of taxes, the payment of the National debt, and the reduction of the size of both army and navy. He refrained from partisanship. "We are all Federalists, we are all Republicans," he said when he was inaugurated, and it was not long before he had won over many moderate Federalists to his party. His Cabinet was a very strong one, and it was in perfect accord with him. In Madison, the Secretary of State, and Gallatin the Secretary of the Treasury, he had two advisers that were almost unequaled.

War with the Barbary States.—The piratical Barbary States of northern Africa had been preying upon American commerce for some years. This brought on a war in 1801. Tripoli was bombarded, and all the Barbary States were brought to terms. Fortunately for the United States, this war gave our sailors valuable training, which was useful a few years later.

Purchase of Louisiana.—The most important act of Jefferson's administration was the purchase of Louisiana. This vast territory, extending from the Mississippi River to the Rocky Mountains, was then but little known to the world. France had ceded it to Spain in 1763, but had regained it in 1800. Napoleon, who was then the ruler of France, planned to send over an army of occupation and to build up a strong rival of the United States. The port of New Orleans was closed to American commerce, so that the Western States were practically cut off from all trade with the rest of the world.

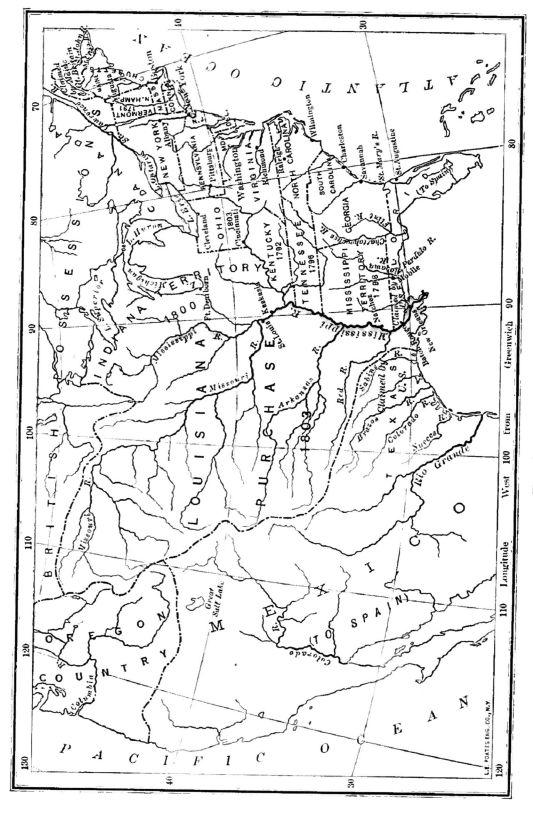

The Louisiana Purchase

Napoleon's plans caused great uneasiness in the United States; and even Jefferson, friendly to France as he was, became alarmed and made up his mind to obtain an outlet into the Gulf of Mexico for the commerce of the great Mississippi valley. Napoleon was soon again at war with England and greatly needed money. As he was unable to defend Louisiana, he agreed to sell it for $15,000,000. By this purchase about one million square miles of territory were added to the United States (see map on page 240). In this purchase of territory, Jefferson overstepped his authority, as defined by the Constitution, and thereby violated his doctrine of strict construction. He knew, however, that he was doing so, and asked that an amendment to the Constitution be passed to give the Administration the right to enter into such a contract in case of urgent need.

The country as a whole approved the action of the President in making the purchase; but very violent opposition to it developed in New England, where there were threats of secession from the Union. This was, however, confined to one section and to one party. The people generally realized how valuable the new possession was.

Admission of Ohio.—In 1803 Ohio was admitted to the Union as a free State. This was the first State to be formed out of the Northwest Territory and the seventeenth to enter the Union. Migration westward was increasing every year. Already there was a growing population in what is now Illinois and Indiana. With the purchase of Louisiana Territory, migration to the Mississippi Territory, now Alabama and Mississippi, increased; and many settlers pushed across the Mississippi River to the new West.

Western explorations. — In Jefferson's administration important progress was made in the exploration of the West. In 1804 an expedition under Lewis and Clark, after ascending the Missouri River, crossed the Rocky

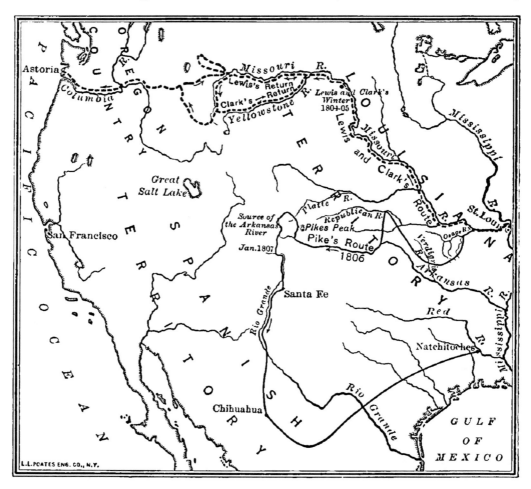

THE ROUTES OF LEWIS AND CLARK, AND PIKE

Mountains, descended the Columbia River, and reached the Pacific Ocean. This expedition gave the United States a strong claim upon the Oregon country.

In the same period Lieutenant Zebulon M. Pike, in attempting to discover the source of the Missouri River, reached the northern limit of the Louisiana Territory, and a year later, after discovering and measuring the peak that bears his name, reached the Rio Grande.

Election of 1804. — In 1804 Jefferson was elected President for a second term, and George Clinton of New York Vice President, by a very large majority over C. C. Pinckney of South Carolina and Rufus King of New York.

Burr's conspiracy.—In 1804 Aaron Burr, who had been defeated for governor of New York through the influence of Alexander Hamilton, challenged Hamilton to a duel and killed him. Burr's term as Vice President expired in 1805, and he went west to escape punishment. There he planned some sort of uprising against the United States, the object of which has never been clearly revealed. The plan fell through, and Burr was arrested by the authorities of Mississippi Territory, but was finally acquitted by the Federal Court at Richmond, Virginia (1807).

AARON BURR

CHAPTER LVIII

STRUGGLE FOR COMMERCIAL RIGHTS

Jefferson's Second Administration, 1985–09

Trouble with England and France.—During the long struggle between England and France, known as the "Napoleonic Wars," American vessels increased in number and obtained more and more of the carrying trade of the world. At that time the British Government, in order to strike a blow at France, ordered the seizure of all vessels carrying goods to France from the French West Indies. This affected American merchantmen. Furthermore, England began again the searching of American ships and the impressment of seamen. In less than a year one hundred American vessels were captured, and nearly a thousand seamen impressed. Jefferson was opposed to war, as he realized the injury it would work to the United States. Consequently, though he protested to England against the outrages on American commerce, he made no preparations to force her to respect our rights on the high seas.

In 1806 Napoleon issued a series of decrees that were intended to cut off Great Britain from all trade with the rest of the world. Great Britain replied by a series of Orders in Council which declared France in a state of blockade and forbade any nation to trade with her. Both sides began to capture all vessels that failed to obey these decrees and orders, and in consequence the business of the United States suffered terribly. Neither France nor England would listen to our protests.

In 1806 a Non-Intercourse Act was passed by Congress; but it was not put into effect for some time, and conditions in the meanwhile steadily grew worse.

The "Chesapeake" and the "Leopard."—The anger of the people of the United States was increased greatly by a British outrage that occurred in June, 1807. The British ship, *Leopard*, acting under orders, held up near the Virginia Capes the American frigate *Chesapeake* and, after firing on her and killing three and wounding eighteen men, searched her and impressed four of her crew. The whole country was indignant, and there was a general demand for war. But Jefferson still clung to his policy of peace, and the only action immediately taken was an order to English ships to leave the United States.

Efforts to avoid war.—Jefferson tried to prevent further trouble with England by a treaty. But the treaty that Pinckney and Monroe made (1806) contained no assurance that England would stop either impressment or the seizure of American commerce bound for France. It was so unsatisfactory to the President that he refused to send it to the Senate for ratification.

Acting on Jefferson's advice, Congress then passed an Embargo Act (1807), which prohibited all American vessels from sailing for foreign ports. It was hoped that England and France would be so much hurt by loss of trade that they would yield. But the United States was more injured than either France or England; for not only were the shipowners deprived of business, but sailors, farmers, merchants, manufacturers, and laborers, all suffered. In some sections of the country business practically stopped.

The embargo proved to be very difficult to enforce. Many vessels slipped away from the home ports despite the law. The Legislature of Massachusetts declared the Act unconstitutional, and in some parts of New England there were discussions urging secession. Public opinion against the embargo was so strong that finally the Act was repealed (1809); and the Non-Intercourse Act, that had been awaiting the President's approval, was signed by Jefferson just three days before the expiration of his term of office.

Jefferson's place in history.—Thomas Jefferson probably had a greater influence on our political life than any other American. He directed the acts of Congress during his Presidency; and after his retirement until his death, his advice was constantly sought by political leaders. His far-seeing statesmanship in the conduct of government —shown, for instance, in the purchase of Louisiana— entitles him to the gratitude and veneration of all his countrymen. He made mistakes, particularly in his foreign policy, but they were far overbalanced by the good he accomplished. One of the greatest acts of his career was performed after his retirement to private life; namely, the founding of the University of Virginia.[1]

JEFFERSON'S HOME, "MONTICELLO"

---

[1] He spent his last days at his beautiful home, "Monticello," near Charlottesville, Virginia. Here he entertained his numerous friends, supervised the building of the University of Virginia, and read the many valuable books in his great library. On his tomb appears the following epitaph, which Jefferson himself wrote: "Author of the Declaration of Independence; of the Statute of Virginia for Religious Freedom, and the Father of the University of Virginia." Jefferson was undoubtedly one of the most learned men of his day. One of his acquaintances said: "When he spoke of law, I thought he was a lawyer; when he talked about mechanics, I was sure he was an engineer; when he got into medicine, it was evident that he was a physician; when he discussed theology, I was convinced that he must be a clergyman; when he talked literature, I made up my mind that I had run against a college professor."

After he retired to private life, Jefferson became reconciled to his old friend and political rival, John Adams; and they carried on a correspondence during the remainder of their lives. Both died on the fiftieth anniversary of the signing of the Declaration of Independence, July 4, 1826.

Invention of the steamboat.—In 1786 James Rumsey of Virginia displayed the model of a steamboat which he had invented. As early as 1788 John Fitch of Connecticut put a steamboat on the Delaware, and in 1790 a steamboat that he invented made regular trips between Philadelphia and Trenton. Seventeen years later (1807) the most notable effort at steam navigation was made by Robert Fulton. His vessel, the *Clermont*, steamed from New York to Albany in a day and a half, and this was at first looked upon as little short of a miracle.

THE "CLERMONT"

Within a few years steam was used generally in propelling rivercraft and even in ocean navigation.

Election of 1808.—Jefferson refused a third term, as Washington had done, and retired to Monticello, his home in Virginia. Largely through his influence, James Madison, his Secretary of State, was chosen to succeed him.

CHAPTER LIX

ENGLAND FORCES WAR

Madison's Administration, 1809–12

Madison's efforts at peace.—After Madison[1] was inaugurated (March 4, 1809), he made further efforts to

---

[1] James Madison was born in King George County, Virginia, March 16, 1751. He was graduated at Princeton and did post-graduate work there. He was a member of the Virginia Legislature, the Continental Congress, and the Federal Convention of 1787. In the latter body he

avoid trouble with England and France. Like Jefferson, he was a man of peaceful disposition, but all his efforts to induce England to withdraw the Orders in Council (page 242) failed. He then made an attempt, through an act of Congress, to persuade France or England to make favorable terms by offering, if one of them would withdraw its restrictions on American commerce, to forbid the United States to trade with the other.

JAMES MADISON

Napoleon, in the meantime, had ordered the seizure of American ships under pretext that they had violated the Embargo Act by leaving American ports. Now, however, he answered Madison that all the offensive decrees had been withdrawn; but when trade began again with a rush, he ordered that American merchantmen be seized and confiscated. Thus fresh injuries were inflicted upon the United States.

The "President" and the "Little Belt."—So great had been England's outrages against the United States that the people became impatient and demanded war. France had been as hostile as England, and there was equal cause for war with her. But England was particularly hated by many of the people. Added to their

---

did the greater part of the framing of the Constitution and exerted more influence than any other member. He also preserved the outlines of the debates in the Convention. He was later a member of Congress, Secretary of State, and President for two terms. He was a writer of ability and was one of the authors of *The Federalist*. He died June 28, 1836.

bitter resentment of recent outrages were their old memories of the Revolution.

About this time the frigate *President* was sent out to protect American vessels. On her way to New York City, she met the British war vessel, *Little Belt;* and a battle followed, in which the *Little Belt* was defeated and badly injured (1811).

Declaration of war.—When Congress met in 1811, it was controlled by a new set of leaders. They were young and enthusiastic and came mostly from the South and the West, where the feeling against England was most intense and where there was a strong desire for war. Prominent among them were Henry Clay of Kentucky and John C. Calhoun of South Carolina. These young men, with their "warhawks" from the South and the West, were tired of submitting to insult and injury; so they forced Congress to a declaration of war. President Madison was still opposed to it; but finally his consent was won, and war was declared, June 18, 1812.

England forced this war by: (1) the sending of British war vessels to the coast of the United States; (2) the capture of hundreds of American vessels; (3) the Orders in Council; (4) the inciting of the Indians to hostility; (5) the impressment of seamen.

Indian troubles.—In 1810 Tecumseh, a remarkably able Indian chief, and his twin brother, "The Prophet," united the Indians of the Northwest into a hostile league. It was thought that the chiefs were under the influence of the English in Canada, and the league threatened the whole western frontier of the United States. In 1811 General William Henry Harrison, taking advantage of the absence of Tecumseh, attacked the Indians near their town, Tippecanoe, on the Wabash River, and defeated them. This feat made Harrison the hero of the West.

End of the Bank.—The Republicans had always opposed the National Bank; and when its charter expired in 1811, they refused to recharter it, on the ground that it was not needed and that it had too much power.

Madison reëlected.—In 1812 Madison and Elbridge Gerry of Massachusetts were elected President and Vice President. The Federalists supported DeWitt Clinton of New York and Jared Ingersoll of Pennsylvania.

Admission of Louisiana as a State.—By 1812 the population of the southern portion of the Louisiana Purchase (the Territory of Orleans) had grown largely. The section had been chiefly French; but many Americans had gone into it, and New Orleans had become an important shipping point for all the West. The Territory was therefore admitted as a State, with a constitution providing for slavery.

CHAPTER LX

FIRST AND SECOND YEARS OF THE WAR OF 1812

Madison's Administration, 1812–13

Situation in the United States.—The United States was not at all prepared for war. The army was small and weak, and the navy had but few vessels, while England had powerful armies and nearly a thousand ships of war. The country was poor, and the revenues were steadily growing smaller. Worst of all, the country

FIRST TWO YEARS OF THE WAR OF 1812   249

was far from being united. The New England States had just been offended by the admission of Louisiana as a slave State (1812). The Northern and Middle States as a whole felt that it would be their interests, rather than those of the South, that would suffer by war, since a great part of their property was invested in shipping or commerce. So strong was the feeling against the war, that Massachusetts, Connecticut, and Rhode Island refused to obey the President's call for the militia. Many men in New England, however, volunteered in spite of the action of their States.

Campaign of 1812.—The first plan of the war was to invade and capture Canada. Three armies were ordered to advance into that country: one under General Hull by way of Detroit, another under General Van Rensselaer by way of Niagara, and a third under General Dearborn by way of Lake Champlain. The armies were to unite and then to seize Montreal and Quebec. Hull, fearing a general Indian massacre, surrendered Detroit and the whole of Michigan without a blow. He was afterward tried for cowardice and sentenced to death, but was pardoned because of his military record in the Revolution. Van Rensselaer was defeated at Queenstown Heights because his militia refused to go into Canada, and Dearborn never reached Canadian soil. This year the efforts of the Americans on land were unsuccessful, with one exception. At Ogdensburg, New York, the British were repulsed by a force of militia under Jacob Brown, a Quaker farmer.

War on the sea.—The discouragements on land in 1812, however, were fully offset by victories on the sea. Great Britain was acknowledged the undisputed mistress of the sea, and no one thought that the vessels of the United

States would have any chance against her power. But in August the *Constitution*, Captain Hull commanding, defeated and destroyed the *Guerrière*. The ships met in the Gulf of St. Lawrence, and the battle was over within half an hour. Two months later, the *Wasp* captured the *Frolic*, and the *United States*, under Captain Stephen Decatur, captured the *Macedonian*. In December the *Constitution*, then under Captain William Bainbridge, destroyed the *Java* and won the name "Old Ironsides." Other victories of less importance were added to these, gladdening the

THE NORTHERN FRONTIER DURING THE WAR OF 1812

hearts of all Americans and amazing the world. Through her navy the United States won the respect of the nations.

After this year the tide turned, and the American vessels were either captured or forced to take refuge in the harbors of their own country. The most famous of the

American defeats was the capture of the *Chesapeake* by the *Shannon*. Captain Lawrence of the *Chesapeake* was killed; and his last words, "Don't give up the ship," became the watchword of the navy. In this war two hundred and fifty American privateers, vessels owned by

"Don't Give Up the Ship"
After the painting by Chappel.

private persons and authorized by Congress to enter the war, scoured the seas, capturing many hundred English merchantmen and inflicting terrible injury upon British commerce.

War in the Northwest.—In 1813 General Harrison, the hero of Tippecanoe, was placed in command in the Northwest and ordered to regain Michigan. Part of his force under General Winchester was captured at Frenchtown, on Raisin River. The British force, under General Proctor, was assisted by a body of Indians under Tecumseh. Proctor promised protection, but his Indian allies fell upon the prisoners and massacred most of them. This "Raisin River Massacre," as it was called, aroused the Northwest as nothing else had done; and Harrison soon had a large force at his command.

Proctor and Tecumseh at once retreated, and Harrison followed them into Canada and attacked them on the Thames River. The battle resulted in an American victory. Tecumseh was killed, but Proctor escaped. By these victories the Northwest was permanently recovered.

Perry's victory on Lake Erie.—In the meantime, Captain Oliver H. Perry, a young naval officer, was busily engaged in building a fleet on the shores of Lake Erie. The British already had a number of vessels on that lake; and on the 10th of September, 1813, the two fleets engaged in battle. Perry had nine vessels, and the British six; but the British vessels were larger and had more and heavier guns. The battle lasted for three hours, and Perry finally lost his flagship, the *Lawrence*, named for the gallant commander of the *Chesapeake*, whose last words were the battle cry of the day.[1] But despite the flying shell, Perry went in a rowboat to the *Niagara*, and in a few minutes the fight was over and won. Perry's message to General Harrison has become famous: "We have met the enemy and they are ours; two ships, two brigs, one schooner, and one sloop."

---

[1] When Perry was ready for the battle, he unfurled a flag, saying: "My brave lads, this flag contains the last words of Captain Lawrence. Shall I hoist it?" His men replied with one voice, "Ay! Ay! Ay!" When the rest of the fleet saw the words, "Don't give up the ship!" they showed their approval of the sentiment by their hearty cheers.

Operations around Lake Ontario.—In April General Dearborn's army captured York (now Toronto) and, to the disgrace of the nation, burned its public buildings. An American attempt to capture Montreal failed. The British then invaded New York. Although they were repulsed at Sackett's Harbor, they did much damage elsewhere. Unfortunately the Americans about this time burned a Canadian village (Newark).

Jackson and the Indians.—In the Southwest, both the British and the Spanish had been stirring up the Indians against the United States. In August, 1813, the Creeks rose and, falling upon the settlers at Fort Mims in Alabama, killed four hundred of them with horrible cruelty. General Andrew Jackson was sent to subdue them. With a force of Tennessee riflemen and militiamen from the Southwest, he inflicted a crushing defeat upon the Indians at Horseshoe Bend. Jackson's men affectionately gave him the title "Old Hickory," in recognition of his endurance.[1]

ANDREW JACKSON IN THE UNIFORM OF 1812

---

[1] On one of his prolonged marches, Jackson had three good horses at his disposal, but gave them over to sick soldiers while he walked with his men. One of the soldiers, observing this, remarked, "The General is tough"; and a second one added, "As tough as hickory." He was ever afterward known as "Old Hickory."

CHAPTER LXI

THIRD YEAR OF THE WAR OF 1812

Madison's Administration, 1814

The third invasion of Canada.—In July, 1814, an American army under General Jacob Brown crossed the Niagara River and invaded Canada. Two American victories followed, one at Chippewa and the other at Lundy's Lane (map on page 250), but no important advantage was gained. In these battles General Winfield Scott won distinction.

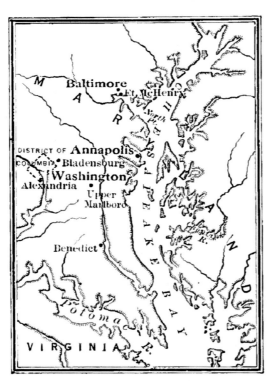

THE CAMPAIGN AROUND WASHINGTON

The English had fixed their attention on the Hudson valley route into the heart of the Republic. Now they took advantage of the fact that a large force of Americans was absent in Canada with General Brown. General Prevost, the English commander in Canada, marched with an army against Plattsburg on Lake Champlain. A British fleet on the lake supported him, but it was defeated and captured by a small American squadron under Commodore Macdonough. Prevost was so alarmed by this that he retreated at once without striking a blow.

The capture of Washington.—During 1814 the English succeeded in blockading the Atlantic coast quite effectively. A number of towns were captured; and finally a fleet under Admiral Cockburn sailed into Chesapeake Bay, and an army under General Ross marched upon Washington. The British army defeated the weak force under General Winder which opposed them at Bladensburg, and occupied Washington. There they brought disgrace to their country by burning the Capitol and all the other public buildings.

A British fleet, in the meantime, threatened Baltimore, but was unable to pass Fort McHenry, which was bombarded for a long time.[1] The British army from Washington advanced upon Baltimore, but was likewise repulsed near the city and retreated to the fleet.

Battle of New Orleans.—Soon after these events a veteran English army was sent under General Pakenham against New Orleans. To defend the city the President chose General Jackson, who was placed in command of a force of volunteer riflemen, chiefly from Tennessee and Kentucky. Jackson fortified his position on the field of Chalmette below the city, and inflicted a terrible defeat upon the British (January 8, 1815). General Pakenham was killed, and the British loss was over two thousand killed and wounded. The American loss was seven killed and six wounded.

The treaty of peace.—If news could have been carried in those days as rapidly as it is to-day, the battle of New Orleans would never have been fought; for the treaty of

---

[1] While the bombardment of the fort was in progress, Francis Scott Key, who was on a boat detained in the midst of the British fleet, composed the National air, "The Star Spangled Banner."

peace had already been signed at Ghent, December 24, 1814.

This treaty did not mention the questions over which the war had been fought; but since the war between England and France had come to an end, most of the questions had ceased to be of importance. Each side gave up what territory it had occupied, and both were glad to see the end of the war.

CHAPTER LXII

THE AMERICAN REPUBLIC RESPECTED ABROAD

End of Madison's Administration, 1814-17

Political results of the war.—Despite the fact that the war had not been a great military success and that the treaty failed to settle the matters in dispute, its results were on the whole very advantageous to the United States. It brought out clearly a national spirit, which was beginning to develop; and it greatly strengthened the general Government. It drew into close relation the different sections of the country, with the one exception of New England, which remained aloof and disapproved.

Fortunately the successful termination of the war put a stop to the efforts of certain New England leaders to induce their States to withdraw from the Union. In 1814, before the close of the war, delegates from these States had met at Hartford, Connecticut, and adopted resolutions condemning the war, asserting the right of nullification, and threatening to secede from the Union if certain demands which they made on Congress were not granted.

But the end of the war came almost at once, and the only effect of the Convention was to kill what remained of the Federalist party. The war caused the American Republic to be greatly respected by European countries; for they saw, to their astonishment, how well the new Republic could resist a great power like England.

Financial results of the war.—The financial condition of the country grew steadily worse during the war, and the Government found it very hard to raise money to carry on the struggle. In 1816 a new National Bank was chartered for twenty years. It was like the old one, except that it was much larger (pages 225 and 248).

Although trade with foreign countries was cut off during the war, manufacturing in the United States proved very profitable, and there was a great increase in the number of factories and their output. But when peace came, the country was flooded with goods from England, where they were manufactured much more cheaply; and the American industries were threatened with destruction. To help the manufacturers, Congress in 1816 passed the first tariff designed primarily for the protection of home industries. That is, the tax thus placed on goods brought into the country made their price so high that American manufacturers could compete with those of foreign countries.

Admission of Indiana.—In 1816 Indiana was admitted to the Union as a free State. It was the second State to be formed from the Northwest Territory and the nineteenth to enter the Union.

Election of 1816.—Madison declined to consider a third term and was succeeded by James Monroe of Virginia, his Secretary of State. The Federalists voted for

Rufus King, who carried only three States. Madison retired to Montpelier, his Virginia home, where he lived to a ripe old age, revered and honored by the whole people.

CHAPTER LXIII

NEW PROBLEMS AT HOME AND ABROAD

Monroe's Administrations, 1817-25

Monroe's Cabinet.—Monroe had been well trained for the Presidency by long public service,[2] and this helped him in selecting good men to assist him in his Cabinet. John Quincy Adams, the son of President Adams, was Secretary of State, William H. Crawford of Georgia was Secretary of the Treasury, John C. Calhoun was Secretary of War, and William Wirt of Virginia was Attorney General. Adams, Crawford, and Calhoun became characters of the first importance in our history.

The Seminole War.—Soon after Monroe came into office, trouble arose in the South. Florida then belonged to

---

[1] Madison was always a popular man. He was never bitter in his manner toward anyone. He had been one of the chief advocates of the Constitution, but never a believer in "loose" construction. Hence, after the Constitution was adopted, he opposed Hamilton's policy and Washington's methods. He was an able debater—the greatest of his time. It was said of him in debate: "When he had finished, nothing remained to be said."

[2] James Monroe was born in Westmoreland County, Virginia, April 28, 1758. He attended William and Mary College and soon entered on long career of public service. He was a soldier in the Revolution, and member of the Virginia Legislature and of the Convention to ratify the Constitution. He was in turn Governor of Virginia, United States Senator, Minister to France and England, Secretary of State, and President for two terms. He died July 4, 1831.

Spain, but there was scarcely any government there. The Seminole Indians were kept stirred up by escaped criminals and runaway negroes from Georgia and South Carolina and by a few Spaniards who lived among them. They would cross the border into the United States to plunder and burn and then hasten back to Spanish territory before they could be punished. In 1818 the President sent General Andrew Jackson against them. Jackson misunderstood the President and thought Florida was to be seized, so he led his army there and captured St. Marks and Pensacola. He captured also two British subjects who had been stirring up the Indians against the United States, and had them court-martialed and executed.

JAMES MONROE

Purchase of Florida.—It looked as if trouble might follow with both Spain and England because of these incidents, and many people in the United States thought that Jackson should be punished for what he had done. But all efforts to start such proceedings failed, and Jackson was more popular than ever. In order to prevent further trouble, the United States opened negotiations with Spain for the purchase of Florida. In 1819 Spain ceded Florida to the United States for $5,000,000, and at the same time settled the Spanish boundary on the west, Texas being conceded by the United States to be part of Mexico.

Settlement of the northern boundary. — In 1818 a treaty with Great Britain was made which settled upon the forty-ninth parallel as the northern boundary of the United States from the Lake of the Woods to the Rocky Mountains. Both Great Britain and the United States claimed the Oregon territory, but it was decided to post-

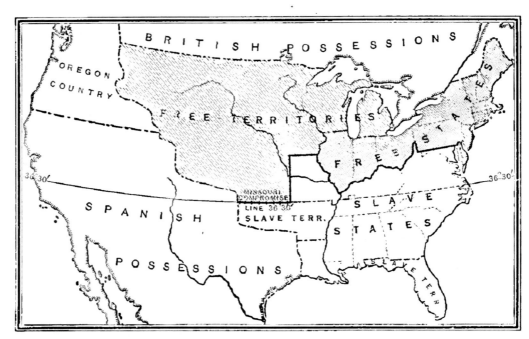

The Territory Affected by the Missouri Compromise

pone the settlement of the boundary there and to have joint occupation of the country for ten years (page 300).

New States admitted. — The western and southern movement of population reached its height in Monroe's administration. By 1817 the population was large enough to justify the division of the Mississippi Territory, organized in 1798, into two parts: one, the present Mississippi, which was admitted as a slave State in December of the same year; the other, the present State of Alabama, which was organized as a Territory. Alabama grew so rapidly that it was admitted as a slave State in 1819. In the Northwest the growth in population was even more rapid, and Illinois quickly followed Indiana as a free State; so that by 1818 three States from the Northwest had been admitted to the Union of States.

The Missouri compromise. — We have already seen that the North was gaining political strength faster than the South, and was opposed to the extension of slavery. This feeling first showed itself clearly when Missouri wished to enter the Union.

Missouri had been settled largely by slaveholders, and in 1819 applied for admission as a slave State. The House of Representatives was willing to admit it only under the condition that gradual emancipation of slaves should take place. The Senate would admit it with slavery. Very bitter debates followed, and the whole country was much stirred up. The matter was finally settled (1820) by a compromise introduced by Senator Thomas of Illinois. Missouri was admitted as a slave State, but the rest of the Louisiana Purchase north of latitude 36°30′, the southern boundary of Missouri, was to be forever free. This compromise was very favorable to the North. About the same time Maine was admitted as a free State, Massachusetts having consented to surrender her interest in this region.

Reëlection of Monroe. — In 1820 Monroe was reëlected without opposition. Only one electoral vote was cast against him, and that by an elector who was in favor of him, but wanted Washington to be the only man who had ever had the honor of unanimous election. Because of this lack of opposition, the period has been called the "Era of Good Feeling." There was at this time only one party, the Democratic-Republican; the Federalists had disappeared.

The Monroe Doctrine.—The most important act of Monroe's administration was the statement of foreign policy known as the "Monroe Doctrine." Shortly before this time Spain's colonies in South America had revolted because of harsh treatment, and their independence had been recognized by the United States. A league called the "Holy Alliance" had recently been organized by the rulers of several European countries, for the purpose of checking republican movements everywhere; and it was supposed that it would aid Spain to regain her colonies. Accordingly, in his message to Congress in 1823, Monroe warned the nations of Europe that North and South America were closed to further colonization by any Old World powers, and that the United States would allow no interference with the affairs of any American Government. This has been the fixed policy of the United States ever since. Its effect at the time was to prevent Spain from receiving any aid in Europe. Russia had already occupied Alaska and was laying claim to California; but when Monroe's message became public, the latter claim was dropped.

HENRY CLAY

The tariff of 1824.—In 1824 a new tariff law was passed, which raised the duties on imports still higher for the purpose of protection. Clay was its chief advocate. Many people in the South were strongly opposed to protection, because they were beginning to see that an agricultural section was injured by it.

Election of 1824.—Four candidates for the Presidency appeared in 1824: William H. Crawford, Henry Clay, John Quincy Adams, and Andrew Jackson. Calhoun had been a candidate, but withdrew and was elected Vice President. When the electoral vote for President was counted, it was found that Jackson had received 99; Adams, 84; Crawford, 41; and Clay, 37. As no one had a majority, the election went to the House of Representatives. Clay's name was dropped because he was fourth, and the House considered the other three. Through Clay's influence, Adams was chosen. Clay was made Secretary of State by Adams, and Jackson and his friends at once said that a "corrupt bargain" had been made between them. The charge was probably false, but it injured Clay during the rest of his political life.

CHAPTER LXIV

THE UNITED STATES IN 1820

Population.—Ever since the Revolution there had been a steady growth of population, and since 1790 it had more than doubled. This growth probably affected the West more than any other section. Settlements in the Ohio and Mississippi valleys had commenced before the Revolution, and by 1820 there were over two and a half million people living there. As has been seen, by 1817 four States west of the Alleghanies had been admitted to the Union; and in 1817 Mississippi came in as a slave State. Illinois as a free State and Alabama with slavery were admitted in 1818 and 1819 respectively.

There were three territories—Missouri, Arkansas, and Michigan.

The East, too, had grown rapidly; for it had received the main body of European immigrants. The South had grown, but mainly from natural increase. Few immigrants went there because labor was already supplied by slavery. Then, too, the South had lost many of its population, who had moved West to get away from slavery.

The westward movement.—Various motives influenced the early settlers to go West: the abundance of fertile land; the love of the wilderness with its rough, unrestrained life; and still more, the opportunity for a man to rise by his own exertions—to "grow up with the country."

The moving to the West was a picturesque sight. Whole families, sometimes whole communities, went together, carrying all their possessions, including furniture, farming implements, cattle, and even the family dog. The men rode horseback; the women and children, in the wagons. At night they camped. The meat for their meals was often secured with the rifle from the abundant game, and the streams supplied plenty of fish. When the western country was finally reached, the bold pioneer would choose a good site for a house and farm, build a cabin, and provide his family with the meager comforts of frontier life.

Internal improvements.—The roads to the West were few and bad, and traveling was difficult. After the Alleghany Mountains were crossed, the rivers helped somewhat by furnishing natural highways; but until steamboats came into use, a journey upstream was very hard. Even after steamboats were used, it was not possible for them to go in shallow depths, and rivers did not always run where the settlers wished to go. Consequently, as the western country was filled, a demand arose for better facilities for communication with the East in order that trade might benefit both sections. The States were so poor that many propositions were made for National aid. As early as 1806 the Cumberland Road from the Potomac to the Ohio had been begun. Other highways also were started, and many canals were planned.

In 1808 Albert Gallatin proposed that the Federal Government build a canal from Boston to the sounds of North Carolina. In 1817 Congress passed a bill greatly extending the work of internal improvements. Madison, who was a strict constructionist, vetoed it on the ground that it was unconstitutional. New York then commenced the construction of the Erie Canal from Lake Erie to the Hudson River, which was completed in 1825. Other States, especially Pennsylvania, made great steps in the building of roads and canals; and Maryland, Virginia, and North Carolina also planned elaborate systems of internal improvements which, however, were never fully carried out.

Life in the West.—Life in the West was primitive, but there was great opportunity for a young man of ability and determination. A new democratic spirit arose there, because all alike began at the beginning, as it were; and this spirit has greatly influenced the development of the whole country. With it grew a new National spirit; for the Western States had been created by the Union and looked upon it as supreme, while most of the older States still regarded the Union as the creature of the States and dependent upon them.

The chief occupation of the West at this time was agriculture. There was little wealth or poverty; but many of the people owned large tracts of land, which later were very valuable. Everyone was deeply interested in politics; and, as property was accumulated, there was a general desire for education. In the Northwest public schools were established early, and there was a vigorous intellectual life.

Development of the East.—While the West was going forward, the East was not lagging behind. With the increase of population went a great increase in wealth, particularly after the War of 1812. Education became more general; and, as transportation facilities were improved, local differences disappeared. Newspapers were established in large numbers, and many of them had wide circulation.

Sectional differences. — The differences between the North and the South, however, became more marked as time went on. Many of these were caused by slavery. At the opening of the Revolution, all the colonies had slaves; but the Northern States soon began to free theirs. Slavery in that section had never paid, and there were very few slaves. There was as yet little feeling that slavery was wrong. New England had continued to monopolize the traffic in African slaves until 1808, when Congress passed a law forbidding it; and even after that New England traders frequently smuggled slaves into the South.

In the South cotton was fast becoming the crop of primary importance, and everything else was neglected for it. Since Eli Whitney's invention of the cotton gin (1794), cotton raising had been very profitable. Slaves were needed for its cultivation, and thus slavery was fastened more tightly than ever upon the South. More and more the North turned to manufacturing and commerce, while the South bent every energy to the production of large crops of cotton. Slave labor was useless in manufacturing; so the South, about 1816, abandoned all hope of establishing manufacturing enterprises. In the North the towns and cities grew and exerted a great influence; while in the South there were few cities, the population being chiefly rural. Wealth was in the hands of a comparatively small class of slaveholders, and they largely controlled politics. Free labor had a very poor chance in competition with slavery, and the South lost thereby.

By 1824 seven of the original States had abolished slavery, and six had retained it. Of the nine new States, five had slavery. Thus there were at that time eleven free States and eleven slave States. As the free States saw less and less of slavery within their own borders, their feeling against it increased.

With the growth of population in the North there was also a large increase in the number of representatives in Congress. Consequently the South had to rely upon the Senate to defeat any legislation hostile to slavery. This was the reason why free and slave States were kept evenly balanced in the admission of new States. In 1824 the South was in control of National politics, but after that the struggle for supremacy grew more bitter. As the years passed, slavery was placed on the defensive; and the South held more and more to the doctrine of strict construction. The North, growing industrially and needing from the Federal Government such aid as the protective tariff, became more National in sentiment.

Education.—In the North there were systems of public education in most of the States. In the South school systems had never been established. But just at this time North Carolina was beginning the movement that led to the establishment in 1840 of a system of public schools. Secondary education in the South at this time was furnished by tutors and private schools.

Both sections had a number of colleges. In the North were Harvard, Yale, Princeton, Columbia, Brown, Dartmouth, Amherst, Williams, Rutgers, and the University of Pennsylvania, most of which had been established prior to the Revolution. In the South were William and Mary, St. John's, Washington College (later Washington and Lee University), and Hampden-Sidney, which were founded before the Revolution; the University of North Carolina chartered in 1789, the University of Georgia founded in 1785, and South Carolina College founded in 1801. Jefferson succeeded in 1819 in his efforts to establish the University of Virginia.

Literature.—By 1824 three American writers were attracting attention by their work. Washington Irving, by his "Knickerbocker's History of New York" and his sketches, had made even England acknowledge that there was a growing American literature. James Fenimore Cooper, the first important American novelist, was writing his tales of American frontier life. With their backwoodsmen and Indians, they pictured scenes altogether new in literature; and the stories they told were quite unlike the tales of English writers. Besides these, a rising American poet, William Cullen Bryant, had written "Thanatopsis."

CHAPTER LXV

FORMATION OF NEW PARTIES

John Quincy Adams's Administration, 1825-29

Difficulties of the administration. — John Quincy Adams[1] had had splendid training for the Presidency; but, like his father, he did not make friends easily. Throughout his term he saw the movement against him, but refused to do anything to strengthen himself. He thought that the President should not stoop to such a thing. Loyal service to the country was his way of "electioneering," but it did not win him friends. Congress would not follow his recommendations, and the people still remembered the charges that had been made against him and Clay.

Jackson's campaign. — Jackson's friends were very angry over his defeat in the election of 1824. They said that the will of the people had been disregarded, and at once directed their energies to securing Jackson's election in 1828, beginning a campaign that lasted four years. Jackson was very popular with the people, and the idea spread rapidly that he would make a good President because he was one of the "plain people." This feeling was particularly strong in the West.

---

[1] John Quincy Adams was born at Braintree, Massachusetts, July 11, 1767. He was graduated at Harvard and was for a time a professor there. He was a lawyer by profession, but spent a large part of his life in public service, being Minister to Holland, Sweden, Prussia, Russia, and Great Britain. He was United States Senator, Secretary of State, and President for one term. After he retired to private life, he was elected to Congress and served for seventeen years, being best known as the strong debater and leader of the antislavery party. He died February 23, 1848.

Policy of Adams.—Adams was particularly interested in internal improvements and urged that the Federal Government should spend money in building roads and canals, but Congress would do little for fear of strengthening the President.

In 1826 a congress of the American republics was called to meet at Panama to discuss matters that concerned all. Adams and Clay were very anxious that delegates should be sent from the United States; but Congress delayed so long in the hope of injuring the President that, when the delegates reached Panama, the congress had adjourned.

JOHN QUINCY ADAMS

Georgia and the Indians.—Within the limits of Georgia at this time lived the Creeks and the Cherokees. The United States had promised to remove them long before, but had failed to do so. The people of Georgia were annoyed at the delay, and now prepared to take control of the lands themselves. They began to try the Indians for offenses against the laws of the State, although by a treaty with the United States the Indians were not under the laws of the State. When Adams warned Governor Troup that he must stop having the Indian lands surveyed, the Governor answered defiantly, and Congress refused to take any action to support the President. As it was near the end of his Presidential term, Adams did nothing more about the matter; and when Jackson became President he refused to enforce a decision of the Supreme Court in favor of the Indians.[1] Later a treaty was made, and the Indians moved west.

The tariff of 1828.—During Adams's administration the manufacturers of New England were calling for a higher tariff to protect their business, and in 1828 the duties were greatly raised. The whole South by this time was strongly opposed to protective tariffs and was particularly outraged by this one, which was known as "the tariff of abominations." A large number of Southern State Legislatures passed resolutions declaring the law unconstitutional. South Carolina in particular was excited, and Calhoun commenced writing against it.

Election of 1828.—The Democratic-Republican Party now began to split into two new and definite parties, headed by Adams and Jackson. The supporters of Adams, who were in favor of the National Bank, a protective tariff, internal improvements, and strong powers in the central Government, called themselves National Republicans. Later they took the name Whigs.

Jackson's party was made up of those who believed in a low tariff and were opposed to the National Bank. From this time it was known as the Democratic Party. The States' Rights men, or those who followed Jefferson in thinking that the States should keep most of the powers of government, also supported him. This party made its appeal to the people and waged a spectacular campaign in which hickory walking-canes and hickory "pole-raisings" played a conspicuous part. As a result, Jackson was elected by an overwhelming majority.

---

[1] Jackson is reported to have said, "John Marshall made the law, now let him enforce it."

CHAPTER LXVI

TRIUMPH OF THE NEW DEMOCRACY

Jackson's First Administration, 1829-33

Meaning of Jackson's election.—The election of Jackson[1] to the Presidency meant that a new era had begun in politics and that, more than ever before, the voice of the people would be heard in political discussions. His inauguration was attended by a great crowd.[2] Out of the West had come a new spirit of democracy, which was strong and honest, but ignorant and prejudiced. Its effect was to make a new party; and never was a party more in accord with the opinions of the mass

---

[1] Andrew Jackson was born in North Carolina, March 15, 1767. His parents were poor Irish immigrants. While a mere boy, he was a soldier in the Revolution. He became a lawyer and removed to Tennessee. There he rose rapidly and was at various times a member of the Constitutional Convention and of Congress, United States Senator, Justice of the Supreme Court of Tennessee, and Major General of militia. In the regular army, also, he rose to that rank. He won distinction by his defeat of the Creeks in the War of 1812 and by his defeat of the British at New Orleans. Later he crushed the power of the Seminoles in Florida. He was defeated for the Presidency in 1824, but was elected in 1828 and again in 1832. He died June 8, 1845. He was one of the most interesting characters in our history, and likewise one of the strongest political leaders.

[2] "Judge Story, who was an eyewitness of the scene, declared that Washington City had never seen such a throng; and Daniel Webster wrote that men came from a distance of five hundred miles to see the 'Old Hero.' On the night following the inauguration, in their eagerness to shake hands with the President, rough men stood with muddy boots upon the costly furniture of the White House and smashed the fine chandeliers which hung overhead. At one time during the reception the press was so great that Jackson was in danger of injury and was rescued with difficulty from the onslaught of his friends."—GARNER AND LODGE.

of the people, or a leader more representative of his party. Jackson's administration may truly be called his "reign," but he reigned because a majority of the people wanted him to. Rough, untrained except by war, hardships, and privations, he had the virtues and the faults of the people; and they loved him.

Untrained as he was, Jackson was a man of unusual ability; and his military habits of leadership enabled him to give the country a strong administration for eight years. But he was always a fighter. His terms of office were filled with a succession of quarrels, in most of which he won.

ANDREW JACKSON
In his last days.

The "spoils system."—The greatest evil of the administration was the establishment of the system of rewarding party service by appointment to public office. The cry of the supporters of Jackson had been "Turn the rascals out!" and when he was elected, he did not forget his friends who demanded office. Removals were made by the wholesale, and the appointment of his friends followed, regardless of their fitness. This system, as can easily be seen, set a bad example for the future.

Jackson's Cabinet.—Jackson's Cabinet was not very strong. Martin Van Buren, a clever politician who had resigned the governorship of New York to become Secretary of State, was probably the most able member. But the weakness of his Cabinet did not make much difference to Jackson; for he soon quarreled with most of its members, either because they were friends of Calhoun, whom he disliked, or because their wives would not visit Mrs. Eaton, wife of the Secretary of the Navy. As a

THE WHITE HOUSE IN JACKSON'S DAY
From a print of 1829.

result, Jackson formed a new Cabinet. But even then he was more apt to take the advice of a number of his close friends who constituted what was called his "Kitchen Cabinet."[1]

Rise of the Abolitionists.—In Jackson's first term the discussion of the slavery question became very bitter. Up to this time a great many people in the South, like Washington and Jefferson, had believed that slavery was an evil and had hoped to get rid of it some day. But as slavery became more profitable because of the growing importance of the cotton crop, there were fewer opponents to be found in the South. We are told that in 1827 the

---

[1] His confidential advisers were so called because they habitually came in to see him by a side door toward the back of the White House. These confidential advisers were some old friends of the President from Tennessee.

South had five sixths of all the antislavery societies then organized in the United States, and that in three years (1824–26) about two thousand slaves were freed in North Carolina alone. In 1831 a bill providing for the gradual emancipation of all the slaves in Virginia was lost in the Legislature of that State by a close vote. But the same year William Lloyd Garrison established in Boston an antislavery paper called *The Liberator;* and the violent opponents of slavery, who were called Abolitionists because they wanted slavery abolished, began to agitate the subject. Garrison declared the Constitution of the United States to be "a covenant with death and an agreement with hell" because it permitted slavery.

At first the Abolitionists were very unpopular in the North as well as in the South, and they were often mobbed. But in time they made converts to their cause in large numbers and began to flood Congress with petitions for the abolition of slavery in the District of Columbia. The Southern influence in Congress was strong enough to keep these petitions from being received; but as this was a denial of the constitutional right of petition, it made many enemies for the South. John Quincy Adams, who had become a member of Congress (1831), was for seventeen years the champion of the antislavery forces.

In the South a slave insurrection under the negro leader, Nat Turner, had caused great horror and alarm. It occurred in Virginia in 1831 and resulted in the death of sixty persons, principally women and children. The blame for it was attributed to the spread of Abolitionist sentiment. To prevent any repetition of such an uprising, the Southern States began to pass strict laws against the Abolitionists and refused to let abolition books and papers come within their borders, whenever they could prevent it. The laws in regard to slaves were made much more strict, and the Southern States that had allowed free negroes to vote, took the privilege away from them.

The Webster-Hayne debate.—In 1830 Senator Hayne of South Carolina made a sharp attack on New England and asserted that a State had a right to nullify any law of Congress that it believed unconstitutional. Daniel Webster,[1] Senator from Massachusetts, a lawyer and orator, made one of his most brilliant speeches in reply. In it he asserted that the Constitution had made a national government, not merely a compact between the States. He closed with the thrilling words, "Liberty and Union, now and forever, one and inseparable!" It was finer oratory than Hayne's speech and struck a responsive chord in the North where feeling against the South was intense, and in the West where the Union had always been considered of more importance than the States. Hayne's theory as to the character of the Constitution was, however, based

DANIEL WEBSTER
Engraving of 1840 from a daguerreotype.

---

[1] Daniel Webster was born at Salisbury, New Hampshire, on January 18, 1782. He was educated at Dartmouth College and later studied law. He was a member of Congress from New Hampshire and then, having changed his residence, from Massachusetts. He was a member of the Constitutional Convention of the latter State and also a United States Senator. He was Secretary of State under Harrison, Tyler, and Fillmore. He died October 23, 1852. He was the greatest orator in our history and one of our greatest constitutional lawyers.

on history, and reiterated the views expressed in the Kentucky and Virginia resolutions (page 233); but Webster's speech was more in harmony with the rising national spirit of the North and West.

Election of 1832.—In 1832 Jackson was elected President by a large majority, and Martin Van Buren was chosen Vice President. The Presidential candidate of the National Republicans, or Whigs, was Henry Clay. A third party, called Anti-Masons,[1] nominated William Wirt.

All the parties in this campaign had nominating conventions. This way of nominating had taken the place of the old method of nominating by a Congressional caucus or by the State legislatures; and as a result it gradually drew every voter into some party organization.

CHAPTER LXVII

NULLIFICATION AND THE BANK

Jackson's Second Administration, 1833–37
Van Buren's Administration, 1837–41

Nullification in South Carolina.—In 1832 the "tariff of abominations" was lowered slightly; but the idea of protection was still uppermost in the law, and the South was greatly angered and almost desperate. Finally, in November, the Legislature of South Carolina called a convention of the people and passed an ordinance declaring

---

[1] It was so called because formed in opposition to the Masons. A man in New York named Morgan wrote a book to reveal the secrets of Masonry and disappeared soon afterwards. The Masons were accused of murdering him, and a political party was formed against them.

the tariff laws of 1828 and 1832 null and void, and forbidding the collection of the duties in the State after February 1, 1833. Secession was threatened in case the United States resorted to force.

Jackson's attitude. — More than a year before that time Jackson had intimated what he thought of nullifica-

THE CITY OF WASHINGTON AND THE CAPITOL IN 1832
From a lithograph of that year.

tion. At a Democratic banquet in Washington on the anniversary of Jefferson's birth, he had proposed as a toast, "Our Federal Union, it must be preserved." This incident showed that Jackson was a man of strong national feeling. But in addition to this he had a personal hatred for the leader of the nullification movement, John C. Calhoun.[1] In reply to the nullification ordinance, Jackson issued a proclamation in which he said:

---

[1] John Caldwell Calhoun was born in the Abbeville District of South Carolina, March 18, 1782. He was graduated from Yale with high honor and began the practice of law. He was a member of the South Carolina Legislature, and afterwards of Congress, serving successively as Represen-

"The laws of the United States must be executed. I have no discretionary power on the subject—my duty is emphatically pronounced in the Constitution. Those who told you that you might peacefully prevent their execution deceive you. Their object is disunion, and disunion by armed force is treason."

Jackson then asked Congress to give him power to enforce the tariff law. This was done by the passage of the "Force Bill." It looked as if bloodshed would certainly follow; but here Henry Clay, the "Great Pacificator," as he was called, introduced a bill providing for the gradual reduction of the tariff for the next ten years. This bill was passed, and South Carolina accepted the compromise.[1] South Carolina had won as far as securing a reduction of the tariff; but, on the other hand, the "Force Bill" became a law, and nullification was dead for the future. Calhoun resigned the Vice Presidency and was elected Senator in order that he might assert in the halls of Congress the right of his State to nullify the tariff laws of the United States

Destruction of the Bank.—As soon as Jackson became President, he attacked the National Bank as unconstitutional. Although its charter would not expire until 1836, those who favored its renewal thought that it would be a good plan to secure another charter in advance. They,

---

tative and as Senator; later Secretary of War, Vice President, Senator and Secretary of State. He was a stanch political follower of Jefferson and for many years was the chief leader of the Southern Democrats. He was an advocate of slavery and one of its earnest defenders. He was a man of patriotism and high character and one of the ablest of the nation's statesmen. He died March 31, 1850.

[1] In reply to a critic who told Clay that this compromise would defeat him for the Presidency, the Great Pacificator uttered the memorable words: "I would rather be right than President."

therefore, had a bill put through Congress in 1832, providing for a renewal of the charter. Jackson vetoed the bill, and thus the bank question became the chief issue in the Presidential campaign of 1832. Many people in the country believed with Jackson that a corporation possessing such large powers over the currency was dangerous. It was charged, too, with using its power in politics, and this made it unpopular. The feeling against the bank was particularly strong in the South and West.

When Jackson was reëlected (1832), after he had vetoed the bank bill, he considered that he had been given full power in the matter and had the Secretary of the Treasury stop depositing Government money in the bank (1833). This forced the bank to go out of business as a National institution. The friends of the bank were indignant at Jackson's high-handed action; and the Senate, which had a Whig majority, passed a resolution censuring him for it.

The Government money was thereafter placed in State banks, called "pet banks" because they were chosen on account of Jackson's friendship for their owners. Many of these banks were weak and unreliable; and, like all other banks in the country, they were issuing notes in great quantities, often without proper security for paying them.

Speculation followed everywhere in the country, but particularly in the West. At this time the Government revenue was so great that the Government could not use it all; and in 1836 it distributed twenty-eight million dollars among the States as a loan. This caused still further speculation. The sales of the public lands increased, but it was soon found that payment for them was being made in bank notes. Many of these were entirely worthless; so, to prevent loss to the Government, Jackson issued an order, called the "Specie Circular," to the effect that only gold and silver should be received in payment for land. This caused a demand for specie, which the banks could not supply; and many banks had to refuse to redeem their notes. This was one of the causes of the panic that came upon the country in 1837.

New States.—In 1836 Arkansas came into the Union as a slave State; and the next year Michigan entered without slavery, making twenty-six States.

Election of 1836.—Jackson could probably have had a third term had he desired it;[1] but he was growing old and wanted to go back to "The Hermitage," his home in Tennessee. So he contented himself with securing the Democratic nomination for Martin Van Buren, who was elected. The Whigs made no nominations, but scattered their electoral vote, General William Henry Harrison, the hero of Tippecanoe, receiving the largest number.

The panic of 1837.—Van Buren[2] had the misfortune to come into office just as the panic of 1837 reached its height. It was due to many causes, but chiefly to speculation in the country and a bad banking system. It was also in part due to the financial disturbances of Jackson's

---

[1] William Wirt said, "My opinion is, that Jackson may be President for life if he chooses."

[2] Martin Van Buren was born at Kinderhook, New York, December 5, 1782. He became a lawyer and politician and served successively as State Senator, Attorney General, member of Congress, United States Senator, Governor of New York, Secretary of State, Minister to England, and President. He was a politician of great ability and he rose to the dignity demanded by the office when he became President. He died July 24, 1862.

administration. Banks failed, factories shut down, and business houses of all sorts closed their doors. There was, as a result, much distress in the country during the winter of 1837, and lack of food was not unusual. The business depression lasted for several years.

MARTIN VAN BUREN

Independent treasury.—To remedy the financial confusion and to take the place of the National Bank in regulating the currency, Van Buren induced Congress to establish an "independent treasury" or "subtreasury" system which directed that all Government money should be placed in Government vaults in different parts of the country. This system, which was first adopted in 1840, is in operation to-day.

Second Seminole War.—An important act of Jackson's administration had been the formation of the Indian Territory as a home for the Indians who were being crowded out of the States east of the Mississippi. In 1835 the Seminole Indians in Florida refused to move to the new reservation. This brought on a war that lasted seven years and cost over twenty million dollars. Osceola, the leader of the Seminoles, was a very able chieftain; and when he was finally captured (1837), it was thought that the war in Florida would stop. But it continued several years longer before the Indians were finally subdued (1842). This was the last Indian war east of the Mississippi River.

Election of 1840.—Van Buren was blamed for all the

evils of the panic and a great many things besides. During his entire term the Whigs were organizing for the next campaign, and they did their utmost to make the Democrats unpopular. But despite the fact that Van Buren had lost strength with his own party, he was renominated. The Whigs nominated General William Henry Harrison of Ohio and John Tyler of Virginia, who had formerly been a Democrat.

The campaign that followed was one of the most exciting in our history. The Whigs were full of confidence and enthusiasm and kept the people interested by speeches, processions, barbecues, and campaign songs. Much attention was paid to Harrison's military record, and "Tippecanoe and Tyler too" was the Whig battle cry. The attention of the

A CAMPAIGN PICTURE OF 1840
Ornamenting a "Tippecanoe or Log Cabin Quick Step, dedicated to Gen. William Henry Harrison."

country was called to the fact that Van Buren was a man of wealth and, as the Whigs said, "a little aristocrat." Harrison, on the other hand, was a poor man who had lived in a log cabin and was fond of hard cider, the poor man's drink. The cabin and the keg of hard cider became Whig emblems, and the campaign was known as the "hard-cider campaign." The result was a sweeping victory for Harrison and Tyler.

CHAPTER LXVIII

DEVELOPMENT OF THE COUNTRY, 1820-40

Area and population.—Between 1820 and 1840 the United States had acquired no new territory, but had spread its settlements over the fertile valleys of the Ohio and the Mississippi. Although only four States had been admitted into the Union during this period—Maine, Missouri, Arkansas, and Michigan—the population of the country had increased from about nine and one half millions to over seventeen millions. Of these seventeen millions over nine and one half millions were in the Northern States, and a little over seven millions (including nearly two and one half million slaves) were in the South. The census of 1830 showed that the center of population was farther South than it had been in any other period of our history, yet from 1830 to 1840 the population in the older Southern States showed only a slight increase. The tide of foreign immigration had set in, and the number of immigrants trebled between 1830 and 1837; yet the increase during this period represents for the most part the natural growth of the native population. In 1840 only eight and one half per cent of the population lived in cities of over eight thousand inhabitants. The largest cities in the order of their size were New York, Philadelphia, Baltimore, and Boston. Cincinnati and Chicago were small towns, and Omaha and Denver had not been heard of. At the end of this period (1840) there were only three millionaires in the country.

Overland routes.—In 1820, at a cost of seventeen million dollars, the Federal Government completed a great road from Cumberland, Maryland, to Wheeling, West Virginia. The road was thirty-five feet wide, and was carefully graded and thoroughly macadamized. At a later date it was extended from Wheeling across Ohio and Indiana. We are told that one hundred and fifty six-horse teams passed daily over parts of this road, besides four or five four-horse coaches, which carried mail and passengers. Thousands of settlers passed over it, moving into the Mississippi valley.

Hardy pioneers were also moving across the western plains, some of them going over the Oregon Trail into the far Northwest, while more than twenty thousand moved into Texas over the Santa Fé and other routes.

Steamboats come into general use.—In no other country were steamboats so quickly introduced and used to such advantage as in the United States. During the period from 1830 to 1840 they plied on all our navigable rivers, gathering up the products of field and forest and carrying them to great centers like New York, Philadelphia, and Baltimore, where they were reshipped to foreign countries.

In 1819 the *Savannah*, the first steamship to cross the Atlantic, sailed from Savannah, Georgia, to Liverpool by the combined use of steam and sails. In 1825 a steamship rounded the Cape of Good Hope and went to India. By 1840 large numbers of steamships were making regular voyages across the ocean without the aid of sails. This new means of ocean travel soon brought throngs of foreign laborers, who greatly increased the population of the country. The use of steam to propel war vessels (1836) revolutionized naval warfare.

Canals.—Communication between interior points in various parts of the country was further improved by the building of canals. The most important of these was the Erie Canal (page 265), which furnished an all-water route between Chicago and New York City. Many had deemed such a canal an impossible undertaking. So, while the canal was being dug, it was dubbed "Clinton's Big Ditch," in ridicule of Governor Clinton of New

A NEW AND IMPROVED CANAL BOAT OF 1830
After a lithograph made from the engineer's drawing.

York, who had enthusiastically supported the enterprise. When completed, the length of this canal was three hundred and sixty-three miles, and its width forty feet. Its depth was at first four feet, but later was increased to seven. It extended through hills and valleys and across swamps and rivers. The completion of the task was announced by the firing of cannon placed five miles apart from Buffalo to New York. A triumphal procession of canal boats bearing Governor Clinton and other celebrated men went over the entire route from Lake Erie to the Atlantic, where a keg of water from the lake was emptied into the ocean to signify that these two great bodies of water had been at last united. Within a year the cost of carrying freight from New York to Buffalo dropped from one hundred dollars to fourteen dollars a ton.

The success of the Erie Canal led to the speedy building of the Ohio Canal, which connected Lake Erie with the Ohio River; and to another, the Chesapeake and

Ohio Canal, which established a water route between Pittsburg and Washington.

Railroad development.—In 1828 the venerable Charles Carroll of Carrollton, the last surviving signer of the Declaration of Independence, inaugurated the work on the Baltimore and Ohio Railroad, which was soon to connect Washington and Baltimore. As he drove the first spade into the ground, he said, "I consider this among the most important acts of my life, second only to that of signing the Declaration of Independence." This was the first great railroad in America. In the decade from 1830 to 1840 the railroads of the United States increased from twenty-three miles to two thousand eight hundred and eighteen miles.

There was at first much opposition to railroads because it was thought they "would do away with the market for oats and for horses, and that stage drivers would seek wages in vain." The earlier roads were built of stone cross-ties and wooden rails. With the discovery of anthracite coal, and its use in smelting iron (1839), railroads were needed to carry the coal from the mines to the smelting furnaces and factories; and railroad building was greatly stimulated. The first American railroad to carry passengers went into operation between Charleston and Hamburg, South Carolina, in 1830, and on it was used in the same year the first American-built locomotive engine.[1] The first railroad to carry the mails ran from Charleston to

---

[1] This engine was built at West Point, New York, and was named "The Best Friend of Charleston." The locomotive engine was perfected by George Stephenson, an English inventor. A member of Parliament who inspected Stephenson's first engine said, "Suppose, Mr. Stephenson, that a cow were to get in front of your engine moving at full speed, what would happen?" The inventor replied, "It would be very bad for the cow!"

Savannah, a distance of one hundred and thirty-six miles. This road when completed (1833) was the longest continuous line in the world.

Express and post.—The express business had its beginning in America in the plan of a young man for carrying packages between Boston and New York. At first he carried all the packages intrusted to his care in a carpet bag. In 1840 he had a strong competitor in the Adams Express Company, which was founded to carry express between the same cities over a different route. In 1833 a horse express, with relays of horses, was established between Philadelphia and New York by the *Journal of Commerce*. This was to enable the *Journal* to publish the news from Congress a day earlier than any other New York paper.

SOUTH CAROLINA RAILROAD IN 1837
Heading of the bulletin in the "Miller's, Planter's, and Merchant's Almanac" for that year.

A few years later letters were sent in envelopes, though postage was still charged according to the distance.

The telegraph.—In 1837 Samuel F. B. Morse was given a patent on the "magnetic telegraph." After successfully sending a message (January, 1838) over a wire three miles long, he applied to Congress for aid to establish a line from Washington to Baltimore. After Morse had waited anxiously for four years in poverty and want Congress finally (1843) voted thirty thousand dollars for this enterprise.[1] The work was completed in the following year. This was the first regular telegraph line.

Agricultural implements.—For a long time the development of agriculture was greatly hindered by imperfect implements for gathering grain. The pioneer farmer used a sickle, with which he could cut only a handful of wheat or straw at a time. His work was made much lighter by the invention of the cradle, with which he could cut a whole sheaf at one stroke. Then came the wonderful grain-reaper, invented by Cyrus Hall McCormick of Virginia, who spent twenty years patiently working on the great problem. But when his invention was patented (1831) and ready for use, the farmers would not buy the machine. He even went to the grain-raising section of the Northwest and urged the farmers to try his new invention. His success was finally assured by the exhibition of his machine at the World's Fair in London in 1851, where it received a Council medal. A London paper declared that

SAMUEL F. B. MORSE

---

[1] The invention was greatly ridiculed in the debate on this bill. One member said that the invention was "fit for nothing"; another proposed an appropriation to construct a railroad to the moon. A member was defeated in the next election because he voted for the appropriation. While the bill was being debated, Morse was "leaning against the railing in the House in great agitation." In reply to words of comfort from a friend he said, as he placed his hand to his head, "I have an awful headache. I have spent seven years in perfecting this invention, and all that I had. If the bill fails, I am ruined. I have not money enough to pay my board bill."

the introduction of this invention alone was worth to the farmers of England the whole cost of the exhibition.

Other American inventions of this period have greatly reduced the cost of planting and harvesting crops. The threshing machine displaced the old hand-flail, thereby enabling farmers to separate and clean their grain with one third of the former cost. Improved plows have saved two thirds; drills for planting seeds, one third; and horse rakes and horse hayforks, one half.

Development of manufacturing. — In this country manufacturing by the factory system began in Lowell Massachusetts. The first factory in that town, now one of the greatest manufacturing centers in the country, was started in 1821. A year later a copper rolling mill, then the only one in America, was established in Baltimore. In 1829 matches began to displace the old tinder boxes. Damask table linen was manufactured in Pittsburg as early as 1828. In that year also paper was made from straw, and planing machinery was introduced. About this time (1829) there was manufactured in Rhode Island figured muslin, probably the first ever made. Before the end of the same year Massachusetts had introduced calico printing and produced the first American cutlery and New York City had begun the manufacture of galvanized iron. The invention of platform scales by the Fairbanks Brothers of Vermont, about 1830, was of inestimable value to the commercial world. Then followed

---

[1] In 1835 some meddlesome persons attempted to hinder a meeting of Democrats in New York by suddenly putting out the lights, but one of the members had "Locofoco matches" in his pocket and quickly lighted the lamps again. This incident caused the Democrats to be called "Locofocos," a name which they held for a period of about ten years.

the discovery of photography and the process of making daguerreotype pictures.[1] In this period pins and hosiery were made for the first time by machinery. The Nasmyth steam hammer was invented in 1838. In fact, the multiplicity of inventions so greatly increased the work of the Patent Office that in 1836 it was made a separate bureau.

Life in the cities.—The difficult problem of supplying fuel for use in cities was first solved by the use of coal. Iron furnaces were invented for burning anthracite or hard coal. There were no official fire departments, and each citizen was required to keep in his front hall a water bucket for use in fighting fire.

A Coach Still in Use in 1830
From a contemporary print.

Instead of having the streets swept at the public expense, every householder was required by law to sweep the walk in front of his own home. The thoroughfares were roughly paved, or not paved at all. In some cities it was ordered that on Sunday, during the hours of service, chains should be stretched across the streets in front of the churches, to prevent the disturbance of clattering vehicles. Illuminating gas used for lighting streets of cities slowly displaced candles and whale-oil lamps. At first everyone seemed to oppose the use of "lamps without wicks." The gas had

---

[1] Dr. John W. Draper, of New York, was "the first person who photographed the human face" (1839).

a bad odor, and some persons argued that by cutting the gas pipes burglars could leave a city in darkness. Although gas was introduced into Baltimore as early as 1816, four years later only three people in that city were using it in their houses. It was introduced into Boston in 1822, New York in 1825, and Philadelphia in 1829.

Prison reforms.—In the earlier years of the Republic thousands of criminals and insane persons were crowded together into dingy and dark prisons, where they were poorly fed and clad and often cruelly whipped. Through the efforts of Edward Livingston, the great reformer, these conditions were exposed, and improvements were soon introduced. In the period from 1820 to 1840 the whipping post, pillory, stocks, branding irons, and other implements of torture, which had been used from time immemorial, were abolished in many parts of the country. Penitentiaries were established at the instance of reformers who claimed that juries often turned criminals loose upon society rather than subject them to the severity of the old forms of punishment. In 1824 New York founded the first separate prison for youthful criminals; and about the same time provisions were made for religious instruction in the prisons of the country.

For many centuries imprisonment for debt was a punishment imposed throughout the civilized world.[1] It was estimated that in the year 1829 the prisons of Massachusetts received three thousand prisoners for debt; New York, ten thousand; Pennsylvania, seven thousand; and

---

[1] One of the saddest and most disgraceful incidents in American history was the imprisonment of Robert Morris (pages 178 and 204), the great financier and statesman. In his old age he met with misfortunes that carried him to a debtor's prison.

other States in like proportion. We are told that the proportion of debtors to other prisoners throughout the country was as five to one. Many of these prisoners were honest debtors who were unable to pay because of misfortunes. In 1831 a man was kept in a Philadelphia prison thirty-two days because of a debt of two cents.

Literary progress. — During the period from 1820 to 1840, Bryant, Irving, and Cooper were still proving our claim to a literature of our own. As our national life pro-

HAWTHORNE   POE   LONGFELLOW   MAURY

gressed away from European ideals, so our literature became still more distinctly American. After 1820 the writers who won a world-wide reputation for themselves and for American literature were, chiefly, Hawthorne, Poe, Longfellow, Emerson, Holmes, Lowell, and Whittier. The great historians of the period were Prescott, Jared Sparks, and George Bancroft; among the scientists were Audubon, Asa Gray, Louis Agassiz, and Matthew F. Maury; and among the writers on legal subjects were Kent, Story, and Wheaton.

CHAPTER LXIX

FAILURE OF THE WHIG PROGRAMME

Harrison's and Tyler's Administration, 1841-45

Death of President Harrison.—President Harrison[1] died one month after his inauguration. He was succeeded by Vice President Tyler. This was the first time in the history of the country that a Vice President had become Chief Executive.

WILLIAM HENRY HARRISON

Tyler and the Whig Party.—John Tyler[2] entered upon his duties as President two days after the death of President Harrison. Everyone was asking the question whether Tyler would carry out the views of the Whig Party. It was generally known that he was opposed to many Whig policies and that he had stated his opposition

---

[1] William Henry Harrison was born in Charles City County, Va., February 9, 1773. His name is chiefly associated with the development of the Middle West. He was successively delegate to Congress from the Northwest Territory, Governor of Indiana Territory, member of Congress from Ohio, and United States Senator. In 1811 he defeated the Indians at Tippecanoe, and in 1813 the British at the Battle of the Thames. He went to Colombia as Minister in 1828. In 1836 he was defeated for the Presidency, but was elected in 1840. He died April 4, 1841.

[2] John Tyler was born in Charles City County, Va., March 29, 1790. He was educated at William and Mary College. He studied law and was at different times a member of the Virginia Legislature and Representative and Senator in the National Congress. He was Governor of Virginia, 1825-27; President of the United States, 1841-45; and member of the Peace Conference and the Confederate Congress, 1861. He died in 1862.

to the bank and internal improvements. Clay, the real leader of the Whig Party, thought that the President could be forced to accept all the party measures, even declaring, "Should the President resist, I will drive him before me." But to the surprise of his party leaders, Tyler vetoed two National Bank bills which they had advocated. He was unjustly accused of bad faith; and all his Cabinet resigned except Webster, the Secretary of State.

JOHN TYLER

The Webster-Ashburton Treaty. —Daniel Webster remained in Tyler's Cabinet until he could make a treaty with England which would settle the boundary between the United States and Canada on the northeast. This treaty, known, after the men who negotiated it, as the Webster-Ashburton Treaty (1842), settled what is now the boundary between Maine and Canada. The treaty contained also an agreement between the United States and Great Britain to suppress the slave trade.

Minor incidents. — In Rhode Island much dissatisfaction was manifested against the old charter, which had served as a State constitution since the Revolution (page 86). It allowed only one third of the men to vote. A popular government was set on foot which drew up a new constitution, chose a Legislature, and elected Thomas W. Dorr Governor. This gave the State two governors and two legislatures. Both sides appealed to the

President for support. Tyler recognized the old government under Samuel King, and this brought to an end Dorr's "rebellion." But the outbreak led to the adoption of a new constitution, giving more men the right to vote.

In Tyler's administration the Mormons, or Latter-day Saints, as they called themselves, moved to Utah under the leadership of Brigham Young. Before this time the Mormons had lived in Missouri and Illinois. The Mormon Church taught that a man should have more than one wife. Under a law passed by the United States Government, the practice of polygamy, as it is called, was finally abandoned (1890).

At this time there was great activity in western exploration. John C. Frémont explored the valley of the Great Salt Lake, and the Oregon country, going as far as southern California. In honor of his work as an explorer, Frémont was called the "Pathfinder."

In 1843 a missionary, Marcus Whitman, who had lived several years in Oregon, led a body of American settlers across the mountains into that beautiful country. Other settlers followed Frémont and Whitman and helped to gain the Far West for the United States.

In 1845 Florida was admitted as a slave-holding State.

Independence of Texas. — In 1820 Moses Austin of Connecticut moved to Texas and secured permission from Mexico to settle in that section. Soon many settlers from the South came, bringing their slaves. Mexico forbade the importation of slaves into Texas and tried to stop the immigration of all persons into that country from the United States. As a result, the Texans under the lead of Sam Houston finally revolted (1833) against Mexico. This brought on a war.

Some brave Texans were besieged in the Alamo, an old Spanish mission building near San Antonio. In spite of the fact that they had only a few bushels of corn for food, their leader answered the demand to surrender with a report from his cannon. They were finally overpowered, and all persons in the fort except a woman, two children, and a negro servant were cruelly put to death. Among the heroes who were slain was Colonel David Crockett. At Goliad five hundred Texans were captured and cruelly murdered by the Mexicans. The war ended with the battle of San Jacinto (1836), where six hundred Mexicans were killed and seven hundred made prisoners, while the Texans lost only two killed and twenty-three wounded. The Republic of Texas was permanently organized with Sam Houston as President (1836). The United States and many European countries promptly recognized the independence of the new nation.

GENERAL SAM HOUSTON

Annexing Texas.—Texas had no desire to remain an independent nation, as nearly ninety per cent of her population had come from the United States. The Southern people were anxious to secure Texas so as to have an outlet for their slave population and thus increase their strength in Congress. For this reason annexation was opposed by the North. Van Buren refused to make a treaty of annexation, but such a treaty was made by Tyler. Although this treaty was rejected by the Senate, a joint resolution of Congress for the admission of Texas was passed on the last day of Tyler's administration. The State finally entered the Union, December 29, 1845.

Presidential campaign of 1844. — The principal issue before the people in the campaign of 1844 was the annexation of Texas and Oregon. The Whig Convention met first and unanimously nominated Clay by acclamation. When the Democratic Convention met, a majority of its members favored the nomination of Van Buren for President; but he was defeated because of his opposition to the immediate annexation of Texas. The Democratic nomination finally went to James K. Polk, of Tennessee, who is generally referred to as the first Presidential "dark horse"; that is, a candidate not considered for the office before the time of his nomination. The Abolitionists, or Liberty Party, nominated Birney.

Everywhere was heard the demand of the Democratic orators for the occupation of Oregon and the annexation of Texas "at the earliest practical period." Clay at first declared against the annexation of Texas, but later wrote letters that seemed to

THE DISPUTED BOUNDARY OF THE OREGON COUNTRY

favor such a policy. This cost him the vote of the State of New York, and the thirty-six electoral votes of that State decided the election in favor of Polk. After the success of the Democratic Party in the election of 1844, President Tyler induced Congress to pass a joint resolution for the annexation of Texas before the expiration of his term of office.[1]

CHAPTER LXX

WAR WITH MEXICO AND ITS RESULTS

First Years of Polk's Administration, 1845–48

The Oregon question.—The first important matter that demanded the attention of President Polk[2] was the settlement of the claim of the United States to what was known as the Oregon country. Spain had surrendered to the United States (1819) her claim to territory north of the forty-second parallel, and Russia had agreed to 54° 40′ as the boundary line between her possessions and those of the United States west of the Rocky Mountains (1825). But the title of the United States between these lines was disputed by Great Britain, and the two nations

---

[1] Texas was admitted on condition that the territory might be divided into five States, if its citizens should so desire. It is the largest State in the Union, being five times the size of England and more than four times as large as all the New England States combined. Its length from north to south is greater than the distance from Chicago to Mobile, and its length from east to west is greater than the distance from Washington City to St. Louis.

[2] James K. Polk was born in Mecklenburg County, North Carolina, November 2, 1795. In 1820 he became a lawyer; was member of Congress for Tennessee, 1825–39; and Governor of Tennessee, 1839–41. He was President, 1845–49. He died June 15, 1849.

agreed to occupy it jointly. In 1844 the Democratic Party raised the popular campaign cry, "Fifty-four forty or fight." But in 1846 it was finally agreed that Oregon should be divided between the two nations, England receiving the territory north of the forty-ninth degree and the United States all the country to the south of it.

Events leading to the Mexican War.—Mexico claimed all the country west and south of the Nueces River, while Texas claimed that her western and southern boundary extended to the Rio Grande. To protect the claim of Texas, Polk sent General Taylor with four thousand men to the Nueces River to meet any force that might be sent from Mexico, that country having already threatened war if Texas should be annexed to the United States.

JAMES K. POLK

General Taylor, acting under orders from the President, finally crossed the Nueces and was attacked by a force of Mexicans. The President at once sent a special message to Congress, saying: "Mexico has invaded our territory and shed American blood upon American soil." Congress promptly declared war by an almost unanimous vote.

Polk had broader schemes than the annexation of this disputed territory. He wished to acquire from Mexico all of what is now New Mexico, Arizona, and California. Congress supported him and put several armies in the field.

General Taylor's army.—After the attack upon his army that led to the declaration of war, Taylor crossed the Rio Grande and defeated the Mexicans in a number of engagements. Finally, he captured Monterey, which was the principal stronghold in northern Mexico, hoping that this would end the war. But Santa Anna, the Mexican general, gathered an army of twenty thousand men and marched against General Taylor, who then had a force of about five thousand men stationed in a mountain defile near Buena Vista. In reply to Santa Anna's demand for surrender, the American commander said, "General Taylor never surrenders." The Mexicans suffered a disastrous defeat, losing nearly two thousand men, including prisoners, while the American loss was about seven hundred and fifty. This great victory made a popular hero of General Taylor, who was henceforth known as "Old Rough and Ready."

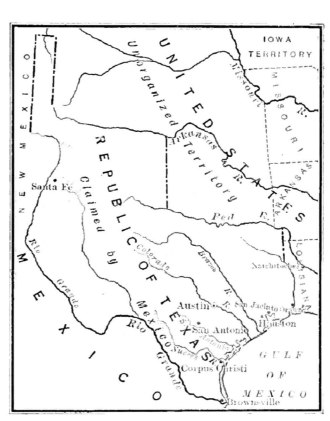

THE DISPUTED BOUNDARY OF TEXAS

Campaigns in the Far West.—General Stephen W.

Kearney was sent upon an expedition against New Mexico and California. He captured Santa Fe without firing a gun. He then went into California where he was met by Frémont,[1] the "Pathfinder," who with Commodore Stockton had taken possession of that country.

General Taylor at Buena Vista

General Scott's campaign.—In March, 1847, General Scott with twelve thousand men captured Vera Cruz and took up his march against the Mexican capital about two hundred miles to the northwest. At Cerro Gordo he defeated Santa Anna at the head of thirteen thousand Mexicans, completely routing him from a strong position, killing and wounding one thousand men and capturing three thousand more. The Americans lost only four hundred

---

[1] Frémont had already been chosen Governor of California by the American settlers. These settlers had driven the Mexicans out of the country before they had heard of the war between Mexico and the United States.

and thirty-one, including sixty-one killed. Santa Anna attempted to escape in a carriage, but was forced to mount

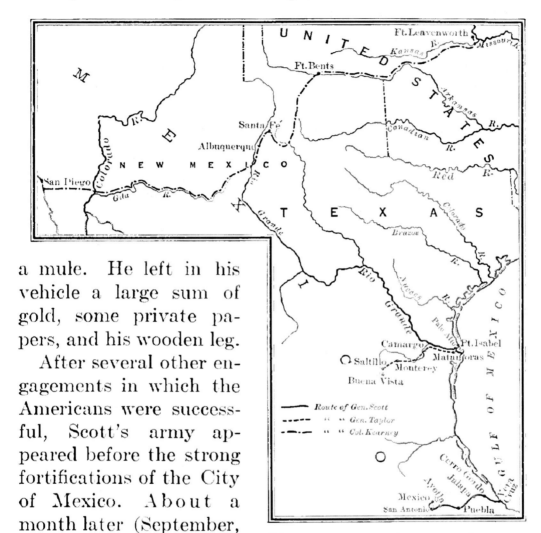

MARCHES OF THE AMERICAN ARMY IN THE MEXICAN WAR

a mule. He left in his vehicle a large sum of gold, some private papers, and his wooden leg.

After several other engagements in which the Americans were successful, Scott's army appeared before the strong fortifications of the City of Mexico. About a month later (September, 1847) the city was taken; and after the fall of their capital, the Mexicans were forced to sign a treaty of peace.

Results of the Mexican War.—The Mexican War afforded excellent training to a number of young officers who were to become distinguished leaders in the future history of the country. Among these were Jefferson Davis and Earl Van Dorn with General Taylor, and Robert E. Lee, Ulysses S. Grant, and Thomas J. Jackson with General Scott.

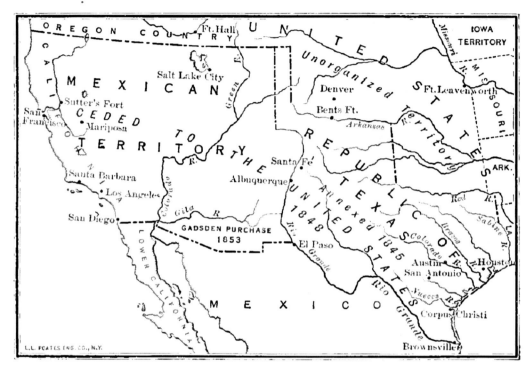

TERRITORY ACQUIRED FROM MEXICO BY THE TREATY OF 1848

By the Treaty of Guadalupe-Hidalgo (February, 1848) Mexico gave up all claim not only to territory north of the Rio Grande, but to New Mexico and upper California, including Arizona, Nevada, Utah, and a part of Colorado. In return for this territory in the Far West the United States paid Mexico $15,000,000.

These accessions were followed by the Gadsden Purchase (1853), by which the United States acquired from Mexico for $10,000,000 the territory that is now part of southern Arizona and New Mexico.

Admission of new States.—Texas came into the Union

in 1845, as a slaveholding State (pages 298 and 299). Iowa was admitted in 1846, and two years later Wisconsin also became a State. As both of these were free States, their admission restored the balance of power between the North and the South, which had been broken by the admission of Florida and Texas as slave States.

CHAPTER LXXI

WESTWARD EXPANSION AND ITS PROBLEMS

End of Polk's Administration, 1848-49

Discovery of gold.—Before the treaty of peace had been made with Mexico, gold had been discovered in California (January, 1848) in a mill race belonging to Captain Sutter. The news spread rapidly, and great crowds flocked to that region. Men from the older States left their work and joined in the mad rush westward. The "forty-niners," as they were called, went in long caravans across the sandy plains and over the rugged mountains, or by water route around Cape Horn, or across the Isthmus of Panama, determined to reach the land of gold. Many of these adventurers lost their lives in the attempt to reach California; and we are told that the emigrant paths across the plains were marked by the bleached bones of horses, oxen, and even of men, and by the broken wagons strewn along the way.

The prices of food and clothing rapidly advanced in this new country. Spades sold for $10 each, and flour for $50 a barrel.

As a result of this westward migration California had,

within fifteen months after the discovery of gold, more inhabitants than many a State; and it was applying for admission to the Union as a State even before it had been organized into a Territory.

The slavery controversy. — Since the first days of William Lloyd Garrison's *Liberator*, antislavery petitions had been sent to Congress. In 1837, Congress had passed a resolution known as the "Gag Law," which laid all antislavery petitions upon the table. This had greatly incensed the antislavery people, who charged the South with attempting to prevent freedom of speech. In 1844, the "Gag Law" rule was abandoned. In 1842 certain citizens of Massachusetts sent a petition to Congress, praying for a dissolution of the Union.

Before the end of the Mexican War, David Wilmot, a Pennsylvania Democrat, had introduced a resolution (1846) providing that in all territory to be obtained from Mexico, slavery should be forever forbidden. This resolution, known as the Wilmot Proviso, failed to become a law; but it greatly aroused the sections and increased their enmity toward each other. Calhoun declared that Congress should not "deprive the citizens of any of the States of this Union from emigrating with their property into any of the territories of the United States."

Presidential campaign of 1848. — The platforms of the Whig and Democratic parties in 1848 contained no reference to slavery, each party having both proslavery and antislavery men. The Whigs nominated General Zachary Taylor of Louisiana, and Millard Fillmore of New York. As Taylor was a slaveholder, he won the support of the Southern people; and his recent military career brought him a large vote in the North. Strange to say, the

Democratic Party, whose strength was principally in the South, nominated Senator Lewis Cass of Michigan, an antislavery man, and William O. Butler of Kentucky. A number of antislavery men formed the Free-Soil Party, which nominated Martin Van Buren of New York, and Charles Francis Adams of Massachusetts.

Although a large Free-Soil vote showed the rapid development of antislavery sentiment in the North, Taylor [1] and Fillmore were elected.

CHAPTER LXXII

THE CALIFORNIA COMPROMISE

Taylor's Administration, 1849-50

California applies for admission as a State.—In 1849 California, without having been organized as a territory, adopted a constitution and applied for admission as a free State. The slavery issue at once became foremost in the minds of the people. It aroused the Southern people, who contended that the Missouri Compromise line of 36° 30′ should

ZACHARY TAYLOR

---

[1] Zachary Taylor was born in Orange County, Virginia, September 24, 1784. He entered the army as first lieutenant in 1808, and rose rapidly. He fought in the War of 1812; defeated the Indians under Black Hawk, 1832, and the Seminoles in 1837, became Commander-in-Chief in Florida and later in the Southwest. He won success in the Mexican War. He died July 9, 1850.

be extended to the Pacific Ocean, and that it should be the dividing line between free and slave territory in the Mexican cession. A long and bitter debate followed, which aroused the angry passions of the representatives of both sections.

The California Compromise.—Henry Clay,[1] the "Great Pacificator," who had retired from public life seven years before, to spend his last days in the quietude of his home at Ashland, Kentucky, was called from his retirement in the hope that he might again bring peace to the country. He responded, and shortly after returning to the Senate introduced a bill, which came to be known as the Compromise of 1850. This bill provided for: (1) the admission of California as a free State; (2) the organization of New Mexico and Utah as Territories without any provision as to slavery; (3) the continuation of slavery, but the abolition of the slave trade in the District of Columbia; (4) the passage by Congress of a more effective fugitive slave law; (5) the purchase from Texas of her claim to a part of New Mexico.

These resolutions contained so many important features that the bill was called the "Omnibus Bill." For a period of seven months it absorbed the attention of the entire country, and it looked as if secession might come at any time.

---

[1] Henry Clay was born in Hanover County, Virginia, April 12, 1777. He removed to Kentucky and was a member of the convention that adopted the constitution of the State. He was United States Senator, member of Congress for many years, and five times Speaker of the House. He was a candidate for the Presidency in 1824, 1832, and 1844, but each time was defeated. He was the author of the Compromise of 1850. Few men in our public life have had such devoted friends and followers. He was the founder of the Whig Party and its leader for many years. He died June 29, 1852.

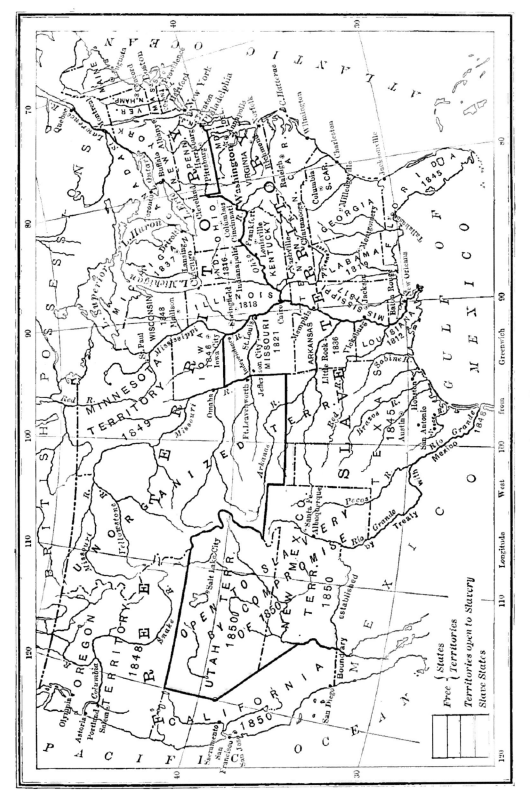

CHANGES IN FREE AND SLAVE TERRITORY FROM 1820 TO 1850

Debates on the great Compromise.—The debates on Clay's bill were conducted by the ablest men in both houses of Congress. When Clay first arose to address the Senate (February 5, 1850), the lobbies and galleries were crowded to overflowing, many people having come several hundred miles to hear his speech. When his friends insisted that he was too ill to speak, he said, "I consider our country in danger, and if I can be the means in any measure of averting that danger, my health and life is of little consequence." For two days he pleaded for toleration and concession. His fervid eloquence, which flowed from a heart filled with love for his country, carried conviction with it and calmed the fierce storm.

JOHN C. CALHOUN

Then came (March 4th) the parting speech of John C. Calhoun, the great Southern patriot, who was everywhere known as the foremost champion of States' rights. As he was too ill to speak, his address was read by Senator Mason of Virginia. The scene was pathetic beyond description. "There he sat, motionless, like a statue, with the hand of death upon him, listening to his own words from another's mouth." He urged the North to concede to the South "an equal right in the acquired territory"; to "do her duty by causing the stipulations relative to fugitive slaves to be fulfilled; and cease the agitation of the slavery question." The concluding words of this great speech were:

"Having faithfully done my duty to the best of my ability, both to the Union and to my section, throughout this agitation, I shall have the consolation, let what will come, that I am free from all responsibility."

Webster followed three days later with his celebrated "Seventh-of-March Speech," for which both

The United States Senate in Session in 1850
From a lithograph of that period.

sides had waited with great anxiety. He began as follows:

"I wish to speak to-day, not as a Massachusetts man nor as a Northern man, but as an American. . . . I have a duty to perform, and I mean to perform it with fidelity. . . . I speak to-day for the preservation of the Union. 'Hear me for my cause.' "

Although he opposed slavery, he criticised the Northern States for not performing fully their constitutional duties in regard to the return of fugitive slaves who had escaped to free soil, saying:

"In that respect, it is my judgment that the South is right and the North is wrong."

In another great speech (July 26th), in which he urged the adoption of his bill, Clay said:

"Will you go home and leave all in disorder and confusion, all unsettled, all open? . . . We shall stand condemned in our own consciences, by our own constituents, and by our own country."

Clay's Compromise finally adopted.—The eloquence of these great men once more brought the sections together; for although Clay's original bill was defeated, its most important features were finally adopted by the passage of separate measures.

The opposition to the bill from the Abolitionists of the North was uncompromising. William H. Seward, of New York, created a sensation by declaring that there was "a higher law than the Constitution," meaning that according to moral law there should be no slavery. Salmon P. Chase, of Ohio, also argued against the Compromise, claiming that Congress had no right to pass a fugitive slave law.

Death of President Taylor.—In the midst of the "Compromise" debate, President Taylor died. Millard Fillmore,[1] the Vice President, thus became the second accidental President in the history of the country.

---

[1] Millard Fillmore was born in Cayuga County, New York, February 7, 1800. He became a lawyer in 1823. He was successively member of the New York Legislature and of the National Congress; Comptroller of the State of New York and Vice President under Taylor. He was President 1850–53, and in 1856 ran again, but was defeated. He died in 1874.

CHAPTER LXXIII

FAILURE OF THE COMPROMISE OF 1850

Fillmore's Administration, 1850-53

Compromise opposed in the North.—For the most part the Southern people accepted the Compromise of 1850 in good faith. It was generally hoped that the country would accept it as heartily as it had accepted the Missouri Compromise in 1820. "Union meetings" were held in both sections, and for a short time everybody except the Abolitionists seemed to forget past differences.

MILLARD FILLMORE

In an effort to carry out the Compromise the Federal Government enacted a law that the United States marshals were to arrest all fugitive slaves and return them to their owners. But the North was greatly incensed every time the law was put into practice. Time and again fugitive slaves were taken from the marshals by mob violence; and usually, whenever the men who interfered with the enforcement of the law were tried, they were acquitted.

"Personal liberty laws."—In addition to this a number of Northern States practically nullified the Fugitive Slave Act by the passage of "personal liberty laws." These laws not only forbade State officials to assist in any way in the arrest of any fugitive, but punished private citizens for doing so. Some States even declared that all slaves who entered their borders were free. The Abolitionists increased rapidly in the North, and they often attacked Southern men who were trying to get possession of their slaves.

"**Underground Railroads.**"—In defiance of the laws made by Congress, the most active opponents of slavery banded themselves together to help runaway slaves in their efforts to get out of the country into Canada. The routes along which the slaves were carried were known as "Underground Railroads." There were stations along these routes from ten to twenty miles apart, where the slaves were hidden during the day to be sent after nightfall to the next station. It is estimated that between three and four thousand persons were engaged in this work, many of them going into the slave States to persuade the slaves to escape.

As a result of this great opposition to the fugitive slave laws, very few slaves who succeeded in getting across the Ohio River were returned to their masters—probably not more than two hundred of them between 1850 and 1856. It is estimated that the South lost thirty thousand slaves as a result of Abolitionists' efforts after the beginning of the slavery agitation.[1]

"**Uncle Tom's Cabin.**"—Northern opposition to slavery

---

[1] An Illinois Abolitionist helped thirty-one slaves to escape from the South in six weeks; another aided four hundred to escape. One Abolitionist boasted that he had helped twenty-seven hundred. It often cost more money to reclaim a runaway slave than he was worth. We are told that the fugitive Burns was recovered at an expense to the Government and his owner of about $30,000. The recovery of a slave by the name of Sims cost his owner $3,000, to say nothing of the expenses of the Federal Government and of friends who aided in the recovery.

was greatly increased by the publication (1852) of a novel entitled "Uncle Tom's Cabin," which was written by Mrs. Harriet Beecher Stowe. It pictured possible abuses that might arise under the slavery system, but the incidents related were exceptional. Nevertheless, the book produced a profound impression upon Northern people who were not acquainted with Southern conditions. Within a year three hundred thousand copies were sold throughout the North, and they made many thousands of Abolitionists. The book was also read abroad, being translated into twenty languages.

Presidential campaign of 1852.—After a spirited contest the Democratic Party nominated Franklin Pierce of New Hampshire for the Presidency, passing by Cass, Douglas, and Buchanan, who were the most celebrated leaders in the party. After fifty-three ballots General Winfield Scott received the nomination of the Whig Party over Fillmore and Webster. The platforms of both parties declared their satisfaction with the Compromise of 1850.

The Free-Soil Party nominated John P. Hale of New Hampshire. Its platform demanded that there should be "no more slave States, no slave territory, no nationalized slavery, and no national legislation for the extradition of slaves."

Pierce received two hundred and fifty-four electoral votes, Scott only forty-two, while Hale failed to carry a single State.

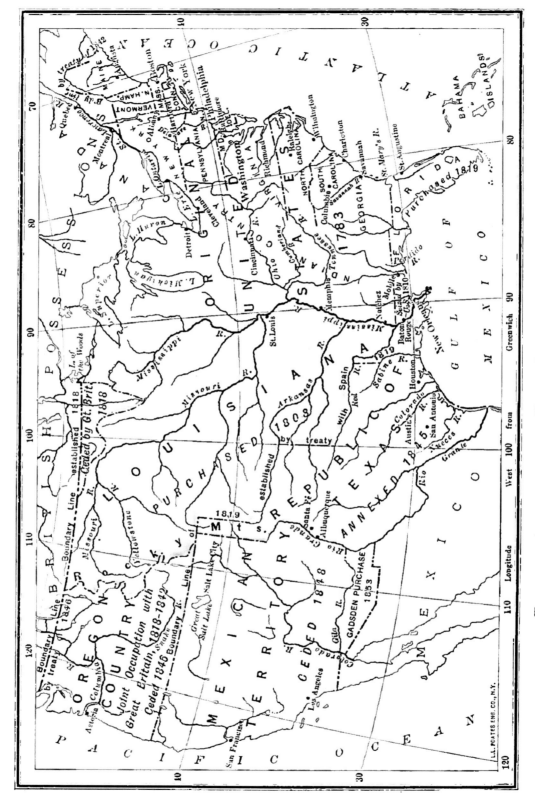

Territory Acquired by the United States from 1789 to 1853

CHAPTER LXXIV

EFFORTS TO ACQUIRE NEW TERRITORY FOR SLAVERY

Pierce's Administration, 1853–57

Pierce's administration. — Although the beginning of Pierce's[1] administration was then spoken of as the "Second Era of Good Feeling," sectional hatred soon broke out anew. The country could not forget the slavery issue.

Foreign relations. — In 1853, James Gadsden of South Carolina, representing the United States, purchased from Mexico (page 304) forty-seven thousand square miles of territory, which was needed for the route of the proposed Southern Pacific Railroad. The same year William Walker attempted to seize Lower California, which belonged to Mexico.

FRANKLIN PIERCE

The year following (1854) some Southern leaders attempted to seize Cuba, which then belonged to Spain. In October the American ministers at the courts of Spain, England, and France met at Ostend, Belgium, and prepared a paper, called the "Ostend Manifesto." This

---

[1] Franklin Pierce was born at Hillsborough, New Hampshire, November 23, 1804. He was successively member of Congress from New Hampshire and United States Senator. He served as a general in the Mexican War. After his Presidential term, 1853–57, he was not conspicuous in politics. He died in 1869.

"Manifesto" declared that Cuba should belong to the United States, and that, if Spain would not sell it for a fair price, the United States should consider the advisability of seizing the island.

Walker and other American adventurers attempted to seize some of the Central American States. All these "filibustering" expeditions, as they were called, were unsuccessful.

In 1852 William A. Graham of North Carolina, Secretary of the Navy, planned a naval expedition to Japan. Under the command of Commodore M. C. Perry the visit was made and a treaty negotiated (1854), opening trade between the United States and Japan. This was the first step toward opening the ports of Japan to the world.

Kansas-Nebraska Bill.—A clause in the Compromise of 1850 permitted the Territories of New Mexico and Utah to decide for themselves whether or not they would have slavery. Many Democrats following the lead of Senator Stephen A. Douglas of Illinois, insisted that, if two Territories were permitted to settle this question for themselves, the same privilege should be extended to all the other Territories. This "Squatter-Sovereignty" idea, as it was called, seemed reasonable to slavery advocates, because it gave the people of new States the same privileges in deciding the slavery question that had been exercised by their ancestors and friends in the older States.

Senator Douglas presented a bill for the organization of the Territories of Kansas and Nebraska (January, 1854). Although slavery had been excluded from these Territories by the Missouri Compromise of 1820, Douglas contended that this prohibition was made "inoperative and void by the Compromise of 1850." The bill affirmed that it was the "true intent and meaning of this act neither to legislate slavery into any Territory or State, nor to exclude it therefrom; but to leave the people thereof perfectly free to form and regulate their own domestic institutions in their own way, subject only to the Constitution of the United States."

In the five months' debate which followed, Seward, Chase, and Sumner, leaders of the Free-Soil Party, attacked the bill, denounced the South, and charged the Democrats with a deliberate breach of faith. However, Douglas, popularly called the "Little Giant," met the attacks of the opposition and succeeded in putting his bill through Congress.

The legislatures of ten Northern States protested against the bill. Douglas was denounced and burned in effigy, and thirty-seven out of the forty-four Northern Democrats who voted with him were defeated in the next election. From this time political parties became more sectional, and the advocates and the opponents of slavery more determined.

Troubles in Kansas.—As soon as the Kansas-Nebraska Bill became a law, there was a mad rush for possession of Kansas. The slaveholders from Missouri, which adjoined the new Territory, were first on the ground. But the people of New England organized a society which gave money and arms to all antislavery settlers who would go into Kansas. The people of Missouri then appealed to their neighbors in the Southern States to come to their aid.

Before the end of a year the proslavery and the antislavery men had made separate settlements in different parts of the State. An election was then held (March,

1855) for a Legislature. The antislavery party met with an overwhelming defeat; but they charged their opponents with bringing Missourians into the Territory, who remained there only long enough to vote and then returned home. When this Legislature met, it passed a law establishing slavery and placing a death penalty on anyone giving aid to a fugitive slave.

THE DIVISION OF THE COUNTRY IN REGARD TO SLAVERY AFTER THE PASSAGE OF THE KANSAS-NEBRASKA BILL

The antislavery party held another election, at which delegates were chosen to a Constitutional Convention. This Convention met at Topeka and made an antislavery constitution. In this way two hostile governments arose in the Territory.

A bloody civil war followed, which was characterized by robbery, murder, and other forms of violence. As a result the Territory was everywhere spoken of as "Bleeding Kansas." The town of Lawrence, which was the center of the antislavery settlement, was partly burned (May, 1856) by Missourians, whom their enemies called "border ruffians." Three days later an antislavery band under John Brown massacred a settlement of slave owners at Pottawatomie.

While these bloody events were taking place in Kansas, Senator Charles Sumner delivered in the United States Senate (May, 1856) a most terrible speech on "The Crime Against Kansas." In this speech he made an attack on Senator Butler of South Carolina. As a result Sumner was personally assaulted and beaten on the head with a cane by Preston S. Brooks, a nephew of Senator Butler, and was left unconscious on the floor of the Senate chamber. These events greatly inflamed the entire country.

CHAPTER LXXV

ACUTE STAGE OF THE SLAVERY CONTROVERSY

Buchanan's Administration, 1857–61

Party changes. — With the death (1852) of the great Whig leaders, Clay and Webster, their party went to pieces. It never rallied after its disastrous defeat in the Presidential campaign of 1852.

About this time the American Party began to attract attention. As its members were bound by an oath to reveal nothing about its organization or plans, they always answered inquiries on these points by saying, "I do not know." Hence they were popularly called "Know-Nothings." Their principal object was to keep all foreigners out of public offices, as is indicated by their motto, "America for Americans." They carried several States in the election of 1854; but after that date they rapidly declined in influence because they refused to take a stand on the slavery question.

After the passage of the Kansas-Nebraska Bill, the dissatisfied elements in the other parties formed (July, 1854) a new party which they called the Republican. It was made up of Northern Whigs, Free-Soilers, and Anti-Nebraska Democrats; and it gained strength rapidly.

Presidential campaign of 1856. — The American, or Know-Nothing, Party nominated ex-President Fillmore; but in stating the principles for which it stood, it still evaded the slavery issue. The Democrats nominated James Buchanan[1] of Pennsylvania. They stated their approval of the Kansas-Nebraska Bill and indorsed the principle of popular sovereignty. The Republicans nominated John C. Frémont of California, and demanded that slavery be excluded from the Territories and that Kansas be admitted without slavery.

JAMES BUCHANAN

This was the most exciting Presidential campaign since 1840. The election showed that the great national parties had become sectional—

---

[1] James Buchanan was born in Franklin County, Pennsylvania, in 1791. He was in turn member of Congress, Minister to Russia, United States Senator, Secretary of State, 1845–49, Minister to Great Britain, and President. In 1866 he published a history of his administration. He died in 1868.

that the North and the West were combining against the South. The Republicans carried every Northern State except five, and the Democrats every slave State except Maryland, which cast its vote for the Know-Nothing candidate. Buchanan received one hundred and seventy-four electoral votes; Frémont, one hundred and fourteen; and Fillmore, eight.

The Dred Scott decision.—A slave named Dred Scott was taken by his owner from Missouri to the free State of Illinois, where he lived two years. He was then carried into Minnesota Territory, where slavery was forbidden by the Missouri Compromise. Two years later his master brought him back to Missouri. Dred Scott then brought suit for his freedom because of his residence in the free State of Illinois and in the Territory of Minnesota. The case was finally carried to the Supreme Court which decided: (1) that a slave was not a citizen of the United States, and could not therefore sue for his freedom; (2) that Congress had no right to keep slavery out of the Territories and that, therefore, the Missouri Compromise was unconstitutional, null, and void; (3) that slaveholders going from one part of the country to another could take their slaves with them just as they could other property.

This decision met with the hearty approval of the Southern Democrats.

The Lincoln-Douglas debates.—In 1858 Stephen A. Douglas was a candidate for reëlection to the United States Senate, from Illinois. The Republicans brought forward Abraham Lincoln as a rival candidate. The two candidates debated national questions throughout the State. Douglas won the election, but the campaign gave Lincoln a national reputation and made him the

Presidential nominee of his party two years later. It also helped to divide the Democratic Party and bring about its defeat in the next Presidential election.

John Brown's raid.—John Brown, the fanatical Abolitionist whose bloody deeds had already attracted attention in Kansas (page 319), attempted to incite a slave insurrection in Virginia (October, 1859). With twenty-two followers he attacked the United States arsenal at Harper's Ferry, Virginia, with the purpose of seizing weapons with which to arm the slaves that he expected would join him. But the slaves did not flock to his standard as he had anticipated; and he was captured by a military force under the command of Colonel Robert E. Lee, an officer in the Federal army. Brown was speedily tried, convicted of treason, and executed.

A majority of the Northern people disapproved of Brown's action. Many, however, regarded him as a martyr for the cause of freedom. On the day of his execution they expressed their sympathy by tolling church bells, lowering flags to half mast, and draping public buildings. The Massachusetts Senate lacked only three votes of adjourning on that day, out of respect to John Brown; and in many Northern cities memorial meetings were held "at which eulogies were pronounced, glorifying Brown's deeds and comparing him to Christ, the Christian martyrs, and the apostles."

Mr. Douglas charged the crimes committed by Brown and his followers to "the matured, logical, and inevitable result of the doctrines and teachings of the Republican Party, explained and enforced in their platform, their partisan presses, their pamphlets and books, and especially their leaders in and out of Congress." Jefferson

Davis spoke of Brown and his raid as "the invasion of a State by a murderous gang of Abolitionists, whose purpose was to incite slaves to murder helpless women and children, and for which he met and deserved a felon's death."

From these facts it will be seen that the two sections had drifted so far apart that there was little hope of a peaceful reconciliation.

Minor incidents. — Minnesota became a State in the Union in 1858. In the following year Oregon was admitted, being the thirty-third State. Both of these States came into the Union with constitutions prohibiting slavery. Attempts were also made about this time to admit Kansas, but the unsettled condition of the Territory in its struggle over the slavery question delayed its admission until 1861.

CHAPTER LXXVI

PROGRESS OF THE COUNTRY, 1840–60

Area and population. — Between 1840 and 1860 the country had acquired Texas, the Oregon Country, and two cessions from Mexico, which increased its area from about two millions to over three millions of square miles. In the same time the population had increased from about seventeen millions to nearly thirty-one and a half millions; and seven new States had been formed, making in all thirty-three States in the Union. The eighteen free States had a population of more than nineteen millions, and the fifteen slave States of a little over twelve millions. As there were nearly four million slaves in the South, the white population of that section was about eight millions, or less than half that of the North.

Large cities had grown up, principally in the North, which had seven out of the ten largest cities in the country. Beginning about 1847, foreign immigration rapidly increased because of a great famine in Ireland and political disturbances throughout Europe. These immigrants crowded into the Northern cities or settled in the rich agricultural region of the Northwest. In 1840 there were in the United States only forty-five cities of eight thousand or more inhabitants; twenty years later there were one hundred and forty-one. In the same period the percentage of city population throughout the country had nearly doubled.[1]

Development of water transportation.—Between 1851 and 1860 twenty-five hundred vessels were built in the United States. In 1853 the New York *Herald* declared that in "both sailing and steam vessels we have surpassed the whole world," and a year later President Buchanan boasted that "our merchant marine is the largest in the world." At the outbreak of the War of Secession no less than fifteen hundred steamships and thousands of sailing vessels were carrying the American flag. The loss of eight hundred lives by steamboat accidents in the year 1851 caused Congress to provide for the inspection of steamboats by Government officials.

Keen rivalry developed between the Cunard line of ocean steamships founded by English capitalists (1839) and the Collins line founded by Americans (1850).

---

[1] New York City had only about two hundred thousand inhabitants in 1830 and nearly eight hundred and six thousand in 1860. Chicago had thirty-three voters in 1833 and over one hundred thousand inhabitants in 1860.

This competition not only increased the comforts, but reduced the cost of ocean travel.

Railway transportation.—The railroad mileage of the country doubled every five years from 1840 to 1860, and between 1850 and 1860 it increased fivefold—from six thousand to thirty thousand miles. Sleeping cars were introduced in 1858. In 1852 trunk-line connection was established between Chicago and the Eastern cities, and

RIVER BOATS AT LOUISVILLE, KENTUCKY, ABOUT 1845
From a lithograph of that time.

five years later St. Louis had railroad connections with Chicago and Baltimore. Plans were being perfected for connecting the Atlantic and Pacific coasts by means of transcontinental lines of railroads. Bridges were built across the Mississippi River at Minneapolis (1855) and Rock Island (1856) and across the Niagara River (1855). These great developments in railroad building cheapened the cost of transportation between the Mississippi valley and the rapidly growing cities of the North and the East. The freight rates on flour from Chicago to New York had fallen from about fifty cents a barrel in 1817 to about ten cents in 1860. The rates on cotton from the South to the North had also decreased in the same proportion.

Street railways were built before 1860, the first in New England being that between Boston and Cambridge (1856). The cars were drawn by horses or mules.

Telegraphic communication.—By the year 1854 about forty telegraph companies had been organized with a combined capital of seven million dollars. Two years later they were bought up, and the great Western Union Telegraph Company was organized. In October, 1861, a telegraph line was completed across the American continent, uniting the California coast with the Atlantic. There were then no less than fifty thousand miles of telegraph wires in the United States.

Just at the close of this period Cyrus W. Field's long-cherished scheme of sending telegraph messages under the water from America to Europe was realized. This idea originated with the great scientist, Commodore M. F. Maury of Virginia. At a banquet given in celebration of the success of this great undertaking, Field said that Commodore Maury had furnished the brains, England the money, and he had done the work. After two expensive though unsuccessful attempts, Field finally succeeded (1858) in laying a telegraphic cable from Newfoundland to Ireland, a distance of seventeen hundred miles. The first message sent over the line was from Queen Victoria to President Buchanan, and read, "Glory to God in the highest, peace on earth and good will to men." Unfortunately the cable parted three weeks later, after four hundred messages had been sent. It was eight years before another cable was laid (1866).

Mail facilities.—The mail facilities were greatly improved by the introduction of steamships and railroads, and in 1860 stagecoaches and post riders carried the mails only to out-of-the-way places. Postage stamps were introduced by the Government in 1847, and in the period from 1840 to 1860 the number of post offices had more than doubled. In 1845 the postage on letters was reduced to five cents for every half ounce for a distance of three hundred miles or less, and ten cents for a greater distance. In 1851 it was further reduced to three cents for a distance of three thousand miles or less, and six cents for a greater distance. We are told that when the first reduction was made, some one prophesied that "before long all the servant girls would be writing letters." In 1861 the rate on letters to France was fifteen cents for each quarter ounce. The "pony express" was used for carrying mails across the Western plains by means of relays at regular intervals, which afforded fresh horses and riders between St. Joseph in Missouri and San Francisco in California.

Progress of discoveries and inventions.—In 1841 a steam fire engine was first used in New York, but the invention was not perfected until 1853. Charles Goodyear of Connecticut, discovered (1844) the process of vulcanizing India rubber, which not only keeps it from melting by heat, but renders it useful in the manufacturing of waterproof goods and other valuable articles. In 1842 ether was first used as an anæsthetic by Dr. Crawford W. Long of Georgia. It has been an inestimable blessing in surgery; for it makes the patient insensible to pain while undergoing an operation. Chloroform was later (1847) used for the same purpose. In 1859 petroleum was discovered in western Pennsylvania. This led to the widespread use of coal oil for lighting purposes. One of the most useful inventions was the sewing machine, patented by Elias Howe of Massachusetts, in 1846. It not only cheapened the cost of clothing and shoes, but lessened the drudgery of the domestic life of women throughout the world. Electric fire alarms were successfully used as early as 1852. About the same time the breech-loading rifle was invented.

The Steam Fire Engine Invented by Captain Ericsson

The cost of printing was greatly reduced with the invention by Richard M. Hoe (1847) of the revolving cylinder press. The Bessemer process of manufacturing steel was first used in New Jersey in 1856. In the following year watches were first made by machinery. The largest number of patents issued in any one year before 1849 was six hundred and sixty; but from that time until 1860 there was an average of about two thousand patents a year.

Telescopes began to be manufactured in the United States about 1850, and in a few years the Americans were making the best telescopes in the world. An American also invented (1853) an apparatus for photographing stars and planets. In this period M. F. Maury founded the new and important science of Physical Geography, which deals with land and water formation, winds, and ocean currents.

Our first World's Fair was held in the Crystal Palace,

New York, in 1853, two years after the London Fair, which was the first international exposition in the world. The Crystal Palace Exposition revealed the wonderful progress of the United States in science and inventions, and gave many new ideas to American inventors.

Progress of manufacturing.—There were in 1860 five times as many spindles in the cotton mills of the country as there had been in 1831. In the ten years from 1850 to 1860 the manufacture of woolen goods increased fifty per cent. In the same period the amount of money invested in manufacturing had increased nearly fourfold, and the number of persons employed had more than doubled. New England led in the manufacture of cotton goods, having in 1860 about four times as many spindles in operation as there were in the Southern States. As a consequence the protective tariff was favored by the North and opposed by the South (page 257).

Progress in literature.—This period has been called the "golden age" of American literature. Most of the great American authors who had received world-wide recognition in the preceding period (page 293) still continued to write. Among the later authors were William Gilmore Simms, Francis Parkman, and George William Curtis.

VII.—WAR OF SECESSION

CHAPTER LXXVII

THE ELECTION OF 1860

Dissensions among Democrats.—In the National Democratic Convention, which met at Charleston, South Carolina, in 1860, most of the Northern members stood by Douglas and his theory of "Squatter Sovereignty." They felt that no other candidate and no other principle could carry the North for the party. The Southern members opposed the nomination of Douglas. They declared that neither Congress nor a Territorial legislature had authority to exclude slavery from the Territories. Upon the adoption of the Douglas platform—that is, the party principles that he upheld—the delegates from six of the Southern States withdrew. As the remaining delegates were unable to agree upon a nomination, they adjourned ten days later to meet again in Baltimore.

The Baltimore Convention nominated Stephen A. Douglas of Illinois, for President. The remaining Southern delegates, after much wrangling, finally nominated John C. Breckenridge of Kentucky. Thus was the Democratic Party hopelessly divided, and its defeat made inevitable at the time of a great national crisis!

Unity in Republican ranks.—The Republican Convention met in Chicago, and on the third ballot nominated

Abraham Lincoln of Illinois, for President. It adopted a platform which declared that the Dred Scott decision was wrong and that it was the right and the duty of Congress to prohibit slavery in the Territories, though it had no right to interfere with slavery in the States. It

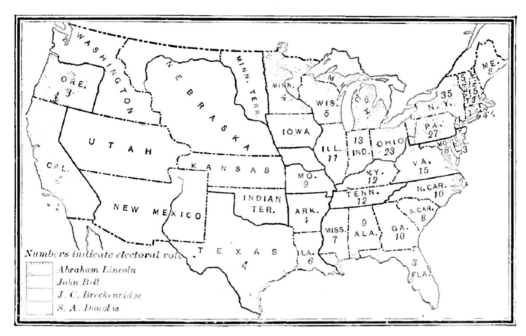

The Electoral Vote of 1860

also denounced the John Brown raid into Virginia as a grave crime.

Effort to revive old parties.—Some Northern Whigs and Southern Know-Nothings united to form the Constitutional Union Party. At a convention which met in Baltimore, this party nominated John Bell of Tennessee, and declared for "the constitution of the country, the union of the States, and the enforcement of the laws"—a platform so vague that it pledged the party to no definite action. Still many Southern people who did not favor a secession movement voted for Bell.

Campaign and Election.—The campaign of 1860, with its great mass meetings, fence rails,[1] and torchlight processions, was one of the most exciting in the history of the country. Lincoln stayed at his home in Springfield, Illinois, and received delegations; but both the Democratic candidates spoke in all parts of the country. When Douglas saw that the Northern States were lost to the Democratic Party, he devoted his attention to the South. In Norfolk, Virginia, he was asked whether he favored maintaining the Union by force. When he said that he did, the South was still more firmly opposed to him. The political leaders of the South had already declared that, in the event of a Republican victory, the "honor and safety" of the Southern States would require their withdrawal from the Union.

The election was an overwhelming victory for the Republican Party. It carried every Northern State except New Jersey, and in that State received four out of the seven electoral votes. Lincoln received two thirds of the entire electoral vote, though he had scarcely one third of the popular votes of the country.

---

[1] At the Republican Convention in Illinois a week before their national convention, two fence rails were displayed with a banner which said that these rails were "part of 3,000 cut in 1830, ten miles south of Decatur, by Abe Lincoln and John Hanks." The people went wild with enthusiasm and shouted themselves hoarse for Lincoln the "rail-splitter"; and after he had made a speech, the convention named him as its choice for the next President of the United States. When asked about the rails, Lincoln said that he had split about 3,000 rails, but that he could not say whether the specimens displayed were among them. He then added, to the great amusement of the convention, "One thing I *will* say—I've made a good many better-looking rails than either of these."

CHAPTER LXXVIII

THE BEGINNINGS OF SECESSION

Withdrawals from the Union.—As soon as it was known that Lincoln had been elected, the Legislature of South Carolina passed a unanimous vote calling for a convention to determine what to do. After a short debate this convention unanimously voted (December 20, 1860) to repeal the ordinance by which, in 1788, South Carolina had adopted the Federal Constitution and thereby entered the Union. This action was approved throughout the State by the waving of palmetto flags, the singing of martial songs, the booming of cannon, and the pealing of bells.

Mississippi then adopted an Ordinance of Secession (January 9, 1861) and unfurled a State flag, which the members saluted as the first flag of the young republic. This incident gave rise to the popular war song, "The Bonnie Blue Flag that Bears a Single Star." Similar ordinances were adopted in Florida (January 10th), Alabama (January 11th), Georgia (January 19th), Louisiana (January 26th), and Texas (February 1st).

A Charleston "Extra" Announcing the Secession

The home coming.—Most of the Southern men in the service of the United States resigned and returned home when their States seceded. These men felt that their first duty was to their State. The parting addresses of senators and representatives retiring from Congress were solemn and impressive. The address of Jefferson Davis was especially noteworthy. After calmly defending the course taken by his State, he added:

"Then, Senators, we recur to the compact which binds us together; we recur to the principles upon which our Government was founded; and when you deny them, and when you deny to us the right to withdraw from a Government which, thus perverted, threatens to be destructive of our rights, we but tread in the path of our fathers when we proclaim our independence and take the hazard. This is done, not in hostility to others, not to injure any section of the country, not even for our own pecuniary benefit, but from the high and solemn motive of defending and protecting the rights we inherited, and which it is our sacred duty to transmit unshorn to our children."

Two hundred and forty-five officers in the Army of the United States resigned, the most conspicuous of whom was Robert E. Lee.[1] In the United States Navy, among the officers to resign was Raphael Semmes.

---

[1] In January, 1861, General Lee wrote: "If the Union is dissolved and the Government disrupted, I shall return to my native State and share the miseries of my people, and, save in defense, will draw my sword on none."

CHAPTER LXXIX

GROUNDS FOR SECESSION

Right of secession.—The South believed that the States were older than the Union and that when they emerged from the Revolution they were separate sovereignties. After mentioning each State in the treaty acknowledging the independence of the United States, the King of England had declared them "free, sovereign, and independent States." When the Constitution of 1787 was made, each State was left free to adopt it and enter the Union, or to remain a separate nation. If the Constitution had forbidden the withdrawal of a State from the Union, it would never have been adopted. Moreover, the right to withdraw from the Union at pleasure had been expressly stated in the resolutions by which three States —Virginia, New York, and Rhode Island—adopted the Constitution.

Scene Outside the Capitol at Montgomery, Alabama, after Secession Was Announced

When the North believed in secession.—The right of secession had been repeatedly asserted by the North. When the admission of Louisiana was under discussion in 1811, Josiah Quincy had said:

"If this bill passes, it is my deliberate judgment that it is virtually a dissolution of the Union; that it will free the States from their moral obligations; and, as it will be the right of all, so it will be the duty of some, definitely to prepare for a separation—amicably if they can, violently if they must."

During the War of 1812, and particularly at the Hartford Convention, the New England States had threatened to secede (page 256). Upon the annexation of Texas the Legislature of Massachusetts had declared that such a step might "drive these States into a dissolution of the Union"; and John Quincy Adams had declared in Congress that New England ought to secede. At the time of the War with Mexico, William Lloyd Garrison of Massachusetts had proposed, amid great applause, that his State should lead in a secession movement.[1]

Opposition to secession.—On the other hand the Union people, North and South, argued that the Constitution

---

[1] Horace Greeley had said in the New York *Tribune* of November 9, 1860: "If the Cotton States shall decide that they can do better out of the Union than in it, we insist on letting them go in peace. The right to secede may be a revolutionary one, but it exists nevertheless."

Edward Everett had said in a Union meeting in Boston, February 2, 1861: "To expect to hold fifteen States in the Union by force is preposterous. If our sister States must leave us, in the name of Heaven let them go in peace."

Wendell Phillips had said in a meeting at New Bedford, Massachusetts, April 9, 1861: "A large body of people, sufficient to make a nation, have come to the conclusion that they will have a government of a certain form. Who denies them the right? Standing with the principles of '76 behind us, who can deny them the right?"

of the United States had been adopted in order to form a stronger government and to take away the powers claimed by some of the States. They cited the decisions of John Marshall, in which he had repeatedly asserted that the Union was indissoluble and that the Constitution and the acts of Congress were the supreme law of the land. As a majority of the Northern States had passed through the Territorial stage in which they were under the control of Congress, they looked upon the Union as supreme. They therefore took the stand that it mattered not what might have been the ideas of the founders of the Government, it was wrong for a great nation to be broken to pieces.

Causes of secession.—By taking advantage of protective tariffs and ship subsidies the North had developed great manufacturing and commercial enterprises, and these had increased its population and wealth. Northern influence had grown rapidly in Congress, and by this means large appropriations had been made for internal improvements throughout that section and the West. As the South still relied principally on agriculture, it was greatly injured by Federal taxes on importations and profited only indirectly by the development of the North and the West.

At least twelve Northern State legislatures had violated the Constitution by passing personal liberty laws or otherwise nullifying the fugitive slave acts [1] of Congress. Northern leaders had expressed a determination to ex-

---

[1] In his celebrated speech at Capon Springs, Virginia (1851), Daniel Webster had said: "If the Northern States refuse willfully and deliberately to carry into effect that part of the Constitution which respects the restoration of fugitive slaves, and Congress provide no remedy, the South

clude slavery from the Territories in spite of a decision of the Supreme Court. These were among the things that caused the South to feel that it would be impossible for the two sections to live together in peace. One by one the strong ties that had held the country together were severed, and the Union fell apart.

CHAPTER LXXX

THE FORMATION OF THE CONFEDERACY

THE SEAL AND FLAGS OF THE CONFEDERACY

The Southern States unite.—At the suggestion of the South Carolina Convention, delegates from all the seceding States except Texas[1] met in Montgomery, Alabama, February 4, 1861, and drew up a Provisional Constitution, adopting the "Stars and Bars" as the flag of the new nation, which they named "The Confederate States of America." They elected Jefferson Davis[2]

---

would no longer be bound to observe the compact. A bargain broken on one side is broken on all sides."

Caleb Cushing, of Massachusetts, had said to his fellow-citizens in 1860: "So long as the State of Massachusetts perseveres in this nullification of the Constitution, she affords, not a pretext only, but a justificatory cause to the State of South Carolina, to that of Georgia, Alabama, Mississippi, or any other State otherwise disposed to secede; for the violation of the fundamental compact of association by one of the contracting parties serves, in morality as well as law, to release the others."

[1] As this State had seceded only three days before the convention met, its delegates did not reach Montgomery in time.

[2] Jefferson Davis was born in Kentucky, June 3, 1808, and, when a child, came to Mississippi with his parents. He was graduated from West Point Military Academy at the age of twenty. He spent seven years in

JEFFERSON DAVIS
From a negative made during the War of Secession
In the possession of H. P. Cook, Richmond, Virginia

2. Members of the Cabinet[1] might be admitted to seats in Congress with the privilege of engaging in debate.

3. Congress was expressly forbidden to lay protective tariffs or give bounties.

4. The foreign slave trade was prohibited.

Buchanan's recommendation.—After the election of Lincoln, President Buchanan realized that a great crisis confronted the country, but he seemed at a loss to know what to do. He claimed that no State had a right to secede, yet he said that Congress had no constitutional power to force a seceding State back. He recommended the adoption of an "explanatory amendment" to the Constitution, making it the duty of the United States to protect slavery in the Territories and providing more effectively for the return of slaves escaping into the free States.

The Crittenden Compromise.—Congress promptly considered these recommendations, and several compromise measures were proposed. The most noteworthy was brought forward by John J. Crittenden of Kentucky, the successor of Henry Clay in the Senate. The Crittenden Compromise proposed:

---

in the practice of law he entered public life, serving as a member of the Lower House of Congress from 1843 until 1859. He was elected to the United States Senate after the war, but was not permitted to take his seat. He again served in the Lower House of Congress from 1873 to 1883.

[1] Two of the most celebrated members of the Confederate Cabinet were Robert Toombs of Georgia, Secretary of State, and Judah P. Benjamin of Louisiana, Attorney-General. The latter was often referred to as "the brain of the Confederacy." After the war Mr. Benjamin settled in England, where he gained great reputation as a lawyer. John H. Reagan of Texas, the Postmaster-General of the Confederacy, was also a man of ability and integrity.

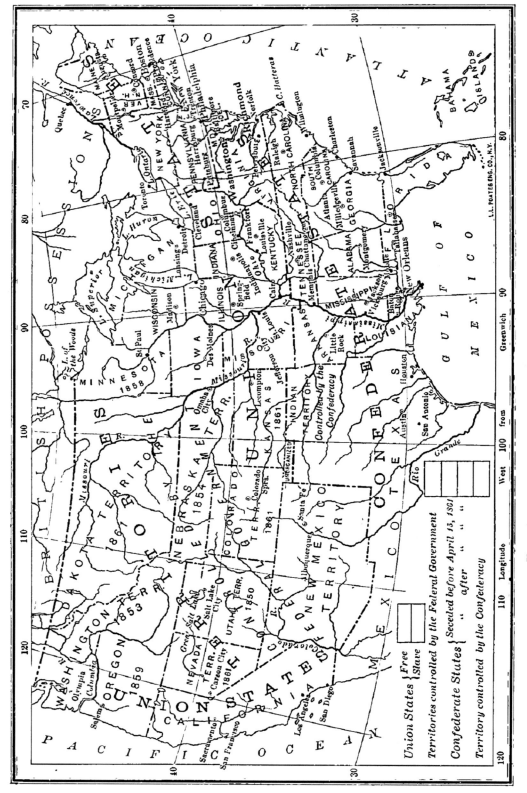

The Union and the Confederate States in 1861

THE FORMATION OF THE CONFEDERACY

1. That the Missouri Compromise line, 36° 30' (page 261), be extended to the Pacific; that slavery be prohibited in all territory north of that line, and that neither Congress nor any territorial legislature be permitted to interfere in any way with slavery south of it.

2. That when new States south of the Compromise line were admitted into the Union, they might decide for themselves whether they would be free or slave.

3. That a Constitutional amendment should be adopted prohibiting Congress from abolishing or interfering with slavery in any State.

4. That the Northern States be requested to repeal their personal liberty laws.

This Compromise was defeated by the opposition of the Northern Senators.

The Peace Conference.—Although twenty or more Southern Senators and representatives in Washington had advised their States to secede, Virginia made a final effort to save the Union that she had taken the lead in forming.[1] In response to a call from her Legislature, delegates from thirteen free and seven slave States met at the National capital on the day the Confederacy was organized at Montgomery. But none of the seceded States were represented at this meeting. After a session of more than three weeks, the convention agreed upon a plan of conciliation, but it was rejected by Congress.

---

[1] Robert E. Lee said: "I can anticipate no greater calamity than a dissolution of the Union. . . I am willing to sacrifice everything, but honor, for its preservation."

CHAPTER LXXXI

THE SOUTH TRIES TO PREVENT WAR

"Star of the West."—After South Carolina seceded, she sent commissioners to Washington to arrange for the peaceful delivery to the State of the Federal forts and other property within her limits. While President Buchanan hesitated about withdrawing the troops from Charleston harbor, a Northern merchant vessel, the

Fort Sumter before the War

Star of the West, was sent with two hundred and fifty men, arms, ammunition, and other supplies for Fort Sumter. The vessel was fired upon by State militia and forced to retire. Although no effort was then made to seize the fort, the President was warned that an attempt to reënforce it would be regarded as an act of war.

Federal property.—As the States withdrew from the Union, they took possession of arsenals, forts, post

THE SOUTH TRIES TO PREVENT WAR 343

offices, and other public buildings in their borders, which had belonged to the United States. The seceding States felt that their safety demanded such a step, and they offered to pay the difference if it was found that they had (within their limits) more than their share of public property. In this way twenty-one forts on the Atlantic and Gulf coasts changed hands, as did also several arsenals with their equipments. But most of the muskets thus acquired had already been "condemned as well-nigh worthless."

This property was given over to the Confederacy when the State in which it was situated joined the new nation. When the Confederacy was formed, the only fortified places in its limits still held by the Federal Government were Fort Sumter at Charleston, Fort Pickens at Pensacola, and Key West in Florida. Confederate Commissioners were sent to Washington to request that the United States give up these forts also.

Inauguration of Lincoln.—As President Lincoln[1] had remained quietly at home after his election, the public did not know what to expect when he should take the

---

[1] Abraham Lincoln was born in Kentucky eight months after the birth of Jefferson Davis. His parents moved to Indiana when he was only seven years of age. They were very poor and unable to give their children school advantages. Young Abraham went to school not more than a year in all. But he borrowed books and read them carefully to improve his mind and to prepare for life's duties. At the age of twenty-one he moved to Illinois. While clerking in a store, he won the title of "Honest Abe" by walking six miles at night to give a woman six cents which she had overpaid him. He read law, was elected to the State Legislature, and then to Congress. In 1858 he was defeated for the United States Senate by Stephen A. Douglas, but his speeches in the campaign attracted national attention and led to his nomination and election to the Presidency.

oath of office. He entered Washington in disguise for his inauguration, which was marked by the assembling of the largest military force ever brought to that city.

In his inaugural address, which was delivered behind a row of bayonets, he said that he did not intend to interfere with slavery in the States; but that, acting on the assumption that the Union was unbroken, he would execute the laws of the Union in all the States as far as possible. He said that he would hold all property of the United States and would collect customs duties throughout the country. In defense of this policy he claimed that the Union was perpetual and that no State had a right to withdraw from it. In conclusion he said:

"In your hands, my dissatisfied fellow-countrymen, and not in mine, is the momentous issue of civil war. The Government will not assail you. You can have no conflict without being yourselves the aggressors. I am loath to close. We are not enemies, but friends. We must not be enemies. Though passion may have strained, it must not break our bond of affection."

Efforts to prevent war.—Several slave States that had not entered the Confederacy were strong in their attachment to the Union. Commodore Maury wrote on the day of Lincoln's inauguration:

"Virginia is not at all ready to go out of the Union; and she is not going out for anything that is likely to occur, short of coercion."

Mr. Baldwin, a leading Union man in Virginia, said to Lincoln while urging him not to attempt to force the seceded States back into the Union:

"Only give this assurance to the country in a proclamation of five lines, and we pledge ourselves that Virginia will stand by you as though you were our own Washington."

Abraham Lincoln

CHAPTER LXXXII

THE BEGINNING OF THE CONFLICT

Fort Sumter reënforced.—The Confederate commissioners who were sent to Washington (page 342) were not officially received; but through private conferences they were led to believe that the Federal troops would be peacefully withdrawn from Fort Sumter. However, instead of surrendering the fort, Lincoln determined to reënforce it, and sent word to that effect to Governor Pickens of South Carolina. About the same time a squadron of eleven ships carrying two hundred and eighty-five guns and two thousand four hundred men, was sent from New York and Norfolk with orders to "reënforce Fort Sumter peaceably, if permitted, but forcibly, if they resist."

THE HARBOR OF CHARLESTON IN 1861

Capture of Fort Sumter.—As the possession of this fort by a foreign power was dangerous to the Confederacy, President Davis demanded its surrender. Major Anderson, the Federal commander, refused to surrender; so, by order of General P. G. T. Beauregard, nineteen batteries opened fire on the fort, April 12, 1861, at four o'clock in the morning. By noon of the next day the fire had burned the fort until the men, one hundred and twenty-eight in number, were almost suffocated by the smoke and were in danger of being blown up by an explosion of the magazine. As the flagstaff in the fort had been cut away and the flag had disappeared, General Beauregard stopped the bombardment to send messengers to find out if the garrison was in distress. It finally surrendered, and the Stars and Bars displaced the Stars and Stripes on the fort.

INTERIOR OF FORT MOULTRIE
One of the batteries that fired on Fort Sumter.

Strange to say, there were no losses on either side in this battle, which was the opening incident of the most bloody war in American history.[1]

---

[1] In his official report of the battle Major Anderson writes as follows: "Having defended the fort for thirty-four hours, until the quarters were entirely burned, the main gates destroyed by fire, the magazine surrounded by flames, ammunition gone, and no provision remaining but pork, I accepted the terms offered by General Beauregard and marched out of

THE BEGINNING OF THE CONFLICT 347

Lincoln's call for volunteers.—President Lincoln then issued a proclamation calling for seventy-five thousand volunteers for three months to suppress the "rebellion," as he called it. Union meetings were held throughout the North. Within a few days ninety thousand volunteers had been accepted by the War Department; and in about ten weeks, more than three hundred thousand men in the North were under arms.

Effect of Lincoln's proclamation in the South.—The South was as eager for the struggle as was the North, and volunteers flocked to the standard of General Beauregard. The question now was: "What will Maryland, Virginia, North Carolina, Kentucky, Tennessee, Missouri, and Arkansas do?" There was still one other slave State, Delaware; but her people merely tolerated slavery and were strongly attached to the Union. Virginia was at first opposed to secession; but when it came to having Northern armies pass over her soil and when she was required to furnish troops to fight her Southern brethren she decided to secede.[1] Her example was promptly followed by Arkansas, North Carolina,[2] and Tennessee.

---

the fort on Sunday afternoon the 14th, with colors flying, drums beating, and saluting my flag with fifty guns."

[1] After Lincoln's proclamation Mr. Baldwin, a former Union man in Virginia, wrote: "We have no Union men in Virginia now. But those who were Union men will stand to their guns and make a fight that will shine out on the page of history as an example of what a brave people can do after exhausting every means of pacification."

[2] The Governor of North Carolina replied to Lincoln's requisition for troops as follows: "You will get no troops from North Carolina for the purpose of subjugating the States of the South. I can be no party to this wicked violation of the laws of the country and to this war upon the liberties of a free people." The Governor of Tennessee replied that his State

Union sentiment and Union forces, however, took possession of Kentucky, Maryland, and Missouri before the seceding element could organize. Thus were the border States saved for the Union, though many a man from these States volunteered for service in the Confederate army.

CHAPTER LXXXIII

THE STRENGTH OF THE TWO NATIONS

Population.—The population of the eleven seceding States was about nine millions, of whom five millions were white. The population of the twenty-two States that remained in the Union was twenty-two millions, and these States had four times as many men for military service as could be found in the South. There was hardly a time when the Confederate enlistments were more than half those of the United States. Furthermore, the South was greatly weakened by the constant fear of a slave insurrection. As the population of the South was so small compared with that of the North, it had to put forth its full strength early in the struggle. In the North industries continued to develop and population to increase because of foreign immigration.[1]

---

would not "furnish a man for the purpose of coercion, but fifty thousand, if necessary, for the defense of our rights and those of our Southern brothers."

[1] An exact statement of the number of troops raised by the South cannot be given. They are estimated at 600,000. Of the troops of the North Dr. Lyon G. Tyler writes: "The total number of men furnished to the United States army from April 15, 1861, to the close of the war was 2,326,168... In the Northern army there were 1,325,297 whites from the North, 316,424 whites from the South [Ky., Md., Mo., W. Va.], 186,017 negroes, 3,520 Indians and 494,900 foreigners.... therefore the foreign and negro elements of the Northern army were greater than the entire army of the South."

THE STRENGTH OF THE TWO NATIONS

Material resources.—As you have already learned, the South was an agricultural section. It had no factories for equipping its soldiers with arms, ammunition, and clothing, or for building and equipping ships. Consequently, at first it had to look entirely to Europe for such supplies. Knowing this, Lincoln declared all the Southern ports in a state of blockade and began the construction of a number of war vessels to prevent blockade runners from carrying cotton to Europe. As a result, the cotton grown in the South could not be sold; the Confederacy was unable to trade with European countries and was greatly crippled. Manufactured goods could not be secured from England.

Financial conditions.—The Confederacy was also seriously embarrassed by a scarcity of money. The large banking centers of the country were in the North, and the gold and silver coin was deposited chiefly in those banks. The South had to rely, therefore, on what coin could be obtained from Europe and upon the issues of paper money which decreased in value as the war continued.

Both sides unprepared for war.—It was about a year after the beginning of the war before the North was prepared to fight. The volunteers had to be trained, and many of them had to be taught to shoot. Very few Union men realized the greatness of the task they had undertaken. Seward prophesied that the trouble "would blow over in sixty days"; and when General Sherman, who had lived in the South, said that it would take two hundred thousand men four years to subdue the South, some one said he was crazy. The South was even more unprepared for the struggle than the North; for not only did it have no standing army, but it had no guns or military supplies.

CHAPTER LXXXIV

THE WAR IN 1861

Plans of action.—Generally speaking, the North was aggressive throughout the conflict, hoping to conquer the Southern States and force them back into the Union. The object of the Southern States was to defend themselves against invasion and to maintain their independence.

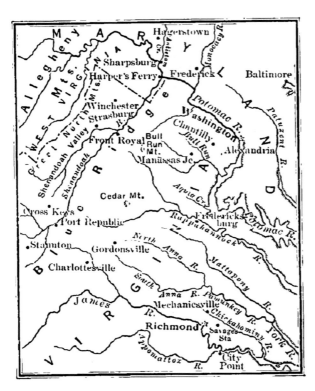

CAMPAIGN IN VIRGINIA IN 1861

There were three plans of action adopted by the Federal Government: (1) to keep up a successful blockade of all the Southern ports and to prevent the Confederates from trading with Europe; (2) to advance upon Richmond, which as soon as Virginia had seceded from the Union became the capital of the Confederacy, and break up the Confederate Government; (3) to get possession of the Mississippi River by destroying the Confederate fortifications and boats which defended it, cut the Confederacy in two, and thus weaken its possibilities of success.

THE WAR IN 1861

Battle of Big Bethel.—Many of the Northern people believed that Richmond could be taken in ninety days, and that this would put an end to the war. The campaign of 1861, therefore, opened with a series of advances toward the Confederate capital. An effort was made (May, 1861) by a Federal force to advance from Fortress Monroe on Hampton Roads; but it was successfully opposed by General Magruder at Big Bethel. This is often referred to as the first battle of the War of Secession. The Confederate force at this point was composed chiefly of North Carolinians and Virginians; and though not trained soldiers, they fought with a bravery that gave promise of a long struggle (map, page 359).

First battle of Manassas.—While General McClellan was in western Virginia trying to organize a new State out of the counties that opposed secession, General McDowell was ordered to advance on Richmond. He was met (July 21st) by a Confederate force at Manassas Junction, about thirty-five miles from Washington. In the early part of the day the Federals were victorious, but toward midday General Thomas J. Jackson[1] rallied the Con-

---

[1] Thomas J. Jackson was born in Virginia in January, 1824. Like Lee and Davis, he was educated at West Point. While there he wrote in his notebook a number of resolutions to govern his life. One of these was, "Through life let your principal object be a discharge of duty." We are told that he rendered very conspicuous service in the Mexican War and that "no officer in the whole army in Mexico was promoted so often for meritorious conduct, or made so great a stride in rank." He was a faithful church member and was so interested in the religious condition of the negroes that he taught a class in the colored Sunday-school that he established at Lexington. He taught in the Virginia Military Institute before entering the army of the Confederacy. His distinguished services in this great conflict will be referred to in other parts of this book. We are told that "he never asked for a day's furlough while he was in the army. In all things he was faithful—to his family, to his country, and to his God."

federates after they had retreated about a mile and a half. Then came Confederate reënforcements under Generals Beauregard, Joseph E. Johnston, and Kirby Smith; and their attack became so vigorous that the Federals were completely routed and fled in disorder toward Washington. It was in this battle that General Bee rushed up to General Thomas J. Jackson, who sat calmly on his horse watching the battle, and exclaimed, "General, they are beating us back!"

GENERAL THOMAS J. JACKSON

"Then, sir," replied Jackson, "we'll give them the bayonet."

A few moments later Bee cried, in rallying his soldiers:

"There stands Jackson like a stone wall." From that time this great leader was popularly known as "Stonewall Jackson."

Retreat to Washington.—Many senators and representatives and private citizens, including ladies dressed "in holiday attire," hired carriages and drove out from Washington toward Manassas to witness the battle. The following account of the retreat was written by one of the spectators, Albert G. Riddle, an eminent lawyer of Cleveland, Ohio:

"There never was anything like it for causeless, sheer, absolute, absurd cowardice, or rather panic, on this miserable earth before. Off they went, one and all; off down the highway, over across fields, toward the woods, anywhere, everywhere to escape. Well, the further they ran the more frightened they grew; and although we moved on as rapidly as we could, the fugitives passed us by scores. To enable them better to run, they threw away their blankets, knapsacks, canteens, and finally muskets, cartridge boxes, and everything else. We called to them, tried to tell them there was no danger, called them to stop, implored them to stand. We called them cowards, denounced them in the most offensive terms, put out our heavy revolvers and threatened to shoot them, but all in vain; a cruel, crazy, mad, hopeless panic possessed them, and communicated to everybody about, in front and rear. The heat was awful, although now about six; the men were exhausted —their mouths gaped, their lips cracked and blackened with the powder of the cartridges they had bitten off in the battle, their eyes starting in frenzy; no mortal ever saw such a mass of ghastly wretches. As we passed the poor, demented, exhausted wretches who could not climb into the high, closed baggage wagons, they made frantic efforts to get onto and into our carriage. They grasped it everywhere, and got onto it, into it, over it, and implored us every way to take them on."

War in the West.—General Frémont had charge of the Union army in the West with headquarters at St. Louis. Under his direction General Nathaniel Lyon tried to secure all of Missouri, but was defeated at Wilson's Creek near Springfield, by General Price, who held southern Missouri for the Confederacy. When the year 1861 closed, the South had been successful in practically every battle.

CHAPTER LXXXV

WAR ON THE SEA

Preparations for naval warfare.—A call from President Davis for privateers to destroy the commerce of the United States was followed by a proclamation from President Lincoln (April 19, 1861) declaring Southern ports in blockade and announcing that all men acting as privateersmen under Confederate authority would be treated as pirates when captured. President Davis answered (April 29th) that if any Confederate privateersmen were put to death as pirates, he would put to death an equal number of Union soldiers held as prisoners.

Treatment of Confederate crews.—Early in June, 1861, the privateer *Savannah* was captured and its crew taken to New York City and placed in jail to await their trial for piracy. President Davis then put in chains some of the prisoners taken at the battle of Manassas. This caused President Lincoln to decide to treat the captives taken on privateers as prisoners of war, and to hold them eligible to exchange as such.

"Trent" affair.—In November, 1861, James M. Mason of Virginia and John Slidell of Louisiana were sent by the Confederate Government to represent it in England and France. They escaped through the blockade and took passage at Havana on the British mail steamer *Trent*. This vessel was stopped by a United States gunboat under Captain Wilkes (November 8th), and Mason and Slidell were made prisoners and carried to Boston. Congress passed a vote of thanks to Captain Wilkes. But the English people were greatly incensed, and declared that the United States had no right to search their vessels. Lincoln was forced to give up the commissioners and to apologize to the English Government. At one time it looked as if England would declare war against the United States, an act which would probably have resulted in the success of the Confederacy.

Attitude of England and France.—Each section of the country expected to get sympathy, if not help, from

Europe. The Confederate Government thought that England would be forced to recognize its independence because the blockade would close the English cotton factories and bring distress to thousands of workmen. But England did nothing more than join with France in recognizing the "war rights" of the Confederacy and in agreeing to take no part in the conflict.

The Last Fight of the "Alabama"

Blockade runners.—As the United States was more able to build ships than was the Confederacy, the blockade of Southern ports became more effective as the war continued. It was soon impossible for Southern ships to take cotton to European markets and bring back guns and other necessary equipment, to say nothing of medicines and common supplies, unless they "ran the blockade." The blockade runners were usually small, swift vessels painted a dark color and otherwise equipped so that they could slip by the Federal boats at night without being discovered. If they passed the blockading vessels, they ran into a foreign port—Nassau, Havana, or some other. After selling their cargoes and buying supplies, they re-

The "Nashville" Running the Blockade at Beaufort, North Carolina

turned home by the same methods they had followed in getting away.

Battle of the Ironclads.—In March, 1862, a desperate effort was made to break the blockade by a new method of naval warfare. When the Confederates seized the Navy Yard at Portsmouth, they raised one of the vessels, the *Merrimac*, which had been sunk by the Union forces. It was renamed the *Virginia* and, after it had been repaired, was covered with a double coat of iron and provided with a great iron prow. This prow was built under the water, to be used in ramming and sinking the wooden vessels belonging to the blockading fleet. The *Virginia* then steamed into Hampton

The "Virginia" Ramming the Federal "Cumberland"

Roads under the command of Captain Buchanan, to attack the Federal fleet. With its prow or "ram" it at once sank the *Cumberland*, and routed the whole Union fleet of five gunboats. The shot and shell from the Federal batteries had no effect on its iron sides.

The next morning the Federal fleet was reënforced by the sudden arrival of another ironclad, the *Monitor*, which

THE "VIRGINIA" CONFRONTED BY THE "MONITOR"

This illustration and the other line drawings picturing scenes of the War of Secession are reproduced from the original wood engravings made from the sketches of the field artists and war correspondents of 1861–65.

was built with its hull under water and a round revolving tower for guns on top. It looked like "a cheese box on a raft." The terrible battle which followed was the first ever fought between ironclads. Neither ship could capture or sink the other. After a desperate struggle of four hours each vessel withdrew, the *Virginia* returning to Norfolk, and the *Monitor* to Fortress Monroe. The *Monitor* refused to accept a challenge to renew the battle with the *Virginia*.[1]

---

[1] Neither vessel rendered any other important service, the *Monitor* being lost in a storm off the Carolina coast and the *Virginia* being blown up by its crew to keep it from falling into the hands of the Federals upon the capture of Norfolk.

The result of this battle was of great importance to naval fighting in the world. It showed that no boats except ironclads could be successfully used in warfare.

Career of the "Alabama."—As there were no important shipyards in the South, the Confederacy could have had few war vessels but for the English ship builders. The first Confederate vessel built in England was the *Florida*, which entered the Confederate service in March, 1862. In August of the same year the most celebrated of the English-built vessels, the *Alabama*, unfurled the Stars and Bars and entered upon her career of destruction, under the command of the brilliant Southern admiral, Raphael Semmes.

RAPHAEL SEMMES, ADMIRAL C.S.N.

After making a few captures near the British coast, the *Alabama* cruised upon the oceans. By the first of November she had taken twenty-two Federal vessels. In the Gulf of Mexico, and off the coasts of South America and Africa, she captured a number more. In less than two years the *Alabama* captured sixty-nine vessels and destroyed ten million dollars' worth of property. Her career was finally brought to an end (June, 1864) by an encounter with a Federal vessel, the *Kearsarge*, off the harbor of Cherbourg, France. Her drowning crew was rescued by a private yacht belonging to an English gentleman.[1]

---

[1] The United States claimed that England had violated the law of nations by allowing Confederate war vessels to be built in her waters.

CHAPTER LXXXVI

THE WAR IN 1862—ADVANCE ON RICHMOND

Plans of action.—After the Battle of Manassas, General McClellan spent over six months in drilling and organiz-

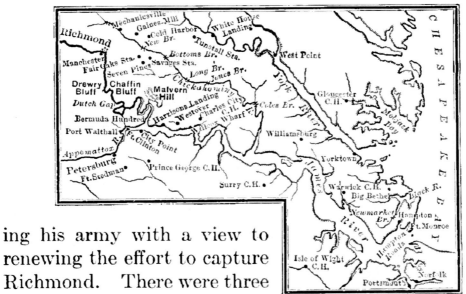

THE PENINSULA CAMPAIGN

ing his army with a view to renewing the effort to capture Richmond. There were three ways of reaching that city from Washington: (1) by the Chesapeake and thence up the Peninsula between the York River and the James River; (2) by a direct route overland; (3) through the Shenandoah valley. General McClellan decided to try the first of these routes, as a great part of the distance could be covered by water. He therefore sailed from Washington with a large army (March, 1862), and took his position at Fortress Monroe.

After many years the "Alabama Claims" were finally (1872) referred to a special court of arbitration, which decided that England should pay the United States fifteen and a half millions of dollars for the damages inflicted on American commerce by English-built Confederate cruisers.

The Peninsula campaign.

As McClellan slowly advanced up the Peninsula, every inch of ground over which he passed was contested with him by the Confederates under Generals Magruder and Johnston. Yorktown was finally evacuated by the Confederates; and after a Federal defeat at Williamsburg, Johnston retired toward

General Robert E. Lee on His Horse "Traveller"

Richmond. He was followed by McClellan's army, which got within sight of the church steeples of the Confederate capital. For two days (May 31st and June 1st) a terrible battle raged between the two armies at Seven Pines and Fair Oaks. The Federals were routed at first, but were saved by the arrival of reënforcements. General Johnston was wounded, and General Robert E. Lee[1] took

---

[1] Robert E. Lee was a son of Henry Lee, the Revolutionary General who was known as "Light Horse Harry." The great Confederate leader was born January 19, 1807. Like President Davis, he was educated at the West Point Military Academy, where he won high rank because of his obedience to orders and his studious habits. He served in the Mexican

1862—ADVANCE ON RICHMOND

command. In this battle Richmond was nearly taken. One corps of McClellan's army got within four miles of the city.

The plan of advance on Richmond and protection of Washington.—If McClellan could have concentrated all his forces, undoubtedly he would have captured Richmond. It was necessary, however, for him to leave a second force under General McDowell to protect Washington and be ready to advance on Richmond by the direct overland route toward Fredericksburg. A third force under General Banks was ordered to occupy the Shenandoah valley to prevent the Confederates from invading Maryland. A fourth force under General Frémont was ordered to keep the Confederates from invading West Virginia. If possible, all these forces were to advance gradually toward Richmond from the North.

"Jackson's Valley campaign."—Johnston sent an army of sixteen thousand men under Stonewall Jackson into the Shenandoah valley to oppose Frémont and Banks, each of whom had a larger force than Jackson. He fell upon

War under General Scott, who said that Lee was the best soldier he had ever seen. When Virginia seceded from the Union, Lee, then a colonel in the United States army, severed his connection with the army and returned to his native State. It is said that before leaving the Union service he was offered the command of the Northern armies, and that he replied, "If I owned the four million slaves in the South, I would give them all up to save the Union; but how can I draw my sword on my native State?" When he accepted the command of Virginia's army of defense, he said, "Trusting in Almighty God and an approving conscience and the aid of my fellow-citizens, I devote myself to the services of my native State." After the war he became President of Washington and Lee University, devoting the remainder of his life to the training of the young men of the South. He said to a Southern mother, "Do not train up your children to be foes of the United States Government. We are one country. Bring them up Americans." Lee died October 12, 1870.

Banks at Winchester and drove him across the Potomac River. He quickly turned to meet Frémont, who had crossed the Alleghany Mountains, and defeated him at Cross Keys near Staunton, Virginia. He then crossed the Shenandoah River and the next day defeated at Port Republic a part of McDowell's army, which had crossed the Blue Ridge Mountains.[1]

SKIRMISHERS ON THE ROAD TO RICHMOND

In the short period of thirty-five days, in May and June, 1862, Jackson had successfully executed one of the most brilliant campaigns recorded in history. He had marched over four hundred miles, won six battles, defeated four armies amounting to sixty thousand men, and inflicted a loss upon his opponents of seven thousand captured, killed, and wounded. Then, with a daring scarcely known in history, he left a small force in the valley and returned to Richmond to aid in the defeat of McClellan. This campaign caused so much fear for the safety of Washington that McDowell was prevented from

---

[1] At one time in this campaign Jackson and his staff were separated from their army with a river between. Finding that a bridge over the river was guarded by a gun in charge of a few Union soldiers, Jackson rode up to the officer and boldly said, "Who told you to place that gun there? Bring it here at once." As the officer thought Jackson was a Federal general, he promptly moved the gun, and the Confederate general and his men dashed across the bridge and rejoined their army before they could be stopped.

joining McClellan in the advance on Richmond and was ordered to hurry his army of forty thousand men to the defense of the Federal capital.

The Seven Days' Battle.—After the battle of Fair Oaks, McClellan's army was inactive, while Lee was preparing for a vigorous attack. In order to learn the strength and location of the Union forces, the dashing cavalry officer, General J. E. B. Stuart, with twelve hundred Confederate horsemen, went entirely around McClellan's army and returned with the desired information. The series of bloody engagements known as the Seven Days' Battle between Lee and McClellan began on June 26th. The Confederates were at first repulsed; but on the next three days Lee, Jackson, and Stuart made decided gains. Although the Federals were finally successful at Malvern Hill, McClellan withdrew his army to Harrison's Landing on the James River, where it was protected by the gunboats; and the attack against Richmond was given up. McClellan lost sixteen thousand men, and Lee twenty thousand; but the Confederates made a successful defense of their capital.

CHAPTER LXXXVII

THE WAR IN 1862—CAMPAIGNS IN MARYLAND AND NORTHERN VIRGINIA

Second battle of Manassas.—After McClellan's defeat President Lincoln called for three hundred thousand new troops. He made General Halleck Commander-in-Chief of the Union army. General John Pope was given command of the forces before Washington, and General McClellan was ordered to withdraw from the peninsula.

Lee and Jackson with fifty thousand men advanced north and inflicted a disastrous defeat on Pope's army of seventy thousand on the old battlefield of Manassas (August, 1862). The Federal army again retreated to Washington. Pope was succeeded by McClellan, who was intrusted with the defense of the city. As there was no

HARPER'S FERRY IN 1862
From a contemporary sketch.

immediate danger of another campaign against Richmond, Lee decided to invade the North.

The Maryland campaign. — Lee quickly crossed the Potomac into Maryland. As he found it difficult to get supplies, he sent Jackson to capture a Federal stronghold at Harper's Ferry and to open up communications with the Shenandoah valley. On September 15th Jackson took Harper's Ferry, capturing twelve thousand prisoners and large supplies of arms and ammunition.

1862—MARYLAND AND NORTHERN VIRGINIA

Two days later McClellan's army of eighty-seven thousand men attacked Lee's army of less than forty thousand near Sharpsburg on Antietam Creek, Maryland. In a bloody battle Lee's small army successfully met every assault and defeated the Federal army at every point. At the end of the day over twenty-three thousand men lay dead and wounded on the field, the losses being almost equally divided between the two armies. The battle was not a decided victory for either side. Although McClellan received reënforcements on the second day, he failed to renew the fight. After waiting on the battlefield twenty-four hours, Lee quietly withdrew his army into Virginia, but McClellan waited five weeks before attempting to cross the Potomac. The Confederates were greatly disappointed because but few Marylanders joined Lee's army; and the Federals were disappointed because McClellan did not make a better showing with the superior force at his command.

Battle of Fredericksburg.—General McClellan was then succeeded by General Ambrose E. Burnside, who at once began to pursue General Lee. The Confederate army was overtaken at Fredericksburg on the south side of the Rappahannock River. Here Burnside made an attack, sending his army across the river in three divisions. Lee's army was again about half the size of the attacking Federal forces. But the result of the battle of Fredericksburg (December 13th) was terribly disastrous to the Federals, each division being almost completely destroyed and driven back in great confusion to the northern bank of the Rappahannock. The Union loss was about thirteen thousand men, and the Confederate loss about five thousand. Burnside, almost frantic with grief, pointed his finger at his dead and dying, and cried, "Oh, those men, those men over there! I am thinking of them all the time."

General Burnside resigned, and General Joseph Hooker, known as "Fighting Joe Hooker," was appointed to succeed him. The Federal army went into winter quarters in northern Virginia and kept up close communication with Washington. Lee occupied the southern bank of the Rappahannock. This ended the war in the East in 1862.

Results of the war in the East in 1862.—For the most part the war in the East in 1862 had been disastrous to the Northern armies. Three campaigns against Richmond had failed: the first, led by McClellan; the second, by Pope; and the third, by Burnside.

CHAPTER LXXXVIII

THE WAR IN 1862—CAMPAIGNS IN KENTUCKY AND TENNESSEE

Plan of action in the West.—Although disheartened by the results of the first year of the war, Lincoln prepared for a vigorous Western campaign in 1862. Edwin M. Stanton, the Secretary of War, was unpopular and disagreeable, but he kept the army well supplied with troops and provisions.

The Federal Government attempted to gain control of Kentucky and Tennessee with a view to opening the Mississippi River. A strong Confederate force under General Albert Sidney Johnston was stationed throughout middle and southern Kentucky, extending from Columbus on the

Mississippi River to the Alleghany Mountains. The western part of Kentucky had also been invaded by a Confederate army under General Leonidas Polk. In northern Tennessee the Confederates had Fort Henry on the Tennessee River and Fort Donelson on the Cumberland. Albert Sidney Johnston was opposed by a large Federal force commanded by Henry W. Halleck, aided by Generals Buell, Thomas, and Grant.

Federal successes in Tennessee.—Starting from Cairo (Illinois), General U. S. Grant advanced up the Tennessee River against Fort Henry, which he captured without difficulty by the aid of a gunboat fleet. He then marched rapidly across the country and surrounded Fort Donelson, which the Confederate General Buckner was forced to surrender (February 16th) with fourteen thousand soldiers, forty pieces of artillery, and a quantity of military stores. This was the first great victory of the North, and it was a severe blow to the Confederate cause. As a result, all of Kentucky and the northern and western parts of Tennessee were practically in the hands of the Federals. The Union forces under General Buell soon occupied Nashville (February 25th). Andrew Johnson, who had been a Democratic senator

FORTS AND BATTLEGROUNDS OF THE WESTERN CAMPAIGNS

from Tennessee and who had opposed secession, was made military governor of that State by President Lincoln.

Turning point in Grant's career.—General Grant was now the hero of the war; but he had practically disregarded his superior officer, General Halleck, by starting toward Nashville without orders. Moreover, he was accused of carelessness in sending in reports as to his movements. General Halleck reported him to the commander of the Federal armies, General McClellan, who ordered Grant to be removed from command. Halleck did not dare take this step, however, because of Grant's popularity. On the other hand, Grant was angry and asked to be relieved of command. But when Grant's reports were in, Halleck expressed his satisfaction, and the matter was dropped. The United States Government thereupon appointed a special agent, Charles A. Dana, to remain with Grant's army and to send daily telegraphic reports of its movements.

Battle of Shiloh.—In the meantime Grant had received reënforcements which gave him an army of about forty thousand men, and he had turned back toward the Mississippi River. Albert Sidney Johnston got together at Corinth an army of about the same number and prepared to attack Grant at Pittsburg Landing, or Shiloh, on the Tennessee River, not far from the boundary lines of Mississippi, Alabama, and Tennessee.

The Confederates had practically defeated Grant in the battle of Shiloh,[1] April 6, 1862, when they sustained a great loss in the death of General Johnston. Unfortunately for the Confederates, Buell, who had been sent by Halleck

---

[1] The battle takes its name from a little log church that stood near the scene of conflict.

Ulysses S. Grant

with twenty thousand men to reënforce Grant, arrived in time to turn the tide of battle and to force Beauregard, who had succeeded Johnston, to retire to Corinth and finally to Tupelo in Mississippi.

CHAPTER LXXXIX

THE WAR IN 1862—CAMPAIGNS IN MISSISSIPPI AND TENNESSEE

Conquest of the upper and lower Mississippi. — Federal gunboats under Admiral Foote took Island No. 10 in the Mississippi River, with five or six thousand prisoners, and then captured New Madrid. Fort Pillow above Memphis then fell (June 5th); and on the day following, Memphis itself was captured by a Federal fleet. These conquests opened the upper Mississippi from its source to Vicksburg.

Meantime Admiral Farragut had entered the mouth of the Mississippi River, passed two Confederate forts and seventeen vessels, and, with the aid of General Benjamin F. Butler, had captured New Orleans (April 25th). The government of the city was intrusted to General Butler, who ruled it "in a manner that has made his name forever odious to the people of the South."[1]

---

[1] On May 15th Butler issued an order which subjected to disgraceful treatment any woman who should by "word, gesture, or movement, insult or show contempt for any officer or soldier of the United States." This order aroused the greatest indignation throughout the South, in England, and in parts of the North. It led to the imprisonment for many months of the mayor and other prominent citizens of the city because they protested against its execution. Butler also hanged a man for removing the Federal flag from the mint.

The fall of New Orleans left only two Confederate strongholds on the Mississippi—Port Hudson and Vicksburg. This loss was a great disaster to the Confederacy, as New Orleans was the most important city in the Gulf States. Its capture meant more than an early overthrow of Confederate authority in Louisiana; it put the Gulf of Mexico under control of the Federal fleet. It also put an end to the gathering of recruits and supplies for the

The Bombardment of Vicksburg by the Combined Fleets of Admirals Farragut and Porter

Southern armies from the important region west of the Mississippi. Thousands of bales of cotton, the shipyards at Algiers across the river, several unfinished vessels, and much other property were destroyed by the Confederates when they saw that the city must fall.

Campaigns against Vicksburg.—After the fall of New Orleans the Confederate Government sent additional guns and troops to defend Vicksburg. When the Federal fleet reached that city and demanded its surrender, the people of Vicksburg said with one voice, "The city must be defended, even if our houses and property are destroyed." About the same time the gunboat fleet from the upper river reached the city. The two great fleets bombarded the city for two months. They were finally dispersed by the Confederate ram, *Arkansas*, which ran out of the mouth of the Yazoo River and, "single-handed, attacked the whole Federal fleet." This attack has been characterized as "one of the most brilliant naval feats recorded in the annals of naval warfare." The Federals then decided that Vicksburg could not be taken from the water front and gave up the effort.

A second campaign against Vicksburg began in December, 1862. General

A Union Transport Forcing Its Way up a Bayou

Sherman in command of a Federal force was sent down the river from Memphis with the fleet to attack the city unexpectedly. General Grant intended to coöperate with him by leading an army across the country from Holly Springs. Both of these plans failed. General Forrest destroyed sixty miles of railroad track over which Grant was supplying his army, and General Van Dorn captured and destroyed millions of dollars' worth of Federal supplies at Holly Springs. This forced Grant to abandon his plan and return to Memphis. General Sherman was disastrously repulsed by General Stephen D. Lee at Chickasaw Bayou, ten miles from Vicksburg (December 29, 1862), and withdrew from before the city a few days later.

Confederate losses west of the Mississippi.—Federal General S. R. Curtis was sent by Halleck to recover southern Missouri and if possible to capture Arkansas. He was opposed by General Van Dorn; but a Union victory at Pea Ridge, Arkansas, left Missouri and northern Arkansas in the hands of the Federals.

Bragg's invasion of Tennessee and Kentucky.—After the Confederate army under General Beauregard retired from Corinth to Tupelo (page 369), Bragg was put in charge, Beauregard being too ill to direct the army. Bragg determined to recover Tennessee and Kentucky for the Confederates, if possible. He marched rapidly through eastern Tennessee across Kentucky and was on the point of attacking Louisville when his army was checked by General Buell at Perryville (October 8th). Thereupon Bragg, fearing that he would be cut off from his supplies, was forced to retreat. Finally he went back to Chattanooga, where he strongly fortified himself; and the Union forces took up their headquarters at Nashville.

Bragg determined to make one more effort to gain a Confederate foothold in Tennessee. He marched against Nashville, but was met at Murfreesboro by the Federal army under Rosecrans, who had been put in Buell's place. After a bloody battle of three days, the Confederates were forced to withdraw from the field (January 2, 1863) and to return to Chattanooga. The Federal army, however, was so badly crippled that it could not follow in pursuit.

Battle of Corinth.—General Bragg left a Confederate force in northern Mississippi under command of Generals Van Dorn and Price, who had crossed the Mississippi River from Arkansas after the battle of Pea Ridge. They made a daring attempt (October 3d and 4th) to recapture Corinth from the Federals commanded by General Rosecrans, but they were repulsed with great losses after they had taken part of the town. The Confederate army then retreated to Grenada, where it was encamped at the time of the second campaign against Vicksburg.

Results of the year in the West.—The war in the West in 1862 had been terribly disastrous to the Confederate cause. Kentucky, most of Tennessee, northern and western Mississippi, Missouri, and northern Arkansas had passed into the hands of the Federals. The fortifications at Vicksburg and Chattanooga were the most important strongholds still held by the Southern army in these States.

CHAPTER XC

POLITICAL AND ECONOMIC CONDITIONS IN 1862

Effects of the blockade.—At the close of 1861 the Confederates had not felt keenly the results of the general blockade of their ports by the Union vessels, but at the close of 1862 the soldiers of the South were suffering greatly for the necessaries of life. Nevertheless, they continued to struggle with such aid as they could get from home; for the women, old men, children, and slaves made homespun clothes and coarse shoes, hats, and underclothing for the army. Coffee and sugar were scarce, though sufficient food for supplies still came from southern

Virginia, the Carolinas, Georgia, and the Gulf States east of the Mississippi.

The South was still hoping for England's interference, since the laboring class in England had been suffering from the shutting down of the cotton mills. But the Federal Government sent over three shiploads of food to help relieve their distress. The supply of cotton in England was so diminished that by September, 1862, it was selling for sixty cents a pound.

Expenses of the war.—As the war was costing the North two millions of dollars a day, the Federal Government was compelled to issue a great quantity of greenbacks to meet this expense. The National Bank system in force to-day was also established to secure money for the Union.

Paper Currency Issued by the State of Alabama in 1863

According to its requirements no man should run a bank and issue notes unless the capital stock of the bank was invested in Government bonds, and these bonds were deposited with the treasurer of the United States. This forced the people to buy the bonds of the Government. State banks were taxed so heavily that they had to go out of business.

Unfortunately the South could not inaugurate such a system; for its Government had little credit, and the money issued by it was, at the close of 1862, not worth half its face value. The banks in the South issued notes at will, which were nothing more than promissory notes without credit to back them. However, money for building new Confederate "rams" was easily obtained in London in 1863, the capitalists of Europe subscribing for three times as much as was necessary for this object.

Political conditions in the North in 1862.—There were certain conditions in the North that were unfavorable to the United States Government.

In the first place, the Republican party was made up of many Democrats and old-line Whigs and Abolitionists. The Democrats and Whigs who had joined this party had done so only to exclude slavery from the Territories. The Abolitionists, on the other hand, had hoped for the total destruction of slavery. Practically all the Northern Democrats had joined with the Republicans in carrying on the war to force the Southern States back into the Union. As yet nothing had been done toward abolishing slavery in the seceded States, though some of the Northern generals had gone so far as to declare the slaves free in the territory the Union army had entered. Of course these decrees were made without any lawful authority, and in each instance they were promptly annulled by President Lincoln.

Secondly, in the summer of 1862 many people demanded that Northern opponents of the war who had denounced Lincoln should be arrested for treason. The President finally (September, 1862) suspended the writ of *habeas corpus*. This was contrary to the Constitution of the United States, but Congress later gave Lincoln full authority in the matter. He could order the arrest and imprisonment of any man in the United States without even informing him why he was arrested. Thousands of men were kept in prison on such charges as "disloyal practice," "discouraging enlistment," and the like. This caused much dissatisfaction in the North.

In the third place, there were charges against the Government of corruption in awarding contracts and favoritism in making military appointments. As a result six Northern States—New York, Pennsylvania, Ohio, Indiana, Illinois, Wisconsin—that had gone Republican in 1860, elected Democrats to Congress in 1862; and the Republicans had only a small majority left in the House of Representatives.

The Emancipation Proclamation. — In March, 1862, President Lincoln recommended that Congress pass a law encouraging the four slave-holding States still in the Union—Delaware, Maryland, Kentucky, and Missouri—to free the slaves by agreeing to pay their owners for them. But, to the disappointment of President Lincoln, these States took no action in the matter, as they were opposed to emancipation. The Abolitionists, by the summer of 1862, developed strength enough to abolish slavery in all the Territories and to free the slaves in the District of Columbia. In order to strengthen the war sentiment in the North, Lincoln finally decided to yield to the Abolitionists' demands that slavery should be entirely abolished.[1] Immediately after the Federal success at Antietam he issued a proclamation (September, 1862) declaring that on January 1, 1863, all slaves in such slave-

---

[1] President Lincoln wrote in August, 1862: "My paramount object in this struggle is to save the Union and is not either to save or destroy slavery. If I could save the Union without freeing any slave, I would do it; and if I could save it by freeing all the slaves, I would do it; and if I could save it by freeing some and leaving others alone, I would also do that."

holding States as had not returned to the Union would be declared free. On January 1, 1863, he issued a second proclamation declaring all slaves in the States then in the Confederacy forever free, except in the territory under control of the United States army. He stated that this proclamation had "no constitutional or legal justification, except as a war measure."

Of course the proclamation had little immediate effect on the slaves in the Confederate States. Many of those who had gone with their masters to the front were faithful to the end of the war, and those who remained at home took care of the women and children and raised provisions to help supply the needs of the Southern armies.[1]

Admission of West Virginia.—As the western counties of Virginia were in sympathy with the Union, their people refused to join in the secession movement. When Virginia seceded, these counties set up a new government and were later admitted into the Union as West Virginia (1863). The admission of West Virginia as a State without the consent of the Government of Virginia was a violation of the Constitution of United States (see Constitution, Art. IV, sect. 3).

The Conscription Law and the Draft Act.—In order to provide soldiers for the Southern army, the Confederate Congress passed a Conscription Law requiring all able-

---

[1] "History has no parallel to the faith kept by the negro in the South during the war. There were often five hundred negroes to a single white man, and yet through these dusky throngs the women and children walked in safety, and the unprotected homes rested in peace. Unmarshaled, the black battalions moved patiently to the fields in the morning to feed the armies their idleness would have starved, and at night gathered anxiously at the big house to 'hear the news from marster,' though conscious that his victory made their chains enduring. A thousand torches would have disbanded every Southern army, but not one was lighted."—HENRY W. GRADY.

bodied men, between certain ages, to enter the service. This law was extended as the war continued, until finally it included old men and boys.

After the disastrous defeats of the Northern armies in 1862 it was difficult to get volunteers to fill the ranks. The Federal Congress then followed the example of the Confederacy by passing a Draft Act (March, 1863), which authorized President Lincoln to make drafts on Northern citizens at discretion. This caused bloody draft riots in several Northern cities. The most violent outbreak was in New York City, where for a period of four days the rioters destroyed houses, hanged negroes, and fought the troops sent to quell them.

CHAPTER XCI

THE WAR IN 1863—CAMPAIGNS IN THE WEST

Third campaign against Vicksburg.—After the failure of the second campaign against Vicksburg (page 371), General Grant was left in charge of the territory about that city. He at once (January, 1863) entered upon a third campaign, which resulted in the fall of that important stronghold, July 4, 1863. He descended the Mississippi River with an army of over fifty thousand men. After spending more than three months in vain attempts to reach the highlands north of Vicksburg and in an unsuccessful effort to

THE VICKSBURG CAMPAIGN

change the course of the Mississippi River by means of a canal, he finally ran his boats past the batteries while he marched part of his army on the Louisiana side to a point below the city. He then crossed the river and entered the State of Mississippi several miles south of Vicksburg.

The Confederate forces in Mississippi were under the command of General Joseph E. Johnston, who occupied Jackson (May, 1863). He was assisted by General Pemberton, who was stationed at Vicksburg. Grant took possession of the surrounding country and prevented the sending of reënforcements to Vicksburg. Thus Johnston's and Pemberton's forces were separated. After capturing Jackson and defeating Pemberton at Champion Hills (May 16th), Grant settled down to besiege Vicksburg.

JOSEPH E. JOHNSTON

The siege and surrender of Vicksburg.—The memorable siege of Vicksburg lasted forty-seven days. During this time the doomed city, containing only seventeen thousand effective Confederate troops, was truly surrounded by "a sheet of bayonets and fire." Grant's army, now increased to over seventy-five thousand men, kept up a continuous fire upon the Confederate fortifications, from the land side, while Admiral Porter's fleet of gunboats on the water front threw into the city, "day and night, the largest shells and shots known in modern warfare." The inhabitants sought refuge in caves dug in the hillsides;

and after the supply of food had been exhausted, the hungry troops ate mule flesh. Hunger and exposure produced disease, and on the day the city surrendered eight thousand men were reported sick. In demanding the surrender of the city, Grant said: "Men who have shown so much endurance and courage as those now in Vicksburg will always challenge the respect of an adversary and, I can assure you, will be treated with all the respect due them as prisoners of war."

With the fall of Port Hudson, a few days later, the Mississippi River throughout its entire length was under Federal control. This severed the Confederacy and hastened its downfall.

Battle of Chickamauga.—While Grant was engaged in opening the Mississippi, the Federals under Rosecrans stood facing the Confederates under Bragg near Murfreesboro, Tennessee.[1] The two forces finally met in battle at Chickamauga Creek, twelve miles from Chattanooga. After a terrible struggle of two days (September 19th and 20th), the Union forces were driven from the field. They would have been totally routed but for the stand taken by General Thomas, which enabled them to withdraw into Chattanooga. From this time Thomas was known as

---

[1] The most famous and daring cavalry raid of the war was that of General John H. Morgan, who was sent by Bragg into Kentucky at the head of twenty-five hundred men. After crossing that State, Morgan continued his raid into Indiana and Ohio, destroying much valuable property and moving day and night to keep from being captured. He was closely followed by a rapidly increasing band of militia and farmers who killed and wounded so many of his men that his band was reduced to about four hundred. Morgan was captured and confined in the penitentiary at Columbus (Ohio), but finally escaped by digging a passage under the walls. The following year he was killed in Tennessee.

A Group of Confederate Generals

John B. Gordon
Braxton Bragg
Nathan B. Forrest

John B. Hood
J. E. B. Stuart

Wade Hampton
Albert Sidney Johnston
P. G. T. Beauregard

the "Rock of Chickamauga." Bragg[1] now fortified Missionary Ridge and Lookout Mountain, and began to besiege Rosecrans in Chattanooga. Unfortunately for the Confederates, Longstreet was sent with a part of the army to attempt the capture of Knoxville. In this effort he failed after a gallant assault and was forced to retire into Virginia and join Lee's army. Grant came to Rosecrans's aid with a part of the army that had captured Vicksburg. The Federals also received reënforcements from Virginia, under General Hooker. General Grant then took command, and began his campaign to drive the Confederate forces from their position.

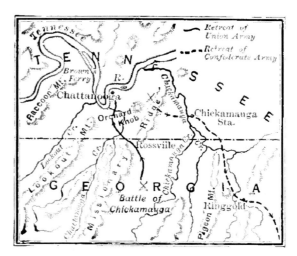

THE CAMPAIGN NEAR CHATTANOOGA

Battles of Lookout Mountain and Missionary Ridge.— Hooker charged up Lookout Mountain (November 24th)

---

[1] General Bragg sent a soldier boy of seventeen, by the name of Sam Davis, to obtain information about the Federal fortifications in middle Tennessee. While on the way back to his command with important papers, Davis was captured by the Federals. When asked who gave him the drawings and specifications, he answered, "A Federal officer, high in command." He was then asked the name of the officer. His reply was, "I shall not tell you." He was condemned to hang as a spy, but was offered his life if he would tell the name of the officer from whom he had obtained the papers. To this proposition the young hero replied with indignation, "Do you suppose I would betray a friend to save my own life? No! I will die a thousand times first." He went to his execution with the courage of a martyr.

and forced Bragg to withdraw and concentrate his forces on Missionary Ridge. The next day General Thomas drove the Confederates from this strong position. Bragg then withdrew his army into Georgia and took up winter quarters at Dalton. This ended the campaign in the West in 1863.

Results of the war in the West in 1863.—The Federals had everywhere been successful. Grant had won for himself a name as a great general and was called to Washington and placed in command of all the armies of the United States. General Bragg was succeeded by General Joseph E. Johnston in command of the Confederate forces in the West.

CHAPTER XCII

THE WAR IN 1863—CAMPAIGNS IN VIRGINIA AND PENNSYLVANIA

Battle of Chancellorsville.—In April, 1863, General Hooker with over a hundred thousand men crossed the Rappahannock River to attack General Lee, who was encamped near Fredericksburg with somewhat over fifty thousand men. A bloody battle was fought at Chancellorsville (May 2d) in which Lee and Jackson outgeneraled Hooker and completely routed his army. But the Confederates sustained a great loss in the death of one of their most beloved commanders, General Jackson. The general was fatally wounded by one of his own soldiers, who, in the darkness of night, mistook him and his staff for a body of Federal cavalry. He died a few days later, his last words being, "Let us cross over the river and rest under the shade of the trees." His death was a great calamity to the South and brought inexpressible sorrow to his devoted followers. General Lee wept in his anguish and said, "I have indeed lost my right arm."[1]

Battle of Gettysburg. — In June, 1863, General Lee made another attempt to carry the war into the North. With an army of seventy thousand men, he crossed the Potomac River at Harper's Ferry and pressed on into Pennsylvania. General George Meade, who had superseded General Hooker, started with an army of a hundred thousand men to check the Confederate advance toward Harrisburg. The two armies met at Gettysburg,

JACKSON AT CHANCELLORSVILLE

where a bloody three days' battle began, on July 1, 1863. On the first day Lee drove back the Union advance and almost destroyed two corps of their army. He then waited for the arrival of the rest of his force. On the

---

[1] As soon as General Lee heard that Jackson had been wounded, he wrote to Jackson: "Could I have directed events, I should have chosen, for the good of the country, to have been disabled in your stead. I congratulate you upon the victory which is due to your skill and energy."

afternoon of the second day a Confederate attack was made on the Union lines, but they withstood the assaults. On the third day the Confederates made a desperate but unsuccessful attempt to dislodge the Federals from their position. After a terrible bombardment of two hours, beginning at one o'clock, Lee issued an order to charge the center of Meade's line on Cemetery Ridge.

Pickett's charge was one of the most daring incidents in military history. As his men, about fifteen thousand in number, started across the open valley, a mile or more wide, between the two lines, there was a lull in the battle. When they had gone about half the distance, the Federal batteries poured a deadly fire into their ranks. But the lines re-formed and swept on, returning the fire until they "rushed to the very mouths of the cannon." They drove back the Federal line and planted the Confederate banner on the breastworks. But the deadly fire of the Federals was too much for human endurance. The Confederates began to fall back, and the battle of Gettysburg was lost just as Longstreet was on the point of congratulating Lee on his great victory. The Federals lost eighteen thousand men, killed and wounded, and the Confederates over twenty thousand.

FROM CHANCELLORSVILLE TO GETTYSBURG

With guns in position Lee waited for a Federal attack during the entire day of July 4th, but the battle was not renewed. Though defeated, he made a masterly retreat and without further loss recrossed the Potomac into Virginia.

Along the Atlantic Coast. –Lincoln's blockade of the Southern ports was very effective in 1863. Only a few "runners" were able to escape the vigilance of the United States vessels and take cotton from the South to exchange for foreign goods. The Federals, however, were able to capture, of the chief cities, only Norfolk and New Orleans. In April, 1863, a fleet of monitors attacked Fort Sumter, but were driven off by the Confederates under Beauregard, and the Federal effort to take Charleston by sea was abandoned.

Results of the war in the East in 1863.—Although the Confederates in the East fought with a heroism that is unexcelled in history, they met with two fatal disasters in 1863. On the eve of their triumph at Chancellorsville they lost one of their greatest commanders, Stonewall Jackson; and in the gory conflict at Gettysburg they were not only repulsed, but suffered a loss of numbers that was irreparable.

July 4, 1863, marks a turning point in the war. On that day the Confederacy sustained the double misfortune of defeat at Vicksburg and at Gettysburg. These events greatly encouraged the North. They silenced many people who had opposed the Draft Act and had demanded an abandonment of the struggle. Although the war was now costing the Federal Government three millions of dollars a day, the conflict was renewed with increased vigor. From this time the Southern army fought on the defensive.

The Southern losses at Vicksburg and Gettysburg kept the European powers from recognizing the independence of the Confederacy and thus destroyed all hope of foreign intervention to stop the conflict.

In after years General Lee said: "If I had had Stonewall Jackson at Gettysburg, I would have won that battle; and a victory there would have given us Washington and Baltimore, if not Philadelphia, and would have established the independence of the country."

CHAPTER XCIII

THE WAR IN 1864—CAMPAIGNS IN THE LOWER SOUTH

Last battles of the war in Mississippi.—After the fall of Vicksburg, all Confederate troops except a small cavalry force were taken from Mississippi. In the spring of 1864 Sherman laid waste the country between Vicksburg and Meridian. In his report he said: "We are absolutely stripping the country of corn, cattle, hogs, sheep, poultry—everything; and the new-growing corn is being thrown open as pasture fields or hauled for the use of our animals. The wholesale destruction to which the country is now being subjected is terrible to contemplate. There are about eight hundred women and children who will perish unless they receive some relief."

General Forrest completely routed a large Federal force at Brice's Cross-Roads (June, 1864), gaining one of the most signal victories of the war for the forces engaged. A month later the fighting in Mississippi came to a close in a series of small engagements, culminating in a bloody battle at Harrisburg, near Tupelo. Although this was a drawn battle, the Federals retreated to Memphis.

1864—CAMPAIGNS IN THE LOWER SOUTH

The Red River expedition.—To complete the conquest of the States west of the Mississippi, a Federal force under General Banks was sent northward from the southern part of Louisiana, and another under General Steele was sent southward from Arkansas. Before they could unite, General Banks was defeated by General Richard Taylor in two battles in central Louisiana (April, 1864) and returned to the southern part of the State. Also, General Steele was defeated by General Kirby Smith in two battles in the northern part of Louisiana and retreated to Little Rock, Arkansas.

Grant's plans for ending the war.—After General Grant's brilliant achievements in the West, the North looked upon him as the "coming man" in the war. In March, 1864, he became Commander-in-Chief of all the armies of the United States. He soon decided on two great campaigns—one against Johnston, to be led by Sherman, who was to march through Georgia and cut off Confederate supplies from the lower South; the other to be led by himself against General Lee, with Richmond as his goal. If these plans were successfully carried out, they would prevent Johnston and Lee from reënforcing each other.

Sherman's attack on Johnston.—In May, 1864, Sherman moved from Chattanooga with over a hundred thousand men. He attacked Johnston's army of about half that size at Dalton, Georgia. As he was unable to defeat the Confederates, he tried by a flank movement to cut them off from Atlanta. This forced Johnston to retreat. For over two months Sherman continued to attack the Confederates in front, attempting at the same time to flank them. In order to delay Sherman's advance and to avoid a decisive battle against great odds in numbers, Johnston slowly retreated toward Atlanta. These movements cost Sherman about twenty-five thousand men by the time Johnston reached Atlanta in July, 1864. President Davis thought that Johnston should have attacked Sherman's army, and therefore removed him from command.

Hood's attack on Sherman.—General John B. Hood was then placed in command of the Confederate forces,

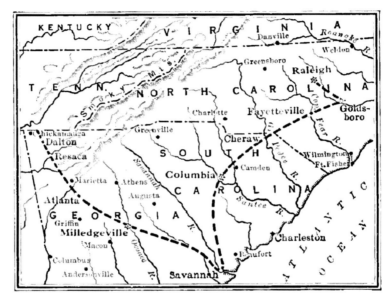

SHERMAN'S MARCH TO THE SEA

with instructions to attack General Sherman and force him back. Hood fought with determination and made three desperate attempts to break Sherman's forces (July 20th to 28th), but in each case he was unsuccessful. He was finally forced to evacuate Atlanta, which was at once occupied by the Federals (September 2d).

Hood then moved around Sherman's army to cut off supplies, and to defeat Thomas, who had charge of the Federal army in Tennessee. If successful in these movements, he planned to join Lee in an attack on Grant in Virginia.

Sherman's march to the sea.—According to Sherman's own report, he had "thoroughly destroyed Atlanta, save its mere dwelling houses and churches." He then started on his "march to the sea" (November 15th), intending to break the remainder of the Confederacy in two and to join in a movement to crush Lee's army. Sherman spread his army over a district sixty miles wide, burning all kinds of public and private buildings, destroying crops, killing horses, mules, cows, hogs, and fowl, tearing up railroad tracks, and twisting the heated rails around trees. After a march of four weeks he reached the sea on December 13th. He estimated that on this raid of about three hundred miles his army had destroyed property in Georgia to the value of one hundred million dollars, one tenth of which he said "inured to our benefit, and the remainder was simply waste and destruction." Savannah was captured after an eight days' siege. From that place he sent the following dispatch to President Lincoln: "I beg to present to you, as a Christmas gift, the city of Savannah, with one hundred and fifty heavy guns and plenty of ammunition, and also about twenty-five thousand bales of cotton." At Savannah Sherman's army went into winter quarters.

Hood's Tennessee campaign.—In the meantime Hood was defeated at the battle of Franklin, but continued his advance on Nashville, where Thomas quietly awaited him. When the Confederate forces failed to dislodge the Federals, Thomas ordered his men forward, took Hood by surprise, and totally defeated him, dispersing the whole army (December, 1864). In a sense this was the most decided Federal victory in the war; for it was the only one in which the Confederate army was so put to rout that it could not be led off in an orderly retreat.

Federal victories on the sea.—In June, 1864, the Confederate cruiser *Alabama* was defeated and sunk by the *Kearsarge* off the coast of France (page 358). In August of the same year, Admiral Farragut captured Mobile Bay, which was the most important harbor on the Gulf Coast left to the Confederacy. As this port had been a safe retreat for blockade runners, its capture was a great loss. In December, 1864, Admiral Porter began an attack on Fort Fisher, which guarded Wilmington, North Carolina. Its fall (January 15, 1865) closed the last port through which the Confederacy could reach the outside world. This completed the blockade proclaimed by Lincoln at the outbreak of the war. By the end of 1864 Charleston and Wilmington were the only important Confederate ports that had not fallen, but they were so strongly blockaded by Federal gunboats, that blockade runners could not get through.

CHAPTER XCIV

THE WAR IN 1864—CAMPAIGNS IN VIRGINIA

Plan for capturing Richmond.—At the opening of the year 1864, Grant devised a plan by which two armies were to advance on the Confederate capital. While he was to move toward Richmond from the north, General B. F. Butler was to approach that city by way of the James River.

Battles in Spotsylvania County.—With a well-equipped army of a hundred and twenty thousand men Grant

A Group of Federal Generals

George H. Thomas	William S. Rosecrans	Joseph Hooker
George B. McClellan	William T. Sherman	Philip H. Sheridan
Don Carlos Buell		George G. Meade

crossed the Rapidan River in May, 1864, to attack Lee's ragged and half-starved army of less than sixty thousand men. Lee's men fought so bravely that Grant was repulsed in a terrible two days' conflict known as the Battle of the Wilderness. But the Federal army was so large that it gradually pushed around the wing of the Confederate army and forced Lee to fall back to Spotsylvania Court House. Here, however, Grant's army was again defeated with heavy losses. At one time in this battle General Lee started to lead the advance in person, but his men refused to move unless he went back beyond the danger line. At a point known as the "death angle," men fought from "the top of heaps of dead men till their own bodies were added to the pile, and others came to take their places." It is said that a tree nearly two feet in diameter was cut down by musket balls and that "not a tree or a sapling was left alive and standing." While the armies were struggling in Spotsylvania County, a party of Federals on a raid tried to reach Richmond. General J. E. B. Stuart intercepted them and drove them back. But the gallant Stuart lost his life. He was succeeded, as Lee's cavalry commander, by General Wade Hampton of South Carolina.

VIRGINIA CAMPAIGN OF 1864-65

Battles around Richmond and Petersburg.—Lee withdrew to Cold Harbor, about thirty miles north of Richmond. Grant tried to penetrate the Confederate center, with the disastrous result that in about ten minutes he lost over twelve thousand men. Grant then swung around the Confederate army and crossed the James River, with the intention of attacking Richmond from the south; but he found himself before the strong fortifications at Petersburg. He attempted to take that city by means of a mine, which he tunneled under a Confederate fort. When Grant attempted to march his forces into the city through the crater that had been made by the explosion of this mine, he lost between three and four thousand men. It is estimated that from May, 1864, to the end of the year, Grant lost in killed, wounded, and missing over one hundred and thirty thousand men—more than twice as many men as Lee had in his whole army.

Throughout the autumn of 1864 he kept his army around Petersburg and Richmond, besieging those two cities. He also extended his lines to the south so as to cut off the railroad connections into North Carolina, by means of which Lee's army had received much of its provisions.

Success of Magruder and Early.—Butler had advanced up the southern bank of the James River to attack Richmond. But he got no farther than the mouth of the Appomattox River, where, to use Grant's expression, he was "bottled-up" by the Confederates.

While these events were taking place around Richmond, the Federals, first under Sigel, then under Hunter, came up the Shenandoah valley for the purpose of cutting off Lee's supplies from that source and approaching Richmond. Every effort was made to keep the Federals back, and even the students of the Virginia Military Institute were led out to battle. Finally, General Jubal A. Early drove the Federals over the mountains into West Virginia. Early then made a bold dash at Washington, defeating the Federals at Monocacy (Md.), and got within sight of the dome of the Capitol, but was forced to retreat.

Sheridan's raid.—Grant sent Sheridan into the Shenandoah valley with instructions to make it a "barren waste." He burned two thousand barns filled with grain,

CADETS OF THE VIRGINIA MILITARY INSTITUTE AT THE BATTLE OF NEW MARKET, VIRGINIA

and seventy mills filled with flour and wheat, and captured four thousand head of cattle. He was surprised by Early at Cedar Creek, near Winchester, and lost about five thousand men, which was about one thousand more than the Confederate general had in his command. But Sheridan rallied his fleeing men and drove Early from the Shenandoah valley.

CHAPTER XCV

LINCOLN REËLECTED—PRISONERS OF WAR

Political conditions in 1864.—As the war continued, political parties again developed in the North. One of them, the Union Party, was composed of Republicans and "War Democrats" who supported the war policy of President Lincoln. The other embraced the Democrats who opposed either the war or the Emancipation Proclamation. The latter party insisted that it stood for the "Constitution as it is and the Union as it was."

Lincoln renominated.—The Union Convention met in Baltimore, and on the first ballot renominated Lincoln for the Presidency. It nominated for Vice President Andrew Johnson, a "War Democrat" from Tennessee. The Radical Republicans nominated General Frémont for the Presidency, but their plans were thwarted by his final withdrawal from the race. The homely expression of Lincoln that it was "not best to swap horses when crossing a stream" was effective in the campaign.

The Democrats nominate McClellan.—The Democratic Convention met in Chicago and nominated General George B. McClellan for the Presidency on a platform which declared that the war had been a failure; also that Lincoln had violated the Constitution, had used the army to control elections, and had shamefully disregarded the sufferings of the Union soldiers in Southern prisons. But in accepting the nomination McClellan declared that the war had not been a failure and should be prosecuted.

Lincoln Reëlected.—Frémont's withdrawal and McClellan's declaration that the war was not a failure gave

1864—LINCOLN REELECTED

assurances of Lincoln's success. Just before the day of the election Federal successes all along the line of battle indicated that the Confederate Government would soon fall. The soldiers everywhere voted for Lincoln; and he carried every State in the Union except New Jersey, Delaware, and Kentucky. Lincoln's second inauguration took place on March 4, 1865.

Prisoners of war.—In the second year of the conflict (July, 1862) both sides signed an agreement to release on parole all prisoners taken in war. As the Confederates had more prisoners than the Federals in the first part of the war, this agreement was advantageous to the Union; but after the summer of 1863 conditions were reversed. The Federals, insisting that the slaves were free, urged the exchange of negro troops who had enlisted in the Northern army. This ended the exchange agreement. An effort was made by the Confederates in August, 1864, to exchange "officer for officer and man for man"; but the offer was declined by General Grant. He said: "It is hard on our men held in Southern prisons not to exchange them, but it is humanity to those left in the ranks to fight our battles. If we hold those caught, they amount to no more than dead men." As a result Southern men were confined in twenty prisons in the North, some of which were in charge of negroes; and the few prisons belonging to the Confederacy were overcrowded with Federal captives. It is estimated that over twenty-six thousand Confederates died in Northern prisons; and over twenty-two thousand Federals, in Southern prisons.

CHAPTER XCVI

THE WAR IN 1865—THE CONFEDERACY OVERCOME

Plan of campaign.—The next movement of the Federal army was to continue Sherman's raid from Savannah through the Carolinas, with a view to joining Grant against Lee. In the meantime Grant was to continue his effort to get in the rear of Lee's army by a flank movement.

Fort Sumter at the Close of the War

Joseph E. Johnston was placed in command of a Confederate force in the Carolinas with instructions to oppose Sherman's advance, while Lee continued to defend Richmond. But sickness and hunger reduced the effectiveness of the Confederate army. Their ranks grew thinner and thinner; and at the time for renewing the spring campaign in 1865, Lee had only about thirty-five thousand men with which to oppose a well-supplied Federal army of over one hundred and fifty thousand soldiers. When Grant's flank movements south of Petersburg threatened to cut off the only remaining source of Confederate supplies and to seize the only route of retreat, Lee wished to abandon Petersburg and Richmond, march southward to help Johnston against Sherman, and then unite the two armies against Grant. This plan had to be abandoned because of the inability of his half-starved horses to pull his cannon and wagons over the roads that had been softened by the winter rains.

Sherman in the Carolinas.—Sherman left Savannah to continue his destructive raid, February 1, 1865. He captured and burned Columbia, the capital of South Carolina (map, page 388). In reporting his march, he wrote:

"As I anticipated, fire and smoke and complete destruction marked our pathway. . . . Not a thing has been left to eat in many cases; not a horse, or an ox, or a mule, to work with. . . . It was not the intention of the commanding officers that the poor people should thus be stripped. But unprincipled stragglers . . . show no mercy or heart."

The Confederate forces quickly evacuated Charleston, and hastened to join Johnston in North Carolina. Into that State Sherman followed, and was confronted by Johnston; but after some fighting he occupied Goldsboro, North Carolina, seizing the railroad that ran south from Richmond. This cut off for Lee the most effective way of escape southward. About two weeks later the news of Lee's final surrender caused Sherman to stop his preparations for attacking Johnston, then at Raleigh, where he was hoping to be joined by Lee.

Evacuation of Petersburg and Richmond. — The last act in the great struggle between Lee's force and Grant's began on April 1, 1865. In his efforts to meet a flank movement of Grant's army, Lee was forced to spread out his lines until in places his men were seven yards apart. Grant then attacked at Five Forks, near Petersburg, a weak place in the Confederate line.

On the morning of this attack, as President Davis sat in his pew at church in Richmond, a Confederate soldier walked up the aisle and gave him a telegram. It was from General Lee, and contained the following words: "Richmond must be evacuated this evening." That night Lee withdrew his army from the city, and on the following day it was entered by the Federal troops.

General Lee made repeated attempts to reach Johnston's army in North Carolina, but found it impossible to cope with the overwhelming forces that were pressing him on every side. He then realized that a continuation of the bloody struggle would be useless.

The Surrender at Appomattox.—Grant and Lee met in a residence near Appomattox Court House to arrange the terms of the surrender. After the two great commanders had shaken hands and taken their seats, they spent a few minutes in general conversation. General Lee then asked for the terms of surrender. General Grant replied that the army should lay down arms and not take them up again during the war.

The terms were quickly written out and signed by Lee, no mention being made of the surrender of side arms or private property belonging to the Confederates. Grant, realizing that the Confederates would need their horses "to put in a crop to carry them and their families through the next winter," instructed his officers "to let every man of the Confederate army who claimed to own a horse or mule take the animal to his home." Lee then said that

ROBERT EDWARD LEE
From a negative made during the War of Secession
in the possession of H. P. Cook, Richmond, Virginia.
Pronounced by a member of his family as the best picture of General Lee.

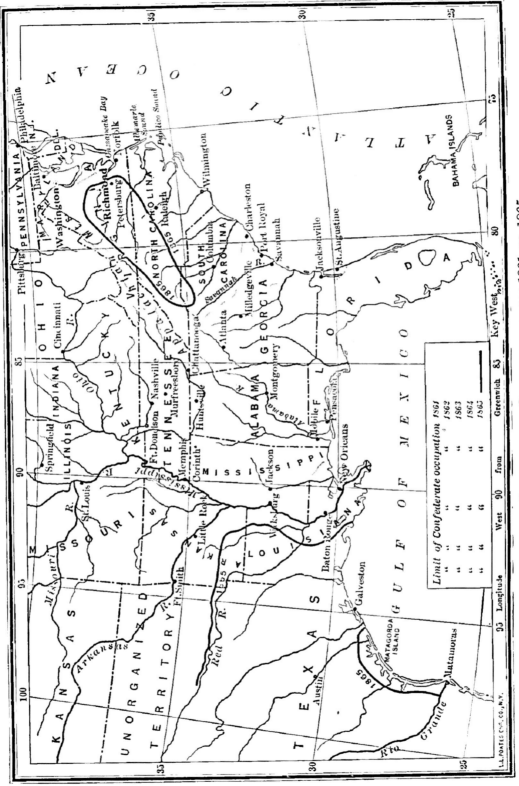

Areas of Confederate Occupation from 1861 to 1865

his men had been living for some days on parched corn exclusively, and that he would have to ask for food for them. This request met with a prompt and favorable response.

When General Lee's faithful soldiers saw that the end had come, they were overcome with grief. To his soldiers Lee said: "Men, we have fought through the war together. I have done the best I could for you. My heart is too full to say more."[1] On the following day (April 10, 1865) General Lee issued his farewell address to his army and returned to Richmond.

Two weeks later Johnston surrendered to Sherman, and with the final surrender of Kirby Smith in Texas (May 26, 1865) the last of the Confederate forces gave up the conflict.

Assassination of President Lincoln.—While the North was still rejoicing over Lee's surrender, the whole country was shocked to hear of the assassination of President Lincoln. He was shot in his box at Ford's Theater in Washington (April 14, 1865) by an actor, John Wilkes Booth, who thought that this wicked deed would be a great service to the South. Lincoln died on the following day. Booth escaped into Virginia, where he was finally killed.

---

[1] The parting scene between General Lee and his army was pathetic beyond description. We are told that when he appeared among his men, "every hat was raised, and the bronzed faces of the thousands of grim warriors were bathed with tears. As he rode slowly along the lines, hundreds of his devoted veterans pressed around the noble chief, trying to take his hand, touch his person, or even lay a hand upon his horse. The General then, with head bare and tears flowing freely down his manly cheeks, bade adieu to the army. In a few words he told the brave men who had been so true in arms to return to their homes and become worthy citizens."

The sudden and unexpected death of President Lincoln removed from the head of the Government the best friend of the bleeding South. At the time of his assassination he was engaged upon the consideration of a plan for a speedy return of the seceded States to the Union.

Capture of President Davis.—After the surrender of General Johnston, President Davis was captured in southern Georgia (May 10, 1865). He was carried to Fortress Monroe, where he was detained in prison for two years under an indictment for treason. He was finally released on bail, and a little later the trial was abandoned. During the greater part of his imprisonment he was harshly treated, irons being at one time placed on his ankles. These sufferings greatly increased the love that the people of the South already felt for their great chieftain.

CHAPTER XCVII

SOME FACTS ABOUT THE WAR

The enlistments of the war.—When the end of the struggle came, the Union army contained over a million soldiers, and the Confederate army about one hundred thousand. All told, the Union had in its service during the war over two million, three hundred thousand men; the Confederacy about six hundred thousand. In short, the North had nearly four times as many soldiers as had the South. When Lee started for Appomattox, his force numbered only about thirty-five thousand men; and when he surrendered, less than twenty-nine thousand men and boys were paroled by Grant. The Union navy closed the war with seven hundred vessels, of which sixty were ironclad. It was at this time the most powerful navy in the world.

In this desperate war over twenty-two hundred engagements were fought. The losses of the four years in killed and wounded on the battlefield were appalling; but the losses from diseases contracted by exposure and army life were even greater. The total deaths amounted to about three hundred and sixty thousand Federals and three hundred and twenty-five thousand Confederates. It may be safely stated that over a million men lost their lives by the war.[1]

Property losses.—The entire loss of the war in money and property is beyond computation.

The Federal Government spent seven billions one hundred and eighty millions of dollars actually paid into the treasury for war purposes. In addition to this, two billions eight hundred millions of dollars were collected by the sale of bonds. The debts of the Northern States and cities were increased, and the pensions of disabled soldiers multiplied. In view of these facts the war must have cost the Federal Government not less than twelve billions of dollars.

The cost of the war to the South cannot even be approximated. There are no figures as to money actually spent by the Confederate Government, and it is impossible to tell how much was raised by bond issues and Confederate notes, all of which became worthless.

Toward the close of the war, instead of trying to buy supplies and stores, the Confederate Government required all the farmers in the South to contribute one tenth of

---

[1] As has been fitly said, "The blood of the Nation was lastingly impoverished by that awful hemorrhage."

their produce for the support of the army; so that they levied a tax in kind. But this in no way lightened the expense of the Confederacy to the people of the South; for, as a rule, the men of the army practically supported themselves, receiving provisions and clothes from their homes. The destruction of property was appalling, to say nothing of the loss from the emancipation of four

THE MANSION AT LOWER BRANDON ON THE JAMES RIVER
Around the door the wall is riddled with bullet holes. Typical of the least of the war's damages in the South.

million slaves, who at a conservative estimate were worth at least ten billions of dollars. It seems very probable that the loss of the South in the war was at least twice as much as that of the North.

Right views of the conflict.—The war settled two important questions in American history:

1. The abolition of slavery. Though the first effort to free the slaves was made by proclamation as a war measure, the slaves were finally freed in a Constitutional

SACRIFICES AND MAKESHIFTS OF THE WAR 403

way. This was by the ratification of the Thirteenth Amendment in 1865. The whole country now rejoices over the removal of this great evil, which had been forced upon the South in colonial times.

2. The right of secession also was settled by the war. This was a natural result of the conflict, since the North fought to preserve the Union and won in the conflict.

Let no child who studies American history be ashamed of the part that his ancestors may have played in this memorable struggle. If he is a Southerner, let him be proud of his country. Let him feel that his ancestors were not traitors; for they fought for the Constitution as they understood it, and for State sovereignty as it was generally accepted at the time of the formation of the Union. They fought for a principle which they believed to be right, and which was finally destroyed by the power of armies. On the other hand, let every Northern child be proud of the part that his ancestors may have taken toward the preservation of the Union. It was a struggle which meant that the United States should not be divided in such a way that its influence would be lost in the history of the world.

There were incidents connected with the conduct of this terrible war, which one must condemn as harsh and even cruel; but they must not be cherished as representing the spirit of either side.

CHAPTER XCVIII

SACRIFICES AND MAKESHIFTS OF THE WAR

Military equipments. — The problem of arming and equipping the Southern armies was a serious one, since the South had few implements of warfare and little means of making them. Plantations and churches gave up their bells to be cast into cannon. The women of the Confederacy undertook to provide material for building ironclad ships by collecting broken pots, pans, and kettles. We are told that in the time of extreme need "the women even offered the hair of their heads to be sold abroad for arms."

An Old Blunderbus Pistol Used by a Confederate Soldier

Clothing.—Perhaps the most important service rendered by the women of the Confederacy was that of supplying clothing for use at home and in the armies. "The hum of the wheel and the thump of the loom were almost as ceaseless as the tick of the clock." Amid the enthusiasm of the earlier days of the war silk dresses had been converted into battle flags; woolen dresses and shawls were then used for making shirts for the soldiers; and carpets, for blankets. Linen curtains, sheets, and tablecloths were used for making lint and bandages for the wounded. These sacrifices reduced the home wardrobes to nothing. The dresses of the women were made of homespun. Buttons were made of wood. Hats were made of straw or palmetto leaves. As the supply of leather was exhausted, shoes were made either entirely of wood or of cloth fastened to wooden soles.

Food supply.—Confederate money depreciated so in value that $60 of it were worth only $1 in gold. Often a barrel of flour sold for $250 of Confederate money. Salt "was the most precious of all commodities," and at times it could not be bought at any price. In one instance thirty teacups of salt were given for thirty cords of wood.

SACRIFICES AND MAKESHIFTS OF THE WAR

Meal sold for $50, corn for $40, and oats for $25 a bushel. Beans were quoted at $50 and black-eyed peas at $45 a bushel. Brown sugar sold for $10; while coffee and tea brought $12 and $35 a pound, respectively. Bits of sweet potatoes, corn, rye, and okra seed well parched, or burnt molasses, were used as substitutes for coffee. Peanuts or "goobers" were parched, ground, and used as chocolate. Dried raspberry leaves or sage leaves were used for making tea. In some places honey was used instead of sugar or molasses in preserving fruit. Soda was often made from the ashes of corncobs. The earthen floors of old smokehouses were dug up; and, by a process of leaching and boiling, the accumulation of salt from the drippings of meat in former years was extracted for table use. A lady who experienced these privations said, "In every emergency there was one unfailing resource—if we could not find a substitute for any article, we could do without it; and this we did, with a fortitude born of the times."

Paper and stationery. — With the continuance of the blockade, printing paper became so scarce that most of the newspapers were reduced to half their usual size. At times they were forced to print the news on wall paper. As the type was badly worn and the ink was of an inferior quality, the papers did not present an attractive appearance.

A Southern gentleman tells us:

"Every available bit of paper, every page of old account books whether already written on one side or not, and even the fly leaves of printed volumes . . . [were] ferreted out and exhausted. Envelopes were made of scraps of wall paper and from the pictorial pages of old books, the white side out, stuck together in some cases with the gum that exudes from peach trees."

Results of the surrender.—There is no experience like the death of one's nation. A Mississippi lady says:

"When the news came suddenly that our country was *dead*, a deep hush fell into our lives, a wordless grief settled on our hearts, a dark foreboding clouded the future. . . . One glint of brightness came to us even in this dark time. The ever-present and all-pervading anxiety concerning the soldiers was ended. They were coming home to stay. The joyous welcome to the returning ones was subdued by the intense longing for those who would never come."

The effect upon the Confederate soldiers was forcibly told by Henry W. Grady, the great Georgia orator:

"Let me picture to you the foot-sore Confederate soldier, as . . . he turned his face southward from Appomattox in April, 1865. Think of him as ragged, half-starved, heavy-hearted, enfeebled by want and wounds. . . . He surrenders his gun, wrings the hands of his comrades in silence, pulls the gray cap over his brow and begins the slow and painful journey. . . . What does he find when he reaches the home he left so prosperous and beautiful? He finds his house in ruins, his farm devastated, his slaves free, his stock killed, his barns empty, his trade destroyed, his money worthless . . . his people without law . . . without money, credit, employment, material, or training; and besides all this, confronted with the gravest problem that ever met human intelligence . . . his liberated slaves.

"What does he do—this hero in gray with a heart of gold? Does he sit down in sullenness and despair? The soldier stepped from the trenches into the furrow; horses that had charged Federal guns marched before the plow, and the fields that ran red with human blood in April were green with the harvest in June."

VIII. PERIOD OF NATIONAL DEVELOPMENT

CHAPTER XCIX

THE PROBLEM OF RECONSTRUCTION

Johnson's Administration, 1865–69

National questions.—The downfall of the Confederacy brought forward several important questions which required immediate settlement. The most important of these were: (1) How should the Southern white people be treated? (2) What should be done with the negroes? (3) How should the seceded States be regarded? About these three questions turns the whole history of Reconstruction.

Treatment of the white people.—As far as the Southern soldiers were concerned, it was evident that most of them could not be punished in any way for their part in the war; for they were protected by the terms of the surrender. There was, however, much discussion in the North as to what punishment should be imposed upon the officers of the Confederate Government. But the only person who was held for trial was President Davis, and the case against him was dropped in 1869. Several members of his Cabinet and a number of the Southern governors also were imprisoned, but were soon released.

Rights of the negroes.—After the beginning of the war, slavery in the border States was abolished by the States themselves; in the Territories by Congress; and in most of the South by the Emancipation Proclamation, supplemented by the Thirteenth Amendment. This Amendment passed Congress in 1865 and was ratified by the States before the close of the year. The slaves were free, but the question of the position of the freedmen before the law still remained to be settled.

Relation of the Southern States to the Union.—The most important question of all was that of the relation of the Southern States to the Union. Were they still in the Union? Or had they, as the Southern people had said, seceded? The theory of the North, throughout the war, had been that the States could not secede; but a new view of the case was generally accepted by the North when the war closed. Four theories were advanced on the subject: (1) The "Presidential" theory, held by President Lincoln; by his successor, President Johnson; and by the Southern people when they accepted the results of the war, which was that the States were still in the Union and that, as soon as they had complied with certain conditions, they would be entitled to representation in Congress and the direction of their own governments. (2) The "State-suicide" theory, advanced by Senator Sumner,[1]

---

[1] Charles Sumner was born in Boston, Massachusetts, on January 6, 1811. He was educated at Harvard and became a lawyer and writer. He served for many years in the United States Senate and had a powerful influence, being a man of ability, although conceited and prejudiced to a great degree. He was the chief advocate in the Senate of a harsh policy toward the South and attempted by law to make the negroes the legal, social, and political equal of the white people. He died March 11, 1874.

THE PROBLEM OF RECONSTRUCTION

which held that the States had by secession lost statehood and were only Territories. (3) The "conquered-province" theory of Thaddeus Stevens, which regarded the South as a province subjugated by war and subject to the will of the conquerors. (4) The "forfeited-rights" theory, which was that the States were still a part of the Union, but had lost part of their rights. This was the one finally adopted.

Lincoln's efforts to restore Southern States to the Union.— President Lincoln in 1863 issued a proclamation which provided that when one tenth of the voters in any Southern State should take the oath of allegiance to the United States, they could set up a State government which he would recognize, and that they could send representatives to Congress. Citizens of Louisiana, Tennessee, and Arkansas accepted these terms; but Congress would not recognize them, receive their representatives, or count their vote for President in the election of 1864. This disagreement between Congress and the President was not settled when Lincoln was assassinated and Johnson became President.

President Johnson[1] was a Southerner, but had refused to go with his State when it seceded. He had been mili-

---

[1] Andrew Johnson was born in Raleigh, North Carolina, December 29, 1808. He was for some years a tailor in Raleigh and then moved to Greenville, Tennessee, where he worked at his trade and entered politics. He served in both houses of the Tennessee Legislature and as a member of Congress. He was then elected Governor of the State and at the close of his second term became United States Senator. He refused to go with his State when it seceded, and at the expiration of his term as Senator he became military governor of Tennessee. He was a man of natural ability and of sterling honesty and fearlessness in the performance of his duty; but he had little tact and made very bitter enemies, especially during his administration as President. He died July 31, 1875.

tary governor of Tennessee and as a War Democrat had been elected Vice President. He was very bitter against the South, and it was feared even in the North that he would be too severe. He, however, followed in the footsteps of his great predecessor and tried to bring about a lasting peace between the sections.

Johnson's plan.—Johnson promptly issued an amnesty proclamation that had been prepared by Lincoln, but altered it so as to exclude a larger number of persons from its benefits. He issued also proclamations appointing new governors for the Southern States and directing that they should establish temporary State governments, which should declare the ordinances of secession null and void, abolish slavery, and repudiate the debts incurred in carrying on the war.

ANDREW JOHNSON

The work of setting up new governments was pushed forward, not only by the President, but by the people of the South who were anxious to see order brought back so that they might begin to repair their ruined fortunes. The commerce of the South was resumed, the mails were carried, taxes collected, and the courts opened. The conventions met and provided for setting up permanent governments. This was done so promptly that when Congress met in December, 1865, representatives and senators were there from every Southern State except Texas.

Radical opposition.—In the meantime opposition to the President's plan of restoring the States to the Union was

THE PROBLEM OF RECONSTRUCTION

growing rapidly in the North. By the time Congress met, there were many who believed that the Southern States should not be restored until something had been done to protect the freedmen from the harsh laws that might be made by these States. Others wanted to see the South punished, and many were even afraid that the Democrats would make their way back into power. Congress therefore refused to admit the senators and representatives from the South, and thus took the question of Reconstruction into its own hands.

The "Black Codes."—In the South the people were striving to settle satisfactorily one of the most difficult problems that any people had ever faced. Four million slaves had become freedmen and were, theoretically at least, independent. Their freedom had been recognized by a great majority of the Southern people, who did not care to bring slavery back. But the negroes were still dependent upon the white people; for they had never had any opportunity to learn how to take care of themselves. In many cases they refused to work, and were becoming burdensome to the white people and the States. Vagrancy laws were therefore passed to make them find employment. Nearly all these laws were copied from those of Northern States. They declared that people who would not work for wages could be fined and forced to work out the fine.

To the North, ignorant of the true condition of affairs and prejudiced in favor of the negroes, these laws, or "Black Codes," as they were called, seemed unjust and like a return to slavery. Congress therefore determined to take some action that would protect the negroes.

CHAPTER C

CONGRESSIONAL RECONSTRUCTION

Johnson's Administration, 1865-69

The Freedman's Bureau.—The Freedman's Bureau was established in 1865. This bureau was under the control of the army. It protected many negroes in their rights, cared for their sick, and furnished food and clothing to the paupers. Yet it did much harm; it made the negroes look to the Government for support; it caused them to want to hold office; and it made them dislike the white people in the South, among whom they had to live and upon whom they were dependent. Some men connected with the bureau made thousands of the negroes believe that the United States was going to give to each one of them "forty acres and a mule," and many waited for the gift instead of going to work.

The Civil Rights Bill; the Fourteenth Amendment.—Early in 1866 (April 9th) the Civil Rights Bill was passed by Congress over the President's veto. This declared the negroes to be citizens and put them under Federal protection as far as their rights of citizenship were concerned. As this did not appear sufficient, the Fourteenth Amendment was then passed; and the lately seceded States were required to accept it before they could have place again in the Union. This amendment made the negroes citizens of the United States. It tried to force the States to give them the right to vote, by providing that whenever a State refused to allow negroes to vote, it should have fewer representatives in Congress. It also prohibited nearly all of the Southern leaders from holding office without a special act of Congress.

Tennessee was the only Southern State that accepted this amendment at first (1866). Her representatives were at once admitted to Congress. The States that refused to accept the amendment had to face still more severe conditions.

Quarrel of the President and Congress.—The President and Congress were now openly and bitterly hostile. Johnson angered the leaders in Congress by speaking harshly of them in his speeches. He hoped to arouse the people and defeat the radicals, as the extreme Republicans were called. But his hope was vain, as the elections of 1866 gave the radicals a two-thirds majority in Congress, and made it possible for them to override him in everything.

The Reconstruction Acts.—In March, 1867, Congress passed the Tenure-of-Office Act, which limited the President in his power of removing from office. . It then passed the first Reconstruction Act,[1] which divided the ten Southern States into five military districts, and placed each district under the command of a general of the United States army, whose duty it was to reconstruct the States in his district. The right to vote was denied to every man who had served the Confederacy after having taken, as an officeholder, an oath to support the Constitution of the United States. At the same time, in direct violation of the constitutions and laws of the States, and without any authority from the Constitution of the United States, all the negroes were allowed to vote. No attention was paid to the fact that in some of the Northern States the ballot had not been given to negroes.

---

[1] Two other Reconstruction Acts were passed later.

Conventions were then called to make new constitutions which had to guarantee to the negroes of all the Southern States equal rights with the white people. The constitution of each State had to be accepted by a majority of its voters, and the first Legislature of each State had to ratify the Fourteenth Amendment. If these conditions were fully met, the State would be allowed representation in Congress and the control of its own government. The men most responsible for these severe and unjustifiable acts of Congress were Thaddeus Stevens[1] and Charles Sumner. Stevens wanted to punish the South and strengthen the Republican Party; Sumner desired to make the negroes the political and social equals of the Southern white people.

Southern Reconstruction.—The conventions in nearly all the States were under the control of negroes and Northern white men who had come South to grow rich. These white men were known as "carpetbaggers," because it was said that they had no more property than they could bring in a carpetbag. In several States the negroes had clear majorities. The old constitutions were set aside; and new ones, like those of Northern States, were adopted.

Readmission of States.—By July, 1868, six States— North Carolina, South Carolina, Florida,[2] Alabama,

---

[1] Thaddeus Stevens was born in Vermont on April 4, 1792. He graduated at Dartmouth College and moved to Pennsylvania, where he became a lawyer. He served in the State Legislature and Constitutional Convention, and was for many years a member of Congress. He died August 11, 1868. He was a man of ability, but was bitterly partisan and was particularly hostile to the South. He was the leader of the radicals in Congress and more than any other man was responsible for the harshness of Reconstruction.

[2] A graphic account of the Florida Convention, which was presided over by a carpetbagger and composed principally of negroes, is given

Louisiana, and Arkansas—had met the conditions imposed by Congress and been restored to the Union. Virginia, Mississippi, and Texas at first refused to adopt new constitutions and were not admitted until 1870. Georgia adopted a constitution, but would not allow negroes to hold office. After being twice refused representation in Congress, that State finally met the conditions and was restored to the Union in 1871. But in the meantime the Fifteenth Amendment, intended to guarantee to negroes the right to vote, had been passed (1869) by Congress; and these last four States were required to ratify this as well as the Fourteenth Amendment before they were admitted. In 1868, the Fourteenth Amendment was declared adopted, and in 1870, the Fifteenth Amendment. No other amendments have since been added to the Constitution.

Impeachment of President Johnson.—The radicals had viewed President Johnson with suspicion for some time, fearing that he was going to interfere with Reconstruction.

---

by one of its members, a negro, from whose writings the following extract is taken: "Some of the lesser lights, ... who could neither read nor write, would be seen with both feet thrown across their desks, smoking cigars, while the convention was in session, and would often address the President: 'I rize to a pint off orter and deman' that the pages and Mess'gers put some jinal on my des.' The President would draw a long sigh and order journals to be carried and laid upon the desks of these eminent statesmen, who would seize them and go through the motions of reading them, perhaps upside down. ... These ridiculous scenes continued for two weeks or more, when a portion of the members seceded, leaving the convention without a quorum.

"On Monday, February 10th, between twelve and one o'clock at night, the seceding delegates ... returned to Tallahassee in a body, broke into the capitol, ... and proceeded to reorganize the convention. This reorganized convention perfected the constitution under which the State entered the Union."

As he vetoed every measure connected with the subject which came before him, their hatred of him was very intense and they commenced to plot his downfall. In 1867 an attempt was made to impeach him, but the plan failed. In 1868, however, their opportunity came. The President and Edward M. Stanton, Secretary of War, were not on good terms; and finally the President asked for his resignation. Stanton was the spy of the radicals in the Cabinet and refused to resign. Johnson at once removed him. But the Senate, under the Tenure-of-Office Act (page 414), would not consent to his removal; and he was reinstated only to be again removed. Stanton declined to surrender his office; and before he could be forced out, the House of Representatives impeached the President for high crimes and misdemeanors.

The impeachment trial was held, according to the Constitution, before the Senate with the Chief Justice of the Supreme Court presiding. After a long trial, marked by great partisanship, the President was acquitted, his enemies lacking only one vote of convicting him.

CHAPTER CI

FOREIGN AND DOMESTIC AFFAIRS

Johnson's Administration, 1865–69

The French in Mexico.—During the War of Secession Napoleon III of France, who was bent upon extending French influence, tried to set up in Mexico an empire dependent upon France. On the throne he placed Maximilian, Archduke of Austria, and established him in power by armed force and against the wish of the Mexicans. As soon as the war was over, the President turned his attention to this open and direct violation of the Monroe Doctrine (page 262) and forced the French to withdraw their troops. The empire at once fell, and Maximilian was captured by the Mexicans and shot.

The Atlantic Cable.—The Atlantic cable (page 326) was in 1866, after much discouragement to those promoting it, successfully laid and operated; and in consequence all parts of the world were benefited.

Purchase of Alaska.—Before the end of the war Russia had offered to assist the United States in case any European power entered the conflict in behalf of the Confederacy. In 1867 Secretary Seward concluded a treaty with Russia by which Alaska was ceded to the United States for $7,200,-000. This was so much more than it was thought to be worth that the valuation was generally considered a way of repaying Russia for her friendship when the nation was in distress.

Admission of Nebraska.—With the close of the war many emigrants went west of the Mississippi River. By 1867 the population of Nebraska had so increased that it was admitted to the Union, becoming the thirty-seventh State.

Campaign of 1868.—The campaign of 1868 had for its main issue whether the Congressional plan of Reconstruction should be continued. But there were several other important questions discussed as well. The Republicans indorsed the Reconstruction policy of Congress and favored the payment of United States bonds in gold. They nominated General U. S. Grant for President, and Schuyler Colfax of Indiana for Vice President. The Democrats denounced the Reconstruction measures and the way they had been carried out, demanded the complete pardon of all who had been connected with the Confederacy, and condemned the granting of public lands to railroads. This party nominated Horatio Seymour of New York for President, and General Frank P. Blair of Missouri for Vice President.

The campaign was very exciting, but the Republicans were too strong and Grant too popular for the Democrats to make great headway. Grant was elected by a large majority.

CHAPTER CII

CONGRESSIONAL RECONSTRUCTION A FAILURE

Grant's First Administration, 1869–73

The Pacific Railroad.—Grant's[1] administration began when the country was at the high tide of the commercial and industrial activity that followed the war. The country was rapidly growing in population and wealth and entering upon the wonderful industrial era that still continues.

The year 1869 saw the Atlantic and Pacific coasts joined by the completion of the Union Pacific Railroad, which had been chartered by Congress in 1862. This was of immense importance in commercial development.

---

[1] Ulysses Simpson Grant was born at Point Pleasant, Ohio, on April 27, 1822. He was educated at West Point and entered the army. He served in the Mexican War with gallantry, but resigned and engaged in business. When the War of Secession commenced, he raised a company of volunteers and rose to the chief command of the Union army. In 1866 he was raised to the full rank of General. In 1868 he was elected to the Presidency and served for two terms. In 1880 he was a candidate for the Republican nomination, but was defeated. He died July 23, 1885. He was a man of kindly and magnanimous nature and was popular with all classes and sections as a man and a soldier. He was a great general, but as President he was not a success.

CONGRESSIONAL RECONSTRUCTION A FAILURE 419

The Geneva award.—In Grant's first term of office, the board of arbitration to which the *Alabama* claims (page 358) had finally been referred met in Geneva to settle the question. The contention of the United States was acknowledged as valid, and England was forced to pay damages amounting to $15,000,000.

At the same time, a long-standing dispute between the two countries on the subject of the boundary between

Driving the Last Spike in the Laying of the Union Pacific Railroad

the United States and British Columbia was referred to the Emperor of Germany and settled by him. This method of settling international disputes commends itself to the world more and more as time passes.

Conditions in the South.—Although the North was prospering, the South had fallen on evil days. As a result of Reconstruction nearly all the States had fallen completely into the hands of those least fitted by character and ability to govern. The leaders of the Republican Party in the South were the "carpetbaggers," and associated with them were two classes of native whites: (1) Those who had joined the Republican Party from fear or with the hope of reward, called by their opponents "scalawags"; and (2) a much smaller number who, having opposed secession, had become Republicans from conviction. Supporting these white leaders and controlled by them were the ignorant and misguided negroes who had been led to abandon their best friends, only to be betrayed by their supposed allies. The negroes were organized by the "carpetbaggers" into a society known as the "Union League," which had been founded at the North before the close of the war to assist in preserving the Union. After the war it was brought South and used as a means of controlling the negro vote. Every community had one or more branches of the society; and they became centers of lawlessness, which made the negroes in the South dangerous to peace and prosperity.

Legislatures of Southern States.—In all the Southern States there were many negroes in the Legislature; in some States they were in a majority. As they were utterly unfit to vote and entirely incapable of making proper laws, the results were not only disgusting, but tragic for the downtrodden South. The party in power was honeycombed with dishonesty, and official extravagance and corruption were general. Millions and millions of dollars were stolen or wasted; the debt of the Southern States was increased by more than $150,000,000 through the issue of bonds for which the States received nothing; and taxation was increased until it was ruinous. Life and property were not safe, and crime and violence of every sort increased rapidly. The negroes, having tasted of idleness, in many cases refused to work, or, if they consented, were likely to break their contracts. Conditions soon became so bad that had it not been for the power of the United States the disgraceful State governments would have been forcibly overthrown by the better class of citizens.

The Ku Klux Klan.—The situation finally became unbearable, and the white people of the South were driven in self-defense to take some decided steps to regain control. In 1867 there appeared, first in Tennessee, and later all over the South, what was known as the Ku Klux Klan, or, as it was also called, "The Invisible Empire," a secret organization used first for protection against violence and later for political purposes. It was made up of small groups, or "dens"; and no one but the leaders knew who were members of other dens. Long processions of white, shrouded figures on white-veiled horses, with horrible badges and mysterious signs and symbols, would suddenly appear and throw the negroes into an agony of superstitious terror. They visited evil-doers, white as well as black, with certain and severe punishment. Night after night they rode, seeking for those they had condemned, and carrying out their decisions even to administering at times the death penalty. By these means they did much to check the wrongs that the South was enduring. In the course of time reckless people were admitted into the Klan and caused it to commit atrocities. The best men then withdrew from the Klan and helped to put it down.

The "Force Acts."—The terror aroused by the Ku Klux, and the false accounts of its violence, which reached the North, led Congress to pass the "Force Acts." These put elections under the control of the Federal Government and provided severe punishment for interfering in any way with the negroes' voting, and furthermore allowed the President to suspend the writ of *habeas corpus* when he thought it necessary. The trouble continued, and Federal troops were sent to many parts of the South to preserve order. A large number of persons were arrested and tried, and some were fined and imprisoned.

Overthrow of Reconstruction.—By 1875 the native whites were in control of the governments in most of the Southern States, and the "carpetbaggers" had been driven out. South Carolina, Florida, and Louisiana, however, because of the interference of the Federal Government, were still in the hands of the Republicans; and their situation was terrible beyond description.

The campaign of 1872.—In 1872 there were signs of a serious division in the Republican Party. The Northern Democrats, who had acted with the Republicans during the war, now that the Union was safe, began to return to their own party. In addition many Republicans were dissatisfied with the administration of Grant because of the corruption that was beginning to appear, and were disgusted with the situation in the South. These classes united in what was called the Liberal Republican Party, which held a convention in Cincinnati in 1872. After adopting a platform demanding amnesty to the late Confederates, universal suffrage, and the reform of the civil service, it nominated for President, Horace Greeley, the founder and editor of the New York *Tribune*, and for Vice President, B. Gratz Brown of Missouri. The Democratic Convention indorsed this platform and the candidates, hoping that by taking advantage of the division in the Republican Party it might defeat the Republican candidate.

The Republicans nominated Grant for President, and

Henry Wilson of Massachusetts for Vice President. The Prohibitionists also put a ticket in the field, but the struggle was between Grant and Greeley. It was soon evident that the latter had no chance of winning; and when the election came off, he carried only six States. Broken down by disappointment and the labors of the campaign, and prostrated by the death of his wife, Greeley died before the electors met.

CHAPTER CIII

A PERIOD OF DISTRESS AND CORRUPTION

Grant's Second Administration, 1873–77

The panic of 1873.—Ever since the war there had been great commercial and industrial activity in the Northern and Western States, and business increased to such an extent that it was more than the country could handle with its limited carrying facilities. As a result, over twenty-five thousand miles of railroads were built in four years, which was more than the population warranted. The prosperity of railroads depends largely upon the population of the territory through which they pass, and many of these roads went through parts of the country that were still only sparsely settled. To carry out these enterprises one hundred millions of dollars of greenbacks had been withdrawn from circulation, thus greatly reducing the supply of money. Another cause increased the shortage of money. In 1871 the imports of the country had so far exceeded the exports that over $50,000,000 in coin left the United States to pay foreign creditors. Fires in

Chicago in 1871 and in Boston in 1872 had caused great losses.

As a consequence of these conditions, business became unsettled; and when in September, 1873, the important firm of Jay Cooke & Co. failed, a great panic followed. During the next year ten thousand business houses failed to the amount of $225,000,000, and by the end of three years the amount had reached $775,000,000. The railroad losses were probably even greater. The failure of the banks carried distress all over the country, and the shutting down of factories threw thousands of men out of employment and left them without means of support.

Demonetization of silver.—In February, 1873, a law was passed that dropped the old silver dollar from the list of coins to be made at the mints free to those who sent the silver there for that purpose. As no silver dollars had been coined for a long time, and none were in circulation, nobody at that time objected to the change. But later, when the silver movement began, this act was called by some, "the crime of '73." The gold dollar thus became the sole standard of value. Now only gold is coined at the mint "free" to the owners of the metal.

Scandals.—It became apparent that many members of Congress had been bribed by the Crédit Mobilier, a corporation formed to build the Union Pacific Railroad. The Whisky Ring, too, was detected. It had been formed by Government officials and distillers, and had defrauded the Government of many million dollars before it was discovered in 1875 and broken up. A number of its leaders were tried and convicted. Secretary of War Belknap was impeached for corruption in office; but before he could be tried by the Senate, President Grant,

A PERIOD OF DISTRESS AND CORRUPTION

who was his warm friend, accepted his resignation, and the matter was dropped. Congress passed the "Salary Grab" Act by which the salaries of Congressmen and of certain high officials were raised from the beginning of their terms of office. Public opinion was so aroused by this that the act was soon repealed. Finally, among the many charges brought against the President, was one that he had put many of his own relatives in office.

Indian troubles.—The rapid settlement and development of the West brought with it fresh troubles with the Indians. Those

CUSTER'S LAST FIGHT

who had already been settled on reservations were cheated by the Government agents and treated very badly. Grant did something to improve Indian affairs, but it was too late to prevent two serious uprisings. The Modocs in Oregon, to avoid being sent to a new reservation, went on the warpath and murdered General

Canby. They were conquered later and sent to Indian Territory. In 1876 the Sioux Indians rose against settlers who had gone among them, seeking for gold. In the war that followed, General Custer was killed; and all his force, except one man, was destroyed by a band of Indians under Sitting Bull. After some time the Sioux were subdued and Sitting Bull fled to Canada.

Elections of 1874.—The corruption in the Government and the panic of 1873 led to a Democratic victory in the elections of 1874, by which the House of Representatives had a Democratic majority of about seventy.

Resumption of specie payments.—In 1875 Congress passed a law providing that after January 1, 1879, the Secretary of the Treasury should redeem in coin all paper money presented at the Treasury. Immediately paper money in circulation had an equal value with coin, and public confidence was greatly increased.

Admission of Colorado; the Centennial Exposition.—In 1876 Colorado became the thirty-eighth State of the Union. The same year a great world's fair was held in Philadelphia to celebrate the one hundredth anniversary of the signing of the Declaration of Independence. Nearly all the States and many foreign countries sent exhibits, which were great object lessons of progress to the thousands who viewed them.

The *Virginius* affair.—For some years the Cubans had been in revolt against the tyrannical rule of Spain. A horrible war had been carried on, marked with great cruelty on both sides. The United States was neutral, but many people in the country sympathized with the Cubans and tried to help them by carrying them supplies of war. In 1873 the *Virginius*, a vessel engaged in

A PERIOD OF DISTRESS AND CORRUPTION

this intercourse, was captured by a Spanish gunboat on the high seas; and fifty-three of its crew, including eight Americans, were shot. Spain promptly paid a large indemnity, and war was averted.

The campaign of 1876. — It was evident from the election of 1874 that the Republicans would have to make a great struggle to maintain their power, and the Democrats had high hopes of victory in the next Presidential campaign. Four parties had tickets in the field — the Prohibition, the Greenback, the Republican, and the Democratic; but, as usual, the struggle was between the two last-named parties. The Republicans indorsed Grant's administration, favored a protective tariff, and nominated Rutherford B. Hayes of Ohio for President, and William A. Wheeler of New York for Vice President. The Democrats nominated Samuel J. Tilden[1] of New York for President, and Thomas A. Hendricks of Indiana for Vice President, and adopted a strong reform platform. Tilden was a particularly suitable candidate for this platform, for he had won distinction in exposing and bringing to punishment the "Tweed Ring" in New York City, which had robbed the government of that city of millions of dollars.

The whole campaign was one of great activity and excitement. The Republicans were fighting with the

---

[1] Samuel J. Tilden was born at New Lebanon, New York, in 1814. He was educated at Yale and at New York University and became a lawyer. He was a member of the State Legislature and the Constitutional Convention of New York and, after playing an important part in breaking up the "Tweed Ring," was elected Governor of the State. His able and honest administration secured for him the Democratic nomination for the Presidency. He died August 4, 1886. He was a man of sterling character, and is to be remembered as a great reformer in a period in which great reforms were needed.

odds against them, and the Democrats were determined to win.

The Contested Election.—When the election was finally over, it was generally thought that the Democrats had been successful; but the Republicans claimed the victory, insisting that they had really carried the three States, South Carolina, Louisiana, and Florida, in which there were disputes as to the returns.[1] In Louisiana and Florida the returns gave large Democratic majorities. Mr. Tilden had beyond any dispute one hundred and eighty-four

THE ELECTORAL VOTE IN 1876

electoral votes, which was only one less than the number required for election. In the three States mentioned, the election returns were in the hands of returning boards that

---

[1] There was also one disputed elector in Oregon. The State went Republican, but one of the electors was ineligible for the position. The Democrats claimed that a Democratic elector should therefore be returned in this place.

had great powers in counting the vote. The returning boards, which were openly and notoriously corrupt, after trying without success to sell the election to the Democrats, threw out votes enough to reverse the result, on the ground that they were fraudulent, and declared for the Republican electors. The fraud was so evident that the Democrats protested vigorously.

The Electoral Commission.—The Senate was Republican at this time, and the House of Representatives Democratic; and as the electoral vote, under the Constitution, must be counted in the presence of both Houses, there was little hope of any agreement. The debates on the subject were very fierce, and for a time it looked as if civil war would result from the situation; but at length a law was passed providing for the creation of an Electoral Commission to decide the dispute. It was composed of five Senators, five Representatives, and five justices of the Supreme Court. Eight were Republicans, and seven were Democrats. Every question that came before the commission was decided by a strict party vote, and Hayes was declared elected.

CHAPTER CIV

SECTIONAL FEELING BEGINS TO DIE

Hayes's Administration, 1877–81; Garfield's and Arthur's Administration, 1881–85

Withdrawal of troops from the South.— Hayes[1] had said that if he became President, he would withdraw the

---

[1] Rutherford B. Hayes was born in Delaware, Ohio, October 4, 1822. He was educated at Kenyon College and became a lawyer. He served

Federal troops from the South. Soon after his inauguration, therefore, he withdrew from the "carpetbag" governments the support of the administration; and, as a result, the Republican State governments in South Carolina and Louisiana quickly gave way to governments chosen by the people. Florida had already redeemed herself, and now the people of all the Southern States were once more in control of their own affairs. In 1879 the use of the Federal troops at the polls was forbidden by law. Prosperity came, and the new South began to rise from the ruins of the old.

RUTHERFORD B. HAYES

As a result of the evil government they had endured during, and immediately following, Reconstruction, the Southern States became solidly Democratic; and they have kept solidly together in politics as a guarantee against the return of the negro to power. Additional steps to prevent such a thing have been taken by the adoption in most of the Southern States of new constitutions, beginning with the Mississippi constitution of 1890. These constitutions in one way or another prevent ignorant men, both white and black, from enjoying the right to vote.

in the War of Secession, rising to the rank of brigadier general. Later he was a member of Congress, and Governor of Ohio for two terms. He became President in 1877 and served one term. He was a good man, but not of unusual ability. Because of the doubt as to his election, he was handicapped during his whole term and was not considered for a second nomination. Hayes died January 17, 1893.

The benefit to both white people and negroes has been very great.

Financial matters.—The resumption of specie payments was to become effective in 1879, and the men who wanted more money in the country turned to silver as their hope. They secured the passage of the Bland Act (1878) which provided for the coinage of not less than two million dollars of silver per month, the weight of the silver dollar to be sixteen times that of a gold dollar. Gold was still the standard, but silver was accepted at its face value.

Labor troubles.—The growth and development of industry in the period following the war led to the organization of great corporations, which grew with wonderful rapidity. To protect the interests of the laboring classes, labor unions were organized; and differences between capital and labor soon developed. These differences often resulted in disastrous quarrels, usually taking the form of "strikes." That is, the laborers refused to work, or allow others to do so, until their demands were granted.

During the administration of Hayes, railroad strikes were frequent because wages were being reduced along with freight rates. The worst of these was at Pittsburg in 1877, when many lives were lost and millions of dollars' worth of property was destroyed. The State was unable to check the disorder, and Federal troops had to be called out. They soon ended the trouble.

Campaign of 1880.—In 1880 the Republicans were afraid that Hayes would be defeated because of the general feeling in the country that he had not been legally elected. General Grant was a candidate for the nomination, but the Republicans nominated General James A. Garfield of Ohio for President, and Chester A. Arthur of

New York for Vice President. The Democrats passed over Tilden and nominated General Winfield S. Hancock of Pennsylvania, and Edward S. English of Indiana. The Greenback and Prohibition parties also nominated tickets. Garfield and Arthur were elected.

JAMES A. GARFIELD

Death of Garfield.—On March 4, 1881, Garfield[1] was inaugurated as President. One of the great evils of the time in government was the spoils system (page 273) by which wholesale removals from office accompanied every change of Presidents. Garfield was besieged by applicants for office and in July, 1881, was shot and mortally wounded by a disappointed and half-crazed office seeker. The President died in September and was succeeded by Vice President Arthur,[2] who proved himself an honest but not a brilliant President.

Civil-service reform.—In the death of Garfield the American people had an object lesson of what the spoils

---

[1] James A. Garfield was born in Orange, Ohio, November 19, 1831. He was graduated at Williams College and became a lawyer. He was a member of the legislature of Ohio for a number of years. He served in the Union army in the War of Secession and became a major general. After the war he was elected to Congress and later became United States Senator. He was an able legislator, but had not shown himself a statesman of the first rank. He died September 19, 1881.

[2] Chester A. Arthur was born at Fairfield, Vermont, in 1830. He was graduated at Union College, then taught, then practiced law. In 1862, he was Inspector-General and Quartermaster-General of New York troops. Later he was Collector of the Port of New York City. He died in 1886.

system might do; and as a result the Pendleton Bill was passed providing for the examination of candidates for certain offices by a Civil Service Commission appointed by the President, and for the appointment of those best qualified. The list of offices coming under the civil service has been extended from time to time, always with good results. Now, not so many officers as formerly are chosen because of party service.

Tariff discussion.—After 1879 a surplus began to accumulate in the Treasury, and the question of the reduction of the tariff arose in consequence. Many prominent Republicans, among them President Garfield, had favored reduction. In 1882 Congress authorized a commission to draw up a bill for the purpose. But Congress amended the bill until the duties, instead of being lowered, were, on an average, decidedly raised.

Engineering feats.—One of the most remarkable engineering attempts of the world was brought to a successful conclusion by the completion of the Brooklyn Bridge from Manhattan Island to Brooklyn, in 1883. It began a new epoch in bridge construction.

Chester A. Arthur

Another notable work, completed about this time, was the Washington Monument, the highest stone structure in the world. It is a shaft five hundred and fifty-five feet high and is a noble tribute to the Nation's greatest son.

Campaign of 1884.—During the administrations of Garfield and Arthur there were factional fights going on in the Republican Party, which did much to weaken it. There was also a feeling in the country that the party had been so long in power that it had grown careless of the rights of the people. Consequently, the Democrats were very hopeful of victory.

The Republicans nominated James G. Blaine [1] of Maine and John A. Logan of Illinois. The Democrats chose Grover Cleveland of New York, and Thomas A. Hendricks of Indiana. This campaign marks the end of the war issues. The attention of the people was directed thereafter to other matters, such as revenue, expenditure, and the protective tariff. Two other tickets, presented by the Greenback-Labor-Anti-Monopoly and the Prohibition parties, attracted no particular attention.

The campaign was one of great bitterness, and many personal charges were made against the candidates. Cleveland was supported by many independent Republicans called "Mugwumps," who refused to support Blaine. The election was very close, and the result was in doubt for some days; but New York gave Cleveland a small majority and decided the contest in his favor. For the first time since 1856 the Presidential candidate of the Democratic Party had been elected.

---

[1] James G. Blaine was born in Washington County, Pennsylvania, January 31, 1830. He was graduated at Washington College and, removing to Maine, became a newspaper editor. He served for some time in the State Legislature and was then elected to Congress. He was speaker of the House of Representatives and Republican leader in Congress, and later, for two terms, a member of the Senate. He was Secretary of State under Garfield and Harrison, being one of the ablest of those who have filled that position. In 1884 he was defeated for the Presidency because many Republicans deserted his standard, the reason being his connection with a number of scandals during Grant's administration. He died January 27, 1893.

CHAPTER CV

DEMOCRATIC TRIUMPHS AND DEFEATS

Cleveland's First Administration, 1885–89; Harrison's Administration, 1889–93

Important legislation.—Although the Republicans still held the Senate, and could thus prevent the Democrats from carrying out any policy to which Cleveland had pledged himself, several important laws were passed during the administration of President Cleveland.[1]

A new law was enacted (1886) arranging the succession to the Presidency in case of the death of both President and Vice President. It provided that the Secretary of State, if eligible, should succeed; or, if not, the next Cabinet officer, considered in the order of the creation of the executive departments.

GROVER CLEVELAND

The Interstate Commerce Commission was established

---

[1] Grover Cleveland was born in Caldwell, New Jersey, March 18, 1837. He became a lawyer and settled in Buffalo, New York. He was sheriff of Buffalo and won reputation as a man of unflinching courage in the performance of his duty. He was reform Mayor of Buffalo and reform Governor of New York. His successful administration of the latter office secured for him the Democratic nomination for the Presidency in 1884, and he was elected. He was defeated in 1888, but was again the Democratic nominee in 1892, when he was elected. His devotion to duty and his firmness in the performance of it won for him the admiration and respect of the whole country; and after his retirement from office, his advice was welcomed by all his fellow-countrymen. He died June 24, 1908.

in 1887. Its duty is to pass on the rates charged for freight and passengers carried from one State to another.

In order that there might never be a dispute about the election of President such as the one in 1876 (page 429), a law was passed (1887) providing that each State should be the judge of its own electoral vote.

For the relief of the laboring classes, particularly on the Pacific coast, who were suffering from competition with cheap Chinese labor, a law was passed (1888) which greatly limited Chinese immigration. In 1892 a still more severe law on the subject was passed. The laws were of some benefit, but many Chinese came in through British America. The smuggling in of Chinese became a profitable industry.

With a somewhat similar intent, a law was enacted (1885) forbidding the importation of laborers who had already entered into contracts for labor.

Strikes.—The labor conditions in the country attracted much attention during this whole period. Several serious riots occurred, the most serious being in Chicago in 1886, when an anarchist outbreak, incited by foreigners, took place. A dynamite bomb was thrown which killed seven policemen. Several of the anarchists were convicted, and four were executed. In the same year there was a strike on the railroads leading southwest from St. Louis, which tied up traffic for some time. These outbreaks, signs of further trouble to come, were viewed with alarm by the people of the country.

The new navy.—At the beginning of Cleveland's administration, the navy of the United States was an object of the world's contempt. But under the direction of his able Secretary of the Navy, William C. Whitney, the building of new ships was pushed forward, and the movement was started which by the close of the century gave the country a powerful navy.

A Battleship of the Atlantic Fleet

Civil-service reform.—Cleveland was a firm believer in the reform of the civil service; and because he would not remove all Republican officeholders, he offended many members of his own party. Because he removed some, the Independents who had supported him were disappointed and displeased. He also gained the hostility of many of the Union veterans by vetoing a large number of pension bills that were unwarranted and extravagant. His disregard of the rules that usually govern politicians made him some bitter enemies; but he won the respect of the people of the country, regardless of political faith.

The tariff question.—Toward the close of Cleveland's administration, the discussion of the tariff was renewed by the action of the President. The National debt had been greatly reduced, and almost all the war taxes had been repealed. The tariff produced much more revenue than was needed to pay the interest on the debt and the running expenses of the Government, and it seemed to many that the time had come when the tariff should be reduced. But manufacturers had demanded the protection of American industries, and nothing had been done in the way of reduction. The surplus produced a very serious condition; for more and more money was thus being drawn from circulation, and Congress was tempted to extravagant appropriations.

So Cleveland in his annual message to Congress in 1887 proposed that the tariff should be lowered and the surplus thereby reduced. The Mills Bill, which provided for a reduction, then passed the House; but it was rejected by the Republican Senate, and thus became the main issue of the next campaign.

Campaign of 1888. — The Democrats renominated Cleveland and chose Allen G. Thurman of Ohio, as their candidate for Vice President. The Republicans nominated Senator Benjamin Harrison[1] of Indiana, the grandson of President William Henry Harrison, and Levi P. Morton of New York. Three small parties also had Presidential tickets. The Republicans wanted a high tariff, and the Democrats a low tariff. Cleveland received a majority of the popular vote, but Harrison was elected. He was inaugurated March 4, 1889.

Some important laws.—The Republicans secured a majority in both houses of Congress in the election of 1888, and were therefore able to put their policies into effect. Several important measures were enacted into law.

The Republican plan of a high tariff to protect home

---

[1] Benjamin Harrison was born at North Bend, Ohio, August 20, 1833. He was graduated from Miami University, and later practiced law in Indianapolis. He served as an officer throughout the War of Secession. He was United States Senator, 1881-87. He died March 13, 1901.

DEMOCRATIC TRIUMPHS AND DEFEATS

manufactures was carried out in the so-called "McKinley Bill." A new pension law greatly increased the amount paid by the Government to the Union veterans. A law known as the "Sherman Anti-Trust Law" was passed as a means of controlling the "trusts" or great business organizations. A law called the "Sherman Act" amended the Bland Act (page 431), so that the Government, instead of coining silver money, had to purchase 4,500,000 ounces of silver every month, and, keeping it in the Treasury, issue on it paper money called silver certificates.

BENJAMIN HARRISON

New States.—In 1889 the States of North Dakota, South Dakota, Montana, and Washington were admitted to the Union. A year later Idaho and Wyoming were received, making a total of forty-four States. The Territory of Oklahoma was also set off from Indian Territory and opened to white settlers, who immediately poured in by thousands to take possession of the rich lands.

A new party.—The Sherman Act was designed to prevent the passage of a bill, providing for the free coinage of silver, which had been stopped in 1873 (page 424). Free coinage means the privilege to anyone of carrying bullion to the mint and receiving its weight in coined money. The bill was introduced by members of the People's Party, a new political organization formed by a combination of the farmers of the West and the South, who had some years before organized the Farmers' Alliance. Prices of agricultural products were low, and the farmers believed that this would raise them. Certain elements of the Labor Party in the silver-producing States of the West had also advocated the free coinage of silver. The silver miners thought that free coinage would raise silver to its old price, while the other members in the party wanted more money. In 1890 they elected a number of members of Congress and carried several States, but the Democrats swept the country and secured a large majority in the House.

Campaign of 1892.—Three parties strove for supremacy in 1892. The Democrats nominated Cleveland for the third time and put Adlai E. Stevenson of Illinois on the ticket with him. The Republicans nominated Harrison and Whitelaw Reid of New York. The People's Party, or Populists, nominated James B. Weaver of Iowa, and James G. Field of Virginia. The chief issue between the Republicans and the Democrats was the tariff; but the People's Party had a number of new demands in their platform, such as the free and unlimited coinage of gold and silver, Government ownership of railroads and telegraph lines, the lending of money by the Government to individuals on the security of farm products, and the repeal of the tax on State banks (page 374). The People's Party also proposed to tax the incomes of the wealthy.

The Democrats carried the country by a large majority, Cleveland receiving 277 electoral votes, Harrison 145, and Weaver 22. For the first time since the war the Democrats had the President and a majority in both houses of Congress.

CHAPTER CVI

DEMOCRATS IN CONTROL OF THE GOVERNMENT

Cleveland's Second Administration, 1893–97

The panic of 1893.—Soon after Cleveland's inauguration there was a panic, due partly to the prospect of a reduction of the tariff, and still more to the small volume of money in circulation. The price of silver had gone down, and the gold reserve in the United States Treasury had fallen below the amount required by law. So many notes had been issued in payment for silver that many persons believed the Government would never redeem them; and this caused uneasiness, which soon brought on the panic. Over three hundred banks failed or were forced to suspend payment, and this caused in turn the failure of thousands of business houses. Business stopped, factories were closed, and many thousands of people were left without employment.

Repeal of the Sherman Act.—President Cleveland at once called an extra session of Congress; and upon his recommendation the Sherman Act (page 439) was repealed, but only after bitter opposition by the silver forces in Congress. Business recovered very slowly, and there was much distress. Labor agitation of an intense kind followed. In 1894 a man named Coxey organized a body of unemployed men to march to Washington to present petitions to Congress. "Coxey's Army," or a small part of it, finally reached Washington, but did nothing of importance there. The repeal of the Sherman Act produced a division in the Democratic ranks, and many people in the South and the West inclined toward the People's Party.

The Wilson Bill.—The chief issue of the campaign had been the tariff, and the Democrats were pledged to its reduction. But the great panic for some time prevented its consideration. In December, 1893, the question was taken up; and the House passed the Wilson Bill, providing for a reduction of the tariff. It also included an income tax, added to satisfy the West and the South, but later declared unconstitutional by the Supreme Court. The bill was greatly altered by the Senate and was so unsatisfactory to President Cleveland that he allowed it to become a law only to carry out the party's pledge, refusing to sign it. It was a failure and did nothing to relieve business conditions; and as the Government needed more money, bonds had to be issued to the amount of $250,000,-000. Owing to the general dissatisfaction in the country, the Republicans were victorious in the congressional elections of 1894.

Strikes.—As a result of the hard times and on account of the troubles between capital and labor, several serious strikes occurred. The one attracting most notice began in the shops of the Pullman Car Company at Chicago (1894). It was caused by a decrease in wages and was followed by a general railroad strike in Chicago. Trains were not allowed to run. Traffic was stopped, and serious destruction of property occurred, accompanied by many other acts of violence. President Cleveland at once sent Federal troops to protect the United States mails, and order was restored.

Hawaii.—In Harrison's administration a revolution had occurred in the Sandwich Islands, by which Queen Liliuokalani was deposed and a republic established. Americans living in the island of Hawaii had done much to cause this outbreak, and marines from American war vessels had protected them and made it possible for the revolution to succeed. The new Government had induced President Harrison to make a treaty of annexation, which was before the Senate when Cleveland went into office for the second time. President Cleveland at once withdrew the treaty until an investigation could be made. He was finally convinced that the United States Navy had been wrongfully used in the uprising, and he declined to resubmit the treaty.

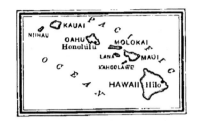

THE HAWAIIAN ISLANDS

The World's Columbian Exposition.—In 1893 there was held at Chicago an international exposition to celebrate the four hundredth [1] anniversary of the discovery of America by Columbus. It far surpassed anything of the kind hitherto attempted. It lasted for six months and was viewed by more than twenty-seven million persons.

Relations with Great Britain.—A second trial of arbitration as a means of settling international disputes was made by the United States and Great Britain in 1893. The question of the right to control the seal fisheries in Bering Sea, claimed by the United States in order to protect the seals, was decided by a board of arbitration against the United States. But the purpose of contention of the United States was practically won, as the board made rules that protected the seals.

For many years Great Britain and Venezuela had been disputing the boundary line between British Guiana and

---

[1] The Exposition could not be completed by 1892.

Venezuela. Great Britain steadily encroached upon Venezuela, and refused to submit the question to arbitration. Finally, Venezuela appealed to the United States. After a fruitless attempt to induce Great Britain to consent to arbitration, President Cleveland sent a message to Congress (1895) in which he held that the United States under the Monroe Doctrine must resist any encroachment by Great Britain and asked the appointment of a commission to investigate the matter. The commission was appointed. But before it began its work, Great Britain consented to arbitration, and the question was settled satisfactorily. For some time it seemed as if there might be war between England and the United States; but the people of the country, as a whole, heartily approved the President's action.

The admission of Utah.—In 1896 Utah, having pledged itself to suppress polygamy (page 296), was admitted to the Union as the forty-fifth State.

Campaign of 1896.—The chief issue of the campaign of 1896 was the money question. The Democratic Party, which was sharply divided on this question, nominated for President William J. Bryan[1] of Nebraska, a young man who was comparatively unknown, though he had served in Congress. His nomination was largely the result of an eloquent speech in the convention. Arthur Sewall of Maine was nominated for Vice President. The platform demanded the free and unlimited

---

[1] William Jennings Bryan was born at Salem, Illinois, March 19, 1860. He was educated at Illinois College and the Union College of Law. He moved to Nebraska and became a lawyer and was for a short time a member of Congress. He has been the nominee of the Democratic Party for the Presidency three times—in 1896, 1900, and 1908. He is the editor of *The Commoner*, a weekly newspaper of Lincoln, Nebraska.

coinage of silver. The People's Party indorsed Bryan, but nominated Thomas E. Watson of Georgia for Vice President. The Gold Democrats nominated General John M. Palmer of Illinois and General Simon B. Buckner of Kentucky. The Republicans chose William McKinley of Ohio and Garrett A. Hobart of New Jersey and adopted a platform favoring a protective tariff and a gold standard.

A heated campaign followed in which the financial and business circles rallied to the support of the Republican Party and contributed an enormous campaign fund. McKinley [1] was elected by a substantial majority.

CHAPTER CVII

THE WAR WITH SPAIN

McKinley's First Administration, 1897–1901

The Cuban situation.—In 1897 the situation in Cuba demanded the attention of the country. The colonial policy of Spain had always been notoriously harsh and grasping and had not improved since the time when her South American colonies had been driven to successful revolt eighty years earlier. The island of Cuba had received particularly harsh treatment, and its inhabitants had revolted again and again. One revolt began in 1868 and lasted ten years, ceasing only when Spain promised

---

[1] William McKinley was born at Piqua, Ohio, April 12, 1827. He served in the War of Secession with gallantry and rose to the rank of major. He then became a lawyer and was for many years a prominent member of Congress. He was, as chairman of the Committee of Ways and Means, author of the tariff law that bore his name. During the time that he was President of the United States he won the admiration, respect, and affection of the whole American people; and his death on September 14, 1901, caused profound regret throughout the country.

reforms. But this promise was never carried out. In 1895 the Cubans, directed by a group of their fellow-countrymen in New York, called the "Cuban Junta," again rose in revolt. Spain attempted to suppress the uprising with a cruelty that put civilization to shame. Much sympathy for Cuba was felt and expressed in the United States, and much private aid was given the revolutionists; but the United States Government remained neutral.

WILLIAM McKINLEY

Loss of the *Maine*.—In the meantime American property in Cuba was being destroyed; and American citizens were being badly treated by the Spanish officers, who resented the American sympathy for Cuba. In 1897 Congress finally appropriated $50,000 to relieve suffering in the island, and in 1898 the battleship *Maine* was sent to Havana to protect American interests. On the night of February 15th the vessel was destroyed by an explosion, and two hundred and sixty-six of her crew perished. Instantly the people of the United States were convinced that the Spaniards were responsible for the blowing up of the *Maine* and demanded war. But before anything definite was done, an investigation was made by a board appointed for the purpose. The board of inquiry found that the destruction of the vessel was due to the explosion of a mine, but went no further. Fitzhugh Lee, our able consul-general in Havana at the time, said: "I think probably it was an act of four or five subordinate officers."

THE WAR WITH SPAIN

General Joseph Wheeler

War declared.—In April, 1898, Congress directed the President to force Spain to leave Cuba. This was soon followed by a declaration of war, in which the United States disclaimed any intention of holding Cuba when the war should close. The regular army of the United States, consisting of about twenty-eight thousand men, was inadequate to engage in war; so the President called first for one hundred and twenty-five thousand volunteers and then for seventy-five thousand additional troops. At the same time the regular army was increased to sixty-one thousand men. The country went wild with excitement and enthusiasm, and the Union and Confederate veterans vied with their sons in hastening to offer their services to their common country. It had only needed such an opportunity to prove that the country was

Admiral George Dewey

General Fitzhugh Lee

thoroughly reunited. Joseph Wheeler and Fitzhugh Lee, two Confederate generals, were appointed major generals by McKinley, and rendered valuable service.

The battle of Manila.—The first battle of the war took place in the far East. Commodore George Dewey, who was in command of the Asiatic Squadron, was ordered to go to the Philippine Islands and attack the Spanish fleet stationed there. Entering Manila Bay early on the morning of May 1st, he destroyed in four hours, without the loss of a man, eleven Spanish war vessels and a fort. He then blockaded the harbor of Manila until August, when an American army under the command of General Wesley A. Merritt arrived. Assisted by Aguinaldo, the leader of the native insurgents, the Americans stormed and captured the city; and the rule of Spain in the Philippine Islands was ended. The victory aroused great enthusiasm in the United States, and Dewey was soon raised to the rank of Admiral.

THE PHILIPPINE ISLANDS

CHAPTER CVIII

FIGHTING IN AMERICAN WATERS

McKinley's First Administration, 1897–1901

Blockade of Cuba.—In the meantime preparations were being made for the invasion of Cuba. Admiral Sampson was sent with a fleet to Cuban waters, and Commodore Schley with a flying squadron was ordered to coöperate with him. The *Oregon*, one of the most powerful ships in the navy, was ordered from San Francisco to the West Indies. After a voyage of thirteen thousand miles, she came in safely and joined the rest of the fleet. The fleet was then engaged in blockading the mouth of the harbor of Santiago, where a Spanish fleet, under the command of Admiral Cervera, had taken refuge. During the blockade the American vessels were frequently fired upon by shore batteries, and Ensign Worth Bagley of North Carolina was killed by an exploding shell. He was the only naval officer to lose his life in the war.

RICHMOND P. HOBSON

It was greatly feared that Cervera would succeed in slipping by the American fleet; and an attempt to prevent this occasioned one of the most gallant actions of the war. Lieutenant Richmond P. Hobson, with six other volunteers, undertook to sink the collier *Merrimac* in the narrow channel leading into the harbor so that the Spanish fleet could not escape. In spite of a terrific fire from the enemy, the vessel was sunk at the harbor entrance; but it did not lie crosswise as planned and so the channel was not blocked. Hobson and his men were captured unhurt and were kindly treated in recognition of their bravery.

Invasion of Cuba.—The army was unprepared for war, and the War Department was incompetent to cope with the difficulties of the situation. Consequently, the troops suffered greatly from sickness and the lack of proper supplies. Hundreds died in the camps, particularly at Chickamauga, where fever was rife. Thus more damage was inflicted upon the army at home than in Cuba.

WORTH BAGLEY MONUMENT
RALEIGH, N. C.

In June, 1898, about fifteen thousand men, under General William R. Shafter, were transported from Tampa, Florida, and landed in Cuba about sixteen miles from Santiago. The march on the city was then begun by two regiments of regulars and the Rough Riders, a volunteer cavalry regiment raised by Leonard Wood and Theodore Roosevelt. In command of the advance was General Joseph Wheeler, whose famous cavalry service under the Confederacy made him an experienced leader. The Spaniards were encountered first at Las Guasimas, in much greater force than the Americans, but were driven back. The main force now came up, and El Caney and San Juan were captured after heavy losses. The fall of Santiago was then certain.

The battle of Santiago.—When it became evident that Santiago would be captured, Cervera was forced by the Spanish authorities to make an effort to escape, though he realized the hopelessness of the attempt. Accordingly, on Sunday, July 3d, his fleet came out of the harbor; and a running fight followed, in which the American fleet under Commodore Schley, Admiral Sampson being temporarily absent, was completely victorious, sinking or capturing every Spanish ship and losing but one man. The Spaniards lost heavily, and all the survivors became prisoners.

ADMIRAL WINFIELD SCOTT SCHLEY

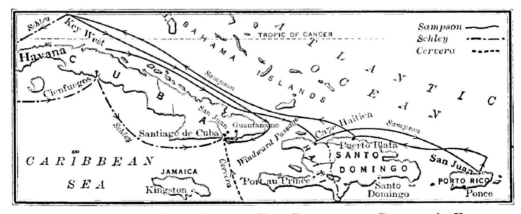

THE WAR IN THE WEST INDIES—THE PURSUIT OF CERVERA'S FLEET

Porto Rico taken.—Two weeks later Santiago surrendered. At once a force under General Nelson A. Miles was sent to occupy Porto Rico, a small but very valuable island which also belonged to Spain. He was marching rapidly to the interior with but little opposition other than light skirmishing, when the war was ended by an armistice, or agreement of both sides to cease fighting.

The treaty of peace.—In the autumn of 1898 a treaty of peace was signed in Paris. The Philippine Islands and Guam, an island in the Ladrones group, and Porto Rico were ceded to the United States, which paid Spain $20,000,000. The United States also assumed a protectorate over Cuba. Many people in the United States were much opposed to the purchase of the Philippines and the retention of Porto Rico on the ground that the country had no need of colonial possessions and no means of governing them, particularly when they were so far away. But a majority of the people were attracted by the idea that expansion would be advantageous to the commercial and industrial development of the country, and the treaty was ratified by the Senate in February, 1899.

Results of the war.—The war brought upon the United States the necessity of expansion. It needed coaling stations in the Pacific. The Hawaiian Islands were annexed in July, 1898 (page 443). In 1899 Wake Island was annexed. The same year saw the occupation of six of the Samoan Islands. Thus the United States began its colonial policy. In consequence of this territorial expansion American commerce was largely increased. Internally, some very interesting results are noticeable:

1. The army and navy have been increased as a matter of necessity. This was much opposed by those who had objected to the retention of the Philippine Islands.

2. The politics of the country entered upon a new phase with new issues. In the union of all parts of the

country to fight Spain, the bitterness resulting from the War of Secession was forgotten, all of it temporarily, some of it forever; and a new national feeling was developed.

CHAPTER CIX

THE PROBLEMS OF IMPERIALISM AND THE PANAMA CANAL

McKinley's First Administration, 1897–1901; McKinley's and Roosevelt's Administrations, 1901–05

The Philippine insurrection.—The Philippine archipelago is made up of over two thousand islands (nearly all of them very small), the most important of which is Luzon. The total area is 115,026 square miles. Some of these islands are very fertile. Their chief products are sugar, hemp, tobacco, coffee, and indigo. The inhabitants number about eight millions, of many nations and of all grades of progress, from savagery to high civilization, the majority being comparatively uncivilized.

Many inhabitants of Luzon firmly expected independence and, when this was refused, under the leadership of Aguinaldo rebelled against American authority. When they found that they could not win by open warfare, they resorted to guerrilla tactics, which prolonged the struggle for a long time. The capture of Aguinaldo, however, struck the revolt a fatal blow; and the islands are now practically subdued. On July 4, 1901, a civil government was established for the islands with Judge William H. Taft at its head. Under his wise administration and that of his successor, General Luke E. Wright, prosperity began; and the natives are rapidly being convinced that they will be benefited by American control and will receive fair treatment.

Cuban affairs.—As soon as the Spanish War closed, the United States took temporary possession of Cuba for the purpose of organizing its government. During the period of American occupation great progress was made in taxation, sanitation, and in legal and judicial reforms. A constitutional convention met and adopted a constitution, modeled after that of the United States; and as soon as the new government was inaugurated, the United States forces were withdrawn (1902). The United States has treated Cuba most generously in every way and has never violated the pledge with which the war was commenced. But a protectorate, with the power of interference in case of internal troubles, is retained.

Porto Rican government.—Porto Rico has been allowed a legislative body; but the island is a dependency of the United States, and its governor is appointed by the President. Free trade between the United States and the island was established in 1901 to its great benefit.

Important legislation.—Although the country was engaged in war during the early part of McKinley's administration, internal matters were considered. In 1897 the Dingley Tariff Bill became a law, which made the duties on imports higher than they had ever been before. The gold dollar was declared the sole standard of value. To meet the cost of the war, special stamp and other internal taxes were levied.

Troubles in China.—In 1900 there began in China a crusade against foreigners, led by the Boxers, a secret patriotic society. The Government of China did nothing to suppress it or to protect the foreigners, and the leading nations of the world hurried troops and vessels there for the protection of their citizens. The United States sent General Adna R. Chaffee with an army from the Philippines, which rendered good service in the invasion that followed. The allies, after severe fighting, stormed Pekin and released the foreigners, who had taken refuge in the legations. China was forced to pay a large indemnity and to put to death certain leaders of the Boxers.

Campaign of 1900.—The Republicans nominated McKinley for President and Theodore Roosevelt of New York for Vice President. The Democrats again nominated William J. Bryan, putting with him on the ticket former Vice President Adlai E. Stevenson. The Democrats denounced "imperialism," as they termed the holding of colonial possessions, and demanded independence for the Philippines. But the money question was again an issue, for the Democrats again called for the free coinage of silver. Many Republicans supported Bryan on the issue of imperialism, but McKinley was reëlected by a larger majority than he had received in 1896.

Assassination of McKinley.—In September, 1901, President McKinley visited the Pan-American Exposition at Buffalo, New York, and while there made a public address. A reception followed, at which thousands of people crowded to meet the President. Among them was an anarchist, who, under pretense of shaking hands with the President, shot him. The wound was mortal. McKinley lingered for more than a week and died September 14th. Theodore Roosevelt [1] then took the oath of office and became President.

---

[1] Theodore Roosevelt was born in New York City, October 27, 1858. He was educated at Harvard. Then he went to the West for his health, and

The Panama Canal.—For many years the United States had considered the project of cutting a canal from the Atlantic to the Pacific, either across the Isthmus of Panama or by a proposed route through Nicaragua. The idea was no new one; for it had been proposed by the Spaniards soon after the discovery of America. It had been much discussed about 1850, and the United States had made several treaties on the subject.

THE PANAMA CANAL ZONE AND ROUTE OF THE CANAL

In 1879 a French company undertook to construct a canal across the isthmus and secured a concession for the purpose from Colombia. The work was carried on for a time, but the company failed and the attempt was abandoned. After the Spanish War, however, the need to the United States of such a canal was greatly increased; and steps were taken to build one by the Nicaragua route. But when the French holders of the Panama concession offered to sell it to the United States (1902), the offer was accepted and their rights purchased

---

while there was a cowboy and hunter. Returning to New York, he entered politics and served in the legislature. He was a member of the United States Civil Service Commission for six years and was Police Commissioner of New York City for two years. He served for a year as Assistant Secretary of the Navy and did much valuable service in preparing the navy for the war with Spain. He resigned in 1898 and raised a regiment of volunteer cavalry known as the "Rough Riders," of which he became lieutenant colonel. In the fall of 1898, he was elected

IMPERIALISM AND THE PANAMA CANAL

for $40,000,000. A treaty with Colombia was then drawn to give the United States proper control of the canal, but Colombia refused to ratify it. Thereupon, Panama seceded from Colombia and set up an independent republic, which, after recognition by the United States, made the desired treaty. Work on the canal then began at once.

Alaska boundary dispute.—Gold was discovered in the Klondike region of Alaska in 1897; and as a consequence, thousands of settlers poured into the country as they had into California in 1849. The boundary with Canada had never been settled; and it now became necessary that it should be determined, as Canada claimed a large part of the

ALASKA AND THE KLONDIKE

Klondike region. In 1903 the decision of the disputed question was referred to a board of arbitration, which decided the matter substantially in favor of the United States.

The great coal strike.—In 1902 the anthracite coal miners of Pennsylvania went on strike over the question of wages. The strike lasted for nearly six months; and there was not only suffering among the miners, but great

---

Governor of New York and in 1900, Vice President. He became President on the death of McKinley and was reëlected in 1904. Few men in our history have been more widely admired, and few have exerted a greater influence.

distress over the whole country because of the scarcity and high price of coal. President Roosevelt intervened, with the suggestion that the quarrel between the mine owners and the strikers should be referred for arbitration to a commission, which he would appoint. As a result, a settlement of the difficulty was agreed upon.

Louisiana Purchase Exposition.—In 1904, in commemoration of the purchase of the Louisiana Territory by President Jefferson, a world's fair was held in St. Louis, the largest city in the purchased territory. In every way it was the most extensive and most successful exposition ever held.

Campaign of 1904.—In 1904 Roosevelt secured the Republican nomination for President, and Charles W. Fairbanks of Indiana was nominated for Vice President. The Democrats nominated Judge Alton B. Parker of New York and Henry G. Davis of West Virginia. The question of regulating "trusts" was the chief issue advanced by the Democrats. The Republicans appealed to the country on their record. Roosevelt was very popular in all parts of the country and was elected by an enormous majority, receiving about two millions more of the popular vote than Parker did.

CHAPTER CX

RECENT EVENTS

Roosevelt's Administration, 1905–09; Taft's Administration, 1909–

Important legislation.—Several important laws were passed in President Roosevelt's second administration. A pure food law was adopted, which provided for the inspection and proper labeling of food products and drugs entering into interstate commerce. The Hepburn Bill provided for the regulation of the rates on all railroads engaged in interstate business. Both of these laws mark increased activity on the part of the Federal Government, and both are designed for the good of the people.

THEODORE ROOSEVELT

The Jamestown Exposition.—To celebrate the three hundredth year since the establishment of the first permanent settlement in America, an international exposition was held near Norfolk, Virginia, in 1907. Among its features of interest was the constant presence of war vessels of many nations in Hampton Roads.

The panic of 1907.—The development of the trusts had excited much discussion and caused great uneasiness for many years. In President Roosevelt's administration a number of prosecutions were begun by the Federal Government under the authority of the Sherman Anti-Trust Act (page 440). These agitations, coupled with the fact that speculation in business during the period of prosperity had caused the manufacture of more products than could be sold, led to loss of confidence in the business and financial world. The result was the panic of 1907, when for a time all kinds of industries were checked.

Admission of Oklahoma.—In 1908 Oklahoma, which had been open to settlement since 1890, and Indian Territory were united, and admitted to the Union as the forty-sixth State, with the name Oklahoma.

The voyage of the fleet.—In 1908 President Roosevelt determined to send a fleet of American war vessels around the world after it should have first visited the Pacific coast of the United States. The plan excited much comment and some opposition, as our relations with Japan were at that time somewhat strained. American citizens living on the Pacific coast had shown hostility toward the Japanese who had settled among them. However, the fleet, after leaving the Pacific coast, went to Hawaii, Japan, the Philippines, and Australia, and returned home by way of the Suez Canal and Gibraltar. The voyage was an entire success and redounded to the credit of the navy and of the United States.

The conference of governors.—In 1908 President Roosevelt invited the governors of the different States to meet with him in Washington to confer in regard to matters for the general good of the country. The meeting was in all respects successful, and brought about a better spirit of coöperation among the States.

Campaign of 1908. — Largely through the efforts of President Roosevelt, his Secretary of War, William H. Taft[1] of Ohio was nominated for President by the Republicans. For Vice President they nominated James S. Sherman of New York. The Democrats for the third time nominated their old favorite William J. Bryan and with him, for Vice President, John W. Kern of Indiana. The Democrats demanded the reduction of the tariff, and the Republicans also pledged themselves to bring it about. As a result of the panic, there was much discussion of financial questions in the campaign, the Republicans favoring a postal savings bank, and the Democrats a system of guaranteeing bank deposits. Taft was elected by a large majority.

WILLIAM H. TAFT

The Aldrich Bill. — Soon after he was inaugurated, President Taft called a special session of Congress to consider the reduction of the tariff; and the Aldrich Bill was passed which, though reducing the tariff on some articles, really made it higher as a whole. An interesting party situation developed during the session,

---

[1] William Howard Taft was born in Cincinnati, Ohio, September 15, 1857. He was graduated at Yale and became a lawyer. He was in succession prosecuting attorney, judge of the Superior Court of Ohio, Solicitor-General of the United States, circuit judge, and Dean of the University of Cincinnati School of Law. In 1898 he was made President of the Philippine Commission, and later Governor of the Philippines. He returned to the United States to become Secretary of War in 1905.

some of the Democrats joining with the Republicans in voting protective duties, and some of the Republicans, called "insurgents," voting for radical reduction of the duties. The insurgents also attacked the growing power of the Speaker of the House of Representatives, evidently determined that the Speaker should do the will of the House rather than that the Representatives should do the bidding of the Speaker.

New Mexico and Arizona.—In 1910, Congress enacted that New Mexico and Arizona should each have the privilege of becoming a state. As soon as these territories have made constitutions acceptable to Congress and the President, they will be admitted to all the rights of statehood. There will then be forty-eight states and no territories within the borders of the United States.

CHAPTER CXI

PROGRESS OF THE COUNTRY, 1865–1910

Some terrible disasters.—Since 1865 the progress of the country has been steady. Labor strikes have at times disturbed the quiet of certain sections of the country (pages 436 and 442), but on the whole the strikes have been settled to the satisfaction of all parties. In April, 1910, there was a great strike of street-car employees in Philadelphia; but the matter was settled so that the daily business of the city went on without much interruption.

Disasters have come to certain localities and have for a time checked progress. In 1886 Charleston, South Carolina, was visited by an earthquake, which took many lives, demolished hundreds of houses, and destroyed, all told, eight million dollars' worth of property. Aid came to the stricken city from all parts of the United States, and soon Charleston was rebuilt, a finer city than it was before.

In 1906 the city of San Francisco was visited by the most terrible earthquake that has been experienced in the United States. Thousands of houses were destroyed, and many hundreds of lives lost. The earthquake was followed by a fire, and the city was practically destroyed. Americans everywhere responded, and trains loaded with provisions and supplies of all kinds were dispatched to the West. Over $5,000,000 was raised for the sufferers.

In 1904 the greater portion of the business section of Baltimore was destroyed by fire; but to-day that section of Baltimore is rebuilt and much improved.

The country has seen two great disasters due to floods. In 1889 Johnstown, a valley town of Pennsylvania, was practically destroyed by the breaking of the dam to an immense reservoir in the mountains above. About two thousand lives were lost, and along the valley much property was destroyed—probably amounting to twelve millions of dollars.

In 1900 a tornado swept over Galveston, Texas, and drove up from the Gulf of Mexico a tidal wave such as has never been recorded before. About seven thousand perished when the city became submerged. Again the whole country came to the aid of the afflicted. Since then a great sea wall has been built around the city, so that there can never be a recurrence of such a calamity.

Race troubles.—Since the days of Reconstruction in the South but little friction has existed between the white people and the negroes. In many places the negroes are making great strides in wealth. They are taking advantage of the free public schools. Here and there slight disturbances have occurred, but each year the hostility between the races is growing less. For the year 1910, we find that the feeling toward the negro is practically the same in the North as in the South, except that among white laborers the opposition to the negro is stronger in the North than in the South. The feeling toward the Japanese and Chinese on the Pacific coast is probably more intense than the feeling in the East against the negroes. In many places there is a prejudice against

Map Showing How the Centers of Population and Manufacture Have Been Moving Westward

the immigrant. This, however, is soon overcome; for the immigrant very quickly adopts American ways of living and thinking. In New Orleans in 1890 occurred an outbreak against the foreign element, during which some Italians were lynched. This followed the assassination of the chief of police of that city, who had caused the arrest of a number of Italian criminals — members of a secret society called the "Mafia."

Population and area. — The epoch that followed the War of Secession was one of great growth along many lines. This is nowhere more apparent than in population.

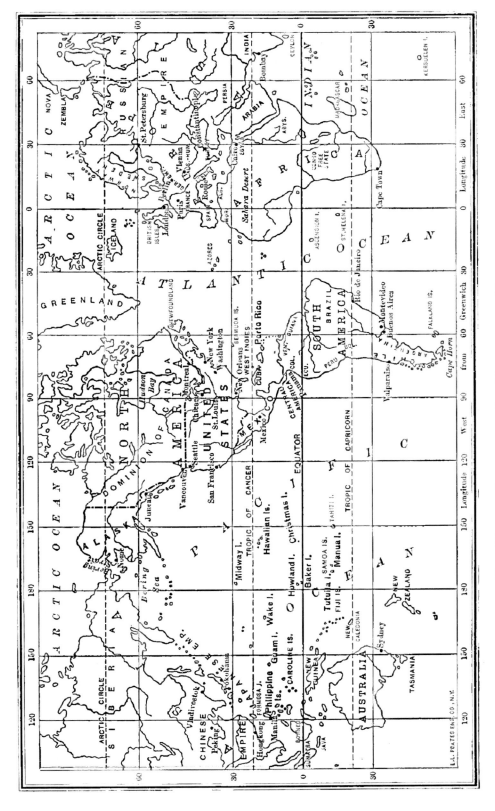

The United States and Its Territorial Possessions

The census of 1870 showed a total population of about 39,000,000 and that of 1900 of about 76,000,000.[1] In this period eight new States were admitted, all of them from the West. During this period increasing numbers of both foreign and native born have been settling in the cities, so that the census of 1900 shows more than seventy-five cities having each a population of over fifty thousand. New York is now the second largest city in the world. For many years immigration from Europe has brought in several hundred thousand people annually. In the main they have settled in the North and the West. The South has received very few because European laborers are unwilling to work side by side with the negro laborers of the South.

In this period many important accessions of territory have increased the area of the country over seven hundred thousand square miles. The purchase of Alaska in 1867 was an important epoch in the expansion of the United States. It marks the first accession of territory lying apart from the States, as well as the beginning of a new form of Territorial government directly under Congress. All the accessions of territory since that date have come under the title "Insular Possessions," that is, territory consisting of islands.[2]

Industrial development. — The era has been one of industrial development. Never has any other nation

---

[1] The estimated population for 1910 is 90,000,000.

[2] These acquisitions are as follows: Hawaii, annexed July 6, 1898; Porto Rico and Guam ceded by Spain, and the Philippines purchased from Spain, February 6, 1899; Samoa ceded by treaty with Great Britain and Germany, February 16, 1900. With the exception of Hawaii, which became a territory (1900), all these accessions have a form of civil government under Congress.

advanced with the rapidity and power of the United States. By the close of the nineteenth century the nation stood foremost among the countries of the world in wealth, energy, and activity. The value of American products exported in 1900-1901 was over a

NAVIGATING THE AIR

An English aviator waiting to start until the American aviator, Mr. Curtiss, already in the air, has passed him.—Photograph by Paul Thompson, New York.

billion and a half dollars, nearly twice the value of the imports.

Inventions and discoveries.—The most notable inventions of the period have been in electricity. The problem of illumination has been satisfactorily solved by electricity, and the methods are being constantly improved. Cars run by electricity have greatly improved transportation and travel, especially in the cities. The first electric street car line was built in Richmond, Virginia (1888). The telephone, first exhibited in 1876, has come into general use, and the telegraph has been much improved. Ocean cables connect all parts of the world. The Pacific Cable between San Francisco and the Philippine Islands was completed in 1903. Wireless telegraphy was made possible at the close of the nineteenth century. It soon came into general use on the sea and has been the means of saving hundreds of lives and a great amount of property. Electric power is also used largely in manufacturing. The world is greatly indebted to Thomas A. Edison, an American inventor, for what he has done toward this development.

In inventions of practical benefit the United States has led the world. In this connection the phonograph and the typewriter are worthy of note. Although the bicycle and the automobile are not American inventions, they have developed in this country great industries with immense capital. American inventors have taken a leading part in perfecting new inventions for aerial navigation.

Science.—The United States has contributed much to the sciences, particularly that of medicine, in which she is probably second only to Germany. In surgery she holds first place, as is the case in the applied sciences generally, and in engineering. In engineering worthy of note, was the building of Brooklyn Bridge (page 433) and the deepening of the mouth of the Mississippi by the "Jetty System" so that boats drawing twenty feet of water can come into the river. The plan, submitted by James B. Eads, was approved by Congress in 1875. The channel of the River was made narrow by "jetties" (great embankments) so that the current flows swiftly and washes out all obstructions. The system is a great success.

Education. — Tremendous progress has been made in education. This is best seen in the public schools, which have greatly increased in number and improved in equipment. There are more and better trained teachers throughout the country, and in 1909 there were nearly twenty million public-school pupils enrolled. A phenomenal growth is to be seen also in the colleges and universities. Millions of dollars have been given to them for endowment and equipment, and their development has been very rapid.

Other educational factors have been the free public libraries, Chautauquas, and summer and correspondence schools, which have reached millions who could not otherwise have enjoyed the priceless benefits of education. The magazines and newspapers have played no small part in general education, and through the medium of the rural free delivery they promptly reach all parts of the country.

Western progress. — During the period following the war the West was put in close touch with the world by the building of railroads, and its population increased by leaps and bounds. By the end of the century it had become in many respects the predominant section of the country. Its rich lands have been occupied rapidly and agriculture is conducted on a scale never equaled in the history of the world. This has been made possible by improved machinery which has revolutionized agriculture everywhere. Grain is grown in tremendous quantities, and cattle-raising is carried on as never before. These two industries, with the packing of meat, have made the West a great food source for all countries.

Nor has the West been left behind in intellectual development. All these States have flourishing schools and colleges, and their State universities are beginning to set the pace for those of the older States in the East.

Conservation of resources.—One of the factors that is becoming daily more important in the development of the West is the Government policy of conserving the natural resources of the country so that they will benefit all the people. Large forest reserves have been made, and every encouragement has been given to settlers to reclaim the arid lands of the West by irrigation. The Department of Agriculture is doing a valuable work in finding out what crops grow best in the various localities, and the results have been of great practical benefit.

Southern development.—The most remarkable development within a short space of time is to be seen in the South. When once the native white people had regained control of affairs, progress commenced; and it showed clearly that the abolition of slavery had freed the South from its greatest burden. Free labor has proved much more productive than slave labor, since it has permitted the introduction of improved methods of agriculture. Larger crops are raised, and planters and farmers have learned how to vary their crops with benefit both to the soil and to the crop. Trucking alone brings to the South every year many millions of dollars.

While the South is still chiefly an agricultural section, momentous changes are to be seen in its industrial life.

Manufacturing has steadily increased. All the cotton, for example, is no longer carried to the North or elsewhere to be made into cloth; but great quantities are used by Southern mills. South Carolina and North Carolina now stand second and third among the cotton-manufacturing States in the Union. Lumbering has become an important industry; also the manufacture of wood products. North Carolina is second only to Michigan in the manufacture of furniture. Coal and iron mines have been opened, and Alabama is second among the States in the production of steel. Water power is being developed, and this will in time change completely the means and methods of manufacturing. With the growth of wealth and prosperity has come a wonderful educational revival in the South. Systems of public schools have been established and improved, and the opportunity of getting an education is given to all. Colleges and universities are growing in wealth, power, and usefulness, and are increasing in number.

In spite of this progress the South has made only a start in the development of its wonderful resources. The present century will show far greater results.

Business development. — One of the most dangerous developments in this period has been that of "trusts," as great business corporations or combinations are called. Through their vast wealth and influence they are able to put small concerns out of business—shut them out of competition and control prices. More dangerous still, the trusts often control legislation. As a consequence, both the States and the United States are taking steps so to limit them by law that their wealth cannot be used to tempt or threaten.

Conclusion.—It will be clearly seen that the progress of the country up to the present time has been largely in industries, inventions, and sciences, and in political expansion. But in the closing years of the last century there was also the beginning of a great philanthropic activity. Now an increasing part of the vast wealth of the country is being used for charitable purposes. In literature, music, and art the country has not taken the highest rank, but it has of late shown such interest and progress in these subjects that we may hope that in the coming years the United States will become also one of the foremost nations in artistic achievement.

QUESTIONS AND EXERCISES

References are here made to the books named in the Library Lists on pages vii and viii, the books being indicated by the names of authors. Williamson I refers to "The Life of General Robert E. Lee" and Williamson II to "The Life of General Stonewall Jackson."

CHAPTER I

MAP EXERCISES.—Find on the maps in your Geography each of the countries and cities mentioned in this chapter.

DEFINITIONS.—Find the meaning of *tenant, sway, emerge, adventure*.

QUESTIONS.—How would civil wars keep Germany from engaging in "discoveries in the western world"? Why was France stronger under Charles VIII than she had been before? What is meant by "the middle class"? How was Italy like Germany in 1492? What evidence does the picture on page 3 give of the wealth and power of Venice? What evidence do you find that England "was probably the best governed" country in Europe in 1492? Name two causes that helped to make Spain "the greatest power in Europe." For what reason (see page 9) did the Europeans try to overthrow Turkish power? What countries were reached by the Norsemen in their wanderings?

REFERENCES.—*Turks:* Guerber, 33; Chandler and Chitwood, 13. *Norsemen:* Guerber, 24–30; Southworth I, 1–9. *Snorri:* Hart, 1–3.

CHAPTER II

MAP EXERCISES.—Find on the map on page 8 a route not mentioned in the text. How far toward the East had traders gone by this route? Which trade route did the Venetians use?

DEFINITIONS.—Find the meaning of *caravan, superstition, visionary, heretic, equator*.

QUESTIONS.—Why was Marco Polo's journey remarkable? Do you think the Bible teaches that the world is flat? Why were the people of Europe anxious to find a new route to India? What was the difference between Mela's idea of the continents and Ptolemy's? For what purpose did Prince Henry the Navigator send out his expedition?

REFERENCES.—*Ideas of the World:* Guerber, 31–33. *Marco Polo:* Southworth I, 10–23. *Prince Henry:* Guerber, 33–36.

CHAPTER III

MAP EXERCISES.—Find mistakes in Toscanelli's map.

DEFINITIONS.—Find the meaning of *speculation, sphere, circumference, decisive, visionary.*

QUESTIONS.—Why was Columbus eager to make his westward voyage? Why are not the people on the opposite side of the earth from us "walking with their feet upward"? What helped and what hindered Columbus in getting aid for his voyage?

REFERENCES.—*Early Life of Columbus:* Gordy, 2–3; Chandler and Chitwood, 14; Guerber, 36–39; Southworth I, 24–31; McMurry, 122–127. *Columbus's Search for Help:* Gordy, 4–9; Guerber, 39–44; Chandler and Chitwood, 5–17; McMurry, 127–133.

CHAPTER IV

MAP EXERCISES.—Find Palos and trace the voyage of Vasco da Gama on the map on page 8. Find where Columbus would have landed in America if he had sailed due west from Palos. Find the Bahama Islands.

DEFINITIONS.—Find the meaning of *rudder, strategy, mutiny, visible, massacre, turmoil, sedition, incentive.*

QUESTIONS.—How did the three evidences noted by Columbus show that his ships were approaching land? By what right could Columbus take possession of the newly discovered lands? What were the causes, principal events, and results of the second voyage of Columbus? The third voyage? The fourth voyage? Did his discoveries prove that the earth is round?

DATE WORTH REMEMBERING.—Discovery of America in **1492** by Columbus.

REFERENCES.—*Voyages of Columbus:* Hart, 4–6; Southworth I, 31–36; Guerber, 44–57; Gordy, 9–21; Chandler and Chitwood, 17–23; McMurry, 133–160. *Death of Columbus:* Guerber, 57–59.

CHAPTER V

MAP EXERCISES.—Find Labrador, Cape Breton, Nova Scotia, Brazil, Strait of Magellan, Philippine Islands.

DEFINITIONS.—Find the meaning of *quest, perilous, expanse.*

QUESTIONS.—What caused the voyages made by the Cabots? By Vespucius? Balboa? Magellan? What regions were visited by each of these explorers? What voyage mentioned in this chapter do you think was most important? Why?

REFERENCES.—*The Cabots:* Southworth I, 37–40; Hart, 7–9; Chandler and Chitwood, 30–33. *Vespucius:* Guerber, 60–62; Chandler and Chitwood, 24–28. *Balboa:* Southworth I, 46–48; Chandler and Chitwood, 24–28; Guerber, 62–64; Hart, 10–12. *Magellan:* McMurry, 161–185.

QUESTIONS AND EXERCISES

CHAPTER VI

MAP EXERCISES.—Find the Azores, Porto Rico, Tampa Bay, Natchez, Mexico, Peru, Chesapeake Bay, St. Augustine.

DEFINITIONS.—Find the meaning of *demarcation, disembark, traverse*.

QUESTIONS.—Why did the Pope exert a great influence throughout Europe? If the world had accepted his "line of demarcation," what might have been the result on the history of America? What led Ponce de Leon to the mainland of North America? What led Hernando de Soto? What important fact was learned from the explorations of De Soto and Coronado? What was the principal aim of the Spaniards in exploring and settling the New World?

REFERENCES.—*De Leon:* Johonnot, 7–9; Southworth I, 41–42; Guerber, 64–65; Chandler and Chitwood, 34–37; McMurry, 222–226. *De Soto:* Southworth I, 50–53; Massey and Wood, 9–10; Guerber, 66–70; Gordy, 22–29; Chandler and Chitwood, 39–42; Hart, 16–19. *Cortez:* Southworth I, 43–46; McMurry, 186–221; Gordy, 52–70. *Pizarro:* Southworth I, 48–50; Hart, 12–16. *Cabeza de Vaca:* Littlejohn, 7–22.

CHAPTER VII

MAP EXERCISES.—Locate Newfoundland, Gulf of St. Lawrence, Montreal, St. John's River, Lake Champlain, Quebec, Albany.

QUESTIONS.—What attracted the French to the region of Newfoundland? Were they the first Europeans to explore this region? (See page 22.) Was their claim to the territory just? Where else did they attempt to settle and why did they fail? Was Ribault's decision to plant a colony at Port Royal wise? Give reasons. What new method of furthering colonization is found in the grant to De Monts? Find three reasons for French colonization in America. Why did the Dutch explore America? What caused them to establish colonies in this country?

REFERENCES.—*Cartier:* Southworth I, 144–148; Guerber, 71–73. *Champlain:* McMurry, 1–34; Southworth I, 153–160. *Verazzano:* Southworth I, 142–144. *Ribault:* Southworth I, 148–152; White, 1–4. *Hudson:* Southworth I, 123–129; McMurry, 35–46; Johonnot, 24–29; Guerber, 102–105; Chandler and Chitwood, 75–78.

CHAPTER VIII

MAP EXERCISES.—Find Chili, Peru, Oregon, Cape of Good Hope, Roanoke Island.

DEFINITIONS.—Find the meaning of *antagonism, pillage, uncouth, booty, forlorn, dire, pacify*.

QUESTIONS.—Why did England take new interest in American colonization in the time of Elizabeth? Can you suggest a reason why Drake did not return from Oregon to Europe by way of the Cape of Good Hope? How would Drake's deeds be considered if done to-day? What change does this show? Was Grenville's scheme wise? Account for Raleigh's interest in America. For the failure of the first colony he sent over. The second colony. What is the most important event given in this chapter? Give your reasons.

REFERENCES.—*Drake:* Southworth I, 54–63; Guerber, 80–82; Hart, 23–25. *Raleigh:* Guerber, 83–86; McMurry, 47–67; Southworth I, 64–72; Connor, 9–15; Gordy, 31–40; Chandler and Chitwood, 44–50. *Lost Colony:* Hart, 165–170.

CHAPTER IX

MAP EXERCISES.—Trace the boundary lines between the three great races of Indians east of the Mississippi River.

DEFINITIONS.—Find the meaning of *savage, barbarous, civilized, subsist, pestle, frequent, feat, stealthy, ambush.*

QUESTIONS.—Why did the Indians bury implements with their dead? Can you think of any proof that the Indian mounds are very old? How did the savage and the barbarous tribes differ as to implements and food? Is there anything about Indian life that is attractive to you? Anything that is repulsive? What advantages and disadvantages did the Indians have in their struggle against the white men? Make an outline classifying the Indian races east of the Mississippi River.

REFERENCES.—*Mounds:* Guerber, 20–23. *Savage Indians:* Guerber, 15–16; Hart, 91–95. *Barbarous Indians:* Guerber, 17–20; Karns, 14–21; Massey and Wood, 1–4. *Esquimaux:* Hart, 20–21. *Indian Life:* Southworth I, 85–88; Hart, 55–57, 91–97, 106–125. *Indian Legends:* 104–105, Massey and Wood, 5–8; Hart, 125–130. *Indian Homes:* Mowry, 17–23.

CHAPTER X

MAP EXERCISES.—Find the mouth of Cape Fear River, Potomac River, Hudson River. Find Cape Charles and Cape Henry.

DEFINITIONS.—Find the meaning of *utensil, overlapping.*

QUESTIONS.—Which reason given for English colonization do you think was the one that most influenced the English? Why? Can you suggest a reason why no settlement was allowed to be established within one hundred miles of the first colony in the "overlapping territory"? How long did it take the Jamestown colonists to make the voyage from London to Virginia? How long would it take now? What makes the difference? What kind of work is most needed in a new colony?

DATE WORTH REMEMBERING.—**1607,** the first permanent English settlement in America.

CHAPTER XI

DEFINITIONS.—Find the meaning of *acquit, relent, discord.*

QUESTIONS.—What strong traits of character were shown by John Smith? What were his moral weaknesses? In what ways did he help the colony? What was the best time of the year for new colonists to arrive? Why? Make a list of the things that hindered the Jamestown colony at first.

REFERENCES.—*John Smith and Pocahontas:* Southworth I, 73–84; Chandler and Chitwood, 51–59; Johonnot, 15–23; Gordy, 42–53; McMurry, 68–101; Guerber, 87–100; Hart, 98–104.

CHAPTER XII

DEFINITIONS.—Find the meaning of *inaugurate, martial, sanction, despite.*

QUESTIONS.—Why was Governor Dale's system of working the lands far better than the old system? What services did Pocahontas render to the Jamestown colony? (See also Chapter XI.) What was the first agricultural product that brought money into the colony? What did Yeardley do for the colony? Why was the "indented-servant" system in the colony good for England? What were the differences between a slave and an "indented servant"? Why was the introduction of the representative assembly the most important event mentioned in this chapter? Why was the London Company overthrown?

DATE WORTH REMEMBERING.—**1619**, first representative assembly, and beginning of African slavery in the United States.

REFERENCES.—*Tobacco:* Hart, 63–64. *Wild Beasts:* Hart, 71–79, 85–89. *Slavery:* Hart, 157–159. *Virginia Children:* Hart, 172–173, 175–177. *Plantation Life:* Hart, 149–152.

CHAPTER XIII

DEFINITIONS.—Find the meaning of *commonwealth, dub, Cavalier, Puritan, allegiance.*

QUESTIONS.—What do you conclude about the Virginians from the fact that they put Harvey out of office? From the fact that many Cavaliers fled to Virginia after the execution of Charles I? Did Virginia have more freedom or less under the Commonwealth than it had had under Charles I? Prove your answer. What does the treaty between Virginia and the Commonwealth prove?

CHAPTER XIV

MAP EXERCISES.—Find the Blue Ridge Mountains, Shenandoah Valley, Alleghany Mountains.

DEFINITIONS.—Find the meaning of *haughty, resent, tutor.*

QUESTIONS.—What three evidences can you give of the independence of the Virginians before the Commonwealth? Why did the Burgesses claim the sole right to levy taxes? Why did the people want to elect Burgesses often? Why did they oppose large grants of land in their colony? What were the causes and results of Bacon's rebellion? Who was at fault in this matter? On which side would you expect to find the rich planters? Why? What hindered education in the early history of Virginia? What aided it?

REFERENCES.—*Berkeley and Bacon:* Gordy, 55–62; Guerber, 155–162; Southworth I, 201–207. *Indians:* Hart, 216–217.

CHAPTER XV

Map Exercises.—Find Holland, Plymouth.

Definitions.—Find the meaning of *ritual, identity, harass, frugal.*

Questions.—What objections did the Pilgrims have to living in England? In Holland? Did these objections justify their removal to America? What was the *Mayflower* Compact? In what respect was the first government of Plymouth superior to that of Virginia? How did this come about? Why could nine Pilgrims conquer a large village of Indians? What does the word "Thanksgiving" signify? Why did the Pilgrims apply to the Plymouth Company for a grant of land? Did they have a grant from the King? Why did they persecute people who did not belong to their church?

Date Worth Remembering.—**1621**, the first English settlement in New England.

References.—*Pilgrims:* Southworth I, 89–91. *Indians:* Guerber, 118–122. *Mayflower:* Guerber, 105–109; Chandler and Chitwood, 60–65. *Plymouth:* Guerber, 109–113; Hart, 133–136. *Miles Standish:* Gordy, 64–79; Southworth I, 92–100. *Thanksgiving:* Guerber, 113–116. *New England:* McMurry, 108–121; Hart, 57–59.

CHAPTER XVI

Map Exercises.—Find Salem, the Charles River, the Merrimac River, Boston, Newtown, Cambridge.

Definitions.—Find the meaning of *blasphemy, stocks, ducking stool, rum.*

Questions.—What was the difference between the Puritans and the Pilgrims? Which body was more favored by the King? Why did the Massachusetts Bay colony succeed better at first than either the Plymouth or the Jamestown colony? What were the good features of the government of Massachusetts? The bad features? What laws made by the Puritans were unjust? Why? Do you think the views of Roger Williams were right? Why? Why was there more trouble over religion in Massachusetts than in Jamestown? Did the Puritans object to slavery? Why were more slaves brought to Virginia than to Massachusetts?

General Exercise.—Make a list of the things that helped, and a list of those that hindered, the Massachusetts colony. Compare Massachusetts and Virginia as to laws, religion, and occupation.

Date Worth Remembering.—**1628**, founding of Massachusetts Bay colony.

References—*Puritans:* Goody, 81–86; Hart, 28–31. *Voyage:* Hart, 25–28. *Boston:* Guerber, 122–125. *Winthrop:* Chandler and Chitwood, 63–65; Southworth I, 101–109; Hart, 201–204. *Birds and Animals:* Hart, 59–63, 88–89. *Travel:* Hart, 67–70.

CHAPTER XVII

Map Exercises.—Find Providence, Portsmouth, Connecticut River, Windsor, Hartford, New Haven, Kennebec River, Lake George, Dover.

QUESTIONS AND EXERCISES

DEFINITIONS.—Find the meaning of *pillage, palisade, dissenter, turmoil.*

QUESTIONS.—Can you prove that Roger Williams was just in his dealings with the Indians? What early settlement was founded by a woman? Why? What is Rhode Island's greatest claim to distinction? Why could not the Dutch and the English live peaceably together in the Connecticut region? In what were the governments of Rhode Island and Connecticut alike? Was the New Haven colony well governed at first? Give reasons for your answer. Were these people in sympathy with the Puritans or the Cavaliers in England? How could Massachusetts be benefited by the possession of New Hampshire and Maine? How did the people of New Hampshire and Maine differ from other New Englanders?

OPEN TEXT-BOOK EXERCISE.—State the names and the services of the greatest men in the early history of New England. Name the colony that you would have preferred to live in and give reasons for your choice.

REFERENCES.—*Williams:* Gordy, 86–90; Johonnot, 32–37; Chandler and Chitwood, 67–72; Guerber, 127–134; Southworth I, 110–114. *Hooker:* Chandler and Chitwood, 72–74. *New Hampshire:* Hart, 192–194.

CHAPTER XVIII

MAP EXERCISES.—Draw a map showing the extent of the New England Confederacy.

DEFINITIONS.—Find the meaning of *confederacy, stupendous, apostle, relic, Quaker.*

QUESTIONS.—What caused the formation of the New England Confederacy? What was the plan of government of the Confederacy? Did John Eliot do anything for the protection of New England? What caused the difference between the treatment of New England and Virginia by the Mother Country during the Commonwealth?

REFERENCES.—*Eliot:* Guerber, 126–127. *Indian Schools:* Hart, 107–111. *Indian Bible:* Johonnot, 44–48. *Pine Tree Shilling:* Johonnot, 77–81.

CHAPTER XIX

DEFINITIONS.—Find the meaning of *harbor, refugee, politic, stockade, revoke, restrain.*

QUESTIONS.—Did Charles II improve the government of Massachusetts? Of Connecticut? Of Rhode Island? Why did Connecticut and Rhode Island hold to their charters instead of making new constitutions when they became independent states? What is meant by the expression "royal colony"? Can you think of any reasons why Charles II wanted to unite so many colonies under one government? Why did the people object?

CLASS EXERCISES.—Tell, as a story, without being questioned, the account of King Philip's War. Of the rule of Andros.

REFERENCES.—*King Philip:* Johonnot, 37–44; Southworth I, 115–122; Guerber, 138–142. *Indian Captives:* Hart, 112–115. *Regicides:* Johonnot, 48–51; Guerber, 136–138. *Charter Oak:* Johonnot, 60–63.

CHAPTER XX

DEFINITIONS.—Find the meaning of *veto, specify, adjust, friction, frenzy, cereal, "manufacturing enterprises."*

QUESTIONS.—What changes did King William make in the New England colonies and what were his reasons for making them? Do the educated people of to-day believe in witches? Why not? Can you suggest a reason why laws were made to forbid the wearing of fine clothes?

CLASS EXERCISES.—Tell, as a story, what you have learned about the witchcraft delusion. About life in New England in 1700.

REFERENCES.—*Education:* Hart, 205–210, 214–215, 220–224, 232–233. *Witchcraft:* Johonnot, 64–66; Guerber, 170–173.

CHAPTER XXI

MAP EXERCISES.—Find Chesapeake Bay, Kent Island, St. Mary's.

QUESTIONS.—What were the first four English colonies in America? Can you explain why Lord Baltimore did not settle in New England? Nor in Virginia? How did his charter differ from all the others that you have studied? In what colonies was the land bought from the Indians? What colonies practiced religious toleration in 1650? What were the causes and results of the troubles between Maryland and Virginia?

CLASS DISCUSSION.—Defend Lord Baltimore's title to Kent Island. Claiborne's title.

DATE WORTH REMEMBERING.—**1634,** settlement of Maryland.

REFERENCES.—*Baltimore and Maryland:* Guerber, 152–154; Chandler and Chitwood, 81–84; Southworth I, 179–186; Hart, 143–144.

CHAPTER XXII

MAP EXERCISE.—Find Annapolis.

DEFINITIONS.—Find the meaning of *deprive, restrict, quell.*

QUESTION.—What evidence can you give to show that Cromwell was a just and liberal man? In what respects did the rebellion in Maryland resemble Bacon's Rebellion in Virginia? Do you think that the majority of Marylanders did right in asking that Maryland be made a royal province? Give reasons for your answer. Was it best that the colonists should be taxed for the benefit of the proprietor?

CHAPTER XXIII

MAP EXERCISES.—Find the Roanoke, the Chowan, and the Cape Fear rivers; the Barbadoes.

DEFINITIONS.—Find the meaning of *proprietary, restriction, discord.*

QUESTIONS.—What were the objects sought by the colonists who settled in the Carolinas? By Charles II in granting the country to the lords-proprietors? Why did the colonists oppose the Grand Model? Were they right?

DATE WORTH REMEMBERING.—**1653,** first permanent settlement in North Carolina.

REFERENCES.—"*A Royal Gift*": Connor, 16-22. *Grand Model:* Chandler and Chitwood, 92-96. *Lords-Proprietors:* White, 4-7, 44-46.

CHAPTER XXIV

MAP EXERCISES.—Find the Ashley River, the Cooper River, Charleston.

DEFINITIONS.—Find the meaning of *migrated, tyranny, prey, piracy, thrifty.*

QUESTIONS.—What evidences do you find that the first settlers of North Carolina were a liberty-loving people? What hindered the progress of that colony? What helped it? How did the people of North and South Carolina resemble? How did they differ? Can you explain why the Huguenots did not settle in French territory? What was then the established church of France? In what way was the existence of different kinds of religious faiths in the same colony a good thing? Why did the colonists oppose the laws of trade? What caused the South Carolinians to spend their summers on their plantations and their winters in Charleston? Why did the governors and proprietors of South Carolina discourage war with the Spaniards?

DATE WORTH REMEMBERING.—**1670,** first permanent settlement in South Carolina.

REFERENCES.—*North Carolina:* Connor, 22-38, 45-52. *Ashley River:* White, 8-10. *South Carolina:* Hart, 65-66, 81-89, 155-157. *Charleston:* White, 11-16. *Edisto River:* White, 17-19; *Foreign Settlers in South Carolina:* White, 47-52. *Trade in South Carolina:* White, 20-22. *Huguenots:* White, 22-27.

CHAPTER XXV

MAP EXERCISES.—Find Savannah, St. Augustine, St. Simon's Island.

DEFINITIONS.—Find the meaning of *dire, deplorable, pauper, designate, savannah, alliance, retaliate, siege, wholesome.*

QUESTIONS.—What unjust laws were enforced in England in 1730? What new motives for American colonization do you find in the founding of Georgia? What new methods of colonization? What helped the growth of the colony? What hindered it? What military service did Oglethorpe render? What work was done by Wesley? By Whitefield?

REVIEW EXERCISE.—Give the origin of the name of each southern colony.

DATE WORTH REMEMBERING.—**1733,** the first settlement in Georgia, the last of the thirteen colonies.

REFERENCES.—*Oglethorpe:* Guerber, 164-166; Chandler and Chitwood, 97-101; Southworth I, 197-200; Massey and Wood, 11-13. *Voyage:* Hart, 52-53; Massey and Wood, 14-17; *The Alligator:* Hart, 79-80. *The Seal of Georgia:* Massey and Wood, 18–19. *Tomo-chi-chi:* Massey and Wood, 20–25. *Salzburgers and Moravians:* Massey and Wood, 26–31. *Troubles with Florida:* Massey and Wood, 32–35. *Silk Culture:* Massey and Wood, 36–37. *Georgia as a Colony:* Massey and Wood, 38–49, 47–48. *Bethesda Orphans' Home:* Massey and Wood, 40–44. *Mary Musgrove:* Massey and Wood, 45–46.

CHAPTER XXVI

MAP EXERCISES.—Find Albany, Philadelphia, New York City, Wilmington (Delaware).

DEFINITIONS.—Find the meaning of *trinkets, peevish*.

QUESTIONS.—What was the principal reason for Dutch colonization in America? What is meant by the "patroon system"? Did it tend to make the colony democratic? Explain your answer. What is meant by the phrase "ruled with a rod of iron"? Why did so many more races settle in New Netherland than in New England? Have you found any American colonists who did not care to have a voice in their government? What great service did Peter Minuit render to his country?

DATE WORTH REMEMBERING.—**1614**, first permanent settlement in New York.

REFERENCES.—*Minuit:* Southworth I, 130–135. *Stuyvesant:* Southworth I, 135–141; Chandler and Chitwood, 77–80; Guerber, 142–146. *New Amsterdam:* Hart, 140–142.

CHAPTER XXVII

DEFINITIONS.—Find the meaning of *burghers, bombardment, entreaty*.

QUESTIONS.—Did England have any claim to the territory of New Netherland? (See page 22.) Were the Dutch cowardly? (Find in Chapter XXVI another reason why the Dutch were willing to pass under English rule.) What changes were made by the Duke of York? Were the Dutch injured by becoming English subjects, or were they benefited? How? What peculiar kind of local government was introduced? Why did the people want a legislative assembly? Why did James II object? What evidence do you find of Leisler's wisdom? Why were pirates numerous in those days? Why not now?

REVIEW EXERCISES.—Which colony had the greatest population in 1700? Which colony had not then been established?

DATE WORTH REMEMBERING.—**1664**, English conquest of New York.

CHAPTER XXVIII

MAP EXERCISES.—Find the Isle of Jersey and Elizabeth (New Jersey).

QUESTIONS.—Why was New Jersey divided? How did Penn's treatment of West Jersey compare with James II's treatment of New York?

REVIEW EXERCISES.—What colonies had trouble with their proprietors about taxes? Make a list of the governments in the colonies that were changed by James II. Repeat all the "dates worth remembering" as far as you have gone in the text and give reasons why each is important.

REFERENCES.—*Penn and the Quakers:* Chandler and Chitwood, 86-88; Southworth I, 187-190; Gordy, 82-88; Guerber, 134-136, 147. *New Jersey:* Hart, 159-162.

CHAPTER XXIX

MAP EXERCISES.—Find Lewes and Wilmington (Delaware).

QUESTIONS.—Why were the Quakers persecuted in England? What facts about Penn's early life prove that he was true to his convictions? How did he acquire Pennsylvania? How did he develop it? Prove that he was just. Who made unsuccessful efforts to get possession of Delaware and why did they fail? Why did Penn want an "open passage to the sea," and how did he get it? How did "Mason and Dixon's Line" originate? Why did so many nationalities settle in the Middle Colonies?

REVIEW EXERCISE.—Make a list of the colonies in which the Indians were paid for their lands? What colonies had religious freedom? In 1762, which was the smallest colony? The largest? The most populous? The oldest? Which had the most slaves? What was the largest city?

REFERENCES.—*Pennsylvania:* Southworth I, 191-196; Gordy, 98-101; Guerber, 148-152; Chandler and Chitwood, 89-91. *Indians:* Hart, 144-148. *Other Explorers:* Pratt, 87-101.

CHAPTER XXX

MAP EXERCISES.—Find Lake Superior, Wisconsin River, Arkansas River, Lake Michigan, Matagorda Bay, Biloxi, Mobile, New Orleans, St. Louis, Detroit.

QUESTIONS.—How did the French and Spanish differ in their treatment of the Indians? Was La Salle's scheme practical? Why did it fail? Was Biloxi a good site for a new colony? What was the difference in the objects and methods of settlement between the French and the English? Why was the possession of the Mississippi River a matter of great importance?

DATES WORTH REMEMBERING.—**1699**, founding of Biloxi, first settlement in Mississippi; **1718**, founding of New Orleans.

REFERENCES.—*Marquette and Joliet:* Southworth I, 161-168; Chandler and Chitwood, 103-105; Guerber, 177-179. *La Salle and Hennepin:* Gordy, 103-114; Guerber, 180-183; Chandler and Chitwood, 105-111; Littlejohn, 25-56; Southworth I, 169-178.

CHAPTER XXXI

MAP EXERCISES.—Find Schenectady, Salmon Falls, Port Royal, Louisburg.

DEFINITIONS.—Find the meaning of *resentment, hostility.*

484 OUR REPUBLIC

QUESTIONS.—What three causes led Louis XIV to desire war with England? What unfortunate result to the colonies followed from the treaty of Utrecht? Why? Where did each of the wars mentioned in the chapter originate? Where was the fighting in America? What colonies participated?

DATE WORTH REMEMBERING.—**1689,** beginning of first conflict between the French and English colonies in America.

REFERENCES.—*Indians:* Guerber, 183–187. *Early French Wars:* Guerber, 187–191; Johonnot, 52–59. *Phipps:* Hart, 32–33. *Troubles with Florida:* White, 27–33. *South Carolina and the Indians:* White, 33–39. *Pirates:* Guerber, 162–164; Hart, 34–51; White, 39–44.

CHAPTER XXXII

MAP EXERCISES.—Find Pittsburg, Alexandria.

DEFINITIONS.—Find the meaning of *encroach, revere, retain, ambush.*

QUESTIONS.—Did the placing of lead tablets establish the French claim to the Mississippi valley? Give reasons for your answer. What early experiences were preparing Washington for his life work? Why was a union of the colonies desirable? Why was it not desired by the colonies? By England? Where did this war between the French and the English begin? Why was the possession of the source of the Ohio especially important to the contending nations? What caused the failure of Braddock's expedition? Why did he refuse to accept the advice of the colonists?

REFERENCES.—*Final Struggle:* Johonnot, 81–85. *Acadians:* Johonnot, 66–72; Guerber, 209. *Washington:* Guerber, 191–199; Southworth II, 24–43; Gordy, 116–134; Johonnot, 84–92; *Franklin:* Southworth I, 208–222; Gordy, 175–185; Johonnot, 108–114; Guerber, 199–205. *Braddock's Defeat:* Guerber, 206–208. *Fort Loudon:* Karns, 29–32.

CHAPTER XXXIII

DEFINITIONS.—Find the meaning of *incompetent, inroad, efficient, compensate.*

QUESTIONS.—What evidence do you find of the great ability of William Pitt? Why did Wolfe succeed? Why was the capture of Quebec one of the greatest events in American history? Who were the Acadians? What do you think of the way they were treated?

DATE WORTH REMEMBERING.—**1763,** end of the long struggle between the French and the English for control of America.

REFERENCES.—*Montcalm and Wolfe:* Gordy, 136–144; Chandler and Chitwood, 112–119; Southworth I, 226–243; Guerber, 210–214. *French Wars and Union:* Fiske, 26–38; Connor, 52–60.

QUESTIONS AND EXERCISES

CHAPTER XXXIV

DEFINITIONS.—Find the meaning of *stern, artisan, sturdy, indenture, lenient, mansion, frugal, clapboard.*

QUESTIONS.—What caused the difference in the way of thinking between the English colonists in the South and in New England? What caused the difference in the way of living? Was the presence of foreigners in the colonies a good thing? Give reasons for your answer. What were the social classes in the thirteen colonies? What were the characteristic amusements in New England? In the Middle Colonies? In the South? What objects do you find in the homes of to-day that were not in the colonial homes? In the kitchens? What was attractive about frontier life? What was unattractive?

GENERAL EXERCISES.—Write an account of the dress, daily life, and homes of wealthy aristocrats in Virginia. In Massachusetts. Of an artisan. Of an "indented servant." Of a slave. Of a frontiersman.

REFERENCES.—*Child Life:* Hart, 152–155, 170–171, 174, 175–188, 192–199, 210–214. *Fuel:* Mowry, 24–57. *Light:* Mowry, 61–76. *Food:* Mowry, 99–116. *Clothing:* Mowry, 143–171.

CHAPTER XXXV

DEFINITIONS.—Find the meaning of *export, relay, tutor, censorship, diversity.*

QUESTIONS.—What were the most important occupations in New England? In the Middle Colonies? In the Southern Colonies? Why was river travel more satisfactory than travel by land? How did the Atlantic Ocean prove a great blessing to the colonies? What can you tell about the first free schools in the colonies? Name and locate each of the colonial colleges. What can you tell about libraries, reading, and newspapers in colonial times? How did the governments of the colonies differ? Name the colonies belonging to each class. Which kind of government was most satisfactory to the colonists? To the King? Is the local government in your state to-day modeled after the New England or the Southern type? What hindered religion in some of the colonies? What arguments can you give in favor of an established church? Against it?

REFERENCES.—*Plantation Life:* Hart, 55–57, 63–64, 149–152, 157–162. *Life in North Carolina:* Connor, 39–44. *Travel:* Hart, 67–70. Mowry, 187–206. *Letters:* Mowry, 247–260. *Indigo:* White, 54–58. *Schools:* Hart, 201–210, 214–233. *Trade in South Carolina:* White, 68–74.

CHAPTER XXXVI

DEFINITIONS.—Find the meaning of *despite, discord, restriction, import, indignant, arbitrary, evade.*

QUESTIONS.—What was the point of dispute in the "Parsons' Case"? What were the results? What grievances did the people have against the royal governors? In each case, which side do you think was right? Was it wise for the King to interfere with colonial laws? Give reasons for your answer. Why did the Southern colonies object to the navigation laws? Why did the New England colonies? What class in England favored them? Why? Why did the colonists object to Writs of Assistance? What objections did Otis urge?

REFERENCES.—*Colonies in 1750:* Fiske, 4–25. *Navigation Acts:* Guerber, 214–217; Hall, 27–36. *Otis:* Chandler and Chitwood, 130–134.

CHAPTER XXXVII

DEFINITIONS.—Find the meaning of *boycott, obnoxious, effigy, exorbitant, designate.*

QUESTIONS.—What dangers confronted the thirteen colonies after 1763? If you had lived in the colonies at this time, would you have approved of a standing army? Why did the colonists oppose it? Was it right for England to pay all the expense of such an army? What was exactly the point of dispute between the colonies and the Mother Country? Why is taxation without representation dangerous? What important services were rendered by Virginia? By Massachusetts? By South Carolina? What were the arguments contained in the Declaration of Rights? Were they sound? What was the Declaratory Act? What were the Townshend Acts? How did the colonies show their disapproval? What conflicts followed? Were the causes of conflict the same in Boston, New York, and North Carolina? How did the speech of Otis, the resolutions of Patrick Henry, and the Declaration of Rights agree?

REFERENCES: *Stamp Act and Revenue Laws:* Fiske, 39–77; Hall, 36–44; Guerber, 218–223; Massey and Wood, 49–51; Connor, 60–67; White, 74–79. *Patrick Henry:* Gordy, 146–154; Southworth II, 1–8; Johonnot, 94–98. *North Carolina Regulators:* Connor, 68–72. *Troubles in North Carolina:* Connor, 73–81.

CHAPTER XXXVIII

MAP EXERCISES.—Find Annapolis, Wilmington (North Carolina).

QUESTIONS.—What caused the repeal of the Townshend Acts? Where and how did the colonists show their opposition to the tea tax? What was the *Gaspee* affair? Why did the colonists sympathize with the smugglers? Was smuggling right? What was the object at which Parliament aimed in the passage of each of the Five Acts? What was done by the first Continental Congress?

REFERENCES.—*The Crisis:* Fiske, 78–85. *Tea:* Guerber, 224–228; Massey and Wood, 51–52. *Samuel Adams:* Gordy, 156–163; Southworth II, 9–23. "*Liberty Tree*": White, 80–84. *South Carolina:* White, 84–89. *Franklin:* Chandler and Chitwood, 165–170.

CHAPTER XXXIX

MAP EXERCISES.—Find Lexington, Concord, Williamsburg, Charlotte.

DEFINITIONS.—Find the meaning of *detest, resent, disperse.*

QUESTIONS.—Was the British commander justified in ordering his men to fire on the colonists at Lexington? What steps were taken against British rule in 1775? What toward independence?

REVIEW EXERCISE.—Make a list of the patriotic services of Patrick Henry.

DATE WORTH REMEMBERING.—**April 19, 1775** (Patriots' Day), first battle of the Revolutionary War.

REFERENCES.—*Minutemen:* Guerber, 228-232. *Paul Revere:* Gordy, 165-174. *Lexington:* Guerber, 233-236. *Putnam:* Johonnot, 98-107. *Allen:* Johonnot, 135-140. *Liberty Boys:* Massey and Wood, 53-59.

CHAPTER XL

QUESTIONS.—What made Washington well qualified to command? What difficulties confronted him when he took command of the Patriot army? Why did he go to Boston? What brought about the Battle of Bunker Hill? What were its results throughout the colonies?

REVIEW EXERCISE.—Give some facts in the early life of Washington.

REFERENCES.—*Washington in Command:* Johonnot, 92-94; Chandler and Chitwood, 149-156; Southworth II, 44-47; Guerber, 242-245; Gordy, 193-195. *Bunker Hill:* Guerber, 237-241. *The Crisis:* Fiske, 85-105. *Canada Invaded:* Blaisdell and Ball, 18-35.

CHAPTER XLI

MAP EXERCISES.—Find Norfolk, Fayetteville, Wilmington (North Carolina).

QUESTIONS.—What were the causes and the results of Dunmore's War? What were the special causes, principal events, and results of the war in North Carolina? In South Carolina?

REVIEW EXERCISES.—What part did Virginia have in the events that brought on the Revolutionary War? What part did North Carolina have? South Carolina? Georgia?

REFERENCES.—*Attack on Charleston:* Blaisdell and Ball, 36-49; White, 96-105. *Independence of South Carolina:* White, 89-95.

CHAPTER XLII

QUESTIONS.—What was Howe's plan of action after leaving Boston? What acts of George III greatly angered the colonists? What were the steps leading to the adoption of the Declaration of Independence? How did Washington show his ability as a general in the events of 1776? What difficulties confronted the Patriots at the close of 1776?

DATE WORTH REMEMBERING.—**July 4, 1776,** signing of the Declaration of Independence.

REFERENCES.—*War in 1776:* Fiske, 104–121; Gordy, 195–202; Guerber, 245–248, 253–262; Chandler and Chitwood, 149–150; Southworth II, 48–54; Johonnot, 131–135. *Jefferson and the Declaration of Independence:* Guerber, 248–253; Southworth II, 108–111; Chandler and Chitwood, 176–181; Gordy, 234–240; Hall, 44–51. *Hale:* Blaisdell and Ball, 50–61. *Mecklenburg Declaration:* Connor, 82–88. *"Hornet's Nest":* Connor, 89–93. *Indians in South Carolina:* White, 105–107. *Henry Laurens:* White, 108–111.

CHAPTER XLIII

DEFINITIONS.—Find the meaning of *aggressive, contributions, recruit.*

MAP EXERCISES.—Find Bennington, Princeton, Brandywine.

QUESTIONS.—What were the results of Washington's victory at Princeton? What caused the failure of Burgoyne's expedition? Can you think of any criticism that might have been made against Washington by the "Conway Cabal"? How was money obtained from foreign countries to aid the American cause?

DATE WORTH REMEMBERING.—**1778**, France gave aid to the thirteen colonies.

REFERENCES.—*War in 1777:* Guerber, 262–271; Fiske, 121–143; Gordy, 202–206; Southworth II, 54–58. *French Alliance:* Southworth I, 223–225; Chandler and Chitwood, 170–174; Fiske, 144–149. *John Laurens:* White, 112–117.

CHAPTER XLIV

QUESTIONS.—What were the hardships endured by the Patriots at Valley Forge? Why did the coming of the French cause Clinton to evacuate Philadelphia? What do you think was the most feasible plan of campaign against the colonies? If you had been an Englishman, would you have approved of the plan to begin this campaign in the South? What other plans had been tried?

REFERENCES.—*Valley Forge:* Guerber, 271–275, 302–303; Gordy, 202–207; Chandler and Chitwood, 151–152; Johonnot, 140–145. *War in 1778:* Fiske, 149–154; Southworth II, 58–60; Guerber, 275–282; Massey and Wood, 60–65. *Burgoyne's Surrender.* Southworth II, 63–74; Johonnot, 146–154.

CHAPTER XLV

MAP EXERCISES.—Find Knoxville, Point Pleasant, Vincennes, Kaskaskia, Cahokia, the Wabash River.

QUESTIONS.—What were the causes of the westward movement of population before the Revolution? What must have been some of the arguments used by Clark in talking to the governor of Virginia about the importance of driving the British out of the Northwest? What difficulties confronted Clark in this undertaking?

QUESTIONS AND EXERCISES

REFERENCES.—*Daniel Boone:* Gordy, 222–233; Guerber, 288–293; Southworth II, 116–122; Chandler and Chitwood, 121–128. *Clark:* Blaisdell and Ball, 1–17; Fiske, 154–156; Guerber, 283–288. *"Traders and Hunters":* Karns, 32–36. *Watauga:* Karns, 37–42. *Robertson:* Karns, 43–49. *Sevier:* Karns, 50–53, 94–95, 270–274. *Tennessee Stories:* Karns, 54–59, 96–98.

CHAPTER XLVI

MAP EXERCISES.—Find the English and Irish Channels.

QUESTIONS.—Can you explain why Washington remained in New York while the British were over-running Georgia? Why was England unable to crush the colonies? What dangers threatened the colonists at the close of 1779?

REFERENCES.—*War in 1779:* Fiske, 156–164; Massey and Wood, 66–68. *Stony Point:* Johonnot, 166–170; Blaisdell and Ball, 77–89. *John Paul Jones:* Johonnot, 115–122; Guerber, 293–297; Southworth II, 84–92. *"First Battle of Chickamauga":* Karns, 60–65. *Settlements in Middle Tennessee:* Karns, 99–119.

CHAPTER XLVII

MAP EXERCISES.—Find Hillsboro, Camden, Charlotte, King's Mountain, West Point.

DEFINITIONS.—Find the meaning of *pillage, mutiny, aggrieved, annihilate.*

QUESTIONS.—Why did the Patriot bands gather in the swampy country? What mistake was made by Gates? Why was the battle of King's Mountain a turning point in the war? Was Washington justified in remaining in New York in the winter of 1779–80? Why did not the British respect Arnold? Were they right in accepting Arnold's offer to surrender West Point?

REVIEW EXERCISES.—How did General Gates make his reputation as a commander? Make a list of all foreigners named in the text who helped the colonists, giving their country and their services.

REFERENCES.—*War in 1780:* Fiske, 164–173; Guerber, 322–315. *Greene:* Southworth II, 75–83; Gordy, 211–217; Connor, 97–101. *Marion:* Guerber, 297–301; Gordy, 217–220; White, 117–137; Johonnot, 126–130. *Sumter:* White, 137–144. *Andrew Pickens:* White, 144–153. *Arnold:* Johonnot, 155–160; Guerber, 304–309. *Tarleton:* Guerber, 309–312. *Champe:* Johonnot, 160–165. *King's Mountain:* Karns, 66–72; Blaisdell and Ball, 90–104; Connor, 93–96.

CHAPTER XLVIII

MAP EXERCISES.—Find Cowpens, Salisbury, Wilmington (North Carolina), Richmond, Petersburg, Yorktown, Hobkirk Hill, Eutaw Springs.

QUESTIONS.—Why did the British withdraw to Wilmington and Charleston? Was the British Invasion of Virginia wise? Give your reasons.

Why did Cornwallis retire to Yorktown? Was it a wise move? Give reasons. Why could not Cornwallis escape from Yorktown?

DATE WORTH REMEMBERING.—**1781**, Cornwallis's surrender at Yorktown.

REFERENCES.—*War in 1781*: Fiske, 173–181; Massey and Wood, 69–74. *Lafayette*: Southworth II, 93–96. *Morgan*: Blaisdell and Ball, 105–122. *Yorktown*: Johonnot, 170–177; Southworth II, 60–62; Guerber, 315–323; Blaisdell and Ball, 123–137.

CHAPTER XLIX

QUESTIONS.—What were the terms of the treaty of peace? What arguments could the soldiers advance for making Washington king? Why did Washington hold his army together so long after the signing of the treaty of peace? What new evidences of Washington's greatness do you find in this chapter? How did the expression "not worth a Continental" originate?

DATE WORTH REMEMBERING.—**1783**, treaty closing the War of the American Revolution—England's recognition of American freedom.

REVIEW EXERCISE.—Account for the success of the colonies in the Revolutionary War.

REFERENCES.—*"Our Greatest Patriot"*: Blaisdell and Ball, 62–76. *"Washington's Farewell"*: Guerber, 323–326. *Revolutionary Heroes and Heroines*: Massey and Wood, 75–81.

CHAPTER L

DEFINITIONS.—Find the meaning of *engross, concede, "face value."*

QUESTIONS.—Why is a written constitution advisable as a basis for government? What caused the delay in adopting the Articles of Confederation? What state sacrificed most for the cause of the Union? Prove your answer. What were the points of weakness in the Articles of Confederation? Why were the people afraid of a strong central government?

REVIEW EXERCISE.—Compare the Confederation with the New England Confederacy.

REFERENCES.—*The South in the Revolutionary War*: Hall, 51–78. *"The Coldwater Expedition"*: Karns, 130–132. *Captives*: Karns, 133–143.

CHAPTER LI

DEFINITION.—Find meaning of *hamper*.

QUESTIONS.—Why is the power to tax necessary for the success of any government? Why were the requests of Congress reasonable? What were the causes and results of the troubles in the States in this period? Why did Washington and others want Congress to have more power? How did Virginia and Maryland lead the way to the Constitutional Convention of 1787?

REFERENCES.—*Troubles of the Confederation:* Fiske, 182–190; Blaisdell and Ball, 138–145. *State of Franklin:* Karns, 76–88. *Settlement of Tennessee:* Connor, 102–108.

CHAPTER LII

DEFINITIONS.—Find meaning of *ratify, restrict*.

QUESTIONS.—Can you suggest a reason why Rhode Island refused to send delegates to the Convention of 1787? What members of this convention have already been mentioned in this text? What members have not been mentioned? What was the opinion of the effects of the Constitution on States rights? What were the principal provisions in the Ordinance for the Northwest?

DATE WORTH REMEMBERING.—**1787,** the making of the Constitution of the United States and the adoption of the Ordinance for the government of the Northwest Territory.

REVIEW EXERCISES.—Compare the methods followed in adopting the Constitution of 1787 with those in adopting the Articles of Confederation.

REFERENCES.—*Convention of 1787:* Fiske, 190–193; Blaisdell and Ball, 145–155; Hall, 78–86. *C. C. Pinckney.* White, 154–160.

CHAPTER LIII

QUESTIONS.—What were the characteristics of the people in each of the different sections in 1789? Why did people move into the Northwest? Why did the North abolish slavery? Why did Virginia favor the antislavery clause in the Northwest Ordinance? What important inventions now in daily use were unknown in 1789?

REFERENCES.—*Frontier Life:* Mowry, 143–147; Karns, 120–129. *Letters:* Mowry, 260–264. *"The First Teacher" in Tennessee:* Karns, 73–75. *"Curious Money":* Karns, 89–93.

CHAPTER LIV

QUESTIONS.—What did the first Congress do toward organizing the new Government? What causes the rise of parties? Is it possible to keep down political parties in a free country? How does a cabinet member come to hold office? What were the five features of Hamilton's financial policy, and what was his purpose in each? How did he succeed in having Congress adopt his policy of assumption of State debts? What were North Carolina and Rhode Island between the inauguration of Washington and their adoption of the Constitution? What did they gain by entering the Union?

REFERENCES.—*Washington's Administration:* Chandler and Chitwood, 154–156. *Hamilton:* Southworth II, 97–107. *Yazoo Fraud:* Massey and Wood, 87–88. *William Blount:* Karns, 144–149. *Indian Attacks:* Karns, 150–156. *North Carolina:* Connor, 109–115. *Thomas Pinckney:* White, 161–168.

CHAPTER LV

QUESTIONS.—What are some of the arguments the Republicans must have used in opposition to Washington's neutrality proclamation? Was the proclamation a wise one? What does "free ships make free goods" mean? What were the grievances the United States had against England in 1793? What were the main points in Jay's treaty? What results followed the invention of the cotton gin? Make a list of them. What arguments were made by the farmers of Pennsylvania against the tax on whisky? Did Washington do right to pardon those who were convicted? Can you think of any advice the people of the United States needed when Washington wrote his "Farewell Address"? Can a President and Vice President belong to different parties to-day?

GENERAL EXERCISES.—Read Washington's "Farewell Address." Make a list of the important events of Washington's administrations.

REFERENCES.—*Washington's Troubles:* Guerber, 38–43. *Eli Whitney.* Southworth II, 123–126; Mowry, 148–152; Massey and Wood, 138–140 *Admission of Tennessee:* Karns, 157–160, 173–175.

CHAPTER LVI

DEFINITIONS.—Find the meaning of *tribute, naturalization, anarchy.*

QUESTIONS.—Why did France consider Jay's treaty "an unfriendly act"? What did Pinckney mean by his reply to the "X. Y. Z." proposition? What was the cause of the new naturalization law? Of the Alien and Sedition Laws? What was the substance of the Kentucky and Virginia Resolutions? Why are they important documents? Why did Maryland present the District of Columbia to the Federal Government for a capital? What predictions were made by the political parties in the election of 1800? How and why did this election affect the Constitution?

REVIEW EXERCISE.—Make a list of the important events of Adams's administration.

REFERENCES.—*Life on the Frontier:* Karns, 161–167, 176–178, 216–225, 229–231, 235–247, 256–258.

CHAPTER LVII

QUESTIONS.—What political principles did Jefferson advocate? What were his policies as President? Can you suggest a reason why the port of New Orleans was closed? Did Napoleon act wisely in selling Louisiana? Give reasons for your answer. How were western explorations beneficial to the Government? What were some of the changes brought about by the introduction of the steamboat?

DATE WORTH REMEMBERING.—**1803,** the purchase of the Louisiana Territory.

REFERENCES.—*Jefferson's Administration:* Southworth II, 111–115; Chandler and Chitwood, 181–186; Gordy, 240–244. *Barbary Wars:* Blaisdell and Ball, 156–168; Chandler and Chitwood, 192–200; Southworth, II, 145–148.

QUESTIONS AND EXERCISES

CHAPTER LVIII

QUESTIONS.—What methods did Jefferson adopt in his efforts to avoid war with England? With France? Do you think he was successful in any of these efforts? Were they wise? What effects did the Embargo have on New England? Why? What was the difference between the Embargo and the Non-Intercourse Act?

REVIEW EXERCISES.—Make a list of important events in Jefferson's administration. Which was the most important?

REFERENCES.—*Fulton:* Gordy, 246–252; Chandler and Chitwood, 187–191; Southworth II, 127–133. *Steamboats:* Mowry, 207–214. *Jefferson's Troubles:* Guerber, 69–71.

CHAPTER LIX

QUESTIONS.—What impression do you get from this chapter about Napoleon's sense of honor? Why was the use of Indians in warfare condemned by the civilized world? Why did the South and the West favor a declaration of war against England? Why did the North oppose it? Would any one of the five reasons for the war be sufficient to bring on war to-day? Can you think of any reason why New England should oppose the admission of Louisiana as a state?

REFERENCE.—*Tecumseh and the Creek War:* Karns, 182–192.

CHAPTER LX

MAP EXERCISES.—Find Detroit, Niagara, Lake Champlain, Queenstown, Ogdensburg, Frenchtown, Thames River (Canada), Lake Erie, Lake Ontario, Sackett's Harbor, Newark (New York).

QUESTIONS.—What was the importance of each of the expeditions planned for the invasion of Canada? What were the reasons for the failure of these expeditions? Were there any reasons in the causes of the war which made Americans fight better on the sea than on the land? Who were the heroes of the first year of the war? What ought Proctor to have done when the Indians attacked the American prisoners at Frenchtown? Why was the destruction of the British fleet on Lake Erie an event of great importance? Why is it disgraceful to burn public buildings in war? Are there any exceptions? Why were the frontiersmen good soldiers?

DATE WORTH REMEMBERING.—**1812,** beginning of the second war with England.

REFERENCES.—*Perry:* Johonnot, 177–186; Southworth II, 140–144; Guerber, 80–86. *"Old Ironsides":* Blaisdell and Ball, 169–184.

CHAPTER LXI

MAP EXERCISES.—Find Plattsburg, Bladensburg.

QUESTIONS.—What connection was there between Brown's invasion of Canada and Prevost's invasion of the United States? What were the results of these invasions? Did the English have any excuse for burning the Capitol at Washington? Give your reasons. How do you account for Jackson's successes in war? How did the peace between England and France remove the principal causes of the War of 1812?

REVIEW EXERCISE.—Make a list of heroes of the War of 1812 and give the services rendered by each.

REFERENCES.—*Jackson and New Orleans:* Gordy, 253-260; Karns, 195-209; Southworth II, 149-156; Chandler and Chitwood, 201-207; Blaisdell and Ball, 185-198; Johonnot, 192-198. "*The Star-Spangled Banner*": Johonnot, 187-192.

CHAPTER LXII

QUESTIONS.—What were the political results of the War of 1812? Which section of the United States derived the greatest benefit from the war? Explain your answer. Name and explain the financial results of this war. Were they all beneficial to the South? Explain your answer.

REVIEW EXERCISES.—Name the Presidents, up to 1816, who had refused a third term of office. Make a list of the Presidents to this time, giving the place and year of birth, time of service as President, and party connections. Make a list of the principal events of Madison's administration.

REFERENCES.—*The South in the War of 1812:* Hall, 86-90. *North Carolina:* Connor, 116-120.

CHAPTER LXIII

MAP EXERCISES.—Find St. Marks, Pensacola, Lake of the Woods.

QUESTIONS.—What section of the country had the greatest power in Monroe's cabinet? (No attempt should be made to learn the names of cabinet officers.) Do you think the United States was justified in waging war against the Seminoles? Can you defend Jackson's seizure of Florida? His execution of the two English subjects? Why was the sale of Florida a wise act on the part of Spain? Can you suggest a reason why the population of Mississippi increased more rapidly that that of Alabama? How do the first settlers generally enter a country? What caused the Missouri Compromise? Why was this Compromise favorable to the North? (See which section gained the more territory.) What caused the Monroe Doctrine to be put forth? What were some of the results? Was this doctrine wise? Was it just to Europe? How does a protective tariff injure an agricultural section?

DATES WORTH REMEMBERING.—**1820,** the adoption of the Missouri Compromise; **1823,** the first assertion of the Monroe Doctrine.

REFERENCES.—*Lafayette's Visit:* Blaisdell and Ball, 199-216; Connor, 121-122. *William Lowndes:* White, 169-174. *Langdon Cheves:* White, 174-178.

CHAPTER LXIV

DEFINITIONS.—Find the meaning of *elaborate, veto, primitive, democratic, supreme, transportation, facilities, monopolize, retain, supremacy*.

QUESTIONS.—What was the principal cause of the growth of population in the East? What class of Southerners were first to move into the West? What motives led people to the West? What dangers did the pioneers face? What hardships? What internal improvements were planned in this period? What is meant by "national spirit"? What caused such a spirit to develop in the West? Did this conflict with the idea of State sovereignty? Why did the Northern States abolish slavery? Why did they at first favor continuing it in the South? Why did the South favor it? What effect upon the poorer classes did slavery have? Manufacturing? Immigration? Was education neglected in the South? Prove your answer.

REVIEW EXERCISE.—Make a list of the States that had been admitted into the Union by 1820, giving the dates of their admission and noting whether they were slave or free.

GENERAL EXERCISE.—Describe a canal.

REFERENCES.—*Canals:* Mowry, 215-222. *Growth of Tennessee:* Karns, 179-181.

CHAPTER LXV

QUESTIONS.—Was there any justice in the complaints over Jackson's defeat in the Presidential campaign of 1824? Can you defend Adams's actions in regard to the Indian trouble in Georgia? What can you say in defense of Governor Troup? What was "the tariff of abominations"? What was advocated by the parties headed by Adams and Jackson?

REFERENCES.—*Henry Clay:* Southworth II, 158-165; Chandler and Chitwood, 225-232. *Indian Troubles in Georgia:* Massey and Wood, 89-93.

CHAPTER LXVI

DEFINITIONS.—Find the meaning of *prejudice, accord, privation, emancipation, nullify*.

QUESTIONS.—How do you account for the success of Jackson as President? Name some of his weaknesses. Can you prove that the South cared little about the slavery question before 1832? What caused Southern sentiment to change on this subject? Why did Northern people mob Abolitionists at first? Why did the South charge the Abolitionists with causing Nat Turner's Rebellion? What means were used by the Abolitionists for spreading their ideas? What was the point at issue in the Webster-Hayne debate? What new parties and methods originated in the campaign of 1832?

REVIEW EXERCISE.—Prove that Northern sentiment about the Union had changed since the Hartford Convention.

REFERENCES.—*Jackson and His Administration:* Southworth II, 156–157; Gordy, 260–262; Karns, 168–172. *Daniel Webster:* Chandler and Chitwood, 233–240; Southworth II, 166–175; Gordy, 264–271. *R. Y. Hayne:* White, 185–188. *McDuffie:* White, 179–185.

CHAPTER LXVII

DEFINITIONS.—Find the meaning of *pacificator, currency, indignant, security, redeem.*

QUESTIONS.—What did Jackson say about the object of nullification? Do you think this statement is correct? Why? What were the principal incidents connected with the nullification controversy? What were Jackson's objections to the National Bank? What did he intend should be the effect of his "Specie Circular"? What caused the panic of 1837? Was the "independent treasury" system better than the National Bank? Why? What were the causes of Van Buren's defeat?

REVIEW EXERCISES.—Compare the first and second Seminole Wars as to causes and results. Make a list of important events since 1820.

REFERENCES.—*Calhoun:* Chandler and Chitwood, 241–246; White, 188–205. *Childhood of Robert E. Lee:* Williamson I, 9–16. *Childhood of "Stonewall" Jackson:* Williamson II, 9–23. *Nathaniel Macon:* Connor, 123–125.

CHAPTER LXVIII

MAP EXERCISES.—Find Cumberland (Maryland), Wheeling, Lowell (Massachusetts).

DEFINITIONS.—Find the meaning of *macadamized, sickle, flail, tinder-box.*

QUESTIONS.—What changes of population took place between 1830 and 1840? Which of these changes can you account for? Was the Cumberland Road as beneficial to Maryland as to Kentucky? Prove your answer. How did the introduction of the steamboat help the farmer? The merchant? The immigrant? What are the important facts in the early history of the Erie Canal? What checked the rapid progress of canal building? What new methods were introduced between 1820 and 1840 for the more rapid transmission of news? Can you suggest any reasons why the farmers were slow to accept McCormick's harvester? Give an account of the development of manufacturing in this period. Since 1840 what changes have taken place in city life? In country life? What were the greatest reforms of this period?

REFERENCES.—*Railroads:* Southworth II, 135–139; Mowry, 223–228. *Erie Canal:* Southworth II, 176–179. *Telegraph and Signaling:* Southworth II, 180–185; Mowry, 265–277; Chandler and Chitwood, 247–251; Gordy, 273–281. *Reaper:* Mowry, 117–123; Chandler and Chitwood, 251–254; Southworth II, 249–251. *The Savannah:* Massey and Wood, 136–137. *Progress in North Carolina:* Connor, 126–133.

QUESTIONS AND EXERCISES

CHAPTER LXIX

MAP EXERCISES.—Find Great Salt Lake, Goliad, San Antonio, San Jacinto. Trace the line 54° 40' from the Rocky Mountains to the Pacific Ocean.

QUESTIONS.—Ought President Tyler to have carried out the Whig policy? Why? What did Webster accomplish by remaining in Tyler's cabinet? What minor incidents occurred in Tyler's administration? Why are they worthy of passing notice? Why did Mexico forbid the importation of slaves into Texas? What idea do you get of the character of the Mexicans in 1836? Of the character of the Texans? Would the annexation of Texas have injured the North? Explain your answer. What prevented Van Buren's nomination in 1844? What defeated Clay in this election?

REFERENCES.—*Sam Houston:* Chandler and Chitwood, 208–216; *Nolan and Bean:* Littlejohn, 59–80. *Austin and His Settlement:* Littlejohn, 83–102. *Sam Houston and Lamar:* Littlejohn, 105–132; Karns, 210–215. *David Crockett:* Littlejohn, 135–147; Karns, 226–228, 248–255. *The Alamo:* Littlejohn, 151–162. *Goliad:* Littlejohn, 165–174. *San Jacinto:* Littlejohn, 177–193. *"Drawing the Black Beans":* Littlejohn, 197–208. *"Castle Perote":* Littlejohn, 211–238.

CHAPTER LXX

MAP EXERCISES.—Find Nueces River, Rio Grande, Monterey, Buena Vista, Vera Cruz, Mexico City, Santa Fé.

QUESTIONS.—How did the Oregon question originate? How was it settled? Why did Mexico oppose the annexation of Texas to the United States? Was Polk correct in saying that Mexico had "invaded our territory"? What were the most important battles of the Mexican War?

DATE WORTH REMEMBERING.—1845–48, War with Mexico.

GENERAL DISCUSSION.—What makes an event important in history?

REFERENCES.—*Polk and the Mexican War:* Karns, 259–262. *Zachary Taylor:* Chandler and Chitwood, 217–224. *Buena Vista:* Johonnot, 199–206. *Georgia and the Mexican War:* Massey and Wood, 94–95. *South Carolina and the Mexican War:* White, 206–209.

CHAPTER LXXI

MAP EXERCISES.—Find Cape Horn, Isthmus of Panama.

QUESTIONS.—What were the dangers encountered by the overland route to California? What were the disadvantages of the Panama route? Of the route around Cape Horn? What caused prices to advance in California? Why did Southerners favor the "Gag Law"? Were they right? Was the Wilmot Proviso wise? Was it just? Why? What strange facts are to be noted about the Presidential campaign of 1848?

REFERENCES.—*The South in the Mexican War:* Hall, 90–97. *Early Manhood of Robert E. Lee:* Williamson I, 18–43.

CHAPTER LXXII

QUESTIONS.—What controversy arose upon the application of California for admission to the Union? What were the five provisions in Clay's compromise measure? In the debate, what did Clay contribute? Calhoun? Webster? Chase? How did the first three of these speeches agree? How did they differ? Why did the Abolitionists object to the fugitive slave law? Could the slave States afford to surrender their constitutional right to demand such a law? Why?

DATE WORTH REMEMBERING.—**1850,** adoption of the great Compromise.

REFERENCES.—"*The South in Olden Days*": Hall, 15–27. *Early Manhood of "Stonewall" Jackson*: Williamson II, 25–77.

CHAPTER LXXIII

QUESTIONS.—Which section first violated the Compromise of 1850? What were the "personal liberty laws"? Compare these with the attempt at nullification by South Carolina. What was the "Underground Railroad"? What were the methods and the effects of its operations? What was "Uncle Tom's Cabin," and what effects did it produce throughout the North? Can you think of any way in which the North might have been induced to observe an effective fugitive slave law? Did the North know the real condition of slave life in the South?

MEMORY GEM.—"*The South*": Williamson I, 181–183.

CHAPTER LXXIV

QUESTIONS.—What part of the Union wanted more territory? Why? What was meant by "squatter sovereignty"? Was it just? Do you think the Compromise of 1850 annulled the Compromise of 1820? (Review these in the text.) Would you have voted for the Kansas-Nebraska Bill? Why? What was the plan of each section for getting control of Kansas? What were the results? Which constitution of Kansas should have been accepted?

REFERENCE.—"*The Sunny South*": Williamson II, 247–248.

CHAPTER LXXV

QUESTIONS.—What were the methods and objects of the Know-Nothing Party? What were the sharp points of difference between the Democratic and Republican parties of 1856? What did this election show? How did the Dred Scott case originate? What was the decision of the Supreme Court? What were the causes and results of the Lincoln-Douglas debates? What were the plans of John Brown and what did he do? What was the effect of his execution on the North? What do you think of Brown?

REVIEW EXERCISES.—Make a full list of "dates worth remembering" in American history to 1860, giving the reasons why each is important.

REFERENCES.—*Slavery in Georgia:* Massey and Wood, 100–103. *Early Causes of Estrangement:* Hall, 146–162.

CHAPTER LXXVI

DEFINITIONS.—Find the meaning of *competition, trunk-line, transportation.*

QUESTIONS.—What caused the rapid increase of population in the North between 1840–60? How did competition affect ocean travel? Make a list of the improvements in railway transportation and of their effects. What great developments were made in telegraphic communication? In mail facilities? What inventions of this period have you seen? What have you not seen? Describe those you have seen. What proof can you give of the great progress of manufacturing from 1840–60? What results followed this development?

REFERENCES.—*Water Travel:* Mowry, 229–234. *Atlantic Cable:* Mowry, 278–285. *Sewing:* Mowry, 172–184. *Food:* Mowry, 124–140. *Light:* Mowry, 77–84. *Printing:* Mowry, 252–257. *Postal System:* Mowry, 260–264. *Ether:* Massey and Wood, 137–138.

CHAPTER LXXVII

DEFINITION.—Find the meaning of *platform* (political).

QUESTIONS.—What caused divisions among Democrats in 1860? What were the main points in the Republican platform? Why were the views of Douglas not acceptable to the North? To the South?

REFERENCES.—*"The Greatest Cause of Estrangement":* Hall, 162–181. *"The Three Sections" of Georgia:* Massey and Wood, 96–99.

CHAPTER LXXVIII

DEFINITIONS.—Find meaning of *compact, hazard, pecuniary.*

QUESTIONS.—What was the immediate effect of the election of Lincoln? Why did Southern men leave the service of the United States when their States seceded? What is meant by "the path of our fathers" in the quotation from Davis's farewell address? What is meant by treason? What is the difference between nullification and secession?

REFERENCES.—*Jefferson Davis:* Chandler and Chitwood, 259–263. *Abraham Lincoln:* Chandler and Chitwood, 265–273; Gordy, 282–300; Southworth II, 186–205.

CHAPTER LXXIX

QUESTIONS.—Can you prove that the States were free to accept or reject the Constitution? What evidence do you find that, when the Constitution was adopted, it was thought the States had a right to secede at pleasure? What evidence can you show that many Northern leaders believed in the right of secession? How can you account for the growth of sentiment against secession? Can you prove that slavery was not the cause of secession? What arguments can you give against secession? In favor of it? If you had lived in 1861, would you have favored secession? Give reasons in full.

REFERENCES.—*Right of Secession:* Hall, 181–192. *Effects of Secession:* Southworth II, 206–209.

CHAPTER LXXX

QUESTIONS.—Why was the Confederate flag called the "Stars and Bars"? Can you prove from the sketch of Davis's life in the footnote that he was patriotic? As far as you can judge from the facts given in this chapter was the Confederate Constitution better than the Constitution of the United States? Was Buchanan's recommendation practical? What were the main features of the Crittenden Compromise? Why did the Northern senators defeat this measure? Why did Virginia want to save the Union? Why was her effort unsuccessful?

DATE WORTH REMEMBERING.—1861, formation of the Southern Confederacy.

REFERENCES.—*"The War":* Hall, 192–196. *"Confederate Battle Flag":* McCarthy, 225–230. *Brown and Stephens:* Massey and Wood, 106–109.

CHAPTER LXXXI

DEFINITIONS.—Find the meaning of *arsenal, aggressor, coercion*.

QUESTIONS.—Did South Carolina want war? Give reasons for your answer. Was the State militia justified in firing on the *Star of the West?* Did the seceding States have a right to Federal property within their borders? Was the seizure of this property wise? Was it possible for Lincoln to carry out, without war, the views expressed in his inaugural address?

REFERENCE.—*The Private Soldier and the Sailor:* Hall, 197–208.

CHAPTER LXXXII

DEFINITIONS.—Find the meaning of *tolerate*. What is the difference between *rebellion* and *revolution?*

QUESTIONS.—Who was responsible for the attack on Fort Sumter? Prove your answer. Can you justify Lincoln's connection with this incident? Davis's connection with it? Can you find evidence to show that Lincoln did not think that the country was entering the greatest conflict in its history? Why did other Southern States join the Confederacy?

GENERAL EXERCISE.—Tell, without prompting, the story of "the beginning of the conflict."

QUESTIONS AND EXERCISES

DATE WORTH REMEMBERING.—**April 12, 1861,** the attack on Fort Sumter.

REFERENCES.—*"Women of the Confederacy"*: Hall, 215–239. *North Carolina:* Connor, 133–137. *Francis W. Pickens:* White, 216–223. *Bonham:* White, 224–231.

CHAPTER LXXXIII

DEFINITION.—What is meant by *material resources?*

QUESTIONS.—How did the population of the two nations compare? How did the South expect to overcome her lack of material resources? Was this hope reasonable? How was the execution of the plan prevented? How did the South expect to overcome her financial disadvantage?

REFERENCE.—*"The Homes That Made Heroes"*: Hall, 98–123

CHAPTER LXXXIV

MAP EXERCISES.—Find Hampton Roads, Manassas, Springfield (Missouri).

DEFINITIONS.—Find the meaning of *aggressive, canteen, frenzy, ghastly, demented, frantic.*

QUESTIONS.—Why was each plan of action adopted by the Federal Government important? Which would you expect would be attempted first? Do you think the capture of Richmond in 1861 would have ended the war? Give reasons for your answer. To what do you attribute the success of the Confederates in the first battle of Manassas? To what do you attribute the panic that seized the Federal soldiers after their defeat?

REFERENCES.—*"The Homes That Made Heroes"*: Hall, 123–145. *"Stonewall" Jackson:* Williamson II, 78–117.

CHAPTER LXXXV

MAP EXERCISES.—Find Nassau, Havana.

QUESTIONS.—Why did Lincoln look upon Confederate privateersmen as pirates? Was President Davis's answer wise and just? What attitude did the Confederate Government expect England to assume in this war? Why? What were the principal events in the career of the *Alabama?* Give an account of the Trent affair. Why was England offended?

REFERENCES.—*"Voice from the Ranks"*: McCarthy, 7–21. *Lincoln and the War:* Southworth II, 209–212.

CHAPTER LXXXVI

MAP EXERCISES.—Find the places mentioned in this chapter. Trace the movements of McClellan in the Peninsula Campaign and of Jackson in his Valley Campaign.

QUESTIONS.—What were the principal events in McClellan's Peninsula Campaign? What were the plans for the movement of the other Federal armies? How were they frustrated? What was the most important battle in the Peninsula Campaign? Why? What caused the failure of the Federal plans in this campaign? What brought success to the Confederates?

REFERENCES.—*Peninsula Campaign:* Guerber, 193-197. "*The Outfit Modified*": McCarthy, 22-34. *Robert E. Lee:* Southworth II, 229-237; Chandler and Chitwood, 274-280; Littlejohn, 259-282. "*Lee and His Paladins*": Hall, 240-252. "*Stonewall*" *Jackson:* Williamson II, 119-173. *Maxy Gregg:* White, 231-238.

CHAPTER LXXXVII

QUESTIONS.—What effects followed the failure of the Peninsula Campaign? Why did Lee wish to carry the war into the North? What disappointments came to both the South and the North as a result of Lee's first invasion of the North? Why was the battle of Sharpsburg, or Antietam, important? What great mistake did Burnside make at Fredericksburg? What was the result?

REVIEW EXERCISES.—Make a list of the different commanders at the head of the Union army in the East. Of those at the head of the Confederate army. Make a list of Confederate victories. Of Federal victories.

REFERENCES.—"*Romantic Ideas Dissipated*": McCarthy, 35-46. "*On the March*": McCarthy, 47-61. *Robert E. Lee:* Williamson I, 45-61. "*Stonewall*" *Jackson:* Williamson II, 175-193.

CHAPTER LXXXVIII

MAP EXERCISES.—Find Columbus (Kentucky), Tennessee River, Cumberland River, Cairo, Nashville, Corinth, Tupelo.

QUESTIONS.—What was the plan of action of the Federals in Kentucky and Tennessee in 1862? Of the Confederates? Why were the forts controlling the Tennessee and Cumberland rivers important? What was the turning point in Grant's career? What saved him from disgrace? Was he right? What saved him from being captured at Shiloh? What territory was gained by the Federals in Kentucky and Tennessee in 1862?

REFERENCES.—*Shiloh and its Heroes*": Hall, 262-265. "*Cooking and Eating*": McCarthy, 62-78.

CHAPTER LXXXIX

MAP EXERCISES.—Find New Madrid, Port Hudson, Vicksburg, Algiers, Holly Springs, Louisville, Perryville, Chattanooga, Murfreesboro, Grenada.

QUESTIONS.—Why was the Mississippi River a source of weakness to the Confederacy? Would this have been the case if the South had had a powerful navy? How was the upper part of the river taken by the Federals? The lower part? Why was the loss of New Orleans a great disaster to the South? Why did the people of New Orleans denounce Butler? Why was Vicksburg more difficult to capture than New Orleans? (Vicksburg is called the "Hill City.") What was the plan of the second campaign against Vicksburg? Why did it fail? What caused the failure of Bragg's plan to retake Kentucky? Tennessee? Why was the battle of Corinth fought?

REVIEW EXERCISES.—Compare the exploit of the *Arkansas* with that of the *Merrimac*. What was the greatest Confederate victory in the West in 1862? The greatest defeat?

REFERENCES.—"*Comforts,*" etc.: McCarthy, 79–99. *Farragut:* Southworth, II, 238–248; Karns, 232–234.

CHAPTER XC

DEFINITIONS.—Find the meaning of *promissory note, habeas corpus, emancipation, quell*.

QUESTIONS.—Why were coffee and sugar scarce in the South at the close of 1862? How did the National banks bring money into the Federal treasury? What did Europeans think about the chances for Confederate success in 1863? What were the three conditions in the North which were unfavorable to the Federal Government? Explain each. What early efforts did Lincoln make to abolish slavery in the four slave-holding states still in the Union? Why did he issue the Emancipation Proclamation? Was it lawful? On what grounds did Lincoln defend his act? How could the slaves have put a speedy end to the war? Were the Conscription Law and the Draft Act just? Why were they necessary?

REFERENCES.—"*Fun and Fury*": McCarthy, 100–122. *North Carolina:* Connor, 138–154.

CHAPTER XCI

QUESTIONS.—Why was it difficult for Grant's army to reach the highlands of north Vicksburg? Why did Grant try to change the course of the Mississippi River? Why did he cross the Mississippi with part of his army? Did he accomplish his object after entering the State of Mississippi Why did he besiege Vicksburg? Could he have taken the city any other way? What took place in the city during the siege? Why did it surrender? Was this step wise? Was Grant angry with the people of the city for resisting him? What were the causes and the results of the battle of Chickamauga? Of Lookout Mountain? Of Missionary Ridge? What caused the success of the Federals in the West in 1863? Can you suggest a reason for Morgan's raid? Why do you admire the conduct of Sam Davis?

REFERENCES.—"*Camp Fires*": McCarthy, 200–224. *Dick Dowling and Dr. Bailey:* Littlejohn, 241–255.

CHAPTER XCII

MAP EXERCISES.—Find the Rappahannock River, Harper's Ferry, Harrisburg, Gettysburg.

DEFINITIONS.—Find the meaning of *anguish, gory, irreparable.*

QUESTIONS.—For what is the battle of Chancellorsville noted? Why was Lee anxious to carry the war into the North? What were the main incidents in the battle of Gettysburg? What was the effect of this battle on the North? On the South? In Europe?

DATE WORTH REMEMBERING.—**July 4, 1863,** surrender of Vicksburg and battle of Gettysburg.

REFERENCES.—*"Jackson and His 'Foot-Cavalry'":* Hall, 253–261. *"'Stonewall' Jackson Mortally Wounded":* Williamson II, 244–245. *"'Stonewall' Jackson's Way":* Williamson II, 248–250. *"Stonewall" Jackson:* Williamson II, 194–238. *Robert E. Lee:* Williamson I, 62–70. *Samuel McGowan:* White, 239–244. *Joseph B. Kennebrew:* White, 244–250.

CHAPTER XCIII

MAP EXERCISES.—Find Dalton, Mobile.

DEFINITIONS.—Find the meaning of *goal, evacuate, disperse.*

QUESTIONS.—What were Grant's plans for ending the war? Why were most of the Confederate troops taken from Mississippi after the fall of Vicksburg? Why did Sherman lay waste the country between Vicksburg and Meridian? Was he right in doing so? Did the fighting in Louisiana at this time exert much influence upon the final outcome of the struggle? What is a flank movement? Was Johnston right in refusing to attack Sherman? Give reasons for your answer. What plans did Hood try to execute? What were the results? Was Sherman justified in the destruction of property in his march to the sea? Why? What was the condition of Southern seaports at the end of 1864?

REFERENCES.—*U. S. Grant:* Southworth II, 217–228; Chandler and Chitwood, 280–287; Gordy, 302–313. *Sherman in Georgia:* Massey and Wood, 112–115.

CHAPTER XCIV

MAP EXERCISES.—Find Rapidan River, Spottsylvania, Cold Harbor.

DEFINITIONS.—Find the meaning of *penetrate, tunnel, crater.*

QUESTIONS.—What was Grant's plan for capturing Richmond? What valuable facts about warfare do you find in the account of the battles of Spottsylvania? What advantages did Grant have over Lee? Lee over Grant? What moves were made to cut off Lee's supplies? What services were rendered by Magruder and Early?

REFERENCES.—*Lincoln and the War:* Southworth II, 212–216. *"The Phantom Host":* Williamson II, 250–254. *Robert E. Lee:* Williamson I, 70–89.

CHAPTER XCV

DEFINITIONS.—Find the meaning of *parole, humanity.*

QUESTIONS.—What political parties arose in the North in 1864? Who were their Presidential nominees and what were their platforms? What

QUESTIONS AND EXERCISES

was the first agreement about exchanging prisoners? What brought it to an end? Was the position of the South on this matter wise? Prove your answer. Was the proposition of August, 1864, just? Which side had the greater number of prisoners? The more provisions? Which side lost more men in prison? What conclusions are to be drawn from these facts?

REFERENCES.—*Robert E. Lee:* Williamson I, 90–98, 169. *Andersonville:* Massey and Wood, 111. "*The Bivouac of the Dead*": Williamson II, 245–246. "*The Lone Sentry*": Williamson II, 239–240.

CHAPTER XCVI

MAP EXERCISES.—Find Goldsboro, Raleigh.

DEFINITIONS.—Find the meaning of *cope, assassination, detain.*

QUESTIONS.—What were the Federal plans in 1865? The Confederate plans? What were the last movements of Lee's army? Why did he surrender? Could he have done anything else? Were Lee and Grant personal enemies? Was Grant a personal enemy of the Confederate soldiers? Were the Confederate and Federal soldiers personal enemies? Why were they fighting? Why did Lee's men love him? Describe the parting scene. Why was the assassination of Lincoln a great disaster? Was Davis a traitor?

REVIEW EXERCISE.—Make a list of the most important battles of the war, giving the significance of each.

REFERENCES.—"*Improvised Infantry*": McCarthy, 123–164. "*After the Surrender*": Massey and Wood, 118–121. *Robert E. Lee:* Williamson I, 99–102. *Micah Jenkins:* White, 250–253. *Nathan Evans:* White, 254–256. *Wade Hampton:* White, 261–279.

CHAPTER XCVII

QUESTIONS.—What were the enlistments and death losses of the war to the North? To the South? What were the property losses of the war to the North? To the South? In what ways was money raised? What are bonds? Greenbacks? Why is paper money worth more now than it was in 1865?

GENERAL EXERCISES.—Write a brief sketch of one of the following: The effects of the war on your country; the part that your grandfather or a neighbor took in the conflict; the experiences of your grandmother or of some other lady during this period; a ruined plantation at the close of the war. Make a list of the ways in which the South suffered more than the North.

REFERENCES.—"*Homeward Bound*": McCarthy, 165–182. *Georgia's Losses:* Massey and Wood, 116–117. "*Conclusion*": Hall, 305–310.

CHAPTER XCVIII

DEFINITIONS.—Find the meaning of *depreciate, ferret, evade, privation.*

QUESTIONS.—What services were rendered the Confederacy by the women of the South, and what hardships did they endure? Why was salt more precious at one time than meal? Make a list of substitutes that were used for well-known articles of food; for printing paper and stationery. Can you account for the faithfulness of the slaves during the war? How did the women at home feel over the news of the surrender? What did the Confederate soldiers do when they returned home after the war?

REVIEW EXERCISE.—Make a list of "dates worth remembering," from 1860–65, noting particularly the reason why each is important.

REFERENCE.—"*Soldiers Transformed*": McCarthy, 183–199.

MEMORY GEM.—"*The Conquered Banner*": Williamson I, 175.

CHAPTER XCIX

DEFINITIONS.—Find the meaning of *amnesty, vagrancy*.

QUESTIONS.—How were the Southern white people treated after the war? What had been done for the negro before the close of the war? What theories were advanced on the relation of the Southern States to the Union? Which seems most reasonable? On what condition did Lincoln think the States should be readmitted? What conditions did Johnson impose? What were the reasons for opposing the President's plan? Were the laws to control freedmen in the South wise? Were they just? Could they have been avoided?

REFERENCES.—"*The South since the War*": Hall, 266–274. *Johnson:* Karns, 263–269.

CHAPTER C

DEFINITIONS.—Find the meaning of *impeach, misdemeanor*.

QUESTIONS.—What can you say in defense of the Freedman's Bureau? Against it? What was the object of the Civil Right's Bill? The Thirteenth Amendment? The Fourteenth Amendment? Were these acts wise? Why were they favored by the North? What reasons can you find in the latter part of this chapter for the passage of the Tenure-of-Office Act? Why did the North give the negro the right to vote in the South? What motive prompted Stevens's actions? What caused the carpetbaggers to settle in the South? To what extent did they care for the interests of the Southern States? What was the status of the several Southern States when they ratified the Fourteenth Amendment?

REFERENCES.—*Reconstruction:* Massey and Wood, 122–128. "*The South since the War*": Hall, 275–304.

CHAPTER CI

QUESTIONS.—How did Napoleon III violate the Monroe Doctrine? Why did he do it? Why did the United States object? Do you think the purchase of Alaska was a wise step? Why? Which ticket do you think you would have voted in 1868? Why?

REFERENCE.—"*Poets of South Carolina and of the South*": White, 282–289.

QUESTIONS AND EXERCISES

CHAPTER CII

DEFINITIONS. Find the meaning of *arbitration, award, tragic, prostrate, shroud, agony, superstitious, atrocities.*

QUESTIONS.—What two great forces had the effect of reducing the size of the United States and of the world? What two disputes were settled by arbitration? Why is this method of settling disputes superior to war? What classes of white Republicans were there in the South? What was the moral difference between them? What were the causes and the results of the presence of negroes in Southern legislatures? Why was the Ku Klux organized? Describe its methods. Why was the Klux successful? What were the objects and results of the "Force Acts"? How did they resemble the Fifteenth Amendment? What was the political condition of the country in the campaign of 1872?

REFERENCES.— *Death and Character of Robert E. Lee:* Williamson I, 103–167. *Reconstruction:* White, 290–297.

CHAPTER CIII

DEFINITIONS.—Find the meaning of *demonetize, balance of trade, standard of value, unprecedented, specie, indemnity.*

QUESTIONS.—What were the causes and results of the great panic of 1873? What effect would reducing the supply of money have on prices? What great scandals arose in Grant's administration? Explain each. What were the causes and results of Indian troubles? Why was paper money worth less than specie before 1875? Does any country own the "high seas"? How do the *Virginius* and the *Trent* affairs resemble each other? What were the differences between parties and platforms in 1872 and 1876? What was the cause of the contested election? Why was a special commission created to settle the case? Which candidate had the better claim on the Presidency?

REVIEW EXERCISE.—Make a list of the important events in Grant's administration.

DATE WORTH REMEMBERING.—**1876,** Hayes-Tilden contested election and appointment of electoral commission.

CHAPTER CIV

QUESTIONS.—Why were Federal troops in the South a great curse? What important service did Mississippi render to the South in 1890? What can you say in defense of labor organizations? Of the strikes? Against them? What prevents the election of a President for a third term? What is the origin and object of the Civil Service Commission? What objections are urged against a low tariff? What caused the election of Cleveland in 1884?

DATES WORTH REMEMBERING.—**1877,** withdrawal of Federal troops from the South; **1890,** Mississippi Constitution disfranchizing negroes.

REFERENCE.—*"Observations of 'Stonewall's' Servant":* Williamson II, 240–243.

CHAPTER CV

QUESTIONS.—Why was each law mentioned in the first section important? What are the causes of strikes? Why are anarchists dangerous to our country? Is a strong navy important? Why? What were the conditions that caused Cleveland to propose a reduction of the tariff in 1887? Was he wise in this? What was the reason for each of the laws passed by Congress in 1888? How did the People's Party originate? What did it stand for in 1892? Which of these measures do you think were wise? Unwise? Give reasons.

REFERENCE.—*North Carolina since the War:* Connor, 155-169.

CHAPTER CVI

MAP EXERCISES.—Find Hawaii, Venezuela.

QUESTIONS.—What were the causes of the panic of 1893? **Explain** each. Why was there opposition to the repeal of the Sherman Act? Who was responsible for the Democratic defeat in 1894? Why? Why did Cleveland refuse to annex Hawaii? What was the cause and the result of the Bering Sea controversy? Was Cleveland right in his position on the Venezuelan affair? What was the principal issue in the campaign of 1896 and what position did the different parties take?

CHAPTER CVII

MAP EXERCISES.—Find Tampa, Santiago, Porto Rico, Philippines, Guam, Wake Island, Samoa.

DEFINITIONS.—Find the meaning of *notorious, grasping, resent, disclaim, vie, collier.*

QUESTIONS.—Can you think of any reasons why Spain oppressed Cuba? Did the United States have any right to try to relieve suffering in Cuba in 1897? What would have been the result if England had attempted to relieve suffering in the South in 1864? Would the United States have been justified in declaring war on account of the *Maine* disaster? Why did the United States announce that it would not hold Cuba? Why was the battle of Manila important?

REFERENCES.—*Leaders in the Spanish-American War:* Gordy, 314-326. *Dewey:* Southworth II, 256-259; Chandler and Chitwood, 297-307.

CHAPTER CVIII

What facts in the history of this war show the importance of the navy? Why did Hobson sink the *Merrimac* in the mouth of Santiago harbor? Make a list of dangers encountered by soldiers. In what respects was the American navy superior to the Spanish? What are the terms of the treaty ending the war? Do you think the United States ought to hold the Philippines? Porto Rico?

DATE WORTH REMEMBERING.—**1898**, war between the United States and Spain.

REFERENCE.—*Clara Barton:* Southworth II, 252–255.

CHAPTER CIX

DEFINITIONS.—Find the meaning of *guerrilla, sanitation, legation, imperialism, intervene.*

QUESTIONS.—Why does the United States hold the Philippines? Should they be given their freedom? Should they be admitted as a State, or as States, to the Union? What obligations does the United States owe to Cuba? What kind of government has Porto Rico? Why did the people of this country pay the stamp tax in 1899 and refuse to do so in 1774? What were the causes and results of the Boxer trouble? What were the issues in the election of 1900? Why should an anarchist wish to kill the President? How did the United States acquire the Canal Zone? What is usually the cause of great labor strikes?

REVIEW EXERCISES.—Make a list of the difficulties of the United States which have been settled by arbitration. Of the principal events since 1865. Of the Vice Presidents who have succeeded to the office of President.

MEMORY GEM.—"*The Sword of Robert Lee*": Williamson I, 7

CHAPTER CX

QUESTIONS.—Why is a pure food law wise? Why does it mark a dangerous tendency? What good results came from the voyage of the United States fleet around the world? What caused the panic of 1907? Why was the conference of Governors wise? Can you think of some important subjects that might be considered by such a conference? What were the principal issues in the campaign of 1908? What evidences of the breaking of party lines do you find in the account of the Aldrich Bill?

REVIEW EXERCISES.—Make a list of great expositions, showing what each commemorated. Of the financial panics in the history of the country and the cause of each. Of the important events in the administration of Roosevelt.

CHAPTER CXI

QUESTIONS. —Why are strikes of comparatively recent date in American history? Do they indicate progress in any line? Do you find any evidence that the country is becoming more closely united? What changes have recently taken place in the condition of the negroes and in the relationship between the white people and other races in this country? Give reasons for these changes. What is the greatest power in this country for preparing foreigners for useful citizenship? In what part of the country do you find the smallest percentage of foreigners? Why? What are some of the most important recent American inventions? What are our most important educational factors? What is the special object of each? What makes the West attractive and prosperous? What makes the South so? Is there any reason why a boy should not become a prosperous and happy man? Why a girl should not be a useful and contented woman? What is necessary for the success of every boy and girl?

REFERENCES.—*Edison:* Southworth II, 260-265; Chandler and Chitwood, 288-294. *Bell:* Chandler and Chitwood, 294-296. *Carnegie:* Southworth II, 266-269. *Southern Literature:* Massey and Wood, 146-150.

APPENDICES

Appendix I

THE DECLARATION OF INDEPENDENCE

In Congress, July 4, 1776.

THE UNANIMOUS DECLARATION OF THE THIRTEEN UNITED STATES OF AMERICA.

When in the Course of human events, it becomes necessary for one people to dissolve the political bands which have connected them with another, and to assume among the Powers of the earth, the separate and equal station to which the Laws of Nature and of Nature's God entitle them, a decent respect to the opinions of mankind requires that they should declare the causes which impel them to the separation.

We hold these truths to be self-evident, that all men are created equal, that they are endowed by their Creator with certain unalienable Rights, that among these are Life, Liberty and the pursuit of Happiness. That to secure these rights, Governments are instituted among Men, deriving their just powers from the consent of the governed, That whenever any Form of Government becomes destructive of these ends, it is the Right of the People to alter or to abolish it, and to institute new Government, laying its foundation on such principles and organizing its powers in such form, as to them shall seem most likely to effect their Safety and Happiness. Prudence, indeed, will dictate that Governments long established should not be changed for light and transient causes; and accordingly all experience hath shown, that mankind are more disposed to suffer, while evils are sufferable, than to right themselves by abolishing the forms to which they are accustomed. But when a long train of abuses and usurpations, pursuing invariably the same Object evinces a design to reduce them under absolute Despotism, it is their right, it is their duty, to throw off such Government, and to provide new Guards for their future security.—Such has been the patient sufferance of these Colonies; and such is now the necessity which constrains them to alter their former Systems of Government. The history of the present King of Great Britain is a history of repeated injuries and usurpations, all having in direct object the establishment of an absolute Tyranny over these States. To prove this, let Facts be submitted to a candid world.

He has refused his Assent to Laws, the most wholesome and necessary for the public good.

He has forbidden his Governors to pass Laws of immediate and pressing importance, unless suspended in their operation till his Assent should be obtained; and when so suspended, he has utterly neglected to attend to them.

He has refused to pass other Laws for the accommodation of large districts of people, unless those people would relinquish the right of Representation in the Legislature, a right inestimable to them and formidable to tyrants only.

He has called together legislative bodies at places unusual, uncomfortable, and distant from the depository of their Public Records, for the sole purpose of fatiguing them into compliance with his measures.

He has dissolved Representative Houses repeatedly, for opposing with manly firmness his invasions on the rights of the people.

He has refused for a long time, after such dissolutions, to cause others to be elected; whereby the Legislative Powers, incapable of Annihilation, have returned to the People at large for their exercise; the State remaining in the mean time exposed to all the dangers of invasion from without, and convulsions within.

He has endeavoured to prevent the population of these States; for that purpose obstructing the Laws for Naturalization of Foreigners; refusing to pass others to encourage their migration hither, and raising the conditions of new Appropriations of Lands.

He has obstructed the Administration of Justice, by refusing his Assent to Laws for establishing Judiciary Powers.

He has made Judges dependent on his Will alone, for the tenure of their offices, and the amount and payment of their salaries.

He has erected a multitude of New Offices, and sent hither swarms of Officers to harrass our People, and eat out their substance.

He has kept among us, in times of peace, Standing Armies without the Consent of our legislature.

He has affected to render the Military independent of and superior to the Civil Power.

He has combined with others to subject us to a jurisdiction foreign to our constitution, and unacknowledged by our laws; giving his Assent to their Acts of pretended Legislation:

For quartering large bodies of armed troops among us:

For protecting them, by a mock Trial, from Punishment for any Murders which they should commit on the Inhabitants of these States:

For cutting off our Trade with all parts of the world:

For imposing taxes on us without our Consent:

For depriving us in many cases, of the benefits of Trial by Jury:

For transporting us beyond Seas to be tried for pretended offences:

For abolishing the free System of English Laws in a neighbouring Province, establishing therein an Arbitrary government, and enlarging its Boundaries so as to render it at once an example and fit instrument for introducing the same absolute rule into these Colonies:

For taking away our Charters, abolishing our most valuable Laws, and altering fundamentally the Forms of our Governments:

For suspending our own Legislatures, and declaring themselves invested with Power to legislate for us in all cases whatsoever.

He has abdicated Government here, by declaring us out of his Protection and waging War against us.

He has plundered our seas, ravaged our Coasts, burnt our towns, and destroyed the lives of our people.

He is at this time transporting large armies of foreign mercenaries to compleat the works of death, desolation and tyranny, already begun with circumstances of Cruelty & perfidy scarcely paralleled in the most barbarous ages, and totally unworthy the Head of a civilized nation.

He has constrained our fellow Citizens taken Captive on the high Seas to bear Arms against their Country, to become the executioners of their friends and Brethren, or to fall themselves by their Hands.

He has excited domestic insurrections amongst us, and has endeavoured to bring on the inhabitants of our frontiers, the merciless Indian Savages, whose known rule of warfare, is an undistinguished destruction of all ages, sexes and conditions.

In every stage of these Oppressions We have Petitioned for Redress in the most humble terms: Our repeated Petitions have been answered only by repeated injury. A Prince, whose character is thus marked by every act which may define a Tyrant, is unfit to be the ruler of a free People.

Nor have We been wanting in attention to our Brittish brethren. We have warned them from time to time of attempts by their legislature to extend an unwarrantable jurisdiction over us. We have reminded them of the circumstances of our emigration and settlement here. We have appealed to their native justice and magnanimity, and we have conjured them by the ties of our common kindred to disavow these usurpations, which, would inevitably interrupt our connections and correspondence. They too have been deaf to the voice of justice and of consanguinity. We must, therefore, acquiesce in the necessity, which denounces our Separation, and hold them, as we hold the rest of mankind, Enemies in War, in Peace Friends.

We, therefore, the Representatives of the united States of America, in General Congress, Assembled, appealing to the Supreme Judge of the world for the rectitude of our intentions, do, in the Name, and by Authority of the good People of these Colonies, solemnly publish and declare, That these United Colonies are, and of Right ought to be Free and Independent States; that they are Absolved from all Allegiance to the British Crown, and that all political connection between them and the State of Great Britain, is and ought to be totally dissolved; and that as Free and Independent States, they have full Power to levy War, conclude Peace, contract Alliances, establish Commerce, and to do all other Acts and Things which Independent States may of right do. And for the support of this Declaration, with a firm reliance on the Protection of Divine Providence, we mutually pledge to each other our Lives, our Fortunes and our sacred Honor.

JOHN HANCOCK.

NEW HAMPSHIRE.
Josiah Bartlett,
Wm. Whipple,
Matthew Thornton.

MASSACHUSETTS BAY.
Saml. Adams,
John Adams,
Robt. Treat Paine,
Elbridge Gerry.

RHODE ISLAND.
Step. Hopkns,
William Ellery.

CONNECTICUT.
Roger Sherman,
Sam'el Huntington,
Wm. Williams,
Oliver Wolcott.

NEW YORK.
Wm. Floyd,
Phil. Livingston,
Frans. Lewis,
Lewis Morris.

NEW JERSEY.

Richd. Stockton,
Jno. Witherspoon,
Fras. Hopkinson,
John Hart,
Abra. Clark.

PENNSYLVANIA.

Robt. Morris,
Benjamin Rush,
Benja. Franklin,
John Morton,
Geo. Clymer,
Jas. Smith,
Geo. Taylor,
James Wilson,
Geo. Ross.

DELAWARE.

Cæsar Rodney,
Geo. Read,
Tho. M'Kean.

MARYLAND.

Samuel Chase,
Wm. Paca,
Thos. Stone,
Charles Carroll of Carrollton

VIRGINIA.

George Wythe,
Richard Henry Lee,
Th. Jefferson,
Benja. Harrison,
Thos. Nelson, jr.,
Francis Lightfoot Lee,
Carter Braxton.

NORTH CAROLINA.

Wm. Hooper,
Joseph Hewes,
John Penn.

SOUTH CAROLINA.

Edward Rutledge,
Thos. Heyward. Junr.,
Thomas Lynch, Junr.,
Arthur Middleton.

GEORGIA.

Button Gwinnett,
Lyman Hall,
Geo. Walton.

Appendix II

THE CONSTITUTION OF THE UNITED STATES OF AMERICA

WE THE PEOPLE of the United States, in Order to form a more perfect Union, establish Justice, insure domestic Tranquility, provide for the common defence, promote the general Welfare, and secure the Blessings of Liberty to ourselves and our Posterity, do ordain and establish this CONSTITUTION for the United States of America.

ARTICLE. I.

SECTION. 1. All legislative Powers herein granted shall be vested in a Congress of the United States, which shall consist of a Senate and House of Representatives.

SECTION. 2. The House of Representatives shall be composed of Members chosen every second Year by the People of the several States, and the Electors in each State shall have the Qualifications requisite for Electors of the most numerous Branch of the State Legislature.

No Person shall be a Representative who shall not have attained to the Age of twenty five Years, and been seven Years a Citizen of the United States, and who shall not, when elected, be an Inhabitant of that State in which he shall be chosen.

Representatives and direct Taxes shall be apportioned among the several States which may be included within this Union, according to their respective Numbers, which shall be determined by adding to the whole Number of free Persons, including those bound to Service for a Term of Years, and excluding Indians not taxed, three fifths of all other Persons. The actual Enumeration shall be made within three Years after the first Meeting of the Congress of the United States, and within every subsequent Term of ten Years, in such Manner as they shall by Law direct. The Number of Representatives shall not exceed one for every thirty Thousand, but each State shall have at Least one Representative; [and until such enumeration shall be made, the State of New Hampshire shall be entitled to chuse three, Massachusetts eight, Rhode-Island and Providence Plantations one, Connecticut five, New-York six, New Jersey four, Pennsylvania eight, Delaware one, Maryland six, Virginia ten, North Carolina five, South Carolina five, and Georgia three.]

When vacancies happen in the Representation from any State, the Executive Authority thereof shall issue Writs of Election to fill such Vacancies.

The House of Representatives shall chuse their Speaker and other Officers; and shall have the sole Power of Impeachment.

SECTION. 3. The Senate of the United States shall be composed of two Senators from each State, chosen by the Legislature thereof, for six Years; and each Senator shall have one Vote.

Immediately after they shall be assembled in Consequence of the first Election, they shall be divided as equally as may be into three Classes. The Seats of the Senators of the first Class shall be vacated at the Expiration of the second Year, of the second Class at the Expiration of the fourth Year, and of the third Class at the Expiration of the sixth Year, so that one third may be chosen every second Year; and if Vacancies happen by Resignation, or otherwise, during the Recess of the Legislature of any State, the Executive thereof may make temporary Appointments until the next Meeting of the Legislature, which shall then fill such Vacancies.

No Person shall be a Senator who shall not have attained to the Age of thirty Years, and been nine Years a Citizen of the United States, and who shall not, when elected, be an Inhabitant of that State for which he shall be chosen.

The Vice President of the United States shall be President of the Senate, but shall have no Vote, unless they be equally divided.

The Senate shall chose their other Officers, and also a President pro tempore, in the Absence of the Vice President, or when he shall exercise the Office of President of the United States.

The Senate shall have the sole Power to try all Impeachments. When sitting for that Purpose, they shall be on Oath or Affirmation. When the President of the United States is tried, the Chief Justice shall preside: And no Person shall be convicted without the Concurrence of two thirds of the Members present.

Judgment in Cases of Impeachment shall not extend further than to removal from Office, and disqualification to hold and enjoy any Office of honor, Trust or Profit under the United States: but the Party convicted shall nevertheless be liable and subject to Indictment, Trial, Judgment and Punishment, according to Law.

SECTION. 4. The Times, Places and Manner of holding Elections for Senators and Representatives, shall be prescribed in each State by the Legislature thereof; but the Congress may at any time by Law make or alter such Regulations, except as to the Places of chusing Senators.

The Congress shall assemble at least once in every Year, and such Meeting shall be on the first Monday in December, unless they shall by Law appoint a different Day.

SECTION. 5. Each House shall be the Judge of the Elections, Returns and Qualifications of its own Members, and a Majority of each shall constitute a Quorum to do Business; but a smaller Number may adjourn from day to day, and may be authorized to compel the Attendance of absent Members, in such Manner, and under such Penalties as each House may provide.

Each House may determine the Rules of its Proceedings, punish its Members for disorderly Behaviour, and, with the Concurrence of two thirds, expel a Member.

Each House shall keep a Journal of its Proceedings, and from time to time publish the same, excepting such Parts as may in their Judgment require Secrecy; and the Yeas and Nays of the Members of either House on any question shall, at the Desire of one fifth of those Present, be entered on the Journal.

Neither House, during the Session of Congress, shall, without the Consent of the other, adjourn for more than three days, nor to any other Place than that in which the two Houses shall be sitting.

Section. 6. The Senators and Representatives shall receive a Compensation for their Services, to be ascertained by Law, and paid out of the Treasury of the United States. They shall in all Cases, except Treason, Felony and Breach of the Peace, be privileged from Arrest during their Attendance at the Session of their respective Houses, and in going to and returning from the same; and for any Speech or Debate in either House, they shall not be questioned in any other Place.

No Senator or Representative shall, during the Time for which he was elected, be appointed to any civil Office under the Authority of the United States, which shall have been created, or the Emoluments whereof shall have been encreased during such time; and no Person holding any Office under the United States, shall be a Member of either House during his Continuance in Office.

Section. 7. All Bills for raising Revenue shall originate in the House of Representatives; but the Senate may propose or concur with Amendments as on other Bills.

Every Bill which shall have passed the House of Representatives and the Senate, shall, before it become a Law, be presented to the President of the United States; if he approve he shall sign it, but if not he shall return it, with his Objections to that House in which it shall have originated, who shall enter the Objections at large on their Journal, and proceed to reconsider it. If after such Reconsideration two thirds of that House shall agree to pass the Bill, it shall be sent, together with the Objections, to the other House, by which it shall likewise be reconsidered, and if approved by two thirds of that House, it shall become a Law. But in all such Cases the Votes of both Houses shall be determined by Yeas and Nays, and the Names of the Persons voting for and against the Bill shall be entered on the Journal of each House respectively. If any Bill shall not be returned by the President within ten Days (Sundays excepted) after it shall have been presented to him, the Same shall be a Law, in like Manner as if he had signed it, unless the Congress by their Adjournment prevent its Return, in which Case it shall not be a Law.

Every Order, Resolution, or Vote to which the Concurrence of the Senate and House of Representatives may be necessary (except on a question of Adjournment) shall be presented to the President of the United States; and before the same shall take Effect, shall be approved by him, or being disapproved by him, shall be repassed by two thirds of the Senate and House of Representatives, according to the Rules and Limitations prescribed in the Case of a Bill.

Section. 8. The Congress shall have Power To lay and collect Taxes, Duties, Imposts and Excises, to pay the Debts and provide for the common Defence and general Welfare of the United States; but all Duties, Imposts and Excises shall be uniform throughout the United States;

To borrow Money on the credit of the United States;

To regulate Commerce with foreign Nations, and among the several States, and with the Indian Tribes;

To establish an uniform Rule of Naturalization, and uniform Laws on the subject of Bankruptcies throughout the United States;

To coin Money, regulate the Value thereof, and of foreign Coin, and fix the Standard of Weights and Measures;

To provide for the Punishment of counterfeiting the Securities and current Coin of the United States;

To establish Post Offices and post Roads;

To promote the Progress of Science and useful Arts, by securing for limited Times to Authors and Inventors the exclusive Right to their respective Writings and Discoveries;

To constitute Tribunals inferior to the Supreme Court;

To define and punish Piracies and Felonies committed on the high Seas, and Offences against the Law of Nations;

To declare War, grant Letters of Marque and Reprisal, and make Rules concerning Captures on Land and Water;

To raise and support Armies, but no Appropriation of Money to that Use shall be for a longer Term than two Years;

To provide and maintain a Navy;

To make Rules for the Government and Regulation of the land and naval Forces;

To provide for calling forth the Militia to execute the Laws of the Union, suppress Insurrections and repel Invasions;

To provide for organizing, arming, and disciplining, the Militia, and for governing such Part of them as may be employed in the Service of the United States, reserving to the States respectively, the Appointment of the Officers, and the Authority of training the Militia according to the discipline prescribed by Congress;

To exercise exclusive Legislation in all Cases whatsoever, over such District (not exceeding ten Miles square) as may, by Cession of particular States, and the Acceptance of Congress, become the Seat of the Government of the United States, and to exercise like Authority over all Places purchased by the Consent of the Legislature of the State in which the Same shall be, for the Erection of Forts, Magazines, Arsenals, dock-Yards, and other needful Buildings;—And

To make all Laws which shall be necessary and proper for carrying into Execution the foregoing Powers, and all other Powers vested by this Constitution in the Government of the United States, or in any Department or Officer thereof.

SECTION. 9. The Migration or Importation of such Persons as any of the States now existing shall think proper to admit, shall not be prohibited by the Congress prior to the Year one thousand eight hundred and eight, but a Tax or duty may be imposed on such Importation, not exceeding ten dollars for each Person.

The Privilege of the Writ of Habeas Corpus shall not be suspended, unless when in Cases of Rebellion or Invasion the public safety may require it.

No Bill of Attainder or ex post facto Law shall be passed.

No Capitation, or other direct, Tax shall be laid, unless in Proportion to the Census or Enumeration herein before directed to be taken.

No Tax or Duty shall be laid on Articles exported from any State.

No Preference shall be given by any Regulation of Commerce or Revenue to the Ports of one State over those of another: nor shall Vessels bound to, or from, one State, be obliged to enter, clear, or pay Duties in another.

No Money shall be drawn from the Treasury, but in Consequence of Appropriations made by Law; and a regular Statement and Account of the Receipts and Expenditures of all public Money shall be published from time to time.

No Title of Nobility shall be granted by the United States: And no Person holding any Office of Profit or Trust under them, shall, without the Consent of the Congress, accept of any present, Emolument, Office, or Title, of any kind whatever, from any King, Prince, or foreign State.

SECTION. 10. No State shall enter into any Treaty, Alliance, or Confederation; grant Letters of Marque and Reprisal; coin Money; emit Bills of Credit; make any Thing but gold and silver Coin a Tender in Payment of Debts; pass any Bill of Attainder, ex post facto Law, or Law impairing the Obligation of Contracts, or grant any Title of Nobility.

No State shall, without the Consent of the Congress, lay any Imposts or Duties on Imports or Exports, except what may be absolutely necessary for executing it's inspection Laws: and the net Produce of all Duties and Imposts, laid by any State on Imports or Exports, shall be for the Use of the Treasury of the United States; and all such Laws shall be subject to the Revision and Control of the Congress.

No State shall, without the Consent of Congress, lay any Duty of Tonnage, keep Troops, or Ships of War in time of Peace, enter into any Agreement or Compact with another State, or with a foreign Power, or engage in War, unless actually invaded, or in such imminent Danger as will not admit of delay.

ARTICLE. II.

SECTION. 1. The executive Power shall be vested in a President of the United States of America. He shall hold his Office during the Term of four Years, and, together with the Vice President, chosen for the same Term, be elected, as follows

Each State shall appoint, in such Manner as the Legislature thereof may direct, a Number of Electors, equal to the whole Number of Senators and Representatives to which the State may be entitled in the Congress: but no Senator or Representative, or Person holding an Office of Trust or Profit under the United States, shall be appointed an Elector.

The Electors shall meet in their respective States, and vote by Ballot for two Persons, of whom one at least shall not be an Inhabitant of the same State with themselves. And they shall make a List of all the Persons voted for, and of the Number of Votes for each; which List they shall sign and certify, and transmit sealed to the Seat of the Government of the United States, directed to the President of the Senate. The President of the Senate shall, in the Presence of the Senate and House of Representatives, open all the Certificates, and the Votes shall then be counted. The Person having the greatest Number of Votes shall be the President, if such Number be a Majority of the whole Number of Electors appointed; and if there be more than one who have such Majority, and have an equal Number of Votes, then the House of Representatives shall immediately chuse by Ballot one of them for President; and if no Person have a Majority, then from the five highest on the List the said House shall in like Manner chuse the President. But in chusing the President, the Votes shall be taken by States, the Representation from each State having one Vote; A quorum for this Purpose shall consist of a Member or Members from two thirds of the States, and a Majority of all the States shall be necessary to a Choice. In every Case, after the Choice of the President, the Person having the greatest Number of Votes of the Electors shall be the Vice President. But if there should remain two or more who have equal Votes, the Senate shall chuse from them by Ballot the Vice President.

The Congress may determine the Time of chusing the Electors, and the Day on which they shall give their Votes; which Day shall be the same throughout the United States.

No Person except a natural born Citizen, or a Citizen of the United States, at the time of the Adoption of this Constitution, shall be eligible to the Office of President; neither shall any Person be eligible to that Office who shall not have attained to the Age of thirty five Years, and been fourteen Years a Resident within the United States.

In Case of the Removal of the President from Office, or of his Death, Resignation, or Inability to discharge the Powers and Duties of the said Office, the Same shall devolve on the Vice President, and the Congress may by Law provide for the Case of Removal, Death, Resignation or Inability, both of the President and Vice President, declaring what Officer shall then act as President, and such Officer shall act accordingly, until the Disability be removed, or a President shall be elected.

The President shall, at stated Times, receive for his Services, a Compensation, which shall neither be encreased nor diminished during the Period for which he shall have been elected, and he shall not receive within that Period any other Emolument from the United States, or any of them.

Before he enter on the Execution of his Office, he shall take the following Oath or Affirmation:—"I do solemnly swear (or affirm) that I will faithfully execute the Office of President of the United States, and will to the best of my Ability, preserve, protect and defend the Constitution of the United States."

Section. 2. The President shall be Commander in Chief of the Army and Navy of the United States, and of the Militia of the several States, when called into the actual Service of the United States; he may require the Opinion, in writing, of the principal Officer in each of the executive Departments, upon any Subject relating to the Duties of their respective Offices, and he shall have Power to grant Reprieves and Pardons for Offences against the United States, except in Cases of Impeachment.

He shall have Power, by and with the Advice and Consent of the Senate, to make Treaties, provided two thirds of the Senators present concur; and he shall nominate, and by and with the Advice and Consent of the Senate, shall appoint Ambassadors, other public Ministers and Consuls, Judges of the supreme Court, and all other Officers of the United States, whose Appointments are not herein otherwise provided for, and which shall be established by Law: but the Congress may by Law vest the Appointment of such inferior Officers, as they think proper, in the President alone, in the Courts of Law, or in the Heads of Departments.

The President shall have Power to fill up all Vacancies that may happen during the Recess of the Senate, by granting Commissions which shall expire at the End of their next Session.

SECTION. 3. He shall from time to time give to the Congress Information of the State of the Union, and recommend to their Consideration such Measures as he shall judge necessary and expedient; he may, on extraordinary Occasions, convene both Houses, or either of them, and in Case of Disagreement between them with Respect to the Time of Adjournment, he may adjourn them to such Time as he shall think proper; he shall receive Ambassadors and other public Ministers; he shall take Care that the Laws be faithfully executed, and shall Commission all the Officers of the United States.

SECTION. 4. The President, Vice President and all civil Officers of the United States, shall be removed from Office on Impeachment for, and Conviction of, Treason, Bribery, or other high Crimes and Misdemeanors.

ARTICLE. III.

SECTION. 1. The judicial Power of the United States, shall be vested in one supreme Court, and in such inferior Courts as the Congress may from time to time ordain and establish. The Judges, both of the supreme and inferior Courts, shall hold their Offices during good Behaviour, and shall, at stated Times, receive for their Services, a Compensation, which shall not be diminished during their continuance in Office.

SECTION. 2. The judicial Power shall extend to all cases, in Law and Equity, arising under this Constitution, the Laws of the United States, and Treaties made, or which shall be made, under their Authority;—to all Cases affecting Ambassadors, other public Ministers and Consuls;—to all Cases of admiralty and maritime Jurisdiction;—to Controversies to which the United States shall be a Party;—to Controversies between two or more States;—between a State and Citizens of another State; between Citizens of different States,—between Citizens of the same State claiming Lands under Grants of different States, and between a State, or the Citizens thereof, and foreign States, Citizens or Subjects.

In all Cases affecting Ambassadors, other public Ministers and Consuls, and those in which a State shall be Party, the supreme Court shall have original Jurisdiction. In all the other Cases before mentioned, the supreme Court shall have appellate Jurisdiction, both as to Law and Fact, with such Exceptions, and under such regulations as the Congress shall make.

The Trial of all Crimes, except in Cases of Impeachment, shall be by Jury; and such Trial shall be held in the State where the said Crimes shall have been committed; but when not committed within any State, the Trial shall be at such Place or Places as the Congress may by Law have directed.

SECTION. 3. Treason against the United States, shall consist only in levying War against them, or in adhering to their Enemies, giving them Aid and Comfort. No Person shall be convicted of Treason unless on the Testimony of two Witnesses to the same overt Act, or on Confession in open Court.

The Congress shall have Power to declare the Punishment of Treason, but no Attainder of Treason shall work Corruption of Blood, or Forfeiture except during the Life of the Person attainted.

ARTICLE. IV.

Section. 1. Full Faith and Credit shall be given in each State to the public Acts, Records, and judicial Proceedings of every other State. And the Congress may by general Laws prescribe the Manner in which such Acts, Records and Proceedings shall be proved, and the Effect thereof.

Section. 2. The Citizens of each State shall be entitled to all Privileges and Immunities of Citizens in the several States.

A Person charged in any State with Treason, Felony, or other Crime, who shall flee from Justice, and be found in another State, shall on Demand of the executive Authority of the State from which he fled, be delivered up, to be removed to the State having Jurisdiction of the Crime.

No Person held to Service or Labour in one State, under the Laws thereof, escaping into another, shall, in Consequence of any Law or Regulation therein, be discharged from such Service or Labour, but shall be delivered up on Claim of the Party to whom such Service or Labour may be due.

Section. 3. New States may be admitted by the Congress into this Union; but no new State shall be formed or erected within the Jurisdiction of any other State; nor any State be formed by the Junction of two or more States, or Parts of States, without the Consent of the Legislatures of the States concerned as well as of the Congress.

The Congress shall have Power to dispose of and make all needful Rules and Regulations respecting the Territory or other Property belonging to the United States; and nothing in this Constitution shall be so construed as to Prejudice any Claims of the United States, or of any particular State.

Section. 4. The United States shall guarantee to every State in this Union a Republican Form of Government, and shall protect each of them against Invasion; and on Application of the Legislature, or of the Executive (when the Legislature cannot be convened) against domestic Violence.

ARTICLE. V.

The Congress, whenever two thirds of both Houses shall deem it necessary, shall propose Amendments to this Constitution, or, on the Application of the Legislature of two thirds of the several States, shall call a Convention for proposing Amendments, which, in either Case, shall be valid to all Intents and Purposes, as Part of this Constitution, when ratified by the Legislatures of three fourths of the several States, or by Conventions in three fourths thereof, as the one or the other Mode of Ratification may be proposed by the Congress; Provided that no Amendment which may be made prior to the Year One thousand eight hundred and eight shall in any Manner affect the first and fourth Clauses in the Ninth Section of the first Article; and that no State, without its Consent, shall be deprived of it's equal Suffrage in the Senate.

ARTICLE. VI.

All Debts contracted and Engagements entered into, before the Adoption of this Constitution, shall be as valid against the United States under this Constitution, as under the Confederation.

This Constitution, and the Laws of the United States which shall be made in Pursuance thereof; and all Treaties made, or which shall be made, under the Authority of the United States, shall be the supreme Law of the Land; and the Judges in every State shall be bound thereby, any Thing in the Constitution or Laws of any State to the Contrary notwithstanding.

The Senators and Representatives before mentioned, and the Members of the several State Legislatures, and all executive and judicial Officers, both of the United States and of the several States, shall be bound by Oath or Affirmation, to support this Constitution; but no religious Test shall ever be required as a Qualification to any Office or public Trust under the United States.

ARTICLE. VII.

The Ratification of the Conventions of nine States, shall be sufficient for the Establishment of this Constitution between the States so ratifying the Same.

Done in Convention by the Unanimous Consent of the States present the Seventeenth Day of September in the Year of our Lord one thousand seven hundred and Eighty seven and of the Independance of the United States of America the Twelfth In Witness whereof We have hereunto subscribed our Names,

G°: WASHINGTON—*Presidt.*
and deputy from Virginia

Attest WILLIAM JACKSON *Secretary*

NEW HAMPSHIRE.

JOHN LANGDON
NICHOLAS GILMAN

MASSACHUSETTS.

NATHANIEL GORHAM
RUFUS KING

CONNECTICUT.

WM: SAML. JOHNSON
ROGER SHERMAN

NEW YORK

ALEXANDER HAMILTON

NEW JERSEY

WIL: LIVINGSTON
DAVID BREARLEY.
WM. PATERSON.
JONA: DAYTON

PENNSYLVANIA

B FRANKLIN
THOMAS MIFFLIN
ROBT. MORRIS
GEO. CLYMER
THOS. FITZ SIMONS
JARED INGERSOLL
JAMES WILSON
GOUV MORRIS

DELAWARE.

GEO: READ
GUNNING BEDFORD jun
JOHN DICKINSON
RICHARD BASSETT
JACO: BROOM

MARYLAND.

JAMES MCHENRY
DAN OF ST THOS. JENIFER
DANL CARROLL

VIRGINIA.

JOHN BLAIR—
JAMES MADISON Jr.

NORTH CAROLINA.

WM: BLOUNT
RICHD. DOBBS SPAIGHT.
HU WILLIAMSON

SOUTH CAROLINA.

J. RUTLEDGE
CHARLES COTESWORTH
    PINCKNEY
CHARLES PINCKNEY
PIERCE BUTLER.

GEORGIA.

WILLIAM FEW
ABR BALDWIN

ARTICLES

in Addition to, and Amendment of the Constitution of the United States of America, proposed by Congress and ratified by the Legislatures of the Several States, pursuant to the Fifth Article of the Constitution.

ARTICLE I.

Congress shall make no law respecting an establishment of religion, or prohibiting the free exercise thereof; or abridging the freedom of speech, or of the press; or the right of the people peaceably to assemble, and to petition the Government for a redress of grievances.

ARTICLE II.

A well regulated Militia, being necessary to the security of a free State, the right of the people to keep and bear Arms, shall not be infringed.

ARTICLE III.

No Soldier shall, in time of peace be quartered in any house, without the consent of the Owner, nor in time of war, but in a manner to be prescribed by law.

ARTICLE IV.

The right of the people to be secure in their persons, houses, papers, and effects, against unreasonable searches and seizures, shall not be violated, and no Warrants shall issue, but upon probable cause, supported by Oath or affirmation, and particularly describing the place to be searched, and the persons or things to be seized.

ARTICLE V.

No person shall be held to answer for a capital, or otherwise infamous crime, unless on a presentment or indictment of a Grand Jury, except in cases arising in the land or naval forces, or in the Militia, when in actual service in time of War or public danger; nor shall any person be subject for the same offence to be twice put in jeopardy of life or limb; nor shall be compelled in any Criminal Case to be a witness against himself, nor be deprived of life, liberty, or property, without due process of law; nor shall private property be taken for public use, without just compensation.

ARTICLE VI.

In all criminal prosecutions, the accused shall enjoy the right to a speedy and public trial, by an impartial jury of the State and district wherein the crime shall have been committed, which district shall have been previously ascertained by law, and to be informed of the nature and cause of the accusation; to be confronted with the witnesses against him; to have compulsory process for obtaining Witnesses in his favor, and to have the Assistance of Counsel for his defence.

ARTICLE VII.

In suits at common law, where the value in controversy shall exceed twenty dollars, the right of trial by jury shall be preserved, and no fact tried by a jury shall be otherwise re-examined in any Court of the United States, than according to the rules of the common law.

ARTICLE VIII.

Excessive bail shall not be required, nor excessive fines imposed, nor cruel and unusual punishments inflicted.

ARTICLE IX.

The enumeration in the Constitution, of certain rights, shall not be construed to deny or disparage others retained by the people.

ARTICLE X.[1]

The powers not delegated to the United States by the Constitution, nor prohibited by it to the States, are reserved to the States respectively, or to the people.

ARTICLE XI.[2]

The Judicial power of the United States shall not be construed to extend to any suit in law or equity, commenced or prosecuted against one of the United States by Citizens of another State, or by Citizens or Subjects of any Foreign State.

ARTICLE XII.[3]

The Electors shall meet in their respective states, and vote by ballot for President and Vice President, one of whom, at least, shall not be an inhabitant of the same state with themselves; they shall name in their ballots the person voted for as President, and in distinct ballots the person voted for as Vice President, and they shall make distinct lists of all persons voted for as President, and of all persons voted for as Vice President, and of the number of votes for each, which lists they shall sign and certify, and transmit sealed to the seat of the government of the United States, directed to the President of the Senate;—The President of the Senate shall, in presence of the Senate and House of Representatives, open all the certificates and the votes shall then be counted;—The person having the greatest number of votes for President, shall be the President, if such number be a majority of the whole

---

[1] Amendments I.-X. were proclaimed to be in force December 15, 1791.
[2] Proclaimed to be in force January 8, 1798.
[3] Proclaimed to be in force September 25, 1804.

number of Electors appointed; and if no person have such majority, then from the persons having the highest numbers not exceeding three on the list of those voted for as President, the House of Representatives shall choose immediately, by ballot, the President. But in choosing the President, the votes shall be taken by states, the representation from each state having one vote; a quorum for this purpose shall consist of a member or members from two-thirds of the states, and a majority of all the states shall be necessary to a choice. And if the House of Representatives shall not choose a President whenever the right of choice shall devolve upon them, before the fourth day of March next following, then the Vice President shall act as President, as in the case of the death or other constitutional disability of the President. The person having the greatest number of votes as Vice President, shall be the Vice President, if such number be a majority of the whole number of Electors appointed, and if no person have a majority, then from the two highest numbers on the list, the Senate shall choose the Vice President, a quorum for the purpose shall consist of two-thirds of the whole number of Senators, and a majority of the whole number shall be necessary to a choice. But no person constitutionally ineligible to the office of President shall be eligible to that of Vice President of the United States.

ARTICLE XIII.[1]

SECTION 1. Neither slavery nor involuntary servitude, except as a punishment for crime whereof the party shall have been duly convicted, shall exist within the United States, or any place subject to their jurisdiction.

SECTION 2. Congress shall have power to enforce this article by appropriate legislation.

ARTICLE XIV. [2]

SECTION 1. All persons born or naturalized in the United States, and subject to the jurisdiction thereof, are citizens of the United States and of the State wherein they reside. No State shall make or enforce any law which shall abridge the privileges or immunities of citizens of the United States; nor shall any State deprive any person of life, liberty, or property, without due process of law; nor deny to any person within its jurisdiction the equal protection of the laws.

SECTION 2. Representatives shall be apportioned among the several States according to their respective numbers, counting the whole number of persons in each State, excluding Indians not taxed. But when the right to vote at any election for the choice of electors for President and Vice President of the United States, Representatives in Congress, the Executive and Judicial officers of a State, or the members of the Legislature thereof, is denied to any of the male inhabitants of such State, being twenty-one years of age, and citizens of the United States, or in any way abridged, except for participation in rebellion, or other crime, the basis of representation therein shall be reduced in the proportion which the number of such male citizens shall bear to the whole number of male citizens twenty-one years of age in such State.

[1] Proclaimed to be in force December 18, 1865.
[2] Proclaimed to be in force July 28, 1868.

SECTION 3. No person shall be a Senator or Representative in Congress, or elector of President and Vice President, or hold any office, civil or military, under the United States, or under any State, who, having previously taken an oath, as a member of Congress, or as an officer of the United States, or as a member of any State legislature, or as an executive or judicial officer of any State, to support the Constitution of the United States, shall have engaged in insurrection or rebellion against the same, or given aid or comfort to the enemies thereof. But Congress may by a vote of two-thirds of each House, remove such disability.

SECTION 4. The validity of the public debt of the United States, authorized by law, including debts incurred for payment of pensions and bounties for services in suppressing insurrection or rebellion, shall not be questioned. But neither the United States nor any State shall assume or pay any debt or obligation incurred in aid of insurrection or rebellion against the United States, or any claim for the loss of emancipation of any slave; but all such debts, obligations and claims shall be held illegal and void.

SECTION 5. The Congress shall have power to enforce, by appropriate legislation, the provisions of this article.

ARTICLE XV.[1]

SECTION 1. The right of citizens of the United States to vote shall not be denied or abridged by the United States or by any State on account of race, color, or previous condition of servitude.

SECTION 2. The Congress shall have power to enforce this article by appropriate legislation.

[1] Proclaimed to be in force March 30, 1870.

PRESIDENTS AND VICE PRESIDENTS OF THE UNITED STATES

NO.	PRESIDENT	STATE	TERM OF OFFICE	BY WHOM ELECTED	BORN	DIED	VICE PRESIDENT
1	George Washington	Virginia	Two terms: 1789–97	Entire Electoral College	Feb. 22, 1732	Dec. 14, 1799	John Adams
2	John Adams	Massachusetts	One term: 1797–1801	Federalists	Oct. 30, 1735	July 4, 1826	Thomas Jefferson
3	Thomas Jefferson	Virginia	Two terms: 1801–09	Republicans [1]	April 13, 1743	July 4, 1826	Aaron Burr / George Clinton
4	James Madison	Virginia	Two terms: 1809–17	Republicans [1]	Mar. 16, 1751	June 28, 1836	George Clinton / Elbridge Gerry
5	James Monroe	Virginia	Two terms: 1817–25	Republicans [1]	April 28, 1758	July 4, 1831	Daniel D. Tompkins
6	John Quincy Adams	Massachusetts	One term: 1825–29	House of Rep.	July 11, 1767	Feb. 23, 1848	John C. Calhoun
7	Andrew Jackson	Tennessee	Two terms: 1829–37	Democrats	Mar. 15, 1767	June 8, 1845	John C. Calhoun / Martin Van Buren
8	Martin Van Buren	New York	One term: 1837–41	Democrats	Dec. 5, 1782	July 24, 1862	Richard M. Johnson
9	William H. Harrison	Ohio	One month: 1841	Whigs	Feb. 9, 1773	April 4, 1841	John Tyler
10	John Tyler	Virginia	3 yrs. and 11 mos.: 1841–45	Whigs	Mar. 29, 1790	Jan. 18, 1862	
11	James K. Polk	Tennessee	One term: 1845–49	Democrats	Nov. 2, 1795	June 15, 1849	George M. Dallas
12	Zachary Taylor	Louisiana	1 year and 4 mos.: 1849–50	Whigs	Sept. 24, 1784	July 9, 1850	Millard Fillmore
13	Millard Fillmore	New York	2 yrs. and 8 mos.: 1850–53	Whigs	Feb. 7, 1800	Mar. 8, 1874	
14	Franklin Pierce	New Hampshire	One term: 1853–57	Democrats	Nov. 23, 1804	Oct. 8, 1869	William R. King
15	James Buchanan	Pennsylvania	One term: 1857–61	Democrats	April 22, 1791	June 1, 1868	J. C. Breckinridge
16	Abraham Lincoln	Illinois	One term, 1mo., 10 da.: 1861–65	Republicans	Feb. 12, 1809	April 15, 1865	Hannibal Hamlin / Andrew Johnson
17	Andrew Johnson	Tennessee	3 yrs., 10 mos., 20 da.: 1865–69	Republicans	Dec. 29, 1808	July 31, 1875	
18	Ulysses S. Grant	Illinois	Two terms: 1869–77	Republicans	April 27, 1822	July 23, 1885	Schuyler Colfax / Henry Wilson
19	Rutherford B. Hayes	Ohio	One term: 1877–81	Republicans	Oct. 4, 1822	Jan. 17, 1893	William A. Wheeler
20	James A. Garfield	Ohio	Six mos., 15 days: 1881	Republicans	Nov. 19, 1831	Sept. 19, 1881	Chester A. Arthur
21	Chester A. Arthur	New York	3 yrs., 5 mos., 15 days: 1881–85	Republicans	Oct. 5, 1830	Nov. 18, 1886	
22	Grover Cleveland	New York	One term: 1885–89	Democrats	Mar. 18, 1837	June 24, 1908	Thomas A. Hendricks
23	Benjamin Harrison	Indiana	One term: 1889–93	Republicans	Aug. 20, 1833	Mar. 13, 1901	Levi P. Morton
24	Grover Cleveland	New York	One term: 1893–97	Democrats	Mar. 18, 1837	June 24, 1908	Adlai E. Stevenson
25	William McKinley	Ohio	One term, 6 mos, 10da. 1897–1901	Republicans	Jan. 29, 1843	Sept. 14, 1901	Garret A. Hobart [2] / Theodore Roosevelt
26	Theodore Roosevelt	New York	Nearly two terms: 1901–1909	Republicans	Oct. 27, 1858		Charles W. Fairbanks
27	William H. Taft	Ohio	1909–	Republicans	Sept. 15, 1857		James S. Sherman

[1] It must be remembered that the original Republican Party changed its name in the time of Andrew Jackson and has since been known as the Democratic Party. [2] Died in office.

GROWTH OF THE UNITED STATES

	STATES		DATE OF ADMISSION	SQUARE MILES	POPULATION 1900
1.	Delaware		Dec. 7, 1787	2,050	184,735
2.	Pennsylvania		Dec. 12, 1787	45,215	6,302,115
3.	New Jersey		Dec. 18, 1787	7,815	1,883,669
4.	Georgia		Jan. 2, 1788	59,475	2,216,331
5.	Connecticut		Jan. 9, 1788	4,990	908,355
6.	Massachusetts	ORIGINAL THIRTEEN RATIFIED THE CONSTITUTION	Feb. 6, 1788	8,315	2,805,346
7.	Maryland		April 28, 1788	12,210	1,190,050
8.	South Carolina		May 23, 1788	30,570	1,340,316
9.	New Hampshire		June 21, 1788	9,305	411,588
10.	Virginia		June 25, 1788	42,450	1,854,184
11.	New York		July 26, 1788	49,170	7,268,012
12.	North Carolina		Nov. 21, 1789	52,250	1,893,810
13.	Rhode Island		May 29, 1790	1,250	428,556
14.	Vermont		March 4, 1791	9,565	343,641
15.	Kentucky		June 1, 1792	40,400	2,147,174
16.	Tennessee		June 1, 1796	42,050	2,020,616
17.	Ohio		Feb. 19, 1803	41,060	4,157,545
18.	Louisiana		April 8, 1812	48,720	1,381,625
19.	Indiana		Dec. 11, 1816	36,350	2,516,462
20.	Mississippi		Dec. 10, 1817	46,810	1,551,270
21.	Illinois		Dec. 3, 1818	56,650	4,821,550
22.	Alabama		Dec. 14, 1819	52,250	1,828,697
23.	Maine		March 15, 1820	33,040	694,466
24.	Missouri		Aug. 10, 1821	69,415	3,106,665
25.	Arkansas		June 15, 1836	53,850	1,311,564
26.	Michigan		Jan. 26, 1837	58,915	2,420,982
27.	Florida		March 3, 1845	58,680	528,542
28.	Texas		Dec. 29, 1845	265,780	3,048,710
29.	Iowa		Dec. 28, 1846	56,025	2,231,853
30.	Wisconsin		May 29, 1848	56,040	2,069,042
31.	California		Sept. 9, 1850	158,360	1,485,053
32.	Minnesota		May 11, 1858	83,365	1,751,394
33.	Oregon		Feb. 14, 1859	96,030	413,536
34.	Kansas		Jan. 29, 1861	82,080	1,470,495
35.	West Virginia		June 19, 1863	24,780	958,800
36.	Nevada		Oct. 31, 1864	110,700	42,335
37.	Nebraska		March 1, 1867	77,510	1,068,539
38.	Colorado		Aug. 1, 1876	103,925	539,700
39.	North Dakota		Nov. 3, 1889	70,795	319,146
40.	South Dakota		Nov. 3, 1889	77,650	401,570
41.	Montana		Nov. 8, 1889	146,080	243,329
42.	Washington		Nov. 11, 1889	69,180	518,103
43.	Idaho		July 3, 1890	84,800	161,772
44.	Wyoming		July 10, 1890	97,890	92,531
45.	Utah		Jan. 4, 1896	84,970	276,749
46.	Oklahoma		Nov. 16, 1907	70,430	700,391

TERRITORIES	ORGANIZED	SQUARE MILES	POPULATION 1900
New Mexico	Sept. 9, 1850	122,460	195,310
Arizona	Feb. 24, 1863	112,920	122,931
Alaska	July 27, 1868	590,884	63,592
Hawaiian Islands	July 6, 1898	6,449	154,001

COLONIAL POSSESSIONS	ACQUIRED	SQUARE MILES	POPULATION 1900
Philippine Islands	Feb. 6, 1899	115,026	7,635,000 (estimated)
Porto Rico	Feb. 6, 1899	3,606	953,343
Guam	Feb. 6, 1899	224	9,000 (estimated)
Samoan Islands	Feb. 16, 1900	84	5,800 (estimated)
Canal Zone	Feb., 1904	474	45,000 (estimated)

Wake Island and other small Islands in the Pacific Ocean were annexed in 1898 as "wild or unexplored territory."

PRONOUNCING INDEX

WITH PRONUNCIATION OF DIFFICULT NAMES

KEY TO PRONUNCIATION

ā as a in sāle	ī as i in kīte
ă as a in hăt	ĭ as i in ĭt
ä as a in färm	ō as o in gō
ạ as a in tạll	ŏ as o in hŏt
ē as e in ēve	ô as o in fôrd
ĕ as e in gĕt	ōō as oo in tōōl
ẽ as e in fẽrn	ū as u in use
g as in g in go	ŭ as u in bŭt

N French nasal, somewhat like ng in tong

Abolitionists, 275, 312, 313, 314, 323, 375, 376.
A cā′ dĭ ä, 129, 135.
Adams, Charles Francis, 307.
Adams, John, 222, 226; biography, 231; administration, 231–236, 244.
Adams, John Quincy, 258, 263; biography, 269; administration, 269–271, 275, 336.
Adams, Samuel, 157, 161, 183.
Agriculture, in 1763, 143, 144; in 1820, 266; 1820–1840, 289, 468, 469.
Aguinaldo (ä-gē-näl′ dō), 448, 452.
Alabama, explored, 28; Indians in, 43, 44; settled at Mobile, 126; ceded to England, 137; migration into, 188, 239; Creek uprising in, 253; a Territory, 260; a State, 263; secedes, 333; in the war, 339, 341, 374, 390; readmitted, 414; industry in, 468.
Alabama, the, 354, 355, 390.
Alabama claims, 355, 419.
Alamance, battle of the, 157.
A′lä mō, siege of the, 297.
Alaska, 417, 457.
Albany, 110, 116, 133.
Albemarle Colony, 99, 100, 101–103.
Albemarle, Duke of, 99.
Aldrich Bill, 461.
Alexander VI, bull of, 25.
Algiers (ăl-jērz′), La., 370.
Al gŏn′quĭn Indians, 43, 44, 45.
Alien and Sedition Laws, 232, 233.
Allen, Ethan, 166, 169.
A′ mă däs, Captain, 37.
Amendments (see Constitution).
America, discovery of, 16; named, 23; first inhabitants of, 42.
Anarchist riot in Chicago, 436; assassination of McKinley, 455.
Anderson, Major, 345–346.
André (än′drā), John, 198.
An′ drŏs, Sir Edmund, 87, 89, 116.
An năp′ ō lĭs, 96, 133, 159, 160, 211.
Annexation, of Louisiana, 238; of

Florida, 259; of Texas, 297; of Oregon, 299; of California and the West, 304; of Gadsden Purchase, 304, 315; of Alaska, 417; of Hawaii, 451; of Wake Island and the Samoan Islands, 451; of Porto Rico, 451.

Antietam (ăn tē' tăm), (Sharpsburg), battle of, 365.

Anti-Federalists, 224.

Ap' pō măt' tox, 398.

Arbitration, of Alabama Claims, 419; of seal fisheries, 443; of Venezuela boundary dispute, 443; of Alaskan boundary dispute, 457.

Archdale, Governor John, 103.

Arizona, admitted, 462.

Arkansas, explored, 28, 125, 240; admitted, 281; secedes, 347, 348; war in, 370, 372, 373, 387; readmission of, 409, 415.

Arkansas, the, 371.

Army, Continental, 168, 169, 177, 178, 179, 184, 194, 198, 204, 205; Confederate, 348, 349, 377, 385, 395, 398, 400, 401, 403.

Arnold, Benedict, 170, 181, 182, 197, 200.

Arthur, Chester A., 431; administration, 432–434; biography, 432.

Articles of Confederation, the, 207–209.

Asia, trade routes to, 8; explored by Marco Polo, 9; search for routes to, 10, 11, 13, 24, 35.

Assembly, first legislation, 60; General, in Massachusetts, 73; in Connecticut, 89; in Maryland, 94; in New York, 115; in Pennsylvania, 122; conflict of governor and, 151; opposition of, to taxation, 155, 156, 158.

Assumption of State debts, 225.

Atlanta, evacuation of, 388.

Atlantic cable, 326, 418.

Aviation, 465.

Ayllon (īl-yōn'), 29.

Bacon's Rebellion, 65.

Bagley, Ensign Worth, 449.

Băl bō' a, 24.

Baltimore Convention, 330.

Baltimore, Lords, 92–98.

Banks, General N. P., 361, 362, 387.

Banks, State, 280.

Barbary States, war with, 238.

Barlow, Captain, 38.

Beauregard (bō-rē-gärd'), General P. G. T., 346, 352, 369.

Bel'knap impeached, 424.

Bellamont, Earl of, 116.

Bennett, Richard, 63, 64.

Bennington, battle of, 181.

Berkeley, Lord, 117.

Berkeley, Sir William, 62, 63, 64, 65, 66, 99.

Bil ŏx' i, settlement of, 126.

"Black Codes," 411.

Blaine, James G., 434.

Blair, Frank P., 418.

Bland Act, 431, 439.

Blockade of Southern ports, declared, 350, 353, 354, 355, 356; effects, 373, 374; completed, 390; raised, 410.

Bon Homme Richard (bo-nom' rē-shär'), the, 193.

Boone, Daniel, 187, 188.

Booth, John Wilkes, 399.

Boston, founded, 71; persecution in, 84; growth of, 91, 144, 145, 288, 292, 326; newspapers in, 146, 275; opposition to British in, 153, 157, 159; Parliamentary acts affecting, 160, 161; in Revolution, 163, 167, 172; fire in, 424.

Boston News Letter, 146.

Boundary disputed between United States and British America, 260, 295, 299, 419; Mexico, 300.

Boxer outbreak, 454.

Braddock, General, 134.

Bradford, William, 69, 70.

Bragg, General, 372, 373, 380, 381.

Brandywine, battle of, 182.

Breckenridge, John C., 330.

Brook, Lord, 77.

Brooklyn Bridge, 433.

Brown, B. Gratz, 422.

Brown, General Jacob, 249, 254.

Brown, John, 319, 322.

Bryan, William J., 444, 455, 461; biography, 444.
Bu chan' an, James, 320; administration, 320-323; biography, 320.
Buckner, General S. B., 367, 445.
Bu'ell, General, 367, 368, 372.
Buena Vista (bwā' nä vēs' tä), battle of, 301, 302.
Bull Run (Manassas), first, 351; second, 363.
Bunker Hill, battle of, 167, 168.
Bur goyne', General, 180, 181, 183, 184.
Burke, Edmund, 156.
Burnside, General A. E., 365, 366.
Burr, Aaron, 234, 241.
Butler, General B. F., 369, 390, 392.
Butler, William O., 307.
Byrd, William, 146.

Cabeza de Vaca (kä vā' thä dä vä-kä), 29.
Cabinet, formation of the first, 223; "Kitchen—," 273; dissensions in, 224, 273, 295, 416.
Cāb' ŏt, John, 22.
Cabot, Sebastian, 22, 23.
Cä hō' kĭ ă, 189, 190.
Calhoun (kăl-hoon'), John C., 247, 258, 263, 271; biography, 278, 306, 309.
California, explored, 36, 296; Spanish in, 31; annexation of, 300, 304; in Mexican War, 302; discovery of gold in, 305; becomes a State, 307, 311; growth of, 326, 327; race troubles in, 436, 463.
California Compromise, 307-311.
Căl' vert, Cecil, 93-97.
Calvert, George, First Lord Baltimore, 92, 93.
Calvert George, Third Lord Baltimore, 97.
Calvert, Leonard, 93, 95, 96.
Camden, 195, 196.
Campbell, Colonel, 186, 191.
Campbell, Colonel William, 197.
Canada, explored, 31; occupied, 33, 34, 124; taken by English, 137; invaded by Continental army, 170; War of 1812 in, 249, 253, 254; boundary adjusted, 295.
Canby, General, 426.
Capital, National, Philadelphia, 180; New York, 222; removed to Washington, 225, 234.
Carolinas, the, first settlements in, 32, 98; origin of name of, 98; grants of, 99; division of, 103, 105; industry in, 144.
Carpenter's Hall, 161, 162.
Carpetbaggers, 414, 419, 422.
Cär' ter et, Sir George, 117.
Cartier (kär'tyā'), Jacques, 31.
Carver, John, 68, 69.
Cass, Lewis, 307, 314.
Caswell, Colonel, 171.
Catholics, 30, 35, 92, 94, 124, 128.
Cavaliers, in Virginia, 62, 63.
Centennial Exposition, 426.
Cerro Gordo (sĕr' rō gôr dō), battle of, 302.
Cervera (Thâr-vā' rä), Admiral, 449, 451.
Chaffee, General Adna R., 455.
Chalmette, battle of, 255.
Champion Hills, battle of, 379.
Champlain (shăm-plān'), 33, 34.
Chancellorsville, battle of, 382.
Charles I, and Virginia, 62, 63; and New England, 80, 82, 83; and Maryland, 92, 95; and the Carolinas, 98, 99.
Charles II, and Virginia, 64, 65, 66; and New England, 80, 85, 86, 87; and Maryland, 96; and the Carolinas, 99.
Charles VIII of France, 3.
Charles IX of France, 32, 98.
Charleston, founded, 103; growth of, 104, 105; in Queen Anne's War, 129; in Revolutionary War, 171, 172, 191, 195, 200; railroad to, 287, 288; convention at, 330; in the War of Secession, 342, 343, 345, 346, 390, 397; earthquake at, 462.
Charleston Mercury, 333.
"Charter oak," 88.
Chase, Salmon P., 311, 317.
Chattanooga, 380, 381.

Cher'o kees, 44, 270.
Cherry valley, massacres in, 186.
Chesapeake, the, 242, 251.
Chicago, fire in, 424; anarchists in, 436; World's Fair at, 443.
Chick a maug' a, battle of, 380.
Chickasaw Bayou, battle of, 372.
China, trouble with, 454.
Chinese, exclusion of, 436; attitude toward, 464.
Chip' pe wa, battle of, 254.
Christiana, Fort, 112.
Church of England (Episcopal Church), 67, 71, 82, 85, 115, 120, 148, 149.
Cibola (sē' bō lä), 29.
Cities, colonial, 114, 143; development of, 218, 284, 324, 465.
Civil Rights Bill, 412.
Civil-service reform, 432, 437.
Clai' borne, William, 63, 94–96.
Clarendon Colony, 100, 103–105.
Clarendon, Earl of, 99.
Clark, George Rogers, 189, 190.
Clark, William, 240.
Clay, Henry, urges war with England, 247; supports tariff, 262; Presidential candidate, 263, 277, 298; introduces tariff compromise, 279; opposes annexation of Texas, 298; introduces Compromise of 1850, 308, 309, 311; biography of, 308; influence of, 319.
Clermont, the, 245.
Cleveland, Grover, 434, 440; biography, 435; administrations, 435–438, 441–445.
Clinton, DeWitt, 248, 286.
Clinton, George, 241.
Clinton, Sir Henry, 185, 195, 200.
Cockburn, Admiral, 255.
Cold Harbor, battle of, 391.
Colfax, Schuyler, 417.
Coligny (kō-lēn'yē) Admiral, 32.
Colonies, life in the, 66, 67, 73–75, 138–148.
Colorado, admission of, 426.
Columbia College, 268.
Columbian Exposition, 443.
Columbus, Christopher, 13–21.

Commerce, to the East, 7–9; English, 49, 105; of New England, 90, 143; laws hindering, 151, 209; in 1789, 217; attacked by England and France, 228, 241–243, 246; in 1820–1840, 285; legislation concerning, 459.
Commonwealth, the, 63. See also Cromwell.
Communication, in the colonies, 144, 145, 161; in 1789, 215, 217, 220; in 1820, 264, 265; 1820–1840, 284–289; 1840–1860, 324–327; since 1865, 418, 456, 466, 467.
Compromise, Missouri, 261.
Concord (kŏnk' urd), fight at, 163–165.
Confederate States, formed, 338; final defeat of, 399; losses and hardships in, 401, 406; reinstatement of, 408–415.
Confederation, New England, 82, 83, 84.
Conference of Governors, 460.
Congregational Church in America, 72, 79, 148.
Congress, first Colonial, 116; Continental, 161, 167, 169, 184, 206, 207; and reconstruction, 411, 412.
Connecticut, 77–80, 256.
Conscription Law, 377.
Constitution, first, written in America, 79.
Constitution of the United States, the first, 207–210; convention to revise the, 211, 212; provisions of the, 212; adopted, 214; interpretation of the, 224; amendments to the, 226, 408, 412, 415.
Constitution, the, 250.
Convention, Annapolis, 133; Albany, 133; Philadelphia, 161; Charlotte (N. C.), 173; Virginia, 173; Constitutional, 211, 212; Hartford, 256; Baltimore, 330.
"Conway Cabal" (kȧ-bäl'), 183.
Cŏr' ĭnth, battle of, 373.
Cornwallis, Lord, 179, 196, 197, 199, 200, 202.

INDEX

Coronado (kō rō nä' thō), 29.
Corporations. See Trusts.
Correspondence, Committees of, 161.
Cor' tez, Her nan' do, 29.
Cotton gin, invented, 230.
Cotton, industry aided by the gin, 230, 266; freight rates on, 326; and war conditions, 349, 355, 370, 374, 389.
County system, 148.
Cowpens, battle of, 199.
"Coxey's Army," 441.
Crawford, William H., 258, 263.
Crédit Mobilier (crā dē mō bē ly a), 424.
Creeks, the, trouble with, 253, 270.
Cro a toan', 40, 41.
Cromwell, Oliver, 62, 63, 80.
Crown Point, 166.
Cuba, early history of, 17, 19, 21, 27; attempt to seize, 426; in Spanish War, 445–452; protectorate over, 452, 454.
Cumberland Road, 285.
Currency, Continental, 178, 204; under Articles of Confederation, 208, 209; specie payments, 426; scarcity of, 423; silver demonetized, 424; Bland Act concerning, 431; Sherman Act, 439, 441; free coinage of silver, 424, 439; Confederate, 349, 374, 404.
Custer, General, 426.

Dale, Sir Thomas, 58, 59.
Dare, Virginia, 39.
Dartmouth College, 268.
Davenport, John, 80.
Davis, Henry G., 458.
Davis, Jefferson, secession address, 334; elected President of the Confederacy, 338; biography, 338; calls for privateers, 353; imprisoned, 400; case dropped, 407.
Dearborn, General, 249, 253.
Debt, the National, 225.
Debtors, in England, 105; in America, 106, 107, 292.
Declaration of Independence, 173–175.
Declaration of Rights, 155.
Declaratory Act, 156.
Delaware, Lord, 57, 58.
Delaware, 112, 113, 122, 123, 347.
Democratic Party. See Party.
Detroit, 127, 249.
Dewey, George, 448.
Dickinson, John, 175, 212.
Dingley Tariff Bill, 454.
Din wid' die, Governor, 132.
Disasters, 462, 463.
Discovery, the, 52.
Dongan, Governor Thomas, 115.
Dorr's Rebellion, 295.
Douglas, Stephen A., 316, 321.
Draft Act, 378; riots, 378.
Drake, Sir Francis, 36, 37, 38.
Dred Scott Decision, 321.
Dress, in New England, 91; in the colonies in the eighteenth century, 142.
Duke of York. See James II.
Dunmore, Lord, 165, 166, 171.
Duquesne (du kān'), 131, 132, 134, 135.
Dutch, exploration, 34; colonization, 109–114; slave ships, 60; in Connecticut valley, 77, 82; in Delaware, 112.

Eads, James B., 467.
Early, General Jubal A., 392, 393.
Earthquakes, 462, 463.
East India Company, Dutch, 35; English, 50, 51.
E' den ton, 159.
Edison, Thomas A., 467.
Education, in the colonies, 66, 67, 75, 91, 145, 146; of the Indians, 83; progress in, 268, 468.
El Caney (ĕl kä' nä), battle of, 450.
Electoral Commission, 429.
Electoral vote, 436.
Electricity, 288, 326, 328, 466, 467.
Eliot, John, 83.
Elizabeth, Queen, 35, 37, 38, 41, 50.
Emancipation Proclamation, 376, 408.
Embargo Act, 243, 246.
Endicott, John, 72.
Engineering feats, 433.

England, in fifteenth century, 4; exploration, 21, 22, 35–42; conditions in, affecting colonization, 49, 62, 67, 71, 92, 105, 119; conflict with Dutch, 77, 82, 113; attitude of, in 1861, 355.
English, Edward S., 432.
Ericson, Leif (līf er' ĭk son), 6, 7.
Erie Canal, 265, 286.
Established Church. See Church of England.
Estaing, d' (děs-tăn'), Count, 186, 191.
Eutaw (ū'taw) Springs, battle of, 200.
Exposition, Crystal Palace, 329; Chicago, 443; Buffalo, 455; St. Louis, 458; Jamestown, 459.
Express business, 288.

Fair Oaks, battle of, 360.
Fairbanks, Charles W., 458.
Făr rā gŭt, Admiral David G., 369, 390.
Federal Hall, 222.
Federalist, the, 223.
Federalists. See Party.
Ferdinand of Spain, 4, 14, 17, 19.
Ferguson, Colonel, 197.
Field, Cyrus W., 326.
Field, James G., 440.
Fillmore, Millard, biography, 311; administration, 312, 320.
Fires, 424, 463.
Fitch, John, 245.
Five intolerable acts of Parliament, the, 160.
Florida, explored, 27; settled, 30; colonial warfare with, 108, 129, 131; ceded to England, 137; Indian uprising in, 258, 259; purchase of, 259; admitted, 296; secession of, 333; readmission of, 414; in 1875, 422.
Force Acts, 421.
"Force Bill," 279.
Forrest, General N. B., 371, 386.
"Forty-Niners," 305.
France, in fifteenth century, 2; exploration, 31–34; occupation of Canada, 124; in western valleys, 124–127, 130; wars with England, 128–137; relations with the United States, 183, 184, 227, 232, 241–243; in Mexico, 416.
Franklin, Benjamin, 133, 183, 184, 212.
Franklin, State of, 210.
Fredericksburg, battle of, 365.
Free Soil Party. See Party.
Freedman's Bureau, 412.
Frémont (frē-mōnt'), General J. C., 296, 302, 320, 353.
French and Indian War, 131–137; effects of, 150, 153, 154.
Frenchtown, massacre at, 251.
Friends. See Quakers.
Frolic, the, 250.
Fugitive slave laws, 308, 309, 311, 312, 313, 318, 321, 337.
Fulton, Robert, 245.

Gads' den Purchase, 304, 315.
"Gag Law," 306.
Gage, General, 163, 167.
Gal' lā tĭn, Albert, 265.
Gama, Vasco da (väs' cō dä gä'-mä), 20.
Garfield, James A., 431, 432; biography, 432.
Garrison, William Lloyd, 275, 306.
Gaspee (gäs pā'), the, 159.
Gates, General Horatio, 181, 183, 196, 198, 199.
Gates, Sir Thomas, 57.
Gĕnet (zhĕ-nā'), Minister, 227.
Geneva Award, the, 419.
Genoa (jĕn o-a), 13.
Geographies, Ancient, 10, 11.
George I, 130.
George II, 106, 130, 182.
George III, 153, 155, 162, 173.
Georgia, name of, 106; first settlements of, 105–109; trouble with Indians, 270; secedes, 333; readmitted, 415.
Georgia, University of, 268.
Gerry, Elbridge T., 212.
Gettysburg (gĕt' ĭz burg), battle of, 383–385.
Ghent (gĕnt), Treaty of, 256.
Gilbert, Sir Humphrey, 37.
Godspeed, the, 52.

INDEX

Goffe, William, 85.
Gold, discovery of, 305.
Golden Hind, the, 36.
Golds' bor o, N. C., 397.
Gō' lĭ ăd, Texas, 297.
Goodyear, Charles, 327.
Gorges (gōr-jĕz), Ferdinando, 81.
Gorges, Sir Ferdinand, 52.
Gŏs' nŏld, Bartholomew, 49.
Gourges, Dominique de (dō' mĕ-nĕk dĕ gōōrg'), 33.
Government, colonial, 147, 150–161. (See also under names of colonies.)
Grā dy, Henry W., 377, 406.
Graham, William A., 316.
"Grand Model," the, 101.
Grant, Ulysses S., in the West, 367, 368; in campaigns against Vicksburg, 371, 378–380; in command of Union armies, 387; in Virginia, 391, 392, 395–398; biography, 418; administrations, 418–429.
Grasse, Count de (dĕ gräs'), 202.
Graves, Admiral, 202.
Great Bridge, battle of, 171.
Gree' ley, Horace, 422.
Greenback Party. See Party.
Greene, General Nathanael, 195, 199, 200.
Grenville (grĕn'-vĭl), Sir Richard, 38.
Guadalupe Hidalgo (gwä' thä-loo'-pā ē thäl go, *or* gü' da-loop hē-däl' go), treaty of, 304.
Guam (gwäm), 452.
Guerrière (ger rē är), the, 250.
Guilford (gĭl'-ferd), Courthouse, battle of, 199.

Habeas corpus, writ of, 375, 422.
Hakluyt, Sir Richard, 50.
Hale, John P., 314.
Hale, Nathan, 176.
Half Moon, the, 35.
Halleck, General, 363, 367.
Hamburg (S. C.), railroad to, 287.
Hamilton, Alexander, 210, 212, 223, 224, 229, 231, 241; biography, 223.
Hamilton, Colonel, 190.

Hampden-Sidney College, 268.
Hampton (Va.), first free school, 145.
Hampton, General Wade, 392.
Hampton Roads, 356.
Hancock, General Winfield Scott, 432.
Hancock, John, 167, 183.
Harper's Ferry, 322, 364, 383.
Harrisburg (Miss.), battle of, 386.
Harrisburg (Pa.), Confederate advance on, 383.
Harrison, Benjamin, nominated, 438; biography, 438; administration, 439, 440.
Harrison, William Henry, defeats Indians, 247; in War of 1812, 251; in election of 1836, 281; nominated, 283; biography, 294; administration, 294–299.
Harrison's Landing, 363.
Hartford (Conn.), 79; convention, 256, 336.
Harvard College, 75, 138.
Harvey, Sir John, 62, 64.
Havana in the Spanish War, 446.
Hawaii (hä wī' ē), revolution in, 442; annexed, 452; voyage of the fleet to, 460.
Hayes, Rutherford B., nominated, 427; biography, 429; administration, 429–431.
Hayne, Robert Y., 276.
Heath, Sir Robert, 99.
Hendricks, Thomas A., 427, 434.
Henry IV of France, 33.
Henry, Patrick, argues Parson's case, 149; opposes the Stamp Act, 155; opposes Governor, 165, 166; Governor of Virginia, 190; in Federal convention, 211.
Henry, Prince, the Navigator, 11, 13.
Hepburn Bill, 459.
"Hermitage," the, 281.
Hessians, the, 173, 181, 193.
Hobart, Garrett A., 445.
Hobkirk Hill, battle of, 200.
Hobson, Lieutenant R. P., 449.
Hoe, Richard M., 328.
Holland, in the Revolution, 194, 203.

"Holy Alliance," the, 262.
Hood, General John B., 388, 389.
Hooker, General Joseph, 366, 381, 382, 383.
Hooker, Thomas, 78.
Horseshoe Bend, battle of, 253.
House of Burgesses. See Virginia, government in.
Houston, Sam, 297.
Howe, Elias, 328.
Howe, General, 167, 173, 175, 182, 185.
Hudson, Henry, 35.
Huguenots (hū' gẽ nŏts), 32, 103, 104, 128.
Hull, Captain Isaac, 250.
Hull, General William, 249.
Hutchinson, Mrs. Anne, 74, 76.

Iberville (ē ber vēl'), 126.
Idaho, admitted, 439.
Illinois, explored, 124; admitted, 261.
Impressment of seamen, 228, 242, 243, 247.
Inauguration day, 214.
Indented servants, 60, 66, 139, 218.
Independence Hall, 167, 174.
Independents, 68.
India. See Trade routes.
Indian Territory, formation of, 282.
Indiana, 127, 189, 257.
Indians, origin of name, 17; Pueblo, 29; Croatan, 41; distribution of tribes, 42–44; life of, 44–48; warfare with, 61, 64, 65, 69, 79, 86, 102, 153, 188, 226, 252, 253, 259, 282, 425; education of, 83; treaties with, 107, 121, 271; as French allies, 116, 128, 129, 131, 134, 135; as Tory allies, 181, 186; in War of 1812, 252, 253; removed to reservations, 270, 282.
Industries, in the colonies, 59, 71, 74, 90, 91, 97, 110, 143, 144; in 1789, 220; in 1814, 257; in 1820, 266, 267; in 1840, 287, 289, 290; in 1860, 327–329; since 1865, 418, 465–470.
Ingersoll, Jared, 248.

Insular possessions, 465.
Internal improvements, 264, 270, 271, 284–288, 324–327, 418.
Interstate Commerce Commission, 435.
Inventions, 220, 288–292, 327–329, 466, 467.
Invisible Empire, the, 421.
Iowa admitted, 305.
Ironclads, battle of the, 356.
Iroquois (ĭr ō kwoi'), 43, 186.
Isabella of Spain, 4, 14, 15, 17, 19.
Italians, in New Orleans, 464.
Italy, in the fifteenth century, 3.

Jackson, Andrew, defeats the Indians, 253; defeats the British at New Orleans, 255; nominated, 263, 269; administration, 272–282; biography, 272.
Jackson, General Thomas J. ("Stonewall"), in Mexican War, 304, 351; biography, 351; in War of Secession, 351, 361 364, 382, 383.
James I, 51, 52, 59, 61, 62, 81, 92.
James II, 87, 88, 114, 115, 116, 118.
Jamestown, 52–57, 66, 459.
Japan, treaty with, 316.
Jasper, Sergeant, 172, 191.
Java, the, 250.
Jay, John, Chief Justice, 228.
Jefferson, Thomas, writes Declaration of Independence, 174; Secretary of State, 223; strict constructionist, 224; Vice President, 231; suggests Kentucky resolutions, 233; elected President, 234; administrations, 237–245; biography, 237; estimate of, 243.
Jesuits (jĕs' ū ĭts), 124, 125, 130.
John, King of Portugal, 5, 14.
Johnson, Andrew, War Governor of Tennessee, 367; administration, 407–418; biography, 409.
Johnston, General Albert Sidney, 366, 367, 368.
Johnston, General Joseph E., at Manassas, 352; in Mississippi, 379; succeeds General Bragg, 382; opposed by Sherman, 387,

388; removed from command, 388; commands in the Carolinas, 396-399.
Johnstown, flood at, 463.
Joliet (zhō'lē ā), Louis, 125.
Jones, John Paul, 192, 193.
Journal of Commerce, the, 288.

Kalb, Baron de, 180, 196.
Kansas, explored, 29; troubles in, 316-319; a campaign issue, 320, 323; admitted, 323.
Kansas-Nebraska Bill, 316-319, 320.
Kās kas' kĭ a, 190.
Kearney (kär' nĭ), General Stephen W., 302, 303 (map).
Kearsarge (kēr' särj), the, 358.
Kentucky, first settlements in, 188; moves to separate from Virginia, 210; admitted, 226; Resolution of, 233; and secession, 348; the war in, 366, 367, 372, 373; and emancipation, 376; raids in, 380.
Kern, John W., 461.
Key, Francis Scott, 255.
Kieft (kēft), Governor Peter, 112.
King, Rufus, 241, 258.
King George's War, 130.
King Philip's War, 86.
King William's War, 128.
King's Mountain, battle of, 197.
"Kitchen Cabinet," 274.
Know-Nothing Party, 319, 331.
Knox, Henry, 223, 224.
Ku Klux Klan (kū klŭks'), 421.

Labor, in 1789, 218, 219; in 1820, 267; in 1877 (organization of unions), 431; imported, 436; troubles, 436, 442, 462; in the South, 469.
Lafayette (lä fä yĕt'), Marquis de, 180, 182, 202.
Lake Erie, battle of, 252.
Lane, Ralph, 38.
La Salle, Robert de (ro' bairr dĕ lä säl'), 125-127.
Las Guās' i mas, battle of, 450.
Laurens, John, 199.
Lawrence, Captain, 251.
Lawrence, the, 252.
Lee, Fort, 176.
Lee, General Charles, 177, 183, 185.
Lee, General Fitzhugh, 446, 447.
Lee, Major Henry ("Light Horse Harry"), 192, 200, 360.
Lee, Richard Henry, 161, 174.
Lee, Robert E., in Mexican War, 304; captures John Brown, 322; resigns from Federal service, 334; quoted, 334, 341, 383, 386, 399; commands Confederate army in Virginia, 360; biography, 360; in Virginia and Maryland, 1862, 363-366; in Virginia and Pennsylvania, 1863, 382-386; opposed by Grant, 387, 390-392, 396-398; surrenders, 398; disbands army, 399.
Lee, General Stephen D., 372.
Legislature. See Congress and Assembly.
Leisler's (lēs' lēr) Rebellion, 116.
Leon, Ponce de (pōn' tha dĕ la ōn'), 27.
Leopard, the, 242.
Lewis and Clark expedition, 240.
Lewis, General Andrew, 189.
Lexington, battle of, 163-165.
Liliuokalani (lē le ōō ō kä lä' nē), Queen, 442.
Lincoln, Abraham, candidate for Senator, 321; in election of 1860, 332; inauguration, 343, 344; biography, 343; and Fort Sumter, 345; calls for volunteers, 347; declares blockade, 353; and captured privateersmen, 354; annuls emancipation decrees, 375; suspends writ of *habeas corpus*, 375; issues emancipation proclamation, 376, 377; and Draft Act, 378; renominated and elected, 394; and prisoners of war, 395; assassination of, 399; and reconstruction, 400, 408, 409, 410.
Lincoln, General Benjamin, 191, 195, 202, 210.
Line of demarcation, 25, 26.
Literature, American, in 1824, 268; in 1840, 293; in 1860, 329.

Little Belt, the, 247.
"Little Giant," the, 317.
Little Turtle, defeats General St. Clair, 226.
Locke, John, 100.
Logan, John A., 434.
London Company, 51, 52, 55, 56, 61, 68.
Long, Crawford W., 327.
Long Island, battle of, 175.
Longstreet, General James, 384.
"Lost colony." See Roanoke.
Louis XIV, 125, 126, 128, 129.
Louis XVI, 184, 227.
Louisburg (lōō' ĭs burg), 130, 135.
Louisiana (Province), claimed for France, 125; ceded to Spain, 137; ceded to France, 238; explored, 240; purchased by the United States, 239; exposition celebrating purchase of, 458.
Louisiana (State), admitted, 248; in War of 1812, 255; in War of Secession, 333, 369, 370, 387; and reconstruction, 409; readmitted, 415; "carpetbag" government in, 422; in the election of 1876, 428; representative government restored in, 430; trouble with "Mafia" in, 464.
Lower California, 315.
Lundy's Lane, battle of, 254.
Luzon (lōō zōn'), 453.
Lyon, General Nathaniel, 353.

McClellan, General George B., 351, 359-366, 394.
McCrea (măc-crā'), Jane, 181.
Macdonough (măc dŏn'ō), Commodore Thomas, 254.
McDowell, General Irwin, 361, 362.
McHenry, Fort, 255.
McKinley, William, nominated, 445; biography, 445; administrations, 445-455; assassinated, 455.
McKinley Tariff, the, 439.
Macedonian (măs ĕ dō' nĭ an), the, 250.
Madison, James, proposes stronger central government, 210; drafts Constitution, 212; proposes Virginia Resolutions, 233; administrations, 245-258; biography of, 245.
Mafia (mä-fē'ä), the, 464.
Magellan (ma-jĕl'ăn), Ferdinand, 24.
Magruder, General J. B., 351, 360, 392.
Maine, 81, 210, 261.
Maine, the, 446.
Mă-năs'săs, 351, 363.
Manhattan Island, 110, 176. See also New York (City).
Manila (mä nil' lä), battle of, 448.
Manufacturing, in 1763, 143; in 1789, 216, 220; in 1820, 267; in 1840, 290; in 1860, 329; since 1865, 470.
Marion, General, 195, 200.
Marquette (mär kĕt'), 124, 125.
Marshall, John, 236, 271, 337; biography, 236.
Maryland, settlement of, 92-98; name of, 92; government in, 92, 93, 97, 98; religious toleration in, 93, 94; claims Delaware, 122; disputes rights to the Potomac, 211; gives District of Columbia, 234.
Mason and Dixon's Line, 123.
Mason, Captain John, 79.
Mason, James M., 354.
Mason, John, 81.
Mason, Senator, 309.
Massachusetts, settled, 68-75; early government in, 72, 85, 89; persecutions in, 70, 84, 85, 90; charter of, violated, 152; loses Maine, 210; ratifies Constitution, 214; nullification in, 243; threatens secession, 336.
Massachusetts Bay Colony founded, 71.
Massachusetts Bay Company, 71, 72.
Măs să soit', 70, 75, 86.
Maumee River (ma mē'), battle at the, 226.
Maury, Commodore M. F., 326, 328, 344.
Maximilian, 416.
Mayflower, the, 68.

INDEX

Mayflower Compact, the, 68.
Meade, General George, 383, 384.
Mecklenburg County (N. C.) declares independence, 173.
Memphis, 371.
Menendez (mă năn'dăth), Pe'dro, 33.
Merrimac, the, in Hampton Roads, 356.
Merrimac, the, at Santiago, 449.
Merritt, General Wesley A., 448.
Methodist Church in America, 108.
Mexico, Spanish conquest of, 29; Texan revolution from, 296, 297; war of United States with, 300–304; French attempt in, 416.
Michigan, in War of 1812, 249, 251; admitted, 281.
Miles, General Nelson A., 451.
Miller, Deputy Governor, 102.
Mims, Fort, 253.
Minnesota, admitted, 323.
Mĭn'u it, Governor Peter, 110, 112.
Minute-men, 163, 164.
Missionary Ridge, battle of, 381.
Mississippi, explored, 28; migration to, 239; admitted, 260; in the War of Secession, 333, 369–373, 378–380, 386; readmitted, 415.
Mississippi River, the, discovered, 28; explored, 124–127; controlled by the French, 127; controlled by the Federals, 369, 380.
Missouri, admission of, 261; in the War of Secession, 353.
Missouri Compromise, 261, 307, 312, 321, 341.
Mobile founded, 126.
Mobile Bay, battle of, 390.
Mŏ'dŏcs, uprising of the, 425.
Monitor, the, 357.
Monmouth, battle of, 185.
Monroe, James, negotiates treaty with England, 243; administrations, 258–268; biography, 258.
Monroe Doctrine, 262, 417, 444.
Montana admitted, 439.
Montcalm, Marquis de, 135, 136.
Monterey (mŏn-tḗ rā'), siege of, 301.

Montgomery, Confederacy organized at, 338, 341.
Montgomery, General, 170, 171.
"Monticello" (mŏn tē chĕl'lō), 244, 245.
Moore's Creek, battle of, 171, 172.
Moravians, 108.
Morgan, General Daniel, 168, 171, 181, 199.
Morgan, General John H., 380.
Mormons, the, 296.
Morris, Robert, 178, 204, 292.
Morse, Samuel F. B., 288, 289.
Morton, Levi P., 438.
Moultrie, Fort, 171, 172, 346.
Moultrie (mōl' trĭ), William, 172.
Mound builders, 42.
Mount Vernon, 204, 230.
"Mugwumps." See Party.
Murfreesboro, battle of, 380.

Napoleon I, 238, 239, 242, 246.
Napoleon III, 416.
Năr ra găn' sett Indians, 76.
Narvaez (när-vä'ăth), 29.
Nashville, battle of, 389.
Nassau, Fort, 110.
National Bank, the, establishment of, 225; discontinued, 248; a new, 257; a campaign issue, 271, 280; charter of, vetoed, 279, 280; abolished, 280; replaced by sub-treasuries, 282; bill vetoed by Tyler, 295.
Naturalization law, 233.
Navigation Acts, 151.
Navy the, beginnings of, 192; department established, 232; respected abroad, 250; in 1865, 400; in 1885, 436; effect of territorial expansion on, 452; in 1908, 460.
Nebraska, admitted, 417.
Necessity, Fort, 132.
Neutrality, proclamation, 227; policy of, 231.
New Amsterdam, 110, 111, 113, 114.
New England, origin of name, 56 (facsimile); united, 82; under Andros, 87–89; in 1700, 90, 91; in wars with the French, 128,

129; in 1763, 142-148; in 1789, 216; and slavery, 249; and secession, 239, 256; and Kansas, 317.
New England Confederacy, 82-84, 87.
New Hampshire, 81, 210.
New Jersey, settled, 117-119, 122; in the Revolution, 177, 179, 185, 186.
New Mexico, organized as Territory, 308; slavery optional in, 316; becomes a State, 462.
New Netherland, 110-114, 122.
New Orleans (ôr'lē anz), founded, 127; port closed, 238; growth of, 248; battle of, 255; "Mafia" in, 464.
New Sweden, 112.
New York (City) taken by the British, 173; evacuated, 203; Draft riot in, 378. See also New Amsterdam.
New York (State) explored, 35; settled, 109-116; in intercolonial wars, 128, 129; in Revolution, 175, 176, 180-182; and secession, 335.
Newspapers, colonial, 146, 153; since 1789, 266, 288.
Niagara (nī ăg ä rä), Fort, 135.
Niagara, the, 252.
Niña (nē'nyä), the, 16.
Nominating Conventions, the beginning of, 277.
Non-Intercourse Act, the, 242, 243.
Norsemen, voyages of the, 6.
North Carolina, first settlements in, 38-42, 100-103; opposition to taxation in, 150; oppression by governors in, 150; loses northwestern counties, 210; ratifies Constitution, 214, 225; emancipation of slaves in, 275; readmitted, 414.
North Carolina, University of, 268.
North Dakota, admitted, 439.
Northwest Territory, occupied by the English, 189, 190; ceded to Federal Government, 207, 208; Ordinance for government of, 214, 215; migration to, 217; slavery prohibited in, 218; education in, 219, 266; in War of 1812, 252; growth of, 261.
Nova Scotia, 129, 131, 135.
Nueces (nwā'sĕs) River, 300.
Nullification, in Virginia and Kentucky Resolutions, 233; in resolutions of Hartford Convention, 256; of tariff law, 271; asserted by Hayne, 276; ordinance in South Carolina, 277, 278; end of, 279.

Ogdensburg, battle of, 249.
Oglethorpe (ō' g'l thôrp), General James Edward, 105-109.
O'Hara, General, 202.
Ohio, first settlements in, 189, 190; admitted to the Union, 239.
Ohio Company, the, 131.
Oklahoma, Territory, 439; State, 460.
"Old Hickory," 253.
"Old Ironsides," 250.
"Old Rough and Ready," 301.
Omnibus Bill, 308.
Opecancanough (ō pĕk ăn kä'nō), 54.
Orders in council, 242, 246, 247.
Ordinance of 1787, 215, 218, 219.
Oregon country explored, the, 36, 240, 296; boundary of, 260, 300; settled, 296.
Oregon, the, 449.
Orleans, Territory of, 248.
Os cē ō' lä, 282.
Ostend Manifesto, 315.
Otis, James, 152.

Pacific Railroad, 418.
Pak'en ham, General, 255.
Palmer, John M., 445.
Pä' lōs, 16.
Panama Canal, 456.
Panama, Republic of, 457.
Pan-American Congress, first, 270.
Pan-American Exposition, 455.
Panic, of 1837, 281; of 1873, 423; of 1893, 441; of 1907, 459.
Parker, Alton B., 458.

Parsons' Case, 149.
Party, origin of, Federalist, 224, 262; Anti-Federalist, or Republican, 224; Democratic-Republican, 262, 271; National Republicans, or Whigs, 271, 319; Democratic, 271; States' Rights, 271; Anti-Mason, 277; Free-Soil, 307; American, 319; Know-Nothing, 319; New Republican, 320; Constitutional Union, 331; Liberal Republican, 422; Prohibitionist, 423; Greenback, 427; Greenback-Labor-Anti-Monopoly, 434; "Mugwump," 434; People's, 440; Labor, 440; Gold Democrat, 445.
Patent office established, 291.
Patriots, use of name, 163.
Pā troon' system, 110, 111.
Paulus (pa' lūs) Hook, 192.
Peace Conference, the (1861), 341.
Peninsula campaign, the, 360.
Penn, Admiral, 120, 121.
Penn, William, and New Jersey, 117, 119; and Pennsylvania, 119–122; and Delaware, 123.
Pennsylvania, Colony of, 120–123.
Pennsylvania, University of, 268.
Pensions, 437, 439.
People's Party. See Party.
Pŏp' per ĕll, Sir William, 130.
Pē' quot War, the, 79.
Perry, Oliver Hazard, 252.
Personal liberty laws, 312, 341.
Petersburg, siege of, 396–398.
Philadelphia, founded, 121; growth of, 121, 145, 216, 218; National Capital, 182.
Philip II of Spain, 39.
Philippine Islands, the, discovered, 25; in Spanish-American war, 448; annexed, 452; insurrection in, 453; government of, 453; fleet at, 460.
Phipps, Sir William, 129.
Phonograph, 467.
Pickens, General Andrew, 195.
Pickett's charge, 384.
Pierce, Franklin, elected President, 314; administration, 315–320; biography, 315.

Pike, Zebulon M., 240.
Pilgrims, the, 67–71.
Pinckney, Charles, 212.
Pinckney, Charles C., 232, 234, 241.
Pine-tree shilling, 84.
Pinta (pēn' tä), the, 16.
Piracy, 105, 116, 238.
Pitcairn (pĭt' kârn), Major, 164.
Pitt, William, 135, 156.
Pizarro (pē-thär' rō), 29.
Plains of Abraham, 136.
Plattsburg, battle of, 254.
Plymouth (plĭm' ŭth), 68–71.
Plymouth Company, 51, 70, 71.
Pŏ cä hŏn' tās, 54, 57, 58, 59.
Political parties, rise of, 224.
Pō' lō, Mär' cō, 9.
Pŏn' tĭ āc's Conspiracy, 152, 153.
Population, in 1700, 66, 75, 91, 116, 119, 123; in 1763, 137, 138, 139, 140; in 1820, 263; in 1840, 284; in 1860, 323; since 1865, 465; westward movement of centers of, 464.
Port Royal (S. C.) settled, 32, 33.
Port Royal (Acadia), 129.
Porto Rico (pōr' tō rē' kō), 451, 452, 454.
Portugal, in fifteenth century, 5, 11, 14, 20, 25, 26; trade with, 74, 91, 143.
Post, the, in the colonies, 146; envelopes for, 288; stamps for, 327.
Pow hä tän', 54.
President, the, 247.
Presidential succession, order of, 435.
Prevost (prĕ vō'), General, 191, 254.
Princeton, battle of, 179.
Princeton College, 146.
Privateers in Revolution, 192; in War of 1812, 251; in War of Secession, 354.
Proctor, General, 252.
Prohibition Party. See Party.
Prō prī' ĕ tā ry government, 147.
Protection. See Tariff.
Providence (R. I.) settled, 76.
Pueblo (pwĕb' lō), 29.
Pū lās' kī, Count, 191.

Puritans, sect and name of, 71; settle Massachusetts, 71–75; settle Connecticut, 80; in Maryland, 95, 96; punishments by, 73; persecutions by, 74, 84, 85, 90.

Quakers, 119; persecution of, in England, 85, 120; in America, 84, 85; settlements by, 117, 119–122; among the Patriots, 178.
Quebec, founded, 34; attacked, 129, 135, 170.
Quebec Act, 160, 189.
Queen Anne's War, 129.

Race troubles, 463.
Races. See Population.
Railroads, development of, by 1840, 287; by 1860, 325; Union Pacific, 418; strikes on, 431, 442.
Raisin River Massacre, 252.
Raleigh (ra' lĭ), Sir Walter, 37–42.
Randolph, Edmund, 223.
Randolph, Peyton, 161.
Rawdon, Colonel, 200.
Reaping machine, invented, 289.
Reconstruction, problem of, 407; theories of, 408; Lincoln's plan for, 400, 409; Johnson's plan for, 410; opposition to, 410; Acts, 413–415.
Red River Expedition, the, 387.
Regicides (rĕj' ĭ sīds), the, 80, 85.
"Regulators," 157.
Reid, Whitelaw, 440.
Religion in the colonies, 148 (see also under names of colonies).
Republican Party. See Party.
Resources, conservation of, 469.
Restoration. See Charles II.
Returning boards, 1876, 428.
Revere, Paul, 163.
Rhode Island, settled, 76, 77; government in, 76, 82, 86, 89; not in Federal Convention, 211; ratifies Constitution, 214, 226; new constitution and Dorr's Rebellion in, 295; specifies right of secession, 335.
Ribault, Jean (zhäN rē bō'), 32.

Richmond (Va.) burned by the British, 200; capital of the Confederacy, 350; objective point of Federal campaigns, 350, 361, 390; fall of, 398.
Rio Grande (rē' o gränd') River, 300.
Rō ȧ noke' Island, 38–42.
Robertson, James, 187.
Rochambeau (rō shäN bō'), Count, 202.
"Rock of Chickamauga," 381.
Rolfe, John, 58, 59.
Roosevelt (rō' ze vĕlt), Theodore, in Spanish War, 450; becomes President, 455; biography, 455; administrations, 456–460.
Rōse'crans, General William S., 372, 373, 381.
Ross, General, 255.
Rough Riders, the, 450.
Rumsey, James, 245.
Russia, occupies Alaska, 262; agrees to boundary lines, 299; attitude in War of Secession, 417; Alaska purchased from, 417.
Rŭt' gers College, 268.
Rŭt' lĕdge, John, 161, 173, 212.

Sackett's Harbor, battle of, 253.
St. Augustine (a' gŭs tēn), founded, 30, 33; siege of, 108; burned, 129.
St. Clair (klâr), General, 226.
St. John's College, 268.
St. Louis, founded, 127.
St. Simon's Island, 108, 131.
Salem (Mass.) witchcraft, 90.
Salz'burg ers, 107.
Sȧ mō' ȧn Islands, 452.
Sampson, Admiral, 449, 451.
San Jȧ cĭn'tō, battle of, 297.
San Juan (hoō än'), 450.
Santa Anna, General, 301, 302, 303.
Santa Maria (sän' tä mä rē' ä), the, 16.
Santiago (sän tē ä' gō), 450, 451.
Sarah Constant, the, 52.
Saratoga, battle of, 181.
Savannah, founded, 107; captured by the British, 191; captured by Sherman, 389.

INDEX 547

Saye and Sele, Lord, 77.
Sayle, William, 103.
"Scalawags," 420.
Schley (slī), Commodore, 449, 451.
Schuyler (skī' ler), General Philip, 181.
Science, contributions to, 327, 467.
Scott, General Winfield, 254.
Secession, threatened by New England, 239, 256; right of, declared by Hartford Convention, 256; threatened by South Carolina, 278; in 1861, 333, 334; grounds for, 335–338.
Sectional differences, growth of, 249, 266.
Seminole wars, 258, 282.
Semmes (sĕms), Admiral Raphael, 358.
Separatists, 68.
Serapis (se rā' pis), the, 193.
"Seventh-of-March Speech." See Webster.
Severn River, battle of, 96.
Sevier (se-vēr'), John, 187.
Sewall, Arthur, 444.
Seward, William H., 311, 417.
Seymour, Horatio, 418.
Shafter, General William R., 450.
Shannon, the, 251.
Shays's insurrection, 210.
Shĕn' ăn dō ah valley, 361, 364, 392, 393.
Sherman Anti-Trust Law, 439, 460.
Sherman, James S., 461.
Sherman, Roger, 161, 212.
Sherman Silver Act, 439; repealed, 441.
Shī' lōh, battle of, 368.
Shipping, in the colonies, 71, 74, 90, 91, 105, 142, 143; laws controlling, 151.
Silver. See Currency.
Sioux (sōō) Indians, uprising, 426.
Sitting Bull, 426.
Slave trade, 60, 74, 91; controlled by England, 129; New England monopoly of, 266; forbidden by Congress, 266.
Slavery, African, introduced, 60; prohibited in Georgia, 107, 108; in the colonies, 66, 91, 97, 104, 116, 137, 139, 142, 143; excluded from the Northwest Territory, 215; Northern States abolish, 218, 219, 226, 266; effect on admission of States, 267; abolished, 408.
Slī-dĕll', John, 354.
Sloughter, Colonel Henry, 116.
Smith, Captain John, 53–57, 59, 68.
Somers, Sir George, 57.
Sons of Liberty, 154.
Sothel, Governor Seth, 102.
Soto (sō' tō), Hernando de, 27.
South, the, in 1789, 216; in 1861, 348, 349; in 1865, 403–406; in 1910, 469.
South Carolina, first settlement of, 100, 103–105; oppression by governors, 150; tea ships at, 159; establishes independent government, 173; and nullification, 271, 276, 277–279; repeals ordinance of 1788, 333; results of secession in, 342, 343; opening of war in, 345; readmitted, 414.
South Carolina College, 268.
South Dakota, admitted, 439.
Southern Company of Sweden, 112.
Spain, in fifteenth century, 4; explorations and settlements, 14–21, 23–31; colonial policy of, 30, 445; rivalry with England, 35; trade with, 74; colonies in America, 262, 445; war with, 445–453.
"Specie circular," 281.
Specie payments, resumption of, 431.
Speedwell, the, 68.
Spoils system, 273, 432.
Spotswood, Alexander, 67.
"Squatter sovereignty," 316.
Stamp Act, the, 153–156.
Stan' dish, Captain Miles, 69.
Stanton, Edward M., 416.
Star of the West, the, 342.
"Star-Spangled Banner," 255.
Stark, General John, 181.
"State-suicide" theory, 408.
States' rights, theory of, 214, 271.
Steamboat, invention of, 245.
Steuben (stū' bĕn), Baron, 180, 184.

Stevens, Thaddeus, 409, 414; biography, 414.
Stevenson, Adlai E., 440, 455.
Stone, Governor William, 96.
Stony Point, 192.
Story, Judge, quoted, 272.
Strikes, 436, 442, 457, 462.
Stuart General J. E. B., 363, 392.
Stuyvesant (stī′ ve sănt), Governor Peter, 112–114.
Sullivan, General, 186.
Sumner, Senator Charles, 408, 414; biography, 408.
Sumter, Fort, 342, 345.
Sut′ter, Captain, discovers gold, 305.
Syms (sĭms), Benjamin, 145.

Taft, William H., Governor of Philippines, 453; nominated for President, 461; biography, 461; administration, 461–462.
Tariff, on interstate imports, 209; on foreign imports for revenue only, 224; on liquor, 225; first protective, 257; increase in, 262; "of abominations," 271; law nullified by South Carolina, 277; laws, 279; discussion, 433, 437, 438; McKinley Bill, 439; Wilson Bill, 442; Dingley Bill, 454; Aldrich Bill, 461.
Tarleton (tärl′ tŭn), Colonel, 199.
Taxation without representation, 112, 149, 150, 153–159.
Taylor, General Richard, 387.
Taylor, Zachary, in the Mexican War, 300, 301, 304; elected President, 306; administration of, 307–311; biography, 307; death of, 311.
Tea tax, 158–160.
Tecumseh (tē kŭm′ sē), 247, 252.
Telegraph, invented, 288; wireless, 467.
Telephone, invented, 466.
Tennessee, first settlements in, 187; admitted, 230; in the War of Secession, 366–373, 380–382, 409 (note); and reconstruction, 409; readmitted, 413.
Tĕn′ure-of-office Act, 413.

Territorial expansion, 452.
Texas, reached by La Salle, 126; Republic of, 297; annexation of, 297; effects of annexation of, 298, 300; war in, 300; not represented at Montgomery Convention, 338; not represented in Congress, 410; readmitted, 415.
Thames (tĕmz) River, battle of, 252.
Thanksgiving feast, the first, 69.
Thirteenth Amendment, 408.
Thomas, General G. H., 380–382.
Thur′man, Allen G., 438.
Ticonderoga (tī kŏn der ō′ gȧ) Fort, 166, 169, 180.
Tilden, 427–429; biography, 427.
Tippecanoe (tĭp pē kȧ nōō′), battle of, 248, 251, 283.
Tobacco, discovered, 38; industry, 59, 60, 97, 139, 142, 144.
Toleration Act, 94.
Tomo-chi-chi, 107.
Tories, 163.
Toscanelli (tōs kȧ-nel′ lē), 12, 13, 25.
Town system, 72, 115, 147, 148.
Towns′hend Acts, the, 156, 158.
Townshend, Charles, 156.
Trade, routes to the East, 8. See also Commerce.
Travel, in the colonies, 144; in 1820, 264; in 1840, 284–288; in 1860, 324–326; since 1865, 467.
Treaty, of Utrecht (ū′-trĕkt), 129; of 1748, 131; of Paris (1763), 137; of 1783, 203; Jay's, with England, 228, 232; of Ghent (gĕnt), 256; Webster-Ashburton, 295; settling the Oregon boundary, 300; of Guadalupe-Hidalgo, 304; with Japan, 316; of Paris (1898), 452; with Republic of Panama, 457.
Trent affair, the, 354.
Trenton, battle of, 177.
Trĭp′ ō lĭ, 238.
Troup (trōōp), Governor, 270.
Trusts, 439, 470.
Try′on, Governor, 157, 187.
Turkey, interference with civilization, 5, 9.
Turner, Nat, insurrection of, 275.

INDEX

Tuscaroras (tŭs kā rôr′ ăs), the, 44, 102.
Tweed Ring, the, 427.
Tyler, John, nominated for Vice President, 283; President, 294–299; biography, 294.
Typewriter invented, 467.

"Underground Railroads," the, 313.
"Union League," the, 420.
United States, the, 250.
Utah (ū′ tä *or* ū′ tȧ). Mormons move to, 296; organized as Territory, 308; slavery optional in, 316; admitted, 444.
Utrecht (ū′ trĕkt), treaty of, 129.

Vagrancy laws, 411.
Valley Forge, 183, 184.
Van Bu′ ren, Martin, Secretary of State, 273; Vice President, 277; biography, 281; President, 281–283; renominated, 283, 298.
Van Rensselaer (văn rĕn′ se ler), General, 249.
Vĕn′ e zuē lä, 443.
Vera Cruz (vā′ rä krōōs), 302.
Vermont, 210, 226.
Verrazano (vĕr rät sä′ nō), 31.
Ves pu′ ci us, A mer′ i cus, 22–24.
Vincennes (vĭn-sĕnz′), 189, 190.
Vĭn′ land, 6, 7.
Virginia, named, 38; colonized, 52–67; "Old Dominion," 64; government in, 53, 55, 56, 58, 60–65, 148; industry in, 59, 60, 67; life in, 66, 67; land claims of, 131, 190; in the French and Indian War, 132–134; opposes governors, 150; denounces the Stamp Act, 155; moves to declare independence, 174; war in, 200; surrenders western lands, 207, 208; calls Annapolis convention, 211; reserves right of secession, 335; tries to save the Union, 341; secedes, 350; readmitted, 415.
Virginia and Kentucky Resolutions, 233.
Virginia Company, the, 51.

Virginia, University of, 268.
Virgin′ i us, the affair of the, 426.
Voyage of the fleet, 460.

Wake Island, 452.
Warren, General, 168.
Washington (City) made the National Capital, 225, 234; burned by the British, 255.
Washington College, 268.
Washington, Fort, 176.
Washington, George, boyhood, 132; in service of Virginia, 132; as commander of Continental army, 167–170, 179, 183, 184, 204, 205; campaigns of, 173, 175–177, 179, 180, 182–186, 190, 191, 197, 202; circular letter to governors, 210; president of Federal Convention, 212; elected President, 221; administrations, 221–231; biography, 221.
Washington, Mary, 132.
Washington Monument, 433.
Washington (State) admitted, 439.
Wasp, the, 250.
Watauga (wä tạ′ gä) Settlements, the, 187, 197.
Watson, Thomas E., 445.
Wayne, Anthony, 192, 200, 226.
Weaver, James B., 440.
Webster, Daniel, in debate with Hayne, 276; biography, 276; negotiates treaty, 295; delivers "Seventh-of-March Speech," 311; candidate for President, 314; quoted, 272, 337.
Webster-Ashburton Treaty, 295.
Wesley, John, 108, 142.
West India Company, the Dutch, 110.
West Indies, the, trade with, 228.
West Point, 198.
Western land claims, 189, 207, 214.
Westward migration, 187–190, 217, 239, 264–266, 284, 305, 317, 325, 468.
Whaley, Edward, 85.
Wheeler, General Joseph, 447, 450.

Wheeler, William A., 427.
Whisky Rebellion, 230.
White, Governor John, 39, 40; drawings by, 40, 48.
Whitefield (whĭt fēld), George, 108.
Whitman, Marcus, 296.
Whitney, Eli, 229.
William III and Mary, 88, 89, 97, 116.
William and Mary, College of, founded, 67.
Williams College, 268.
Williams, Roger, 73, 74, 75-77.
Wilmington (Del.), 112, 122.
Wil'mŏt Proviso, 306.
Wilson, Henry, 423.
Wilson Bill, 442.
Winchester, General, 251.
Winder, General, 255.
Wingfield, Edward Maria, 54, 55.
Winthrop, John, 72.
Winthrop, John, Jr., 77.
Wirt, William, 277.
Witchcraft, 89.
Wolfe, General James, 135-137.
Wood, General Leonard, 450.
Woodford, General, 171.
Wright, Luke E., 453.
Writ of *habeas corpus*, 375, 422.
Writs of Assistance, 151.
Wyoming admitted, 439.
Wyoming Valley massacre, 186.

Yale College, 146.
Yamacraw Indians, 107.
Yeamans, Governor, 103.
Yeardley (yērd' lĭ), Governor George, 60.
York (Canada), 253.
Yorktown, in the Revolution, 202, 203, 204; in 1812, 360.

Breinigsville, PA USA
17 January 2011
253484BV00003B/7/P